GREENHOUSE

RESEARCH IN LAW AND SOCIOLOGY

Volume 1 • 1978

RESEARCH IN LAW AND SOCIOLOGY

An Annual Compilation of Research

Editor: RITA J. SIMON, Director
Program in Law and Society
University of Illinois

VOLUME 1 • 1978

 JAI PRESS INC.
Greenwich, Connecticut

CONTENTS

THE POLITICAL ECONOMY OF SMACK: OPIATES,
CAPITALISM AND LAW

ASCRIPTIONS OF DANGEROUSNESS: THE EYE (AND
AGE, SEX, EDUCATION, LOCATION AND POLITICS) OF
THE BEHOLDER

LAW AND SOCIAL STATUS IN COLONIAL NEW HAVEN,
1639 – 1665

JUSTICE, VALUES AND SOCIAL SCIENCE: UNEXAMINED
PREMISES

CAUSAL ANALYSIS AND THE LEGAL PROCESS

SCHOOL DESEGREGATION AND SOCIAL SCIENCE: THE
VIRGINA EXPERIENCE

THE USE OF A PERSONAL SERVICE ASSISTANT IN THE
TREATMENT OF MENTAL HEALTH PROBLEMS:
A PROPOSAL AND SOME SPECULATIONS

ADOPTION FOR BLACK CHILDREN: A CASE STUDY OF
EXPERT DISCRETION

FOREWORD

This volume, which is the first in an annual series, contains fourteen invited essays by scholars representing five disciplines. The articles cover a wide range of topics, issues, and methods. The common theme is the importance all of them attach to the working relationship between law (making, interpreting, and enforcing) and social institutions, values, and public opinion. The contents of this volume as well as the style in which the articles are written should appeal to an academic and professional, as well as an interested lay audience. None of the pieces is overburdened by mathematical, statistical, or legal symbols or jargon. All address issues and topics about which persons trained in law, the social sciences, and the humanities might be interested. Almost all of them have theoretical as well as public policy import.

Of the twenty authors who have contributed to this volume, four are law professors, six are political scientists, five are psychologists, one is a historian, and four are sociologists. The volume is divided into four major sections. In part, the first section continues a debate on function and significance of law in developing countries. It contains a long essay by Seidman which takes issue with the position assumed by David Trubek and Marc Galanter in their earlier article on that topic which appeared in the *Wisconsin Law Review* (1974), Trubek's and Galanter's response to Seidman, and Seidman's brief response to Trubek and Galanter. Included in this first section are also pieces by Claude and Strouse on the relationship between human rights and economic development in developing countries. It is followed by Rothman's theoretical analysis of the historical and judicial responses that have been made to the dilemmas posed by the First Amendment to the United States Constitution, and it concludes with a piece by Simon and Barnum that reports the results of surveys concerning public attitudes and support for civil liberties in the United States and Israel.

The second section deals mostly with substantive issues of criminal law. It includes a piece by Gibbs in which he asks whether we can meaningfully identify deterrence as a goal of our penal policy. A piece by Chambliss, who claims that one must examine the political and economic forces that shape the laws governing the manufacture, distribution, sale and technology of drugs, because the policy that our government, or any capitalist system assumes vis-à-vis a given drug is a function of whether the system can profit from that drug. Monahan and Hood focus on definitions of dangerous acts as perceived by jurors. They compare jurors' beliefs about which types of acts are most dangerous against criminal psychiatric standards. Baumgartner has gained access to court records from seventeenth-century New Haven and uses the information they contain to assess the relationship between the inhabitants' social status and the rates of conviction, acquittal, and sentences in that colony.

The third section contains essays with strong methodological implications. The Nagel and Neef piece demonstrates concepts and methods for determining causality in the legal process. The thrust of Seidman's essay is to urge social scientists in general, and those working on issues affecting criminal justice and law enforcement in particular, to re-examine the premises that underlie the selection and formulation of their research problem, to generate alternative conceptualizations, and to thoroughly examine the intended and unintended social consequences of their research.

The last section contains three essays that stress the interaction between the written law and social practice. The articles examine and expose the degree of consensus and conflict between legal and social science expertise. Adolph Grundman examines Appellate Court responses to social scientists as expert witnesses and to social science data in the Virginia school desegregation cases heard in the late 1960s. Kirk Schwitzgebel explores the use of personal-service assistants to help persons function more effectively in their natural social environments. Jacqueline and Stewart Macaulay trace the law, the conflict, the current status, and the various alternatives to the placement of black children in adoptive family settings. They contrast the relative stability of the formal law against the more turbulent living law.

The pieces by Seidman, Trubek and Galanter, and Claude and Strouse concentrate on the appropriateness or the exportability of American concepts of law, due process, and legal liberalism to developing Third World nations. Responding to an earlier article by Trubek and Galanter, in which they expressed despair for the value and the usefulness of legal liberalism to help restructure those societies, Seidman takes them to task for the ethnocentrism of their views and model. Seidman's theme is that scholars whose research is guided by models that explain the world of the middle-class American academic will not be likely to serve the disinherited of Brazil, India, or other Third World countries. He urges scholars to do research on law and development problems by focusing on genuine existential problems in the Third World.

Trubek and Galanter respond that Seidman has distorted their original position. They claim that their entire article was devoted to showing that the method of legal liberalism was fundamentally wrong; that it was based principally on comparing their world institutions against an idealized model of Western law. But, they argue, Seidman has stood their original thesis on its head and in his essay accuses them of holding the very position they attacked. In Seidman's brief response, he pleads not guilty to the charge of distorting Trubek's and Galanter's thesis, and holds to his original view that Trubek and Galanter do not offer appropriate or useful tools for testing the model of liberal legalism.

There is a good deal of bitterness and name calling in the exchange. When they are all through, both sides seem to agree that appropriate methods have not yet been developed for testing the model, and that more work mostly of a methodological nature needs to be done.

Claude and Strouse trace the record of human rights of advanced industrial democracies against those of the developing countries. They show that economic development rates are negatively associated with social development and communications, particularly among those countries which sustain high standards of civil liberties and political rights. They posit a model that offers a base for predicting relationships between human rights (political rights and civil liberties) and economic, social, and political development.

The essay by Rozann Rothman shifts the locale to the United States as she identifies the contradictory historical and judicial responses that have been made to questions posed by the First Amendment. She assesses the competing demands of an absolute principle governing First Amendment questions against the exigencies of politics and collective security.

In the last essay in Section 1, Simon and Barnum report the results of two surveys of a cross section of American and Israeli publics concerning attitudes toward civil liberties issues in those societies. Civil liberties in the United States are guaranteed by the Constitution and by federal statutes. The rights specified in those documents are protected from recall or revision by enormously complicated mechanisms. Israel, on the other hand, is a society that has a substantial body of law which permits or legitimizes serious violations of individual rights, and lacks a written constitution. One of the purposes of the surveys was to explore the extent to which the Israeli and American publics are interested in and supportive of civil liberties and to determine the extent to which the written laws and formal mechanisms reflect or are at odds with popular sentiments in each society.

The essays in the second section focus on matters pertaining to criminal law and procedure. Three out of the four have explicit public policy directives. For example, in the first essay, Jack Gibbs writes that "to speak of crime prevention as a goal of penal policy is virtually meaningless without identifying the preventive mechanisms (e.g., deterrence, incapacitation, normative validation) by those who make penal policy." He observes that the validity of the deterrence doctrine could depend in large part on the amount of agreement between legal officials and the public as regards conceptions of crime. Thus, Gibbs concludes, "how much the public knows about criminal law is an important but underresearched issue."

Chambliss begins with the claim that "basic changes in law are a reflection of qualitative and quantitative changes in the political economy of a historical period and not simply the forces within a particular country." As Chambliss indicates early on, he plans to trace the development of legislation and law enforcement practices with respect to opium and its derivatives as illustrative of a model of rule creation that will be useful for analyzing law from a macro-political economic perspective. The bulk of the paper traces the policies that various governments pursued (the Portuguese, the British, the American) vis-à-vis the trade in opium. Chambliss concludes that "the heroin industry is a mainstay of the political economy of much of the capitalist world and it shall not be eliminated any more readily than will the automobile, banking, or construction industries."

The third essay in this section by Monahan and Hood has as its topic one of the most controversial issues in American criminal justice—that of operationally identifying and treating persons who are believed to be dangerous to themselves or to others. The first part of the article is concerned with definitions of dangerous behavior and the second part reports the results of an empirical study in which jurors (as representatives of the general citizenry) rated various behaviors (from having committed murder to using marijuana) as to how dangerous they are. After presenting the jurors' ratings, Monahan and Hood show how the ratings vary as a function of the jurors' social characteristics and how they vary or are consistent with clinicians and court officials who make decisions about treatment and confinement of persons considered dangerous.

The last piece, by M. P. Baumgartner, analyzes data based on 389 cases (148 civil and 241 criminal) heard in the colony of New Haven between 1639 and 1665. Baumgartner focuses on the relationship between the social status of the defendant and the litigant, and the verdicts and sanctions awarded them. She finds that in both the civil and criminal cases, principals who enjoyed high status were more likely to receive favorable treatment by the court.

The third section contains two essays that on initial inspection seem quite unrelated. The first one by Edward Seidman, a community psychologist whose most recent work has been the organizing and evaluating of a juvenile diversion program, is a critical and subjective analysis of the social and political implication of much of the research currently being done in law and criminal justice. Seidman claims that most of the research and theorizing that is done in this area functions to perpetuate the status quo. In his words, "it seems to do little more than reify existing legal and criminal justice policies, practices, and inherent values. Often the process is both insidious and unworthy." The first error that social scientists make, in Seidman's view, is the error of conceptualization—they select the "wrong problem for study." Seidman concludes by providing a set of guidelines for examining the premises underlying the selection and formulation of research problems.

Unlike Seidman, Nagel and Neef do not question the value premises that underlie problem formulation and conceptualization in research in law and society but believe that persons working in this field need more technical skills so that they can ferret out and better understand causal relationships. With the help of several detailed examples, the authors illustrate and explain how one can determine different types of causal analyses: co-effects and intervening variable causation, joint causation, and reciprocal causation. According to Nagel and Neef, the reasoning they ask their readers to apply is useful whether one is attempting to explain the outcomes of cases, the behavior of judges or attorneys, the treatment of defendants, or the effects of regulatory laws. Thus, in this section, Seidman urges researchers to re-examine the premises by which they choose to work on different problems and to carefully assess the social consequences of their output, and Nagel and Neef exhort researchers to gain more technical skills so that they can understand more fully what it is their data mean.

The essays in the last section examine the division of labor between law and social science, the conflict that arises between legal and social experts, and the contribution that various specialties make to the solution of social problems. Using *Brown vs. The Board of Education* as his point of departure, Adolph Grundman, a student of American constitutional history, shows how two major social science documents, "The Coleman Report" and "Racial Isolation in the Public Schools" (a study sponsored by the U.S. Commission on Civil Rights), were reviewed and treated by the Appellate Court in deciding school desegregation issues in Virginia. Grundman's essay concludes on a note of pessimism as he scans the future interest that the Appellate Courts are likely to have in social science and the influence that social scientists are likely to exert on appellate decisions. The pessimism stems largely from the breakdown of consensus which Grundman notes has occurred among social scientists in their assessment of the impact of segregated and desegregated schools on the self-image and emotional well-being of black children.

Schwitzgebel's piece is an exploratory essay on the feasibility of developing the role of personal-service assistants to help "ordinary persons" (not limiting the service to mental patients and "stars") function more effectively in their natural social environment. Schwitzgebel reviews studies that have shown the success that nonclinical volunteers have had working with mental patients in getting them to manage their business and personal affairs and the practice developed by prominent persons and stars in the entertainment world for using "agents" to negotiate for them. The division of labor between the service assistant and the client, and the characteristics of the contractual relationship between them are considered in this essay.

The final essay, by Jacqueline and Stewart Macaulay, provides a brief history of the rise and fall of transracial adoption in the United States as it traces the various alternatives and proposed solutions that have been put forth by the law, the social work profession, adoption agencies, and the black community to the problem of providing adequate homes for black children who cannot live with their biological parents. They review subsidized adoption schemes, describe the advocates and opponents of transracial adoption, probe the underlying values that have determined various adoption policies, assess which groups have had decision-making powers and how they exercised those powers, and finally offer criteria for deciding how prospective adoptive parents and homeless Black children might be united. The essay evaluates the worthwhileness of expert discretion as a tool for solving important social problems.

Before concluding, I would like to express a few thoughts about the content and organization of subsequent volumes that may appear in this series. While the essays that appear in this volume can be separated into four sections, each of which shares a common method and/or substantive theme, the editor did not plan for that to occur. For this volume, she contacted individual scholars and negotiated each contribution without regard for the overall package. What she wanted was thoughtful work on important issues that covered a wide range of topics in the field. That seemed an appropriate format for a first volume. But for the second and later volumes, other formats will be given serious consideration. For example, a volume might be composed of comparative studies, dealing with law and social institutions in different societies. Another might deal with a common substantive interest in criminal behavior and its control, or the function of law in social movements, conflict, and change. A volume organized around various methods for collecting and analyzing data might also be appropriate for a later time.

In this volume, the reader will find considerable variation in the length of the essays. More uniformity might be imposed on later volumes with an emphasis on fewer longer pieces or a greater number of shorter contributions. To a large extent, the critical and market reception that this first volume receives will influence the form, content, and organization of subsequent ones.

Rita J. Simon

THE LESSONS OF SELF-ESTRANGEMENT: ON THE METHODOLOGY OF LAW AND DEVELOPMENT

Robert B. Seidman[1], BOSTON UNIVERSITY SCHOOL OF LAW

The Attorney-General of the United States, in his earlier incarnation as President of the University of Chicago, remarked to an entering law school class in 1974, that

> if law is a mediating discipline with respect to the craftsmanship which is useful and the relevance of what is perceived as current knowledge or opinion, then it is important that the higher learning in law search out those techniques and theories of knowledge most relevant to the correction or direction of law [Levi (14)].

This essay is a modest response to Professor Levi's call.

Its immediate concerns are the problems of law and development in the Third World. Its locus of concern is not accidental. Every country of course uses the legal order (that is, the rules promulgated by government

Research in Law and Sociology — Vol. 1, 1978, pages 1–29.

officials, and their activities in their roles) as an instrument to induce social change. Nowhere, however, is its use so striking as in the poorer countries of the world, that are trying through the legal order[2] to transform their societies. The "correction or direction of law" in these countries lies on the urgent agenda.

The occasion for these reflections is a fascinating article by Professors David M. Trubek and Marc Galanter [Trubek and Galanter (29)], hereinafter "T-G." That article describes what its authors believe to be a general sense of self-doubt among scholars concerned with the issues of law and development. It proposes an explanation, and then suggests alternative solutions.

I take issue with them with respect to their explanations and solutions for the perceived difficulty. To explain why I do and what I would substitute, I must first summarize their article. In its nature, this paper is somewhat polemical. It expresses a sharp disagreement, going, as I see it, to the very roots of the enterprise. In a nutshell, I disagree with T-G about the "techniques and theories of knowledge most relevant to the correction or direction of law" of which Professor Levi spoke.

I

T-G are quite right to observe that law and development studies in this country are in crisis. Funding is almost dead. Student interest in courses not particularly relevant to bar exams is all but dead. Foreign students have dwindled to a trickle. Practically none of us who began the enterprise are left doing it as a full-time academic exercise, if at all.

But that is also the story of law and society studies in this country. Interest there, too, is dying. Scholars everywhere question the relevance of social science to legal studies.

T-G offer an explanation for the current malaise in law and development studies. Briefly restated (too briefly: their argument is elegantly put, with rich and intriguing detail), they argue that law and development studies in this country began with a model or paradigm of law in society, which they call "liberal legalism" [Trubek and Galanter (29), pp. 1070–1072]. This, they claim, was shared by "most" of the scholars in the field. It consisted of the following propositions:

1. Society is made up of individuals, voluntary groups and the state; the state is seen as "a process by which individuals, principally through their membership in . . . voluntary groups, formulate rules for mutual self-governance . . . and since individuals consent to the state, including its coercive features, state control furthers individual welfare."

2. "The state exercises its control over the individual through law—bodies of rules that are addressed universally to all individuals similarly situated." The state coerces violators, "but only in accordance with rules by which the state itself is constrained."

3. "Rules are consciously designed to achieve social purposes"—that is, the purposes of society as a whole, not merely limited groups within it. "Rules are made through a pluralist process which enables all individuals to secure rules favorable to them, while ensuring that the rules respect the vital interests of all others." "No single group . . . dominates the process of formulation of legal rules, and no special characteristic of individuals or groups, such as wealth or race, gives them systematic advantages or disadvantages in rule making."

4. These rules are enforced equally for all citizens, and in a fashion that achieves the purposes for which they were consciously designed.

5. The courts normally have the final say in defining the social meaning of the laws; they are the central institutions of the legal order. The "basic, typical, decisive mode of legal action" is adjudication (the application of rules by courts or court-like institutions). In so doing, the courts produce an autonomous body of learning. It is this body of learning which determines the outcome of adjudication.

6. The behavior of social actors tends to conform to the rules: officials are guided by the rules, not personal class, regional or other bases of decision-making; a large portion of the rules will be internalized by most of the population.

T-G understood "development" to involve not merely increased rationality in man's control of his world and increased material well-being, but also "greater equality, enhanced freedom, and fuller participation in the community" [Trubek and Galanter (29), p. 1073]. Law, following the paradigm of liberal legalism, held the promise of accomplishing all these at once. It was rational and purposive, and hence could achieve the "instrumental" goals of increased material well-being. If "law"—as defined by liberal legalism—were thus used, the other goodies would necessarily follow.

This paradigm was associated with a research agenda that focused on "instrumental" research designed to ascertain the legal changes required to achieve some specific developmental goals. The assumption that T-G say they made was that "the growth of an instrumental perspective would generate legal development, which would in turn foster a system of governance by universal, purposive rules, and would accordingly contribute to the enhancement of liberty, equality, participation and rationality" [(29), p. 1076]. Above all, they tell us that they assumed that "any activity that was designed to change the legal institutions of the Third World countries to make them more like those of the United States would be an effective and morally worthy pursuit." [(29), pp. 1079–80.] They assure us that they were *sincere*—as if anyone doubted that. "We believed in the model. Liberal legalism was not a cynical sham hastily constructed to be palmed off on the world's poor. It was, on the contrary, a clear reflection of the basic ideas about the relationship between law and society and between the United States and the Third World that prevailed in United States universities in the late 1950's and 1960's" [(29), p. 1088].

It did not work that way. T-G assert that scholars (of course they mean themselves) "have come to see that legal change may have little or no effect on social economic conditions in Third World societies and conversely, that many legal 'reforms' only deepen inequality, curb participation, restrict individual freedom, and hamper efforts to increase material well-being."

That is to say, they came to believe on the basis of experience that the promises of legal liberalism were false, as well in the Third World as at home. The state does not represent all of us. It represents particular classes or elites pro tempore in control. It exercises its control only partly through general rules, but partly through arbitrary particularism. Government is at best only fitfully constrained by the law, as Watergate has driven home. The purposes of the rules are ineluctably the purposes of particular strata or classes. The pluralist dogma depends upon equal access, which is patently a myth. The rules are certainly not enforced equally for all citizens. The courts are peripheral to the legal order. The gap between the law-in-the-books and the law-in-action is systematic, not aberrational.

The paradigm having been overthrown, T-G find themselves self-estranged from their subject. They seek to find a solution for their malaise. They offer a set of alternative solutions [(29), pp. 1097–1100]. (1) Legal isolationism—i.e., to abandon the whole law and development enterprise, on the supposedly moral ground that the American lawyer has nothing to offer. (2) "A-legal developmentism"—i.e., to abandon the study of law in favor of those aspects of the developmental process that lie "outside the center of professional, legal concern, but seem at the heart of the effort to secure greater participation, equality and material welfare." (3) "Pragmatic problem-solving," i.e., to abandon the search for theories of law and development, and merely help solve problems as perceived by Third World people. (4) "Positivistic pure science"—i.e., "pure empirical research," devoid of any policy or moral purposes. (5) "Eclectic critique—i.e., to retain the whole vision of liberal legalism, but to treat its propositions as problematical rather than as factual statements of what is the case, and to use them as "critical standards." (They choose the last of these, but accept the others as possible solutions.)

T-G suffer the contemporary *Angst*. Stripped of the moral certainties, like all of us, they see themselves condemned, lost in an unending miasma of doubt and fear, threatened by visions of unending catastrophe, a lifework called into question, alienated from the very subject to which they have both dedicated fruitful professional lives. Of course they are self-estranged.

II

Their explanation for their self-estrangement is, I believe, insufficient. Like every explanation, it has a major premise, here explicit. If I were to "explain" (to propose a ridiculous example to make a point), the existence of plea-bargaining in courts by the assertion, "Policemen wear blue uniforms," the explanation would fail. It would fail because the implicit major premise is false (i.e., that the color of the uniform of the arresting officer determines the procedure used to determine the case). The validity of the major premise—the underlying hypothesis—in part determines the validity of the every explanation.

T-G take their major premise from T. S. Kuhn's monumental *The Structure of Scientific Revolutions:*

> Confronted with anomaly or crisis, scientists take a different attitude towards existing paradigms, and the nature of their research changes accordingly. The proliferation of competing articulations, the willingness to try anything, the expression of explicit discontent, the recourse to philosophy and to debate over fundamentals, all these are symptoms of a transition from normal to extraordinary research [(29) p. 1093].

Therefore, T-G tell us, they are estranged.

By the word "paradigm" Kuhn meant to suggest that "some accepted examples of actual scientific practice—examples which include law, theory, application and instrumentation together—provide models from which spring particular coherent traditions of scientific research [Kuhn (13), p. 10]. Included in that notion of "paradigm" is, of course, a general statement of the researcher's understanding of how things fit together ("theory")—the molecular theory of matter, for example. T-G follow not Kuhn's definition of "paradigm," but the currently fashionable one that identifies it with such a general statement. (Hereafter, I use the word "paradigm" in this second and more usual sense.)

Legal liberalism was such a paradigm. Unlike the equivalent sets of propositions in natural science, however, it was on its face normative as well, because it clearly suggested what ought to be the case as well as what is the case. That is inevitable in the social sciences. As Dewey has argued, every statement about what we *ought* to do is based upon some perception of what *is* [Dewey (5), p. 74]. Every statement of what is the case, therefore, can be understood as a truncated proposal to do something. Thus, T-G's propositions of liberal legalism led them to the belief that it would be a good thing to imitate U.S. legal institutions elsewhere in the world.

Their invocation of Kuhn is therefore both erroneous and revealing. It is erroneous not only because their definition of "paradigm" was very different from his, but also because Kuhn was discussing the physical sciences—a distinction that T-G note but do not pursue. In those disciplines, there is for long periods a dominant paradigm within which what Kuhn calls "normal science" takes place. In social science, however, there are always competing paradigms. Adam Smith presented one model of capitalist society, Karl Marx another. Both have existed for generations. In the same way, all during the short day of law and development studies there were competing models. The model of legal liberalism was never held by every scholar in the field[3] [Trubeck and Galanter (29), p. 1062]. That there are always competing paradigms in social science should teach us all that we must justify the one we adopt, not assume its validity. Had T-G sought to justify legal liberalism, they would necessarily have treated it problematically, instead of taking its propositions for granted.

The reference to Kuhn is interesting for another reason. Kuhn argues that in hard science paradigms are not commensurable, that is, it is impossible to compare two competing paradigms by the use of the scientific method. (This proposition has been vigorously attacked [Phillips (18)].) The adoption of a new paradigm is therefore in Kuhn's view an act of faith, not of reason, even in the hard sciences. The discontent and malaise that accompany the time of paradigm change arise because scientists are then called upon to question their faith, not to determine by experiment and data whether propositions are false. Questioning one's faith leads to self-doubt and self-alienation.

T-G's anguish arises for the same reason. If they had by research falsified a middle-level hypothesis concerning law and development, as competent social scientists and lawyers no doubt they would have been delighted. Karl Popper has shown [Popper (20)] that we learn nothing from data that are *consistent* with a hypothesis. We learn nothing about the proposition that water boils at 100° C. by boiling yet another open pot of water at sea level, and solemnly measuring its temperature. We only learn when we attempt to falsify the proposition—by boiling it at 5,000 feet, for example, or in a closed pot. The spirit of inquiry requires us to seek falsification, and to abandon the notion that we can ever be *sure*.

Instead of treating the propositions of legal liberalism as problematic propositions, subject to disproof (i.e., "hypotheses"), however, T-G, fortified by what I believe to be their misreading of Kuhn, took them as articles of faith. Having, as they tell us, falsified them, they have in fact added to the sum total of knowledge. That ordinarily is an occasion for celebration, not self-doubt, discontent and *Weltschmertz*. The explanation for their anguish, however, is not merely that they are undergoing the heartache of paradigm change. Paradigm change for them led to anguish because they accorded a completely different epistemological status to ordinary hypotheses, and to those of the sort embodied in legal liberalism. A principal thrust of my argument here is that that is the principal source of what I believe to be their error, Kuhn notwithstanding.

Theories of knowledge and how to acquire it—that is, epistemology and methodologies—must be addressed to the particular sorts of knowledge required by the problems at hand. Before I can discuss T-G's methodology (and offer a substitute), I must examine the sorts of problems to which I believe law and development as a discipline is addressed.

III

Perhaps I may be forgiven a brief personal digression. I had practiced law for fourteen years before going to Africa in 1962—that was my first teaching post. Far from going there to do research or to carry the torch for liberal legalism, I went out of an acute sense of Peace Corps-itis (a dread disease to which liberal Americans are very susceptible). I believed then that my chief job was to teach whatever professional expertise I had to law students, in aid of people with whom I empathized.

Ghana from 1962 to 1966 was a strange place. Nkrumah's rhetoric expressed farsighted and humanistic notions of development. Their implementation was, however, sadly ineffective. Ghana was a classic example of what Gunnar Myrdal later called "soft development," a condition where much is said but little actually accomplished.

The study of soft development led me quickly to the study of law as a system of social engineering. I came to define the central problem for law and development research as how to use the tools of social and juridical science to remake the world: no modest task. How to acquire knowledge for that task, of course, is what Professor Levi called for in his University of Chicago speech. It is a domain of study dictated by the nature of society, development and law.

Society is a society (rather than anarchy) because its members behave in repetitive, organized patterns. Those patterns can be defined in the vocabulary of role theory. Repetitive patterns of behavior identify a *role*. The rules that define patterns of repetitive behavior are *norms*.

To define a society is to define its roles. Tanzania is Tanzania in part because farmers there use short-handled hoes and not tractors. The United States is the United States in part because farmers here use tractors, not short-handled hoes. Each set of farmers follows its own norms of behavior. The difference between the set of norms followed in each country defines the difference between the two societies.

When a society changes, the repetitive patterns of behavior change. Farmers come to use tractors rather than short-handled hoes. Social change is a change in the set of norms defining the society. Development, whatever else it may be, is a form of social change.

The legal order is the tool most easily available to politically organized society to bring about purposive social change. Law does this by redefining norms so that, if the new rules in fact induce the behavior which they prescribe, new patterns of social interaction will ensue. Society will be to that extent changed.

Of course, people are not infinitely plastic, nor is the legal order an infinitely flexible tool. It has its limits. The core of the study of law and development, I believe is to define those limits. Knowledge concerning them is essential if the laws to be formulated are to induce the desired behavior, and not other sorts—that is, if soft development is to be avoided. Since the limits of the legal order are in the main defined by society, to study the limits of the legal order is to study the way in which it is related to society.

That is only part of the problem, however. Another aspect of the study of law and development is to discover what sorts of changes in the legal order might be helpful in generating the processes of development. An adequate study of law and development must lead not only to general propositions describing the limits of the legal order, but also to specific proposals for new laws that might be helpful in the circumstances of the Third World [Seidman, (27)].

T-G also perceived these as the tasks of law and development research. They defined a dual role for themselves. On the one hand they describe themselves as "social theorists of law," who "saw Third World nations engaged in the massive use of law to carry out rapid changes in society, thus presenting a fruitful area of theoretical inquiry into the role of law in social change" [Trubek and Galanter (29), p. 1068]. On the other hand, they were humanists. They perceived that "law was . . . both a necessary element in 'development' and a useful instrument to achieve it". They sought to enhance "liberty, equality, participation and rationality" by engaging in "instrumental research designed to ascertain the legal changes needed to achieve some specific developmental goal".

It is a problem with an ancient provenance. How to relate theory and practice? How to provide understandings about how things are, and at the same time to generate specific solutions for specific problems? Lawyers are, after all, not living in ivory towers. They are professionals engaged in practice. The bottom line in law and development studies must be specific laws which will induce developmental activity, designed in such a way that the sum of these solutions for particular problems does not emerge as the biggest problem of all. That requires both a social theory of law, and real-world problem-solving, ending in rules apt to induce development.

(That is not to say that, among scholars, a division of labor is not possible or desirable. Some may emphasize one, some the other task.)

Justice theory, too, is concerned with what the law ought to be. Professor Levi's question poses the problem not only of a theory of knowledge concerning law, but a theory of justice as well: How do we go about acquiring knowledge about what is a just law and a just legal order?— always remembering that a rule which is in the books but not reflected in action is generally neither just nor unjust, but merely futile.

IV

In the mainstream of U.S. social science, "theoretical" research is sharply distinguished from "policy" or "instrumental" research. T-G made the same distinction.[4] That distinction arose from their epistemology.

In that mainstream, these two sorts of research are discrete. Most social scientists assume a discontinuity of the Is and the Ought. Ends—what ought to be the case—are a matter of "values" or even "taste." What they are depends not upon data or science, but the sort of person one is. Means depend upon what is the case. That can be determined by an examination of the real world. The determination of goals is irrational. It is a matter of will. The determination of means is scientific. It is a matter of reason. Values enter into policy choice only at the point of deciding upon ends, not in determining the means.

Now we all carry about in our intellectual baggage what Alvin Gouldner has called "domain assumptions" [Gouldner (9)]. These domain assumptions are, as T-G put it, a "cognitive map of relations among social phenomenon." Implicitly or explicitly, they serve to support some set of values—i.e., ends. They explain "the goodness or potency of some feature of social life" [Trubeck and Galanter (29)]. T-G say that their paradigm of liberal legalism was a set of such domain assumptions.

Precisely because they are normative, such domain assumptions are, in mainstream social science, perceived as epiphenomena of one's "values." Values, whether expressed in normative propositions or as a set of prizings, are not susceptible of empirical warrant or falsification. The Is cannot prove the Ought. One adheres to such domain assumptions not because one is persuaded by data (an act of reason) but because that is the sort of man one is (an act of will). Therefore, such domain assumptions do not arise as the outcome of research. They need not be held hypothetically or problematically, for neither proof nor falsification is possible. Rather, they are believed. The set of one's domain assumptions is one's model or paradigm of society. They define one's understanding of how things are, and suggest the ends toward which one should strive.

The essence of the scientific temper is to hold *every* proposition problematically. It has three important characteristics. "The first may be called the hypothetical spirit, the feeling of tentativeness and caution, the respect for probable error. . . . The second ingredient is experimentalism, the willingness to expose ideas to empirical testing, to procedures, to action. . . . These two features, plus the corrective of criticism, are what is meant by the methodological rules of science; it is the *spirit of inquiry.* a love of truth relentlessly pursued, that ultimately creates the objectivity and intelligent action associated with science" [Bennis (2), p. 48].

Mainstream methodology abandons the scientific temper precisely at the point where it is most required in the policy-making process—that is, in the determination of ends. It does not propose any substitute methodology. It could not, for it teaches that belief in such paradigms depends on the sort of man one is—and *that* is not easily changed.

On the other hand, mainstream social science holds that it is possible to discover general statements about the world that hold true in every time and place. There are, it is believed, universal laws (in the scientific sense) governing the relationship between the legal order and society, as true in Nairobi as New York [Friedman and Macauley (8), pp. 915–16]. It is a theory of knowledge that takes as its model the physical sciences, for atoms do behave the same in Nairobi and New York. T-G, for example, propose as a possible alternative solution for law and development scholarship, "positivistic pure science," devoted to study only "the facts," with a task of "explanation, not evaluation" [(Trubek and Galanter (29), p. 1098]. Description and the analysis of causes, in this view, have no moral component, just as the search for means is presumably value-free. In this arena the scientific temper holds sway, for these empirical propositions are subject to test and falsification.

T-G believe, in accord with mainstream notions, that a theory of law and society will be built out of such empirical research. They distinguish such research from "pragmatic problem-solving." The pragmatic problem-solver, they claim, "denies that his work involves any theory of law and development." Instead, he merely lends his skills in aid of the people of the less developed world. It is a solution bought, in T-G's view, at a price: "It denies that a theory of law and development is possible," and "the scholar must admit that his work can make no contribution to any body of general knowledge".

T-G reject for themselves both "positivistic pure science" and "pragmatic problem-solving." They believe, however, that both are possible. Both are consistent with their epistemology. It is that epistemology that, I believe, has brought T-G to their present muddle. They made sharp cleavages between "description" and "analysis," which are scientific but not a matter of values or ethics; "policy," which is all values and ethics, but not science; and "problem-solving," which is none of the above. It gave them no clue about how to generate a new paradigm, for that is a matter of faith, not reason. Faith may move mountains. Conversely it takes a mountain to change faith. Collisions with mountains do tend to create moments of self-doubt.

V

When I began to try to understand soft development in Ghana, I brought to the task the ordinary philosophical and jurisprudential tools of American lawyers of my generation. American legal realism taught that there was likely to be a divergence between the law-in-the-books and the law-in-action. It taught that the premise of T-G's legal liberalism, that behavior tended to match the norms of the law both for officials and for ordinary citizens,[5] was false. Soft development also concerned the difference between the words of the law and the action which it was supposed to induce.

Soft development as a domain of study led to the study of the legal order as a system of social engineering. That immediately raised the question of values. Like T-G, I then accepted as given the dichotomy between ends and means. Fourteen years of practice in the United States, however, had persuaded me that the legal order in the United States was warped in favor of the rich and the powerful.[6] Anybody who represented blacks or the poor in criminal cases in Connecticut in that period knew in his bones that that was the case. There was obviously a vast difference between the perceptions about the legal order held by those on top and those who viewed the system from its seamier underside. Far from accepting the ends of liberal legalism and urging the replication of American legal institutions overseas, it seemed clear to me that one had to fashion institutions that were adapted to their African milieu, and which overcame what I perceived to be the biases of our own legal order.[7]

What ends or objectives should the legal order then serve? American experience taught that far from there being a consensus on values, conflict prevailed. If that were so, then whose values should control? Plainly, not my own personal ends, drawn from my personal, American experience, but the values of Africans ought to determine the shape of the law's commands to them.

Pound's notions of jural postulates seemed to offer an appropriate intellectual framework. Pound held that from the claims and demands made by the population upon the legal order one could distill propositions—the jural postulates—which together made up the value-sets of the subjects of the law. Any just legal order must fit those jural postulates [Pound (21)].

It was self-evident, however, that African society, like American, did not contain any jural postulates upon which there was a consensus. The African legal order is a plural system. Customary law guides most of the jural relationships of most Africans. The received English law controls those relationships among non-Africans, and among most of the Westernized elite. (Legislation, of course, may override both.) Claims are made on each of these systems.

My first effort was to try to state the conflicting jural postulates underpinning each of them. These I labeled Status (concerning rights arising out of the customary order), Contract (concerning rights claimed by those who adhered to a more or less laissez-faire notion about how to organize the society), and Plan (relating to socialist concepts). T-G's legal liberalism is, in that tripartite model, one form of a Contract perspective [Seidman (28)].

My attempt to use Pound's method failed. It fell apart because of the impossibility of discovering what the jural postulates of the different strata in fact were. I found myself asking the silly question, What jural postulates would *I* hold if *I* were an African of a certain sort?

Like T-G today, I began to cast about for some other way to approach the problems of law and development. I found answers that seemed to me to be satisfying in the writings of John Dewey. Most of the remainder of this essay concerns that alternative epistemology.

I argued above that T-G's malaise arose because they gave a different epistemological status to the sorts of propositions they labeled legal liberalism than they gave to those derived from "instrumental research." If one accepts as true the notion that ends and means are discontinuous, and that ends can only be evolved out of the subjective "values" of the individual, then T-G were quite right in giving them a different epistemological status. Given the assumption, that was inevitable. If so, they have correctly explained their discontents, and their catalogue of proposals for solutions seems complete. If, however, the concepts of ends and means do not represent reality, but only ways in which people try to understand reality, there may be another way of conceptualizing the problem which avoids the dilemmas that T-G have encountered. In that case, there is another path out of their puzzlement.

In short, I argue here (1) that the concepts of ends and means are not statements about what is the case, but concepts developed by man in his constant effort to understand the world; (2) that they are therefore not inevitable or necessary categories, but must be justified in terms of their utility for the task at hand—and T-G have demonstrated their inutility; and

(3) that there is another set of concepts and methodology that avoids the difficulties of the ends-means schema. I propose such a set of concepts and methodology below.

VI

Before undertaking to suggest an alternative epistemology and methodology, it may be useful to suggest an explanation for the deep attachment that so many have to the means-ends schema. We are all brought up in that schema. So deeply are we indoctrinated in it that many regard proponents of any other quite mad.

It is probably inevitable that we so believe. Everywhere, society teaches us the difference between ends and means. Our political structures are bureaucratic. Bureaucracies are inherently instrumental. They are supposed to achieve ends determined by the political process. Our political institutions determine ends by processes involving power, not reason—the power of the majority, of elites, of pressure groups. Inevitably, we assume that the institutions we live in are as they are because they could not be otherwise. That our societies determine ends by power teaches that they cannot be determined by reason.

Our system of property law contributes to the same belief. The law endows the owner of productive goods with the power to determine the uses to be made of them [Renner (23)]. The rest of us are employees, part of the means of achieving the ends determined by the owners. In corporate law, for example, the directors are supposed to determine "policy" (i.e., ends); the employees determine how to achieve them (i.e., means). Again, our institutions argue *sub silentio* that the distinction between ends and means is immanent in the objective world.

Finally, our intellectual history similarly persuades us. Western man emerged from the heady excitement of the American and French revolutions in the belief that now, after the long night of oppression, superstition and unreason, science and enlightened human reason would make a better world. It did not work that way. Poverty and oppression continued. Charles Dickens's England embodied horrors no less terrible than those that preceded it. War killed more people by far after the Enlightenment than before. Events proved false the great promises of the revolutionary era.

Social science then undertook to explain why man, seemingly so rational, ended with so irrational a social environment. Pareto spoke of "residues," Weber of "values," Freud the superego and the id. Man might be rational and scientific in dealing with means, but the ends were determined by dark, irrational currents holding sway in the inaccessible recesses of the mind [Hughes (11)].

The source of these irrational forces was held to be society itself. We are all acculturated by our social circumstances to the values which we hold. They are, as it were, implanted upon our neurons, as an electric circuit is printed upon a plate [Kluckhohn (12), p. 396]. In final analysis, mainstream social science taught us that society—man's creation—is out of man's control. It was a pathological view of human society [Gouldner (9)].

History repeated itself in the Third World after World War II. Liberation from the old bonds of colonialism gave rise to the hope that the new leadership would use reason and science to develop rational, humane societies. They did not. The Development Decade in Africa culminated in the worst starvation in recent memory. In much of the Third World, military putsch replaced democratic elections, fascist-like regimes emerged triumphant, torture and oppression and poverty if anything increased. It was easy to see in these horrors verification for the explanations earlier advanced by mainstream social science.

Given the weight of institutional example and intellectual history, most of us come to believe in the discontinuity between ends and means, and the inevitable irrationality involved in the choice of ends. T-G's epistemology was in the mainstream. Their self-estrangement arose because it instructed them that general models are "assumed." They are mere epiphenomena of "values and attitudes." When their models no longer fit, their methodology did not suggest an agenda of steps to take to devise a new one. Nevertheless, they must scratch for a replacement. That search is wrenching and anguished.

Their mood reflects the crisis of modern man: Endowed with the tools of science, man is nevertheless unable to use them, it seems, to structure his social world. Mainstream social science and society itself shout in unison that the lamentable result is inevitable. Irrational forces, not science, control society.

If that chorus be telling us the truth, then the whole enterprise of law and development—that is, the use of science and reason to help restructure society—is a lost cause. In that event, T-G are quite right to feel estranged.

That is not, however, necessarily the case. We invent words (and therefore concepts) to explain the world. Our culture everywhere distinguishes between the roles and functions of deciding policy, and implementing it. We develop a vocabulary to mark off those discrete functions: the Is and the Ought, means and ends, descriptive and normative, implementation and policy. Once we have developed such a vocabulary, we necessarily think in those terms. We "explain" the inevitability of the institutional structure by the very existence of the words to which the institutional structure itself gave rise.

Words impose their own tyranny. If I say the word "chair," I can point to a chair as one of the class of things referred to by the word "chair." It is precious easy to come to believe that because we have a word for something, it must exist in the real world. We too easily believe that the words "ends" and "means" stand for something as "real" as a chair.

The contrary, however, may be the case. The institutions which gave rise to both our vocabulary of ends and means, and the explanations for social irrationality given by mainstream social science, may have arisen because particular individuals, classes, or elites have seized power and used it to mould institutions and history so as to maximize their own interest.[8] Social scientists from Marx to C. Wright Mills (19) so argued. In that view, rather than our institutions reflecting on inevitable dichotomy between means and ends, that supposed dichotomy reflects the institutional structure. John Dewey insisted that far from being discontinuous, means and ends form a continuum [Dewey (7)].

I do not propose here to enter upon the controversy concerning the origins and functions of social institutions. To demonstrate that mainstream epistemology is not inevitable, I need only suggest an alternative that does not rest on the claimed cleavage between the Is and the Ought, and which therefore unifies the search for knowledge and the search for justice. I attempt in the following sections to sketch such a methodology in briefest outline.

VII

I begin with what I think is the great paradox of social science, the problem of learning from experience. That problem arises out of the complexity and consequent unpredictability of the human circumstance.

Physical science concerns things without consciousness. Atoms do not think. One atom is like another.

People are different. They have consciousness. Now consciousness plainly arises out of the material world. We are a very long way from being able to describe in detail how that works; the mind-body problem remains, I believe, largely unsolved. To the extent that it remains unsolved, our knowledge about the "laws" of human behavior must remain very scanty indeed. If so, the notion that in our present state of knowledge we can discover "laws" of socio-legal behavior, analgous to the laws of the physical sciences, as true in Nairobi as New York, cannot be true. (I leave open the question whether such laws are in principle discoverable.)

I see the moon from a different angle than you do. My experience is always different from yours. Peter Winch goes so far as to say that "when we speak of the possibility of scientific predictions of social developments of this sort, we literally do not understand what we are saying. We cannot understand it, because it has no sense" [Winch (31), p. 94].

On the other hand, if we cannot learn predictable patterns of human behavior, purpose disappears from the world. Every time we attempt conscious intervention in human events, in order to bring about desired change, we must rely upon what we have learned from experience about how things happen.

The problem, therefore, is to learn from experience. By that I mean to extract from one set of circumstance those variables ("causes") that seem to have been both amenable to human manipulation and to have affected the results in that case, and then use that knowledge in a new situation. To the extent that we cannot yet derive "laws" about human behavior, to learn from experience is a paradoxical notion.

The paradox, I think, can be resolved by treating propositions about the social behavior of human beings as *heurisms*. By that I mean that such propositions are never reliable predictions about how human beings will behave in any new situation. Rather, they tell us only that experience teaches that in other cases facts of the categories described in the independent variable seem to have had a described relationship to facts in the categories in the dependent relationship, and that therefore it would be sensible to investigate facts in the relevant categories in the case at hand to see if the same relationship might hold true in the new case. As Marx put it, theory is not a dogma, but a guide to action.

As every common lawyer who has dealt with the problem of precedent knows, it is logically impossible to proceed from one particular set of circumstances to another without formulating a general rule to subsume at least those two circumstances. Knowledge consists of these general propositions. Suppose that in a case study of a government corporation in Zambia, for example, it appears that the directors were powerless to control management, and that this seems to arise because they are part-time directors. The general proposition, "part-time directors of government corporations are ineffective in controlling management," is a plausible major hypothesis for an explanation for the Zambia difficulty. That becomes an item of knowledge—hypothetical, tentative, problematical, to be sure—that may be useful in other cases.

Such propositions are not, however, "laws" in the sense that physical science generates "laws," no matter how often that seems to explain new situations. They are, instead, heurisms. That characterization arises out of the inevitable complexity of historical situations.

An engineer building a bridge in Nairobi can use the same principles of physics and engineering there as he can in New York. A steel girder of a specified sort will have the same strength in the one place as the other. When he examines a bridge which has failed, he can rely upon his stock of knowledge of such propositions to explain why the particular bridge failed.

In the social sciences, in the present state of the art, that is not true. Their analogous propositions can do no more than to point to the categories of particular data that should be examined to find a likely explanation for the event in question. So, if seeking to explain the behavior of a government corporation in Kenya, one could never assert without research in Kenya that "part-time directors of government corporations are ineffective in controlling management." That proposition only advises the researcher that he ought to investigate the amount of time spent by directors on corporate affairs in Kenya, and their effectiveness there in controlling management.

Such general propositions in social science have an analogous function in devising solutions for problems. The laws of physics are predictive. They advise the engineer in Nairobi, as in New York, that if he uses a steel girder of a certain sort it will bear a certain load. That is not the case with social science. There are too many possible intervening variables. If one is creating a public corporation in Ghana, it would be daft to insist that without more than part-time directors, controlling management will be useless, merely because that seems an adequate explanation for the difficulties of public corporations in Zambia and Kenya. Instead, that proposition now advises that there is likely to be a difficulty with respect to the control of management by part-time directors, and that therefore the researcher must investigate the actual situation of directors and managers in the Ghanaian context to see if that result is also likely there.

General propositions in the social sciences are indispensable as guides to research into specific cases. They do not of themselves solve any specific problems. Chairman Mao put it neatly: "No empirical investigation, no right to speak" [Mao (16)].

Even if, therefore, T-G's notions about legal liberalism had been explanations tested by empirical investigations in the United States, T-G would not have been warranted in assuming that therefore they would result in the same consequences in the Third World as in the United States. That assertion is supported by a consideration of the way in which law influences behavior.

It is plainly the case that people rarely behave as they do merely because the law commands them to do so. The simplest and also the most general model of society is that of individuals and collectivities making choices about what to do [Barth (1)]. To explain their choices, one must first explicate the constraints and resources within which they choose (i.e., their range of choice), and second, the reasons for their choosing as they do within that range [MacIntyre (15)]. The legal order is only one of the many sets of constraints and resources in the human environment. I drive on the right hand side of the road only in part because I may feel obliged to do so [Hart (10)] or because I may be arrested if I do not. Mainly I choose to do so because otherwise I may be demolished by another automobile.

The constraints and resources that face different people in different historical situations are enormously varied, for each situation is unique. Even if the laws in any two historically different situations be on their face the same, the varying social contours of the two situations make the range of choice in each case different. As a result, the behavior that ensues in each case can be similar only by serendipity.

That means that a law that induces a particular sort of behavior in one time and place likely will not, save by accident, induce the same sort of behavior in another time or place. I have elsewhere (in a moment of egomania) called this the Law of Non-Transferability of Law [Seidman (25)]. Even if it were true that the institutions of legal liberalism resulted in liberty, democracy and rationality in the United States, they would have had the same effect in Brazil or India only by chance. The notion that it made sense (I do not advert to ethnocentrism or morality) to copy U.S. legal institutions elsewhere was a loser from the start.

VIII

Lawyers are a singularly down-to-earth lot. They deal with existential problems in the real world, not with abstract ideas for their own sake. Our research inevitably begins not with a variable to be tested, or an interest in developing general theory. Usually, for lawyers, it begins with some problem which is causing somebody some difficulty: that public corporations are not operating very well, that existing land tenures seem to be blocking agricultural development, and the like. That requires a preliminary selection of the existential problems to be investigated.

The choice of problems to be investigated requires one to decide, *whose* problems? Does one begin with the problems of the U.S. investor? The elite? The investors in the stock market? The poor? Or the problems of U.S. academics?

Now we all start with general paradigms of some sort. That paradigm directs attention to what is to be investigated. The paradigm of liberal legalism tells us that law represents society as a whole, not merely limited groups within it. It tells us that most laws are applied evenhandedly. It asserts that most rules have been internalized by most of the populace. That is to say, it asserts that society everywhere on the whole consists of a general consensus on the legal order. With such a paradigm, the question of *whose* troubles to examine does not arise, for it holds that the legal order affects all of us equally.

I think that, on the contrary, it is plain as a pikestaff that there is no consensus—ever—on the legal order. Any particular law is inherently incapable of representing all our interests equally. Every such rule ineluctably must favor some and disfavor others, whatever its apparent evenhandedness. The law which commands us to drive on the right side of the road rather than the left at least favors those who presently own left-hand-drive vehicles. (How much is a secondhand left-hand-drive car worth the day after a country decides to change its rules to drive on the left side of the road?)[9]

If one adopts the notion that every rule of law makes a choice as to whom to favor, then the researcher too must make a choice. The most important choice is to decide whose troubles one ought attend to. That depends upon one's point of view. With whom does the researcher empathize? Whose interests will he seek to advance? That choice cannot be evaded so long as conflict exists in the world. In that sense, all research in law and society is necessarily committed research, for by the very choice of the trouble to investigate one has made a commitment.

(A caveat: The same set of facts can constitute different sorts of troubles for different people. Wide-scale poverty is a difficulty for the rich and powerful, because it threatens unrest and riot. For the poor, it means hungry bellies. Research on the problem of the threat to elite rule likely will lead to explanations and solutions apt to solve the threat to power. Research on the problem of hungry bellies will, we hope, lead to explanations and solutions looking to more food for the poor.)

That means that one cannot approach the problems of law and development—or, I suggest, of law anywhere—in the detached, passionless, bloodless temper of T-G's "social theorists of law." If one wants to learn about the real world, one must examine real problems. To do that requires that we examine the problems of real people [Trubek and Galanter (29), p. 1097]. (I exclude academics from that category.) The people in the Third World are concerned with hunger, disease, brutality, vulnerability, early death. They are surely unconcerned with the academic question, why liberal legalism failed as a model for social change. To do meaningful research concerning the problems of the Third World requires that we commit ourselves to someone's notion of what is a difficulty worth remedying. That calls neither for despair, world-weariness, and estrangement, nor for cold-blooded "objectivity." It calls for engagement, for empathy, for concern—in short, for passion.

IV

To say that one must begin research with genuine, existential problems is to say that policy research begins with a look at what is the case. That is in sharp contrast with T-G's methodology, which began with "ends" or "goals," expressed in the model of legal liberalism. These goals, conceived before they ever set foot on airplanes to whisk them off to far corners of the earth, came from the American experience. They were prepared to use science to discover the "means" ("instrumental research"), but their goals they took as articles of faith.

They still do. The stance of what they call "eclectic critique," so far as I can understand it, asserts that they will simultaneously (1) retain the whole of the "vision" that underlies their notion of the law and development enterprise—i.e., liberal legalism but now (2) transforming that vision to "critical standards," which they will hold "problematically." Exactly how they propose to do this I must confess I find difficult to understand. If I read them correctly, however, the question they propose to examine is the gap between the legal systems of the Third World and the model of legal liberalism. I suppose that means that they will seek to explain that gap and to propose solutions to make it more likely that reality will conform to the model. (I think that that is the consequence of their statement that in "eclectic critique" the assumptions of liberal legalism "are purified of the admixtures of descriptive assertion; they are completely and self-consciously normatized" [Trubek and Galanter (29), p. 1099].

This seems to me, despite T-G's claims, simply to repeat what they did earlier. In the end, they will generate proposals to make over the Third World in the model of legal liberalism. To continue to assert the ends specified in that model, after seeing where they in fact lead, denies the principle of falsification.

I would have thought that having seen that their gods have feet of clay, it would be better at least to cast about for new objects of adoration. Better yet would be to find a procedure for doing law and development research that avoids all these difficulties.

There is, I believe, an alternative implicit in the methodological writings of authors seemingly so diverse as Dewey (7), Popper (20), Sartre (24), and Marx (17). It can be conceptualized as consisting of four stages: The selection of a troubled situation; its explanation; the proposal of a solution; and its implementation.

The first task is to determine what real-life troubled situation one will investigate. The first task of empirical research is to ensure that what we define as a trouble is in fact based upon accurate data. A law professor may be quite sure that his students are not studying very hard. Empirical research may discover that in fact they are working very hard indeed.

It is sometimes urged that the very definition of a trouble is merely a reflection of the researcher's "values"—that is, his subjective notions of what is prized or valued. I am concerned with oppression and poverty, it is said, because I hold the values or ends of freedom and prosperity. The argument is circular. The evidence that I hold those values or ends is my concern with oppression and poverty. An "explanation" whose proof is the very event it is supposed to explain means nothing. The statement, that one "values" freedom and prosperity, is only another form of words for stating one's aversion to oppression and poverty. Of course, the choice of subject matter is discretionary. I discuss the control of that discretionary choice below.

That is a very different thing from stating that one values specific ends of the kind defined by legal liberalism. Such specific ends always rest upon a variety of factual propositions, assumed or warranted. John Dewey called "ends" such as freedom and prosperity "generalized ends," and "ends" such as those defined by liberal legalism "ends-in-view". Ends-in-view are specific plans about what to do. They are (or ought to be) the end result of research, not its beginning. T-G were motivated by a concern for equality, freedom, participation, "generalized ends." By assuming at the outset the propositions embodied in legal liberalism, they in effect defined their generalized ends by those propositions. They thus placed them beyond the reach of research. They began, as it were, at the wrong end. Such propositions ought to be the conclusion of the research enterprise, not its beginning.

Secondly, having defined a specific trouble, one must propose alternative explanations for it. Explanations require both a major and a minor premise (as T-G sought to explain their estrangement by reliance upon Kuhn's general proposition). The task is to generate as many such candidate explanations as possible, and then systematically try to eliminate them. There are a variety of criteria by which to make the choice between potential explanations—generality, parsimony, logical form, and so forth. The most important are, I believe, the criteria of falsifiability and empirical falsification. An explanation which is not in principle subject to falsification is either definitional (that is, merely another way to state the trouble), or it rests upon mysticism or intuition (neither of which is falsifiable). One cannot use experience to determine its validity. One can only learn through experience in an organized way if one generates alternative·explanations which are in principle falsifiable, and then conscientiously tries to falsify them by empirical research. The most arduous task of research, of course, is the effort systematically to falsify candidate explanations.

Thirdly, having eliminated most of the candidate explanations and thus identified the "causes" of the trouble, one can propose alternative solutions addressed to those causes. The choice between those alternative solutions depends upon the constraints and resources of the situation, and a notion of their probable consequences. Again, empirical research will be required to discover what are in fact the constraints and resources, and to make an educated guess of what the outcomes of the proposed solutions will likely be, both desired and undesired.

Finally, the research is not complete until one has tried to implement the proposed solution and monitored its success or failure. The success of the action taken will either be consistent with ("warrant") or falsify all the previous steps. Building the bridge that works warrants not only the actual design of the bridge, but the rules of physics upon which it is based. Thus we learn by doing (Dewey). Marx and Sartre called it *praxis* [Bernstein (3)]. (Of course, no rule of law ever works precisely as designed. That it does not is a new trouble, calling for new explanations, new solutions, new efforts at implementation, and therefore—new troubles. Life is indeed one trouble after another.)[10]

In the course of proposing explanations, we must articulate general propositions as major premises. If they work in one case, these propositions have some status as knowledge—i.e., as useful heurisms for further research. The principal task in the generation of knowledge thereafter is to falsify the general propositions suggested, and to amend them or to propose new ones. The general stock of knowledge consists in the main of these "middle level" propositions or theories, all of them heurisms, all of them never more than problematical.

It is these propositions that, in my view, together constitute a social theory of law. The methodology proposed, therefore, does not distinguish (as do T-G) between the tasks of developing general theory, and proposing "instrumental" solutions. We generate theory in the course of solving problems.

X

Now there are discretionary choices to be made in the course of such research. Whose trouble to attend to? What stock of propositions should we draw upon to put forward a candidate explanation? What proposals for solution should we try? What counts as adequate or successful implementation? In this sense all social science is value laden—not only in the selection of the troubles to be examined, but at every stage, except one. That exception is in the conscientious search for falsifying evidence. The scientific temper implies a commitment to truth. If we cannot falsify explanations by data publicly accessible, which any two scientists using the same methodology must accept, then knowledge itself is impossible. That one critical point aside, every step in the research agenda is discretionary.

It is dependent upon "values." Since that is so, the policy advocated as the result of research depends upon those "values."

Mainstream social science generally abandons the scientific enterprise at that stage. Max Weber taught that all that social science can do is to tell one the probable consequences of alternative courses of action. What sort of choice I make depends upon what sort of man I am [Weber (30), pp. 52–3]. That is (as Pound called it) a give-it-up philosophy.

How to impose intellectual controls over these discretionary choices made in the course of research? I believe that the answer can be found in the functional equivalence in the course of research of values, ends, paradigms (models), and explanations.

Large-scale ends in view are to models or paradigms of society as proposals for solutions are to explanations, as proposed in the agenda for decision-making that I have earlier put forward. Explanations, it will be recalled, set forth probable causes of the difficulty under examination. Proposals for solutions must be designed to treat those causes. It is this relationship between causal explanations and proposals for solutions that makes descriptions of what is the case changed to what ought to be the case [Dewey (5)].

Models or paradigms of society are causal explanations of how social systems work. Adam Smith did not write a propaganda tract for capitalism. (In the vocabulary I use here that would be a proposal for solution). Rather, he wrote an explanation for the wealth of nations. Karl Marx in *Capital* did not write an exhortation for socialism. Rather, he set out an explanation for the political economy of nineteenth-century England.

What are commonly called "ends" (I mean here ends-in-view, not generalized ends) are proposals for solutions. Capitalism is a solution for the difficulties examined by Smith, responding to the explanation he advanced. Socialism is a solution for the troubles investigated by Marx, based upon his explanation for capitalist society. Every so-called "end" or "value" in principle rests upon an explanation, implicit or explicit. For every end, therefore, it is possible to discover an explanation upon which it must rest.

The function of values, ends, paradigms and explanations in the research enterprise is the same: They guide the discretionary choices that must be made in deciding upon what troubles to examine, what candidate explanations to test, what solutions to offer. For example, it does not matter whether I make those choices because I adhere to socialism as an end, or because I believe the Marxist explanation for underdevelopment to be true. The choices will be the same.

The great difference is that explanations are in principle falsifiable. They are propositions about matters of fact. Ends are not. They are expressed in propositions about matters of faith. The bulk of the *Wealth of Nations* is data to support the explanations advanced. So is the bulk of *Capital*. The choice between the two ought not to depend upon the sort of man one is, but upon the persuasiveness of the data. Passion is all very well in the research enterprise—I think it is required—except at the point of assessing data. There, an icier mood is appropriate.

The function of large-scale explanations (that is, paradigms) in policy research is to guide the search for a just (and therefore also practical) solution to a specific trouble. The success or failure of that solution to resolve the difficulties which excited the research is the warrant or falsification not only of the particular research, but of the paradigm which shaped it, just as the success or failure of a bridge warrants or falsifies not only its particular design but the underlying principles of physics upon which it is based. The activity of implementation generates data to test every aspect of the research. The systematic examination of experience converts it from mere ongoing activity into activity whose purpose is in part at least to generate knowledge—that is, into experiment.

T-G's experience nicely demonstrates the argument. Casting that experience into the methodology I propose, they believed that in the United States we had achieved a reasonable facsimile of freedom, equitable treatment, and justice. They explained that state of affairs by the propositions set forth in legal liberalism. Looking at the Third World, they saw oppression, inequality of treatment, and injustice. Instead of making an independent investigation of those difficulties, however, they assumed that the reason for them was that the legal institutions of the Third World failed to meet the standards set forth in legal liberalism. To state as the cause of some unsatisfactory state of affairs the *absence* of particular institutions is in fact to assume that the creation of those institutions will remedy the difficulty. The articles of legal liberalism therefore became for T-G not testable explanations, but articles of faith—"ends". And their epistemology taught them that ends cannot be the subject of empirical research.

Had they understood their paradigm as embodying an explanation, they might have tried to falsify it in a variety of ways. (The simplest, of course, would have been to test it against data drawn from the United States experience, before flying off to distant lands. That might have saved a lot of grief.) T-G did it by experiment. They invoked ends derived from their model (that is, to replicate U.S. legal institutions in the Third World) as guides to research in far places. It did not work. The programs proposed by their research failed to bring about equality, freedom and participation— that is, to alleviate the troubles which gave rise to the research. The data generated by the activity falsified not only the particular research, but also the set of explanations embodied in legal liberalism from which their ends were drawn. *Praxis* disproved their explanations, and hence their ends. The Is proved the error of their Ought. Data falsified their "values."

T-G's catalogue of possible solutions for their difficulties is incomplete. There is another: policy-oriented, problem-solving research that in the course of solving particular problems, generates analytical, "middle-level" propositions that in sum constitute a theory of law and society, solves the particular problems at hand, and tests in the implementation of the solutions proposed not only the middle-level hypotheses and the solutions, but the most overarching paradigms of human society, and hence the ends and "values" which derive from them. Good research scratches where people itch. Starting on the most mundane level, seized by the scientific temper, we may yet test against data our dearest faiths. We *can* measure the Ought by the Is. Life tests it daily.

XI

There is one point where the methodological agenda suggested above falls down. It argues that every step in the process of generating a policy proposition is testable by scientific means, even to the point of testing the larger models which guide the research itself.

The test of such models, I argued, was ultimately whether they guided choice to successful solutions to emergent troubles. What is a "successful" solution, however, depends upon one's point of view. The Brazilian generals no doubt find that their solutions for social problems are successful—they remain in power. Others might have a different opinion.

The generalized explanations for the world that we hold are invariably aimed at explaining the world *as it appears from a particular point of view*. That flows from the nature of explanations, which must be addressed to some problem. Overarching explanations are addressed to overarching problems. Whose problem one's general paradigm purports to explain determines whose point of view it embodies. Any paradigm, as applied in problem-solving, if valid must lead to solutions tending to favor the point of view it represents. That is why in social science there are always alternative paradigms, for there are always alternative points of view.

The selection of a point of view is, I believe, not something over which one can obtain intellectual control. That is a matter of gut reaction. The problem is not serious for anyone but middle-class academics. The poor peasant in Brazil knows his troubles. So do the generals. It is only we middle-class academics, and especially expatriates, who have genuine choice.

Yet we do have choice. Unless we consciously choose whose troubles we will study, we fall prey to the choices made for us by the paradigms we adopt.

That is what happened to T-G. Liberal legalism purports to explain why it is that the United States treats its citizens equally, through laws applied evenhandedly, by a government that represents all our interests. The very subject that it purports to explain is a comfortable middle-class picture of our legal order. Blacks facing police brutality; the unemployed; welfare recipients: they have a different perception of legal reality in this country. For the middle class, however, it is all true: the police are polite; the economic system and the legal supports for it work; the bureaucracy is evenhanded and obedient to the rules. Liberal legalism purports to explain *our* world, not *theirs*.

That, I think, is the final and deepest root of T-G's self-estrangement. They entered the lists armed with a paradigm of law and society which explained the middle-class world of the United States academic, one of the highest-status roles in the nation, comfortably lodged in the top fraction of income earners. But, they were more than cold-blooded social theorists of law. They were seized by a kind of passion for equality, freedom, participation. Armed with a theory that purported to explain their own comfortable circumstances, they campaigned for those decencies in vastly different societies. Research guided by a model which explains the world of the middle class U.S. academic will not likely serve the disinherited of Brazil and India. T-G replicated for lawyers the experience of economists, educationalists, sociologists, and political scientists, many of whom also uncritically sought to use paradigms drawn from the experience of the metropolitan countries to guide the development of the LDCs.

There, too, lies the general malaise not only of law and development, but of law and society studies generally. So long as these studies celebrated the myths of legal liberalism, funding was abundant, and American academics could bask in the approval of the power structure. But, as Gunnar Myrdal says, facts kick. Once the legal liberalism model is overthrown, we must take sides. We must commit ourselves. Few academics commit themselves consciously to the side of the rich and powerful. We are all humanists nowadays. We cannot shut our ears to the primal scream of the disinherited. Our research, both here and abroad, requires us in "the relentless pursuit of truth" to adopt their point of view. That requires us either to confront authority, or to pursue triviality. In either case, funds dry up, research clearances get harder to obtain, and despondency settles on us all like a fog.

In this view, T-G's malaise is, in final assessment, to their credit, whatever my disagreements with their methodology. Their self-estrangement arose out of their genuine democratic and humanitarian feelings. They might have spared themselves their *Angst,* however, had they adopted a scientific temper and methodology that reached all, not just a part of their research endeavors. In science, we must never assume the truth of any proposition.

Justice Holmes put it beautifully in another context, long ago:

> But when men have realized that time has upset many fighting faiths, they may come to believe even more than they believe the very foundations of their own conduct that the ultimate good desired is better reached by free trade in ideas—that . . . the truth is the only ground upon which their wishes safely can be carried out. That, at any rate, is the theory of our Constitution. It is an experiment, as all life is an experiment.[11]

Holmes had the answer. *All life is an experiment.* The alternative to self-estrangement, the answer to Professor Levi's call for a theory of knowledge that is also a theory of justice, lies in activity, in procedures, in life itself. It lies in *systematically* learning through doing.

FOOTNOTES

1. I am indebted to Banks MacDowell, Robert Liberman, W. B. Harvey, Judy Seidman, J. C. N. Paul, Alan Feld and Richard Abel for useful criticisms of an earlier draft. Need I say that responsibility for errors is mine?

2. D. J. Black uses much the same sort of a definition: Law is "governmental social control" [Black (4), p. 1096].

3. The assertion that legal liberalism was a dominant paradigm in law and development studies during the sixties is one of the most contentious of the statements made in T-G's article. They first state that "many scholars and assistance officials shared a tacit set of assumptions" (Trubek and Galanter, 1964: 1070). They concede that to try to state these assumptions is frequently "to say things the writers themselves did not." One can doubt that there is any methodology that can take bits and pieces from a variety of writers, and construct from them a set of propositions which can then be claimed to have been held by most of the writers in the field—none of whom ever asserted more than a small part of it. It seems particularly hazardous to try to infer from the unexpressed thoughts of a variety of writers what they believed was "fundamental" or what was "most widely accepted." For example, they cite an article of my own [Seidman (26)] for the proposition in legal liberalism that "rules are consciously designed to achieve social purposes or effectuate basic social principles" [Trubek and Galanter (29), p. 1071]. They then go on to assert—without reference to *any* article, that these purposes are those of the society as a whole, not of limited groups within it, the rules being made by a pluralist process "which enables all individuals to secure rules favorable to them, while at the same time insuring that rules respect the vital interests of all." As I point out below, while of course I believe that law is "instrumental," that notion was coupled in my own article with a clear statement that law could not, in its nature, represent the views of "society as a whole," because there is no such thing. The question must always be, whose notions of what the law should be manage to get embodied into law?

Nor is it a meaningful proposition, that liberal legalism "prevailed" in United States universities [Trubek and Galanter (29), p. 1083.] The period at issue was, it will be recalled, the era of the civil rights movements, the great developments in criminal procedure, and Vietnam. The scholars who wrote the Reports of the President's Commission on Law Enforcement and the Administration of Justice, and of the National Commission on the Causes and Prevention of Violence, refuted many of the propositions of liberal legalism. There were other writings to the same effect, to a few of which T-G refer [(29), pp. 1081, 1083 *et seq.*]. Scholarship is carried forward not by counting heads, but by considering competing propositions and the evidence and arguments in support of and against them.

4. Research Advisory Committee on Law and Development of the International Legal Center (1974). Both Professors Trubek and Galanter were members of that committee; Professor Trubek was the chairman. I was a consultant to the committee.

5. Trubek and Galanter (29), p. 1072. At p. 1072 n. 30 T-G cite as an example of writing that supports the notion that behavior tends to match the norms of the law, an article of mine [Seidman (26)]. I plead not guilty.

6. T-G to the contrary notwithstanding, in my experience this is common currency among practicing American lawyers, and even academics.

7. Among the many American law teachers that I met in Africa during eight years there, only a tiny minority would have disagreed with the proposition in the text. English-trained African academics were usually much more likely to agree with something akin to legal liberalism than American lawyers who had been washed in the acid of legal realism.

8. That is the basic thrust not only of explicitly Marxist writers but of the "development of underdevelopment" school. See Trubek and Galanter (29), n. 3, p. 1095.

9. A very few laws seem to falsify this statement. It is hard to see who is disadvantaged by a law requiring three rather than two witnesses to a will. (That there is a law requiring that wills be executed with significant formality, on the other hand, plainly disadvantages those who desire quickly and informally to leave directions about their estate). Most such laws, I think, are trivial, almost by definition.

10. Professor Robert Liberman has pointed out that this methodology is correlative with the familiar *Rule in Heydon's Case,* 3 Co. Rep. 7b (1584). (In construing a statute there were four things to be considered: "1st. What was the common law before the making of the act. 2d. What was the mischief and defect for which the common law did not provide. 3rd. What remedy hath the Parliament resolved and appointed to cure the disease of the common-wealth. And, 4th. The true reason for the remedy.")

11. Dissenting in Abrams v. U.S. 250 U.S. (1919). I am indebted to Professor Gordon Baldwin, who called my attention to this quotation in this context long ago.

REFERENCES

1. Barth, F., *Models for Social Organization, Royal Anthropological Institute Occasional Paper No. 23,* The University Press, Glasgow (1966).
2. Bennis, W., "Beyond Bureaucracy," in Bennis and Slater (eds.), *The Temporary Society,* Harper and Row, New York (1969).
3. Bernstein, R. J., *Praxis and Action,* University of Pennsylvania Press, Philadelphia (1971).
4. Black, D. J., "The Boundaries of Legal Sociology," *Yale Law Journal* 81 (April 1972): 1086–1100.
5. Dewey, J., *Essays on Experimental Logic,* University of Chicago Press (1916).
6. ———, *Logic: The Theory of Inquiry,* Holt, Rinehart and Winston, New York (1938).
7. ———, *Theory of Valuation,* University of Chicago Press (1939).
8. Friedman, L., and S. Macauley (eds.), *Law and the Behavioral Sciences,* Bobbs-Merrill, Indianapolis (1969).

9. Gouldmer, A., *The Coming Crisis of Western Sociology*, Avon Books, New York (1970).
10. Hart, H. L. A., *The Concept of Law*, Clarendon Press, Oxford (1962).
11. Hughes, H. S., *Consciousness and Society: The Reorientation of European Social Thought*, Random House, New York (1958).
12. Kluckhohn, C., "Values and Value-Orientations in the Theory of Action," in Parsons, M. J., and E. Shills (eds.), *Toward a General Theory of Action: Theoretical Foundations for the Social Sciences*, Harvard University Press, Cambridge, Mass. (1952).
13. Kuhn, T. S., *The Structure of Scientific Revolutions*, University of Chicago Press (1964).
14. Levi, E. H., "An Approach to Law," address to the entering class at the University of Chicago Law School, October 2, 1974.
15. MacIntyre, A., "A Mistake about Causality in Social Science," in P. Laslett and W. G. Runciman, *Philosophy, Politics, and Society*, (2nd ser.), Barnes & Noble, Scranton, Pa. (1962).
16. Mao Tse-tung, *Quotations from Chairman Mao Tse-tung* (2nd ed.) Foreign Language Press, Peking (1967).
17. Marx, K., *Writings of the Young Marx on Philosophy and Society* (Easton, L. D. and K. H. Guddat, eds.), Doubleday, New York (1967).
18. Phillips, D. L., "Paradigms and Incommensurability," *Theory and Society*, 2.
19. Mills, C. W., *The Power Elite*, Oxford University Press, New York (1956).
20. Popper, K., *The Logic of Scientific Discovery*, Harper & Row, New York (1959).
21. Pound, R., *Contemporary Juristic Theory*, Claremont College Press, Claremont, California (1940).
22. ————, *Social Control Through Law*, Shoestring Press, Hamden, Conn. (1968).
23. Renner, K., *The Institutions of Private Law and Their Social Function*, (trans. O. Kahn-Fround), Routledge and Kegan Paul, London (1949).
24. Sartre, J. P., *Search for a Method* (trans. H. E. Barnes), Knopf, New York (1963).
25. Seidman, R. B., "Administrative Law and Legitimacy in Anglophonic (Africa: A Problem in the Reception of Foreign Law," *Law and Society Review* 5 (November 1970): 161–204.
26. ————, "Law and Development: A General Model," *Law and Society Review* 6 (February 1972): 311–342.
27. ————, "Law and Development: The Roles at the Interface Between Policy and Implementation," *Journal of Modern African Studies* 35, 4 (1975): 641–652.
28. ————, "Law and Economic Development in Independent, English-Speaking Sub-Saharan Africa," *Wisconsin Law Review*, (Fall 1966): 999–1070.
29. Trubek, D. M. and M. Galanter, "Scholars in Self-Estrangement: Reflections on the Crisis in Law and Development Studies in the United States," *Wisconsin Law Review* (Fall 1974): 1062–1102.
30. Weber, M., *Max Weber on the Methology of the Social Sciences* (trans. E. A. Shils and H. A. Finch), Free Press, Glencoe, Ill. (1949), pp. 52–53.
31. Winch, P. *The Idea of a Social Science and Its Relation to Philosophy*, Routledge & Kegan Paul, London (1958).

SCHOLARS IN THE FUN HOUSE: A REPLY TO PROFESSOR SEIDMAN

David M. Trubek, UNIVERSITY OF WISCONSIN

Marc Galanter, UNIVERSITY OF WISCONSIN

Reading about ourselves in Professor Seidman's essay made us feel as if we had entered a carnival fun house full of distorting mirrors. We could recognize ourselves in his discussion of our essay on the crisis in law and development studies, but our ideas seemed strangely misshapen. Reflected in the mirrors of Professor Seidman's article, we seemed to be too tall, too fat, too legalistic, too naive, too unreconstructed, too academic; in short, everything but ourselves.

Professor Seidman's criticism of our views is based on distortions of what we said and meant. Since he objects not to what we said, but to what he mistakenly thinks we said, it is hard to respond to his criticisms. We could, alternatively, choose not to reply to his criticisms of "us," but rather to comment directly on the views he puts forward as his own theory of the nature of "law and development" studies. But this task seems

Research in Law and Sociology—Vol. 1, 1978, pages 31–40.

equally difficult because we are unable to discern a clear position in his essay. It defies criticism: if one takes objection to a point he will find the refutation of that same point in another part of the essay.

Accordingly, we have chosen merely to point out some of the more egregious distortions of our essay and the most glaring self-contradictions in his position. For the rest, we commend the reader to our original essay.

Seen in the mirrors of Professor Seidman's fun house, we seem to be rather strange creatures. What did we actually say? We criticized those scholars and actors who looked at the world through the lenses of what we called "liberal legalism." Liberal legalists, we claimed, believed that the establishment in the Third World of legal systems similar to those of the United States and Western Europe promoted development because they would foster equality, enhance participation in public life, and lead to more effective mastery of the world. These views were apparent in scholarship about law and development, and in reform projects.

We felt that unreflective liberal legalism was bad scholarship and led to bad reform projects. We analyzed the underlying assumptions of liberal legalist thought, demonstrating that it was based on an underlying "paradigm" fusing normative and descriptive elements, which oriented the thought of law and development scholars and actors. Our principal criticism of liberal legalists was that they failed to question these assumptions, and that as a result were incapable of grasping the complexity of legal life in the Third World. We condemned their method, which we saw as based principally on comparing Third World institutions with an idealized model of Western law and prescribing changes that would remove gaps between this model and the legal rules and institutions (e.g., courts, professional structures and law schools) in Asia, Africa and Latin America.

Despite our repeated criticism of liberal legalism and explicit rejection of its method, Professor Seidman concludes that we are unreconstructed liberal legalists. We will, he says, "repeat what they [we] did earlier . . . in the end, they will generate proposals to make over the Third World in the model of legal liberalism" (p. 20). Even readers unfamiliar with the earlier debates over law and development studies will recognize the intellectual acrobatics reflected in this passage. Professor Seidman has taken a concept we devised ("liberal legalism") and a critique we developed (liberal legalism's failure to question its assumptions and its effort to change the world to fit its prescriptions) and, on the basis of no evidence whatever, condemns us for conspiring to repeat errors we had exposed!

This distortion of our position is so extravagant that the issue is not to refute it, but to explain it. Why, we have asked ourselves, is Professor Seidman so eager to attack our position that he accuses us of being the exact opposite of what we are?

One explanation may be that he is unwilling to acknowledge partaking in the errors we all committed in the early days of law and development activity. We have openly admitted that our own writings and reform efforts were imbued with "liberal legalism." Professor Seidman seems especially anxious to prove he never shared this outlook; the record, we submit, shows otherwise.[1]

A second explanation of his distortion is that he simply failed to understand the stance we adopt at the end of "Scholars in Self-Estrangement," which we called "eclectic critique." This position was offered as an alternative to the several "competing articulations" which we saw emerging as the liberal legalist paradigm unraveled. Professor Seidman asserts that we saw these as "alternative" and "possible" solutions (p. 4). Quite to the contrary, we presented them as (a) mutually contradictory and (b) all unsatisfactory [*Scholars* (6) pp. 1096ff]. "Eclectic critique" was offered as an alternative to all of these insufficient responses to the crisis.

After sketching this approach, we noted that our article itself was an example of such critique and trusted that the careful reader would understand our approach.[2] While we recognized that details of the idea might remain unclear, it never occurred to us that anyone would be able to conclude, as Professor Seidman does, that it proposed we should "examine the gap between the legal systems of the Third World and the model of liberal legalism" (p. 20). Since our *entire* article had been devoted to showing that this was the method of "liberal legalism" and was fundamentally wrong, we were unable to imagine that anyone would attribute such a position to us. Professor Seidman has proved that we were wrong.

Since Professor Seidman's magic mirror makes us look like liberal legalists, it is easy for him to criticize the distorted image of "T-G" he sees, because he can use our own arguments against us. But as the reader of "Scholars in Self-Estrangement" will see, the method of eclectic critique is the very opposite of the project of comparing Third World systems against the liberal legalist model. As we described "eclectic critique," it takes as a starting point those broad goals articulated by liberal legalism: increased equality, enhanced participation in public life, and greater mastery of natural and social forces. These are values so general as to be held by most persons involved in development work— certainly they are shared by Professor Seidman. But we go on to suggest that the relationship between the normative ideals of the law and development movement and specific legal arrangements is problematic. In other words, we have tried to conserve the most basic normative concerns that animated law and development scholarship while rejecting the claim made by liberal legalism that specific legal institutions or the rule of law in general will necessarily promote these normative goals in the Third

World. Our position is *eclectic* in that it offers no pat formula for pursuing equality, participation, and more effective mastery of the world. As we indicated in "Scholars in Self-Estrangement," we are prepared to find that these goals may be as readily secured through deprofessionalization, the spread of popular tribunals, and reliance on informal dispute processes as through the more professional and formal "legal development" programs put forth by liberal legalists. Our position is *critical* in that it subjects the claims of all institutions—law, legal professions, governments and scientific communities—to critical analysis in terms of these general values and the more detailed specifications of them that are relevant to particular situations. Thus our approach not only rejects the method of liberal legalism—it also led us to question many of the specific conclusions on law and policy which it had produced.

Our failure to develop this position in detail seems an insufficient explanation of Professor Seidman's willingness to take such desperate liberties with what we said. However, a clue may be found in his disagreement with the view of social science that emerged from our critique—a view that seems especially troubling to Professor Seidman.

Professor Seidman objects strenuously to our use of the Kuhnian paradigm notion. We used the concept of a paradigm to *describe* the way social scientists and social actors behave. That is, we asserted that the law and development movement—which included scholars, actors, and actor-scholars—shared a paradigm which included a set of presuppositions or domain assumptions which were, as a matter of fact, not normally subject to testing. The propositions of liberal legalism we developed were our effort to make these basic assumptions visible so they could be tested.

"Paradigm," as we use it, connotes both more and less than a set of propositions. It is a cluster of cognitive dispositions on the part of a scholarly community, "the entire constellation of beliefs, values and techniques and so on shared by members of a given [scientific] community" [Kuhn (1) p. 175].[3] At the same time, these dispositions need not be present in the form of propositions. We attempted to illuminate the underlying assumptions by presenting them in the form of propositions. But the power of paradigm assumptions to shape our work is precisely that for the time being they frame our inquiry rather than occupy the center of the visual field.

Professor Seidman seems undecided on whether he would admit the paradigm notion at all. He tells us that it is inapplicable, for there is no dominant paradigm and thus no "normal science" in the social sciences (p. 6). But then he employs something very much like it when he attributes our myopia to adherence to "mainstream social science"[4] (p. 10).

Professor Seidman's major complaint about our use of Kuhn's paradigm notion is that we took for granted what he would have treated as problematic. It is our failure to treat "the propositions of liberal legalism as problematic propositions, subject to disproof" (p. 6) that is "the principal source of . . . [our] error" (p. 7). The thrust of our article was that these were indeed not treated as problematic by law and development scholars. Instead, they served as presuppositions or domain assumptions—that is, they were taken for granted and largely left unexamined.

Professor Seidman does not dispute our claim that some law and development scholars failed to question these assumptions, although he disagrees with us on how prevalent this may have been.[5] But he seems to infer that because we used the notion of a paradigm consisting of unquestioned domain assumptions to describe liberal legalist behavior, we must be commending this behavior, and that we think that these assumptions *ought* to have been left untested.[6] He seems unwilling to accept what strikes us as a modest and indisputable observation about scholarly communities and individual scholarly work, namely, that at any given time in the course of an inquiry some things are in fact taken for granted.

Professor Seidman believes that "the essence of the scientific temper is to hold *every* proposition problematically" (p. 10). His insistence that all propositions remain open to disproof is indisputable but irrelevant to the actual conduct of inquiry. He fails to distinguish between being open in principle to testing and being actively subjected to testing. (Presumably his own general assertions about science and law are problematic in the sense of being open to testing even when they are not actively being tested.)[7] Nowhere do we suggest that a paradigm is necessarily believed by its adherents to be beyond testing. Rather, the paradigm notion was meant simply to imply that while you are busy observing x, you take for granted many things about x and about your activity of observing. These assumptions need not be present in the form of articulated propositions. What distinguishes paradigm propositions from others is not that they are not testable, but that testing them has a very low priority, if it is a visible option at all, since they provide the framework of the undertaking and seem unproblematic.

It seems to us Professor Seidman has confused our descriptive use of the paradigm notion with a prescriptive use of the idea. We said that liberal legalists adhered to domain assumptions that were not tested. He seems to conclude that we meant that they were justified in doing this, and that accordingly we believe that the propositions of liberal legalism should not be questioned. Of course, the error of this characterization is patently obvious to any reader of our essay. But why has Professor Seidman made what seems to be such an elementary error?

In criticizing liberal legalism, we suggested that its shared presuppositions were related to the values and social positions (e.g., expatriate reformers in less developed countries) of liberal legalists. Thus the notion of paradigm was linked with the notion that the values, prior experience and institutional needs of scholars helped to determine what was left unquestioned. But if social thought is framed by deep presuppositions and these in turn reflect the values and social position of the theorist, the question naturally arises: What is "scientific" about such forms of social inquiry as law and development studies? That such a question might arise seems, to Professor Seidman, to cast an ominous shadow over the law and development enterprise. We have trouble following his argument, but it appears that he believes that if the values of a scholarly community affect its propositions and prescriptions, then the idea of science itself is threatened, and with it the law and development enterprise which is based on science. In a key passage in his article, he sets up a dichotomy between a "science" which has transcended the distinction between fact and value, and "irrational forces." Thus he says that if one admits any "discontinuity between ends and means," then the choice of ends must perforce be irrational. And he concludes that if that is the case, then "irrational forces, not science, control society . . . [and] the whole enterprise of law and development—that is the use of science and reason to help restructure society—is a lost cause" (p. 14). Professor Seidman, in his devotion to saving the cause, centers his attack on our use of the paradigm concept because he perceives it as undermining the scientific credentials he regards as essential to the law and development enterprise.

Although we find this perception unfounded, we do not regard his concern about the implications of our analysis to be frivolous. He is apprehensive that the view of science that lies behind our critique of law and development studies may lead to an amoral, irrational relativism which discredits all efforts to use social science to guide social reconstruction. (If we read him right, he opposes us not because we are liberal legalists, but because he fears we have no real alternative to liberal legalism.)

We share his concern about this problem. We wish to avoid amoralism as ardently as we want to eliminate the errors of liberal legalism. Our concept of eclectic critique as an alternative method was our solution to this dilemma. Behind it lies the hope for a self-critical scholarly community which can test proposals and propositions against ideals of general acceptance and careful evaluations of empirical situations. We tried to avoid amoralism by looking for values that are widely shared. We felt that the law and development movement had properly identified such values as social equality, enhanced participation in public life, and technical mastery of nature and human institutions. We tried to avoid unquestioning identification of these values with specific legal rules and arrangements (e.g., a more instrumentally oriented legal profession) by insisting that all relations between ideals and institutions be subjected to critical scrutiny. We believe that a scholarly community committed to these approaches could make a contribution to the lives of the people of the Third World. We expressed no view on whether such methods should be called "science" since we felt labels like this answer no questions.

We are aware that such an approach is fraught with difficulties and we would welcome thoughtful criticism of it. Unfortunately, Professor Seidman has done far less than this while attempting to do far more. On the one hand, he has failed to grasp our analysis of the problem or to criticize our proposed solution to it. On the other, he has offered what purports to be an alternative theory of social science and of law and development which he claims resolves the perplexities we are still struggling with. We cannot debate the merits of his position because we do not think it contains a coherent notion of social science in general or of law and development studies in particular.

Professor Seidman seeks to transcend the notion that science proceeds from and includes unexamined commitments because he thinks that such a view undermines hope for the "use of science and reason to help to restructure our society" (p. 14). He portrays himself as the proponent of a rival and superior epistemology which by overcoming mainstream social science's "supposed dichotomy" (p. 14) of is and ought, fact and value, is able to "unify . . . the search for knowledge and the search for justice" (p. 14), thus overcoming "the crisis of modern man" (p. 14). Having congratulated himself for overcoming the divorce of the normative and factual (p. 12), he then reintroduces it asserting that propositions about matters of fact are "in principle falsifiable [but] ends are not. They are . . . matters of faith" (p. 23). Even so, he asserts, science is not condemned to an unbridgeable fact-value dichotomy, for ends or values can be tested by "policy-oriented, problem-solving research" and indeed by "life"[8] (p. 24). But such testing in turn appears to be dependent upon "a point of view . . . [which] is a matter of gut reaction" (p. 25). At least it is for most people, "only we middle-class academics . . . especially expatriates . . . have genuine choice (p. 25)." Unfortunately Professor Seidman refrains from telling us the principles by which we would guide such "genuine choice." Are the grounds for the exercise of the choice the is of scientific evidence, or the is of commitment and empathy (p. 20)? "To do meaningful research concerning problems of the Third World requires that we commit ourselves to someone's notion of what is a difficulty worth remedying. . . . It calls for engagement, for empathy, for concern—in short, for passion" (p. 19). But, there are many passions and many someones. Are some passions more scientific than others? Is empathy with some someones a firmer basis for science than empathy with other someones? His displacement of the leap of faith from the shared (and eventually debatable) assumptions of a scholarly community to the gut reactions of the self-appointed problem-solver, does not dispel our suspicion that inquiry is powerfully shaped by untested (and perhaps untestable) suppositions.

Nor does his vision of law and development persuade us that he has a viable replacement for liberal legalism. Professor Seidman's view of research proceeds from a fervid embrace of "real people" (p. 20), while patronizing them as universal victims and creatures of determinism.[9] It is a view that credits the outsider, uniquely free of the limits of place and class with an ability to intervene unilaterally on the basis of empathy with real people, like a bountiful Tarzan who lends his superior power to aid the hapless natives. It resurrects a dream of skillful intervention from above on behalf of the "real people" that recurs throughout colonial history and that animates much recent "development" activity. This vision of the untrammeled intervenor equipped with science is juxtaposed with a statist and technocratic view of law as governmentally managed social engineering (pp. 2, 7). Although he tells us that we must "confront authority," (p. 26) there is nothing here or elsewhere to suggest that Professor Seidman's view of law and development departs from enabling governments—at least those approved by his gut—to "induce the desired behavior" (p. 8) more effectively.

The lessons of liberal legalism do not permit us to share Professor Seidman's complacency with his sanguine instrumentalism. Professor Seidman generously reveals to us the secret of his robust immunity to self-doubt: to avoid *"Angst"* and self-estrangement, he counsels us, we need but adopt "a scientific temper and methodology that reached all, not just part of [our] research endeavors" (p. 26). Although skeptical about a program of questioning everything at once, we thought that in "Scholars in Self-Estrangement" we managed to make problematic some of the key assumptions of the tradition within which we found ourselves. When Professor Seidman undertakes to subject his own statist, instrumentalist version of liberal legalism to a comparable critical analysis, we will be avid and appreciative readers.

FOOTNOTES

1. Professor Seidman's essay might be regarded as a claim for unacknowledged intellectual priority. Since we all agree that the assumptions which we call liberal legalism should be tested, he seems to be saying that his recognition of this antedates our own. Since Professor Seidman acknowledges that he went off to the law and development wars with the "ordinary philosophical and jurisprudential tools . . . of [his] generation" (p. 5) it is not clear whether he is suggesting that he never was a votary of the false gods of liberal legalism or that he long ago abandoned them for the true faith while other liberal legalists are still wandering in the wilderness. That he never accepted "the ends of liberal legalism" (p. 5) is implied by his

observation that "American lawyers . . . washed in the acid of legal realism" were unlikely to "agree with" liberal legalism. The argument of our article was not that liberal legalism was something that people "agreed with" but that it was a pervasive way of seeing law, society and development—it posed questions and suggested what might be the answers. Awareness of the biases and imperfections of American law does not seem incompatible with the presence of a liberal legalist perspective on law and development.

We do not pretend to a detailed mastery of Professor Seidman's voluminous writings on law and development. Inspection of two publications on the subject which appeared roughly contemporaneously with "Scholars in Self-Estrangement" does not suggest to us that Professor Seidman has strayed far from the liberal legalist view of the legal system as an integrated purposive entity employing state power, centered on courts (especially appellate courts), controlling behavior by rules and modifying it by their alteration (cf. [Scholars (6), p. 1072]—preferably by alignment of Third World practice with foreign models. One of these recent pieces [Seidman (3)] consists of an emphatic restatement of the view that law and development consists of the designing of rules by lawyers "to induce new patterns of behavior" (3) p. 644. The other (2) tells us that the failure of constitutional democracy in Africa resulted in part from the weakness of the courts in protecting fundamental freedoms, a weakness due in turn to the "Formal Style" of opinion writing prevalent in the appellate courts. This style, it is noted, has been superseded in the United States by a realist style in which "judges . . . write their opinions frankly addressing the policy issues" (2), p. 844). The Realist Style is a welcome resurrection of an earlier Grand Style which had prevailed in both the United States and in England. Professor Seidman argues (2), p. 844, that "[t]he justification of opinions can . . . match the imperatives of modern Africa . . . only when the bench and bar of Africa have come to accept the legitimacy of Grand Style justifications" and have abandoned the fallacious Formal Style.

2. A further example may be found in Trubek (5).

3. In its broad sense the paradigm constitutes a "disciplinary matrix"—a constellation of group commitments made up of conventions of symbolism, shared values for judging scientific work, examples of successful problem solutions and shared commitment to a variety of models, ranging from heuristic to ontological that "supply the group with preferred or permissible analogies and metaphors," "help to determine what will be accepted as an explanation and as a puzzle solution . . . assist in the determination of the roster of unsolved puzzles and in the evaluation of the importance of each." [Kuhn (1) p. 184].

Professor Seidman's assertion (p. 5) that we use the notion of paradigm in the restricted sense of a theoretical model, rather than in the broader sense that we intended, points to an ellipsis in our argument. We introduce the paradigm notion in terms of a model of law in society and try to enrich it later by discussing other elements under the heading of the "amalgam" of ideas about science policy and moral actions (6), p. 1096. We hope that readers were not misled by our omission into thinking that the notion of paradigm was exhausted by the earlier theoretical model.

4. Later still Professor Seidman agrees that "we all start with general paradigms of some sort . . . that direct attention to what is to be investigated" (p. 18). But he declares our invocation of Kuhn "erroneous . . . because Kuhn was discussing the physical sciences . . . [where] for long periods a dominant paradigm within which what Kuhn calls 'normal science' takes place" (p. 6). But as Kuhn (1). p. 208, himself notes theses of "scientific development as a succession of tradition-bound periods punctuated by non-cumulative breaks . . . are undoubtedly of wide applicability. But they should be, for they are borrowed from other fields. Historians of literature, of music, of the arts, of political development, and of many other human activities have long described their subjects in the same way."

5. See his footnote 16. It is not clear whether he means to exonerate any others besides himself.

6. His unwillingness to distinguish description and prescription in this case seems a curiously mechanical application of the view that descriptions of what is the case are *always* truncated ought statements (p. 22).

7. Professor Seidman tells us that social science is incapable of formulating general propositions with explanatory power and is limited to heurisms which serve as guides to research (p. 16). Yet his paper is liberally sprinkled with unqualified general assertions about social phenomena, including the legal process. For example, we are told about the nontransferability of law from one social setting to another (p. 17) and that ". . . it is plain as a pikestaff that there is no consensus—ever—on the law. Law is inherently incapable of representing all our interests equally" (p. 19). Are these descriptive generalizations which have survived empirical testing? Or are they at least in part components of a way of looking at legal phenomena akin to the "domain assumptions" or paradigm propositions which we found in liberal legalism?

8. We are solemnly counseled that life is an experiment (not, as we had earlier thought, a fountain) and that the alternative to self-estrangement lies in "life itself." The enduring appeal of this locution is illuminated in [Treuhaft (4)], p. 37.

9. He reminds us that "The people in the Third World are concerned with hunger, disease, brutality, vulnerability, early death" (p. 19). It seems to have escaped his attention that they are also concerned with wealth, pleasure, status, salvation, and even knowledge!

REFERENCES

1. Kuhn, Thomas S., *The Structure of Scientific Revolutions,* University of Chicago Press, 2d ed. (1970).
2. Seidman, Robert B., "Judicial Review and Fundamental Freedoms in Anglophonic Independent Africa," *Ohio State Law Journal* 35 (1974): 820–50.
3. ———, "Law and Development: The Interface Between Policy and Implementation," *Journal of Modern African Studies* 13 (1975): 641–52.
4. Treuhaft, Decca [Jessica Mitford], "Lifeitselfmanship," *Mainstream* 9 (1956): 36.
5. Trubek, David M. "Complexity and Contradiction in the Legal Order: Balbus and the Challenge of Critical Social Thought About Law," *Law & Society* 11 (1977).
6. ———, and Galanter, Marc, "Scholars in Self-Estrangement: Source Reflections on the Crisis of Law and Development Studies in the United States," *Wisconsin Law Review* (1974): 1062–1102.

A REPLY TO PROFESSORS TRUBEK AND GALANTER

Robert B. Seidman, BOSTON UNIVERSITY SCHOOL OF
LAW

T-G put forward originally an explanation for the crisis in law and development studies that I believe was seriously mistaken. It was mistaken
because they sought to explain that crisis by the model or paradigm of
liberal legalism that, they argue, was held by practically every scholar in
the field. I disagreed (a) that the model of liberal legalism was held by
every scholar in the field, and, more importantly, (b) that the nub of the
crisis lay in the model (although we are presently in agreement about its
inutility). I argued that the methodology which T-G adopted left them
without any tools for testing their model. When they came to discover its
inappropriateness, they were, therefore, dejected, alienated, self-
estranged. The nub of the matter is methodology, not the paradigm held.

Theirs is a mainstream position, stated perhaps most clearly by Max
Weber. Value judgments and propositions about matters of fact are dis-

Research in Law and Sociology—Vol. 1, 1978, pages 41–44.

continuous. Ends and means are separately decided by very different methodologies and very different criteria. Models contain value judgments or ends, which cannot be tested. The observers are outside the system, cold-bloodedly peering at a static world, and (in the case of T-G), assessing it according to their values. That methodology is inherently authoritarian and manipulative, for it postulates observers outside the system, using their values to assess subjects within it.

(An aside: T-G now tell us that they propose to use the values of "increased equality, enhanced participation in public life, and greater mastery of natural and social forces" as a "starting point." Benjamin Disraeli, Joseph Chamberlain, Winston Churchill, and Theodore Roosevelt no doubt would have agreed with T-G and myself in affirming their devotion to these values. How can values so vacuous that everyone subscribes to them serve to guide research?)

My view of the process of social inquiry, on the contrary, is in the tradition of such otherwise disparate philosophers as Dewey, Marx, Sartre, and Popper. We learn through doing, through *praxis*. Values and facts, ends and means, policy and science, prescription and description are all continuous, not discontinuous phenomena. Models, like all explanations, are therefore testable. Knowledge does not catch the real world; rather, it consists of heuristic propositions that serve to guide problem-solving in a constantly evolving material milieu. ("Theory is not a dogma, but a guide to action.") Knowledge arises out of the practice of problem-solving. One begins research not with big words like "equality" or "participation," selected out of the consciousness of the researcher and given concrete definition by his (usually unexpressed) residues, but with real-life problems of people "out there." It is an inherently participatory methodology, for the researcher is perceived as being part of the client system. Only so can one learn through doing.

Now the choice between these two broad methodologies is an important issue, I believe. Success in the development enterprise depends ultimately upon what we know. The substance of the dispute between T-G and myself is how to acquire that knowledge. The choice of methodology lies at the core of the research enterprise.

I did not dream up either of these two methodologies. They have both been clearly and repeatedly stated in the literature. Each has its practitioners. Because of its central importance to the research enterprise, methodology must be discussed, debated, tested. T-G do not do this. They say in so many words that the issue is not to refute my position, but to explain why I adopt it. So, they respond to my paper principally with vituperation and attacks *ad hominem*. Just as some neoclassical economists refuse to discuss the merits of their position with institutionalists or Marxists, so do T-G simply label my position a "statist, instrumentalist version of liberal legalism," as though that disposed of everything.

Nothing could be more boring than the sight of more or less antique professors snarling impolite vituperation at each other. (I refer to myself when I say "more" in that sentence.) T-G charge me with all sorts of dreadful misdemeanors.[1] They have a constitutional right to do so, I suppose, just as they have a constitutional right to respond to my criticisms of their article by calling me names.[2] Their principal complaint seems to be that I do not join them in their *mea culpas;* I regret that I cannot accommodate them. I cannot believe, however, that disagreements about who misquoted whom advances the scholarly enterprise. Those disagreements can be readily resolved, if anyone thinks them important, by reading the original texts. In the event, we pass like ships in the night. So long as T-G respond to criticism merely with name-calling, however, for so long do they incapacitate themselves from examining their methodology critically. For so long, I believe, do they condemn themselves to their self-proclaimed self-estrangement.

And thus we end precisely where this whole tedious disputation began.

FOOTNOTES

1. A principal complaint made by T-G is that I did not understand their notion of "eclectic critique". They said in their original article that eclectic critique

retains the whole of the vision that underlay the law and development enterprise, but shifts the nature of its commitment to that vision. Eclectic critique transforms the central assumptions underlying the law and development enterprise into critical standards. They always were this in part, but the belief that they were also actually descriptive involved the scholar in premature and uncritical commitment to particular institutions and policies. In eclectic critique the assumptions are purified of the admixture of descriptive assertion; they are completely and self-consciously normatized [Trubek and Galanter (29) p. 1099].

They now say that what they meant was that

eclectic critique . . . takes as a starting point those broad goals articulated by liberal legalism, increased equality, enhanced participation in public life, and greater mastery of natural and social forces. . . . But we go on [in the original article] to suggest that the relationship between the normative ideals of the law and development movement and specific legal arrangements is problematic. In other words, we have tried to conserve the most basic normative concerns that animated law and development scholarship while rejecting the claims made by liberal legalism that specific legal institutions or the rule of law in general will necessarily promote these normative goals in the Third World.

I think that what they are now saying is that they meant to reject all the propositions of liberal legalism, retaining only the broad goals or values which they believe underlay it. I appreciate their clarification. I confess, however, that I remain unable to see how their present position "retains the whole of the vision that underlay the law and development enterprise." I should think it would have been more clear to have said simply that they now believe that they should abandon liberal legalism, and do their research guided by the broad values.

2. T-G had my article in hand for about a year. I sent it to them in part so that they could object if I had misquoted them. We are, after all, not unacquainted. I would have thought that if they were really so concerned about being misunderstood, an appropriate letter might have set me straight, or at least required me to consider whether I was misquoting them. Their very first response, however, was their reply printed above.

HUMAN RIGHTS
DEVELOPMENT THEORY

Richard P. Claude, UNIVERSITY OF MARYLAND

James C. Strouse, UNIVERSITY OF MARYLAND*

Comparison between developing and developed countries in the field of human rights is a legitimate exercise, according to Julius Nyerere of Tanzania, since the Western model of rights development may not be entirely unique to industrialized democracies. Nyerere comments: "Freedom and development are as completely linked as chickens and eggs. Without chickens you get no eggs; and without eggs you soon have no chickens." He concluded that "without freedom you get no development; and without development, you soon lose your freedom" (1968:1). Precision in sorting out the differences between the human rights record of advanced industrial democracies and that which would be feasible for developing countries has largely been an untended research task. Descriptive first steps have been taken in the works of David Bayley (1964) and Robert Martin (1974).

Incremental, gradual, and long-term: these have been the hallmarks of

Research in Law and Sociology—Vol. 1, 1978, pages 45–58.

economic development in the industrialized democracies [Blondel (5), Moore (25)]. Likewise, the classical path of human rights development in Western constitutional democracies has also been marked by the slow evolution of distinct stages [Jellinek (16), Krieger (18), 1962]. The common experiences of these developed countries supply a paradigm linking three varieties of human rights policies with three categories to which political economists refer as "public choice processes": market choice, bargaining choice and centralized choice.

First, property rights, liberty of contract, free expression, the right to travel, and related *civil liberties,* emerged side by side with processes of choice involving a largely decentralized exchange of goods, services and ideas concomitant with relatively free market conditions. Second, the *political and civil rights* stage of policy development which followed was linked with changing processes that emphasized collective choice: competing labor, political, associational, and social groups engaged in a variety of bargaining processes including competition, compromise, persuasion and electoral participation. Third, the positive *socio-economic rights* policies emphasizing health and welfare considerations have become associated in a subsequent stage of human rights development with centralized choice processes where authority is concentrated and where the hierarchical choice processes emphasize planning.

In his *History of European Liberalism,* de Ruggiero (11) links the three policy fields of human rights noted above with changing ideological commitments. Relying on de Ruggiero's broad historical view, elements of the classical model of human rights development are brought together in Table 1 below. The model would lend itself to further historical empirical investigation in terms of the analytical framework of Binder, et al. (4) in their *Crises and Sequences in Political Development*—an important contribution to linking historical and political science research in macro-analytic

Table 1. The Classical Model of Human Rights Development

HISTORICAL PERIOD OF DEVELOPMENT	HUMAN RIGHTS POLICIES	UNDERLYING VALUE STANDARD	ASSOCIATED PUBLIC CHOICE PROCESSES	REQUISITE IDEOLOGICAL TRANSFORMATION
18th century	Civil liberties	Liberty	Market choice	Secularized ideology of the rightful basis of limited political authority
19th century	Civil and political rights	Equality	Group bargaining	Legitimacy of ameliorating stratified social inequalities by reliance on inclusion of new groups into civic life
20th century	Socio-economic rights	Welfare	Centralized planning	Recognition of the need for universal sharing of the risks of industrial development

terms. An historical-stage model could offer a suitable basis for exploring similarities and differences between human rights development in economically advanced democracies and developing countries [Claude (7)].

With respect to promotion of economic development spurred by rights and liberties, rather little has been written [Rheinstein (33)]. However, Frederick Hayek (15) celebrates and Giovanni Sartori (35) details how the development of standards of rights—"legal guarantism" in Sartori's terms—offered the promise of minimizing individual insecurity wrought by government interference. Without the security of expectations assured by the law in the form of the institutions of property and civil liberties, people are seen from the historic liberal perspective to be less motivated to work, save, and invest. But just as insecurity among the mass of citizens promotes economic stagnation, so does privilege among the few. Electoral rights which encourage participation and civil rights which extend equality and freedom from discrimination help to break down privilege and vested interests which dampen the incentive to attempt change, entrepreneurial risk, and economic development [Kuznets (19)]. Modern economic development associated with industrialization requires the aggregation of capital. Where, for purposes of concentrating capital, multiple sources of private financial reserves contribute to the aggregation needed for investment, processes of public choice may usefully rely upon market and bargaining interactions [Adelman and Morris (1)].

But what about developing countries? They often lack pluralized private investment sources. Where the accelerated concentration of capital must rely upon hierarchical choice processes, traditional civil liberties and civil rights may not be seen by government elites as congenial to economic development [Cooray (9)]. In the words of Sankar Ghose, Indian Minister of State for Planning: "When the laws of a social organization are incompatible with its dominant needs, the outmoded laws have to be dicarded. It is the dynamics of the social system that has to determine the nature of the legal system, and not the other way around" (*New York Times*, September 15, 1976, p. 22, col. 1).

Laissez-faire has been virtually abandoned in the West; development command economies exist in the socialist bloc; thus developing nations today almost inevitably lean toward a high degree of government economic involvement [Trubek(41)]. Government-to-government economic aid encourages such concentration of power in recipient developing countries, and impact studies have not been done to discern the consequences of such external intervention, however well motivated.

The efficacy of American aid to developing countries has been debated in these terms. On the assumption that economic aid can extend constitutional democracy, the Foreign Assistance Act of 1961 specifies U.S. policy in the following terms. Aid to foreign countries should seek "to foster private initiative and competition, to encourage the development and use of cooperatives, credit unions, and savings and loan associations, to discourage monopolistic practices, to improve the technical efficiency of their industry, agriculture and commerce, and to strengthen free labor unions." In 1966, the legislation was amended in Section 281 (Title IX) to focus emphasis "on assuring maximum participation in the task of economic development on the part of people of developing countries, through the encouragement of democratic private and local governmental institutions." As detailed by Robert A Packenham, later legislation, with equally unproved results, has required the administrators of U.S. aid to take into account the degree to which recipient countries are making progress toward respect for rule of law, freedom of expression and of the press, and recognition of the importance of individual freedom and private enterprise.

Most ambitious has been the Foreign Assistance Act of 1976. Under it, individual human rights reports must be submitted to Congress with all new requests for security assistance (affecting about eighty countries). The statute provides that no security assistance should be given to any country engaging in a consistent pattern of gross violation of human rights. After receiving reports from the State Department, Congress by majority vote of both houses may reduce or terminate security aid to a country that violates human rights. South Korea, Chile, and Uruguay were thus affected in 1976 by aid reductions (*Washington Post*, October 4, 1976, A2, cols. 1–2).

There is no scholarly consensus on identifying the circumstances under which foreign aid can improve the human rights situation in a recipient country. Fostering greater pluralism may be done in part by programs which contribute to the influence of out-of-power "have-not" groups. On the other hand, increased pluralism may challenge established authority—inviting the ironic effect of stimulating human rights abuses against the new emerging forces—as the experience attests of *campesino* unions in Central America.

Another thorny problem for implementation of new federal law involves the definitional difficulties inherent in the human rights field. While there may be some rights, such as the freedom from government abuse by torture which are not relative, generally there are priority gradations of political and civil rights. It is unrealistic to insist that specific models of parliamentary democracy or party competition are essential everywhere, even if desirable.

What rights? and whose? These are pressing questions for aid administrators. Essential choices cannot be avoided, yet the state of human rights theory and empirical impact research offers neither compass nor guide. For example, the benefits from different types of human rights may be obviously limited to certain classes or groups in the population [Karst and Rosenn (17)]. This can be the result of differences in economic and social status. Some, as a practical matter, pertain only to limited urban elites. Interference with the right to publish a big-city newspaper is an illustration for India, with its widespread poverty and illiteracy. On the other hand, for such a country, how should American aid administrators face up to human rights dilemmas not encountered in developed countries. For example, the remoteness of the village folk and rural poor from centers of communication, sources of capital formation, and persons of influence means that they suffer degradation where basic socio-economic needs and positive human rights are concerned, while the rest of the world hears only of the urban-based problems of press censorship. The "state of the art" in empirical human rights research is not prepared to help in terms of such problems (Claude, 1975). Nevertheless, constructive and relevant normative debate is under way, and the related problem of analytical conceptualization has advanced, for example in the contrasting work of John Rawls (32) and Brian Barry (2).

In a significant law review article on human rights, law and society, and American economic intervention by foreign aid, Trubek and Galanter have issued a healthy warning against the chauvinism of "liberal legalism" (p. 1062). Moreover, American social scientists have expressed appropriate modesty in noting that empirical research on the socio-economic and political correlates of human rights can be criticized for carrying liberal normative biases [Connolly (8)]. Indeed, Theodore A. Sumberg's monograph (39) has a patently "cold war" flavor.

Serial data on comparative rights and liberties have been published annually since 1972 by Raymond D. Gastil for Freedom House in New York. Gastil's *Comparative Survey of Freedom* seeks "to refine a universal standard for measuring the level of human rights in every nation and dependent territory." The *Survey* was relied upon by former United States Ambassador Daniel Patrick Moynihan in November 1976, when he introduced to the United Nations his resolution calling for amnesty for all political prisoners. In *Survey*, human rights scores do not take into account socio-economic rights, but rely instead upon seven-point scales for civil liberties (with indicators emphasizing free expression and fair trial rights) and civil and political rights (with indicators emphasizing political participation rights and nondiscrimination toward political opposition). While these ratings have proved both interesting and useful, they have not been analyzed in terms of hypotheses linking human rights to various social correlates such as the development of communications systems, economic development, cultural systems, etc.

Some efforts along these lines have been conducted by the present authors who have been able to rely upon pre-existing analysis of the sociology of advanced industrialized societies accumulated in terms of associated systems of communciation. Daniel Lerner (20) has led the way by describing communications development as a source of political and economic change. Lerner stresses that in the context of industrializing countries, urbanization exposes the uneducated to the media with consequent development of literacy—equipping them to perform the varied tasks required in a modernizing society. "Out of this interaction," he observes, "develop those institutions of participation (e.g., voting) which we find in all advanced modern societies (20), p. 60." Although efforts to operationalize Lerner's thesis have especially relied upon mass media indicators, communications development may be also usefully thought to be made up of technical means for transmitting personal or business messages, e.g., by domestic and foreign mail and by telephone. In Table 2 below these latter communications indicators, along with urbanization, literacy and professionalization data, all correlate positively with economic development, especially among those twenty-two countries which score most highly on the Gastil rights scores.

Many communications scholars, including Lucian Pye (31) and Karl Deutsch (12) have underscored the importance of communications systems in analyzing nation-states. Indeed, Deutsch argues that the communications system forms a central nerve system from which one can predict system-stability, social cohesion, and many other aspects of the political system. Strong communications systems keep the citizen informed of both national and international events, and they condition the political system to be responsive to demands for political rights and civil liberties. The relationships between communications variables and political and civil liberties, as analyzed by the present authors, include telephones per capita, mail per capita, and literacy [Taylor and Hudson (40)]. They are all significantly related to civil liberties and political rights, and they are among the highest correlations reported.

In Table 3, we can see from the cumulative "R Square" that the independent variables taken together explain over 50 percent of the civil liberties variance. The regression equation, shown at the bottom of the table, describes the influences shaping the configuration of the regression slope. All the slopes are strong ones, pointing to considerable change in the dependent variable for each one unit change in the independent variable. All of the positive slopes in the Strouse-Claude analysis involve communications indicators: domestic mail per capita with a beta weight of 7.4; telephones per capita (2.3) and foreign mail per capita (2.1). The economic development variables have a depressant effect upon civil liberties, at least where rapid growth is concerned. This set of relationships may seem perplexing. On the one hand, R. B. Nixon has published statistics that show that among economically developed countries, there is generally a

Table 2. Simple Correlations Between Selected Independent Variables with High Rights Scores (N = 22) and Low Rights Scores (N = 100)*

| | SOCIAL DEVELOPMENT — COMMUNICATIONS | | | | | | | | | | | |
| | Professional-Technical % | | Literacy | | Foreign Mail (per capita) | | Urbanization | | Domestic Mail (per capita) | | Telephones (per capita) | |
	High Rights	Low Rights	High Rights	Low Rights	High Rights	Low Rights	High Rights	Low Rights	High Rights	Low Rights	High Rights	Low Rights
POLITICAL DEVELOPMENT												
Legal Executive Transfer	-.32	-.05	-.16	.38	.10	-.09	-.11	.07	-.05	-.01	-.37	.04
Irregular Power Change	.02	-.03	.10	-.05	.04	-.09	.08	.02	.15	.01	-.04	-.13
ECONOMIC DEVELOPMENT												
Aggregate Energy per Cap.	.60	-.09	.15	.21	-.21	-.12	.38	-.03	.56	.02	.42	-.07
Fixed Domestic Capital	-.12	.09	.41	.08	.25	.13	-.13	.05	.02	.20	.13	.12
Gross National Product	.59	-.06	.16	.63	-.23	-.11	.38	-.01	.57	.01	.41	-.02
Food Supply (Calories)	.36	.43	.59	.27	-.09	.21	.51	.54	.50	.57	.25	.60
Energy per Capita	.51	.36	.63	.39	.07	.64	.40	.40	.72	.31	.61	.54
GNP per Capita	.57	.48	.74	.50	-.09	.68	.28	.46	.62	.43	.90	.65
ECONOMIC DEVELOPMENT RATES												
Growth Rate per Capita	-.20	.39	.01	.05	-.17	.26	.25	.01	-.11	.53	-.39	-.04
Growth Rate, Energy p/C	-.06	.22	-.08	.16	-.42	.18	.34	.24	-.12	.30	-.27	.18
Growth Rate	-.46	.20	-.53	-.05	.06	.41	-.16	-.10	-.39	-.06	-.52	.03

*Italicized relationships indicate statistical significance. Levels for significance are different for the low rights. (.43) and the high rights states (.20) because of the number of countries in each group.

Source. Rights data: Raymond D. Gastil (14) p. 4; no. 20 (1973), p. 14; no. 23 (1974), p. 8; no. 26 (1974), p. 15. The twenty-two countries which had the highest scores in the civil liberties and political rights fields from 1972–1975 were: Australia, Austria, Barbados, Canada, Costa Rica, Denmark, France, West Germany, Iceland, Ireland, Italy, Jamaica, Japan, Luxembourg, Netherlands, New Zealand, Norway, Sweden, Switzerland, United Kingdom and the United States. Independent variables: Taylor and Hudson, *World Handbook*, pp. 128–35; 150–53; 219–21; 232–35; 236–38; 239–41; 326–31; 341–43; 332–37; 306–21; 256–58.

Table 3.   Stepwise Regression between Civil Liberties and
Independent Variables (N = 122)

	Multiple R	R Square	R Square Change
INDEPENDENT VARIABLES			
Foreign mail per capita	.5259	.2766	.2766
Telephones per capita	.5796	.3359	.0593
Professional/ Technical %	.6053	.3663	.0303
GNP per capita growth	.6185	.3826	.0162
Irregular power change	.6436	.4143	.0316
Domestic mail per capita	.7109	.5054	.0911

Civil Liberties (Y) = + 2.12 Foreign mail per capita ($\times 1$)
+ 2.3   Telephones per capita ($\times 2$)
− 3.0   Professional/Technical % ($\times 3$)
− 3.8   GNP per capita ($\times 4$)
− 4.6   Irregular power change ($\times 5$)
+ 7.4   Domestic mail per capita ($\times 6$)

Source. James C. Strouse and Richard P. Claude, "Empirical Comparative Rights Research: Some Preliminary Tests of Development Hypotheses," p. 59, in Claude (38).

greater level of civil liberties (using free speech and press as his reference) than among the less well developed states [Nixon (27)]. On the other hand, the regression analysis notes a negative relationship between civil liberties and economic growth rates. The apparent paradox may be resolved by emphasizing that, while economic development provides the conditions under which greater civil liberties become feasible, nevertheless, rapid development encourages the strengthening of government controls which may preempt more democratic systems of communications. Wilbur Schramm (36), p. 55, has put this point in other terms: "Whereas it is easier for a developed country to have a completely free press and free communication, it is much harder for a country in the early stages of development to do so." The political instability that is sometimes associated with Third World countries is also reflected in Table 3. The strongest negative slope involves irregular executive transition (−4.6). The violence, coups, and irregular procedures reflected in this indicator are often ad hoc and episodic; by definition they reflect the exception rather than the rule. They may not necessarily reflect long-term trends. For all of these reasons, it is not surprising that, while important, this factor explains only 3 percent of the variance in civil liberties changes (see "R Square Change"). Nevertheless, when such events occur as the establishment of decree rule in Brazil or the displacement of regular democratic constitutional forms in Uruguay, the effect on civil liberties in the countries involved is dramatic and deep.

The regression equation in Table 4 shows that the communications variables associated with political participation rights are very strong, and all have a positive impact upon rights related to the electoral process. Economic development variables are not carried forward by the regression program to show substantial explanatory power. This result is in harmony with recent cross-national studies in this area. In 1959, Seymour Lipset published a well known study of "social and economic requisites" of democracy in which he concluded that the more well-to-do a nation, the greater the chances that it will sustain democracy. The suggestion that the more economically developed a country is the more democratic it is also misleadingly persists in a cross-national comparative study by [Philips Cutright (10)]. Dean Neubauer (26), however, has more recently made clear that while economic development is important, it constitutes a threshold phenomenon where such liberal democratic institutions as free elections are concerned. Once over the economic development threshold, other factors such as communications are more important in determining the prevalence of political rights. A newer analysis of this data in terms of causal modeling has been done by Donald J. McCrone and Charles F. Cnudde in which the importance of communications variables is made clear where democratic political development is involved. Against the background of these findings, the absence of strong positive economic development influences is understandable. The negative influence of rapid economic growth (in terms of growth rate per capita of GNP) sup-

Table 4. Stepwise Regression Between Political Rights and Independent Variables (N = 122)*

INDEPENDENT VARIABLES	Multiple R	R Square	R Square Change
Telephones per capita	.6193	.3836	.3836
Literacy	.6698	.4487	.0651
Foreign Mail per capita	.7053	.4975	.0476
Growth Rate per capita	.7214	.5204	.0229
Domestic Mail per capita	.7517	.5651	.0447

Political Rights (Y) = + .52 Telephones per capita ($\times 1$)
    + .44 Literacy ($\times 2$)
  + 1.29 Foreign Mail per capita ($\times 3$)
  − 2.2 Growth Rate per capita ($\times 4$)
  + 1.69 Domestic Mail per capita ($\times 5$)

*Source: Strouse and Claude, (38) p. 61.

ports the presumption that rapid economic growth, far from being the source of domestic tranquility it is sometimes supposed to be, is rather a disruptive and destabilizing force that leads to political instability [Olson (29)].

The point that economic dislocation involved in intensive growth often causes a regime to be more repressive for the sake of economic development is illustrated by the deplorable treatment of the Uganda Asians in the early 1970s, by the imposition of press censorship under suspension of constitutional rights in India between 1975 and 1977, and by the detention without trial of political dissidents in Chile, Uruguay, and Argentina in 1976. Chilean policy, it should be noted, was altered in November 1976, when political prisoners were released in connection with a Ford Administration abstention from voting on a U.N. condemnation of Chile and after a threat by President-elect Carter to cut foreign assistance in Chile on account of human rights abuses (*New York Times,* Nov. 16, 1976, p. 32, col. 3).

While it is encouraging to note such short-term positive consequences of foreign-aid intervention on behalf of human rights, the long-term pull of socio-economic forces may be expected to have more enduring consequences. According to our research, as reflected in the preceding tables, economic development rates are negatively associated with social development and communications, particularly among those countries which sustain high standards of civil liberties and political rights. Low-scoring countries, where rights information are concerned appear to have traded off liberal political goals—at least temporarily—to place social development at the service of rapid economic modernization. In these countries, the growth rate variables are predominantly positively associated with social development and communications variables. The economic development variables seem to have a correlation pattern in the low-scoring countries which is diminished compared to the high-scoring countries. The reciprocal relationship between social development communications and economic modernization is not as strong among developing nations as it is in the economically mature liberal democracies. Precisely why this should be the case raises a question for subsequent research [Emerson (13)].

While empirical human rights development theory is still an academic fledgling, it is not too early to posit a heuristic model on which to build subsequent research. In Figure 1, below, each of the variables is composed of several factors previously discussed, and each of the main elements in the model interact in positively (+) or negatively (−) reinforcing relationships. In these terms, the model, known as a "Signed Digraph," supplies a preliminary basis for predicting relationships where data is ill-developed. As used by Roberts, Brown and Spencer (34), the model relies on stability theory for criteria in awarding plus and minus signs pointing to functional and dysfunctional relationships, and curved lines indicate significant feedback reinforcement loops.

Of course, the crucial point of the digraph methodology is the specification of the system and the stipulation of relationships among the variables. Where, as in the comparative human rights field, data gathering has barely begun and theory is primitive, the use of delphi panels of experts may be critical for digraph analysis. Once the variables are selected by the delphi panel, they are grouped into composite variables, as in Figure 1. The delphi experts assess whether the relationships between all two-variable groups are positive, negative, or neutral [Linstone and Turoff (21)]. All the variables are paired and analyzed iteratively. Several rounds of decisions by the panel are necessary before the Signed Digraph Model is constructed. The model becomes a working model which is tested by introducing events (e.g., a decline in GNP) or policies (e.g., U.S. foreign aid sanctions) for impact indications. The model is continuously analyzed, updated and reformulated until the "best" model emerges. The approach

Figure 1. A Digraph Model of Comparative Human Rights

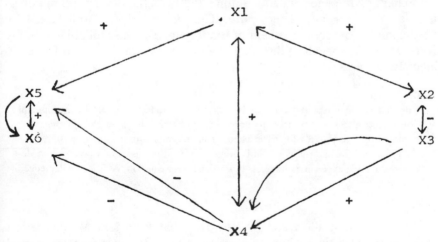

X1 = social development
X2 = political development
X3 = economic development
X4 = economic development rates
X5 = civil liberties
X6 = political rights

suggested here, of course, is similar to techniques already familiar to economists who have developed computerized models of national economic systems.

Political systems of every description must respond to a wide spectrum of changing stimuli [Unger (43)]. But among those countries which adhere to human rights, only in the extreme (for example under circumstances of external threat or economic adversity) is the response one of the suppression or withdrawal of rights [Spinrad (37)]. To the extent that freedom, equality and recognition of human dignity are perceived by legal actors to contribute to public order and general welfare, they will be not only encouraged by the system, but vigorously guarded as well. Where relative economic development prevails and where a communications infrastructure permits multidirectional exchange, it becomes possible for the political system to reach a position of comparative equilibrium. However, if the system is to maintain this homeostatic position, the contending concepts of freedom, equality, and welfare must be channeled so that destructive oscillations from the steady state can be controlled. That mechanism is to be found in the balancing effect of rights and duties, and in the integrative functions of politics.

This problem of balance between political stability and economic development on the one hand, and human rights on the other hand, involves both a *challenge* and a *dilemma*. The *challenge* was well stated by Ferdinand E. Marcos. President of the Republic of the Philippines. In his April 21, 1977, speech to the Board of Governors of the Asian Development Bank, he said:

> In many Third World countries, there is great urgency today for national development to affirm and give real substance to our avowals in favor of human rights. Without any concrete effort to provide for basic needs, and the minimum of human welfare, our commitment to human rights would become a farce. But we cannot procure our development at the expense of the rights of those whom we are, in the first place, pledged to liberate.

The *dilemma* is illustrated by the fact that President Marcos spoke these words at a time when he had imposed a stringent form of martial law, including the postponement of elections, the suspension of the writ of habeas corpus, and the imposition of international travel restrictions on Philippine citizens, especially those who had expressed dissenting views on government policy. Nevertheless, Marcos concluded his address on "Human Rights and Economic Development" with the memorable proposition: "There can be no trade-off between economic development and human rights."

REFERENCES

1. Adelman, Irma, and Cynthia Taft Morris, *Economic Growth and Social Equity in Developing Countries,* Stanford University Press, Stanford, Cal. (1973).
2. Barry, Brian, *The Liberal Theory of Justice,* Clarendon Press, Oxford (1973).
3. Bayley, David, H., *Public Liberties in the New States,* Rand McNally, Chicago (1964).
4. Binder, Leonard, James S. Coleman, Joseph La Palombaro, Lucien Pye, Sidney Verba, and Myron Weiner, eds., *Crises and Sequences in Political Development,* Committee on Comparative Politics of the Social Science Research Council, Princeton University Press, Princeton, N.J. (1971).
5. Blondel, Jean, *Comparative Political Systems,* Praeger, New York (1972).
6. Claude, Richard P., "Comparative Civil Liberties: The State of the Art," *Policy Studies Journal* 4 (1975): 175–80.
7. ———, "The Western Tradition of Human Rights in Comparative Perspective," *Comparative Judicial Review* 14 (1977): 3–137.
8. Connolly, William E., *The Bias of Pluralism,* Atherton Press, New York (1969).
9. Cooray, Joseph A. L., *Constitutional Government and Human Rights in a Developing Society,* The Colombo Co., Colombo, Sri Lanka (1969).
10. Cutright, Phillips, "National Political Development: Measurement and Analysis," *American Sociological Review* 28 (1963): 253–64.
11. deRuggiero, Guido, *The History of European Liberalism,* (translated by R. G. Collingwood) Beacon Press, Boston (1959).
12. Deutsch, Karl W., *The Nerves of Government,* The Free Press, New York (1966).
13. Emerson, Rupert, "The Fate of Human Rights in the Third World," *World Politics* 27 (1975): 201–26.
14. Gastil, Raymond D., "Comparative Survey of Freedom," *Freedom at Issue,* No. 17 (1973) and subsequent issues.
15. Hayek, Friedrich A., *Constitution of Liberty,* Henry Regnery, Chicago (1972).
16. Jellinek, Georg, *System der subjektiven öffenlichen Rechte,* B. Mohr, Freiburg (1892).
17. Karst, Kenneth L., and Keith S. Rosenn (eds.), *Law and Development in Latin America,* University of California Press, Berkeley (1976).
18. Krieger, Leonard, "Stages in the History of Political Freedom," *Liberty, Nomos IV,* Carl Friedrich, (ed.), Atherton Press, New York (1962).
19. Kuznets, Simon, *Modern Economic Growth,* Yale University Press, New Haven (1969).
20. Lerner, Daniel, *The Passing of Traditional Society: Modernizing The Middle East,* The Free Press, New York (1958).
21. Linstone, Harold A., and Murray Turoff, (eds.), *The Delphi Method,* Addison-Wesley, Reading, Mass. (1975).
22. Lipset, Martin Seymour, "Some Social Requisites of Democracy: Economic Development and Political Legitimacy," *American Political Science Review* 53 (1959): 69–105.
23. McCrone, Donald J., and Charles F. Cnudde, "Toward a Communication Theory of Democratic Political Development: A Causal Model," *American Political Science Review* 61 (1967): 72–79.
24. Martin, Robert, *Personal Freedom and the Law in Tanzania,* Oxford University Press Nairobi (1974).
25. Moore, Barrington, *Social Origins of Dictatorship and Democracy,* Beacon Press, Boston (1966).
26. Neubauer, Deane E., "Some Conditions of Democracy," *American Political Science Review* 51 (1969): 1002–1009.
27. Nixon, Russell B., "Factors Related to Freedom in National Press Systems," *Journalism Quarterly* 37 (1950): 13–28.

28. Nyerere, Julius, *Freedom and Development,* Government Printer, Dar es Salaam (1968).
29. Olson, Mancur, "Rapid Growth as a Destabilizing Force," *Journal of Economic History* 23 (1963): 527–47.
30. Packenham, Robert A., *Liberal America and the Third World,* Princeton University Press, Princeton, N.J., (1973).
31. Pye, Lucian W., (ed.), *Communications and Political Development,* Princeton University Press, Princeton, N.J., (1963).
32. Rawls, John, *A Theory of Justice,* Harvard University Press, Cambridge, Mass. (1971).
33. Rheinstein, Max (ed.), *Max Weber on Law in Economy and Society,* Harvard University Press, Cambridge, Mass. (1954).
34. Roberts, Fred S., "Building an Energy Demand Signed Digraph I: Choosing the Nodes" (Santa Monica: The Rand Corporation, R-927/1-NSF, April 1972); "Building an Energy Demand Signed Digraph II: Choosing Edges and Signs and Calculating Stability," (R-927/2-NSF, May 1972); Fred S. Roberts, T. A. Brown, and J. Spencer, "Pulse Processes on Signed Digraph: A Tool for Analyzing Energy Demand," (R-926-NSF, March 1972).
35. Sartori, Giovanni, *Democratic Theory,* Praeger, New York (1965).
36. Schramm, Wilbur, "Communication Development and the Development Process," in Lucian W. Pye, ed., *Communications and Political Development,* Princeton University Press, Princeton, N.J. (1963).
37. Spinrad, William, *Civil Liberties* (New York: Quadrangle Books, 1970).
38. Strouse, James C., and Richard P. Claude, "Empirical Comparative Rights Research: Some Preliminary Tests of Development Hypotheses," in Richard P. Claude (ed.), *Comparative Human Rights,* Johns Hopkins University Press, Baltimore (1976).
39. Sumberg, Theodore A., *Freedom in the Third World,* Georgetown University Center for Strategic and International Studies (Washington, D.C. 1975).
40. Taylor, Charles Lewis, and Michael C. Hudson, eds., *World Handbook of Political and Social Indicators,* 2d ed., Yale University Press, New Haven (1972).
41. Trubek, David M. "Toward a Social Theory of Law," *Yale Law Journal,* 82 (1968): 1–50.
42. ———, and Marc Galanter, "Scholars in Self-Estrangement: Some Reflections on the Crisis in Law and Development Studies in the United States," *Wisconsin Law Review* (1974): 1062–1102.
43. Unger, Roberto M., *Law in Modern Society,* Macmillan, New York (1975).

*Richard P. Claude is associate professor of Government and Politics, University of Maryland, and editor of *Comparative Human Rights* (Johns Hopkins University Press, 1976). James C. Strouse is research associate in the Office of Advanced Systems, Social Security Administration, Department of Health, Education and Welfare.

THE FIRST AMENDMENT: SYMBOLIC IMPORT— AMBIGUOUS PRESCRIPTION*

Rozann Rothman, UNIVERSITY OF ILLINOIS

INTRODUCTION

The First Amendment to the Constitution has symbolized the American commitment to liberty and its corollary, a system of free expression. Yet the most cursory glance at American history reveals incidents which raise disturbing questions concerning application of the guarantees of the Amendment to dissenters. The First Amendment is typically perceived as a link in a fence of protection for the individual, but the perception does not invalidate the sovereign right to impose legitimate constraint on citizens for the protection of the community. The claims of the community present a continuing challenge to the values of the Amendment in that

*An earlier version of this essay was presented at the American Political Science Association Meeting, Chicago, September 2–5, 1976.

Research in Law and Sociology—Vol. 1, 1978, pages 59–80.

they suggest the necessity of modifying its prescriptions to suit the fears, interests, and expectations of a particular historical period. The disparities have been thoroughly dissected, analyzed, and criticized. Fiery denunciations and congratulatory rhetoric compete for public attention and support, and a firm unyielding standard of interpretation of the Amendment remains elusive.

The purpose of this essay is to identify and analyze the dilemmas generated by the juxtaposition of opposing values. Analysis of the basic assumptions which are the source of controversy, and identification of the relationship, interaction, and persistence of competing values suggest the need for a different approach to the classic problems of politics. The tempting assumption, and the one usually made, at least tacitly, is that there exists in principle some optimal effective legal or linguistic resolution of contradiction and that the task of scholars, philosophers, or jurists is to find or at least approximate it. In contrast, this analysis suggests that the contradictions are enduring; they reflect different values as well as different interpretations of the facts. Changes in historical circumstances do not eliminate the classic discrepancies; they are embedded in and integral to the political process.

American institutions have developed techniques to meliorate conflict; these techniques, over time, take on the characteristics of ritual and cushion the impact of contradiction. For example, the judicial function has been defined as the principled accommodation of competing values, and Supreme Court decisions on First Amendment questions provide excellent examples of ritualistic responses which obscure the implications of conflict. Court decisions, even on the "hard questions" posed by the First Amendment, facilitate the transformation of politics into a process of adaptation.[1] In support of this interpretation, this essay identifies the elements of persistent conflict, describes the factors which lead to accommodation, and examines the extent to which elite practices facilitate public acceptance of the persistence of conflict.

PRESENTATION OF THE PROBLEM

Debates and criticism of Supreme Court decisions on First Amendment questions polarize around competing value assumptions: some scholars and jurists firmly insist on extension of the guarantees to derive the fullest protection for speech,[2] while others just as firmly insist that the priority of different objectives—national security or the pursuit of the good[3]— implies limitation of the guarantees of free speech. Theories such as clear and present danger and interest balancing, as well as definitional approaches, are used by the Court to adjudicate conflicting rights, but the persuasiveness of any theory and its usefulness remain subject to the perceptions and concerns of a given historical period.

Efforts to define or maintain a firm, unyielding standard of interpretation founder on the difficulties of assigning weight to competing imperatives. The First Amendment, read literally, seeks to define and protect an area of liberty beyond the reach of government. Yet the very meaning of sovereignty includes the state's right or power to impose legitimate constraint. Conventional interpretations of the First Amendment pose the question, "What are the limits of legitimate constraint?" This question is the point of departure for every effort to construct or devise a standard of interpretation, but a definitive answer is beyond reach. Fear, expectations, and anticipations are inherent in the calculations; relative priorities are shaped by complex and ambiguous perceptions (Erskine and Siegel, 1975; Lawrence, 1976), and the answer varies accordingly.

The conflicts created by dissent touch and involve the basic values of American society. Examination of the intensity of conflict in the marketplace of ideas reveals the problematic character of First Amendment guarantees. The intensity which impels a gesture, such as burning a draft card, or motivates a Henry David Thoreau to urge action from principle and exhort the minority to clog the system, shatters the reassurances of routine procedures and reasoned arguments. The challenge to existing institutions is overt and threatening, and conflict quickly escalates and appears to escape from proscribed channels.

In contrast, much of the argument over competing rights has ritualistic overtones. Concentration on legal argument relegates to the background the intensity of opposing truths. Just as judicial procedure regularizes the shattering impact of murder by providing a consistent body of rules to measure intent and mete out punishment, so judicial doctrines—clear and present danger, balancing of interests and definitional approaches—attempt to routinize the conflicts created by dissent. Resort to the authority of a Jefferson or a Holmes is juxtaposed against pleas for realism and sufficient governmental power to cope with actual or potential threats to valued norms or established custom. The ritual serves to strengthen the value commitments of contending partisans even as it polarizes the participants.

Development of a ritual implies stylized behavior patterns and a routinization of conflict. Competing rights are reconciled, albeit imperfectly, and disputes stay within prescribed channels. The powerful symbolic reassurances offered by ritual result in public quiescence. The arguments have been heard before. They will be repeated the next time a problem arises and the major result will be additional certitude for the values and norms of American society [Edelman, (10), chapters 8 and 9].

The demand for an absolute principle to cover First Amendment questions is one facet of the quest for stability and certainty, but the elusiveness of the principle and the difficulties of application are indications of the problem's intractability. The motivation behind the search for an absolute prohibition governing First Amendment questions derives from the natural rights background of the Amendment and symbolizes American beliefs about necessary limitations on the power of government. The exigencies of an interdependent society and the consequent expansion of government pose a continuing challenge to these beliefs. The irony of the dilemma is illustrated by contemporary efforts to place speech, religion, press, and the right of assembly beyond the reach of government. The efforts depend for success on the active cooperation of at least one branch of government, the judiciary. To expect government to enforce limits on its actions assumes a self-discipline which has not been regularly demonstrated in political action.

The gap between the absolutist prohibitions of the First Amendment and the exigencies of politics—as well as the stark contrasts between the rationality of law and the passion of dissent—cannot be bridged either by philosophic or legal logic. However, legal and philosophic responses to dissent offer confirmation of pervasive norms and values, and in this way facilitate acceptance of ambivalence. Recognition of the symbolic import of the Amendment is the first step towards achieving greater clarity concerning the multiple meanings of the Amendment and its implications for constitutional government.

SYMBOLIC IMPORT

The symbolism of the First Amendment derives from the basic assumptions of American citizens. For most of our history, and for most Americans, certain political beliefs have appeared as natural and self-evident. The Declaration of Independence declared that certain truths are self-evident and that government imposes limitations on official action: officials are elected and, in theory, are responsive and responsible to the people. American rhetoric, American institutions, and the American model of citizenship offer reassurances that constitutional democracy is a fact of American political life.

Supreme Court decisions on First Amendment questions conform with and reinforce public belief in these basic assumptions. Holmes's majority opinion in Schenck v. U.S. (249 U.S. 47 (1919)), his dissent in Abrams v. U.S. (250 U.S. 616 (1919)) and the majority and dissenting opinions in Gitlow v. N.Y. (268 U.S. 652 (1925)) focus attention on freedom of expression as part of the fundamental rights and liberties of the American people. In each of these cases, the fate of the dissenter—who went to jail—was relegated to the background, and did not contradict the Court's claim to have set the limits of legitimate government constraint.

Later cases concerning First Amendment freedoms continued to provide reassurance about the ultimate purposes of American government. Justice Murphy in Thornhill v. Alabama expressed the faith when he noted that "The safeguarding of these rights to the ends that men may speak as they think on matters vital to them and that falsehoods may be exposed through the processes of education and discussion is essential to free government" (310 U.S. 88 (1940):95). Justice Jackson in West Virginia State Board of Education v. Barnette added:

> if there is any fixed star in our constitutional constellation, it is that no official, high or petty, can prescribe what shall be orthodox in politics, nationalism, religion or other matters of opinion or force citizens to confess by work or act their faith therein. If there are any circumstances which permit an exception they do not now occur to us (319 U.S. 624 (1943):642).

Many First Amendment opinions, majority as well as dissents, affirm the preeminence of liberty, particularly freedom of expression, in the constellation of American values. Each example represents an argument over competing priorities and their relative preeminence, and the structure of these opinions conforms to an increasingly explicit formal pattern. The value of free trade in ideas is weighed against the value of security, of preserving the peace of a community, or of the government's right to forbid a substantive evil. The arguments affirm freedom of ideas but they also convey reservations concerning the effects of expression on the lawful and pressing purposes of government. The paradoxes and contradictions in the process are masked by the formal structure of a Supreme Court decision which defines the political situation in terms of long-established and widely accepted norms. The resultant decision, whether it upholds or rejects a dissenter's claim, is of secondary significance; rather, its conformance to widely accepted norms strengthens the symbolism of the Amendment.

Every decision of First Amendment questions reaffirms the common sense conception of the Court's role as arbiter of the limits of legitimate constraint. Widespread acceptance of the Court's role serves to obscure perception of alternate strategies for resolution of the conflict between dissent and the functions of government. Individuals in any society grant some degree of reality to the normal, self-evident routines of everyday life. This grant of reality is labeled common sense.

> The reality of everyday life is taken for granted as reality. It does not require additional verification over and beyond its simple presence. It is simply there, as self-evident and compelling facticity. I know that it is real. While I am capable of engaging in doubt

about its reality, I am obliged to suspend such doubt as I routinely exist in everyday life. . . . The world of everyday life proclaims itself and when I want to challenge the proclamation, I must engage in a deliberate by no means easy effort [Berger and Luckman (3) p. 23].

Although disagreements arise concerning the disposition of a particular case, the rationale which rejects the dissenter's claim is as readily at hand as the rationale which upholds that claim. The latter rationale is obvious: a statement of the preferred position or a reference to the literal meaning of the Amendment with the emphasis on the "no" of "make no law."

A rationale to legitimate rejection of the dissenter's claim is more complex but no more difficult to devise. A change in circumstances, the exigencies of the times, or a national emergency minimize whatever logical contradictions might arise between the protections afforded by the First Amendment and the fate of a Debs, a Schenck, a Gitlow, or a Dennis. Although the First Amendment guarantees freedom of speech, some dissenters pay a price for exercising these rights.

Logical contradictions which arise from the unsatisfactory reconciliation of competing interests are scattered through court opinions. Although criticism of inadequate rationales for decisions is common, scholarly concern about the future of constitutional democracy is rare. The rhetoric reinforcing primary assumptions is sufficiently compelling that decisions which erode First Amendment guarantees appear to be supportive of these guarantees.[4]

The discrepancies between ideal and incompatible practices are more apparent in mass behavior, and social scientists have been dismayed by the findings of survey opinion research. Prothro and Grigg compared respondents in Ann Arbor, Michigan, and Tallahassee, Florida, and found strong approval of the principles enunciated in the First Amendment. However, only a slim majority (51.4 percent) of respondents in Ann Arbor and a minority (33.3 percent) in Tallahassee would permit a Communist to speak. The contradictions generated concern about the efficacy of the fundamental assumptions of democracy (Prothro and Grigg, 1969: 236–252).

Rita J. Simon discussed the trend of public attitudes toward civil liberties and noted that

Over the span of three decades from 1940 to 1970, the Public was consistent in its response to the issue of freedom of speech. Most respondents favored it, but not unequivocally . . . most people favored imposing limitations and conditions on freedom of speech that served the national interest and prohibited radical expressions or sentiments [Simon (30), pp. 106–107].

In a recent study, Erskine and Siegal (12) reproduced data that the National Opinion Research Center (NORC) collected over twenty years on public willingness to extend First Amendment rights to extremists.

The percentage that was willing to allow a Communist to speak has doubled in twenty years, but there is little cause for celebration. The narrow scope of the question "clouds the question of whether there has been an overall growth in American tolerance or only less expressed intolerance of the particular kinds of people who were the objects of these questions" (12) p. 19. Other studies, primarily Gallup surveys, support the assumption that the "public holds widely varying and often contradictory opinions of different kinds of freedom at any one time" (12) p. 19.

David G. Lawrence investigated the relation of procedural norms and tolerance and found that tolerance relates to issues. He noted that "consistency in applying tolerant general norms to unpopular issues and groups increases with education" (19), p. 99. Education increased consistency between ideals and attitudes but 40 percent of NORC respondents in 1974 remained unwilling to tolerate speech by a Communist. The public that holds intolerant views is either unaware of the contradiction or has weighed objectives and found a principle more important than First Amendment freedoms. In either case, there is a discrepancy between ideal and widely accepted attitudes.

Michael Kammen discussed the paradoxical aspects of American attitudes and concluded:

Table 1. Willingness to Grant First Amendment Rights to Extremists[a]

Type of freedom	Year	Admitted Communist (percent)
To speak	1954	27
	1972	52
	1973	60
	1974	58
To have book in library	1954	27
	1972	53
	1973	58
	1974	58
To teach	1954	6
	1972	31
	1973	39
	1974	42

NOTE: 1954 data were collected for Stouffer by Gallup and NORC; 1972; 1973 and 1974 data were NORC replications.

[a]*Source:* Hazel Erskine and Richard L. Siegel (12), pp. 2, 15.

We are comfortable believing in both majority rule and minority rights, in both consensus and freedom, federalism and centralization. It may be perfectly reasonable to support majority rule with reservations, or minority rights with certain other reservations. But this has not been our method. Rather, we have tended to hold contradictory ideas in suspension and ignore the intellectual and behavioral consequences of such "double-think" (1972: 280).

The discovery of paradox should be the start of inquiry, not the conclusion. Explanation of the paradox begins with the realization that insufficient attention has been paid to the impact on attitudes of the symbolic reassurances offered by law and by judicial authority. The symbolism of the First Amendment is engraved in American consciousness and generates self-fulfilling expectations. As long as the purposes of government are taken for granted, the public can assume that specific governmental actions conform to stated intentions, whether or not in fact they do. Scholars may understand that the objectives of policymakers as defined in laws or enunciated in court decisions are open to interpretation, but the public is unlikely to perceive the ambiguous aspects of law. The same effort that is needed to doubt common sense is required to challenge the official, seemingly definitive, statement of the political situation which is embodied in law.

Some justices of the Supreme Court have recognized the intellectual consequences of "double-think." The decisions of Justices Black, Douglas, Murphy, and Rutledge offer examples of efforts to attain a closer approximation to the ideal, but many of these decisions also reflect the strain of weighing competing values in specific situations. For most justices, the task is easier. They use the clear and present danger test, balance interests or adopt a definitional approach to reconcile opposing views. If the strategy is successful, contradictions are explained and the dilemmas are relegated to the background.

From this perspective, the inconsistency of public attitudes, the strong adherence to the norms and values of constitutional democracy and the unwillingness to extend to a Communist the right of free speech is analogous to the Court's use of the various tests to determine the limits of legitimate constraint. The justices, who dissent on First Amendment cases, do not resign; they remain on the Court to render decisions on future cases. The contradiction posed by one case is not sufficient to shake the foundations of the judicial system. Similarly, unwillingness to extend rights to a Communist is not sufficient to destroy public belief in the efficacy of the values and norms of constitutional democracy.

Further indication of the strength of First Amendment symbolism is found in the relatively short collective memory concerning the treatment of dissenters. The memory is limited by the situation: the abolitionists were one case, the pacifists another, and the anarchists still another. There seems to be little suspicion on the part of the general public that the pattern of behavior is other than that officially stated in the Amendment or that these incidents occur other than randomly. An explanation for this phenomenon lies in a comparison of the salience and intensity of the incident and the value which is contradicted by it. When the immediate experience of a conflict-laden incident has dissipated, the First Amendment remains, and all can adhere to it as before. The incident becomes a brief and easily overlooked note in the history texts, while the value is reinforced and reconfirmed by education, socialization, and the web of relationships of an ongoing society.

Evidence of the strength and pervasiveness of the symbols of the First Amendment as the expression of American norms and values is found in the opinions of justices, the rhetoric of officials, and even in the critical analyses of scholars. The strength of the symbolism derives from the natural rights origins of the First Amendment. The constant repetition of these principles reassures both elites and the public concerning the purposes and limitations of government. However, the concept of natural rights no longer possesses the same quality of self-evident truth that it possessed when the Declaration of Independence was written. Consequently, the task of securing an absolute limitation on government becomes more difficult and the ambiguity of First Amendment prescriptions becomes more widely recognized.

THE SEARCH FOR AN ABSOLUTE FOR FIRST AMENDMENT QUESTIONS

Ironically, Americans have come to terms with the absence of universally applicable standards in the Constitution as a whole. The Constitution has been praised for precisely the flexibility which has generated criticism of First Amendment interpretations. The dicta in McCulloch v. Maryland praised flexibility in the name of principle. A "living constitution" demanded that "only its great outlines should be marked, its important objects designated, and the minor ingredients which compose these objects be deduced from the nature of the objects themselves" (4 Wheat. 316 (1819):420). Law was presented as developing from principle and the connections were sufficient to support the belief that change was evolution [Rothman (27), pp. 40–41].

In contrast, flexibility, adaptation of the First Amendment to differing circumstances, has been criticized rather than legitimated; [Professor Berns (4) pp. 129–162] finds the lack of a standard of interpretation a source of ever deepening confusion. Professors Kalven (15) pp. 21–23,

Linde (21), pp. 1169–1182, and Strong (31) p. 4, deplore the lack of predictability of decisions as well as the inadequate rationales for decision. The
difference is due to the contrasting purposes of the Constitution and the
Bill of Rights.

The Constitution was written to establish a government with power.
Although checks and balances were designed to prevent the abuse of
power, agreement existed on the need for sufficient power to cope with
the tasks of government. The First Amendment was added to the Constitution to limit the power of a new government. The words of the Federal Farmer summarize the intention behind the demand for a Bill of
Rights. The Constitution was a fundamental compact between the people
of the United States and their rulers. "It is proper that national laws
should be supreme and superior to state or district laws; but then the
national laws should yield to inalienable or fundamental rights . . ." The
Constitution, particularly Article I, Sections 9 and 10, established a partial
bill of rights which "the federal legislators and officers can never infringe
. . . this bill of rights ought to be carried farther, and some other principles
established, as a part of this fundamental compact between the people of
the United States and their federal rulers" Lee (20), pp. 120–122; cf.
Justice Hugo Black (6), pp. 554–555.

The Declaration of Independence proclaimed the self-evidence of certain truths, the right to life, liberty and the pursuit of happiness. It also
proclaimed that governments are instituted to secure these rights. The
obvious corollary of these principles is that there are some acts which
government ought not to commit. The First Amendment derives from that
tradition. It proclaims that "Congress shall make no law . . ." Given this
background, flexibility becomes the recognition of temporary exigencies
or deviation which cannot be condoned. Belief in natural rights is the
mainstay of efforts to secure an area of liberty beyond the reach of government. Attempts to secure freedom of speech on principles other than
natural right exhibit conceptual and practical difficulties.

John Stuart Mill wrote *On Liberty* to secure the sovereign right of the
individual over his own body and mind. Eschewing an appeal to natural
law, inalienable rights or the pure light of reason, Mill sought to defend
liberty with the principles of Utilitarianism. Robert Paul Wolff demonstrated the inadequacy of this strategy by showing that the application
of utilitarian principle requires an empirical judgment on existing conditions. If perceptions differ about the facts of a situation, utilitarianism
does not secure individual liberty. Wolff contends that perception of the
facts has changed in this century.

Insofar as our enterprises are inherently social, the public private, interference non-
interference model of human relationships breaks down. The central problem ceases to

be the regulation of each person's infringement on the sphere of other persons' actions and becomes instead the coordination of the several actions and the choice of collective goods (35), p. 50.

Contemporary acceptance of the inherently social basis of action and of the significance of government in the common life is at the root of the difficulty in utilizing John Stuart Mill to defend an area of individual liberty from the ever expanding claims of the state.

John Rawls's discussion of "Tolerance and the Common Interest" presents a similar difficulty. Justice as fairness provides strong arguments for an equal liberty of conscience. The parties of the compact that creates the state have good grounds for adopting the principle, but

> liberty of conscience is limited, everyone agrees, by the common interest in public order and security. . . . First of all, acceptance of this limitation does not imply that public interests are in any sense superior to moral and religious interests; . . . The government has no authority to render associations either legitimate or illegitimate any more than it has this authority in regard to art and science. These matters are simply not within its competence as defined by a just constitution. Rather given the principles of justice, the state must be understood as the association consisting of equal citizens. It does not concern itself with philosophical and religious doctrine but regulates individuals' pursuit of their moral and spiritual interests in accordance with principles to which they themselves would agree in an initial situation of equality.
>
> Granting all this, it now seems evident that, in limiting liberty by reference to the common interest in public order and security, the government acts on a principle that would be chosen in the original position. For in this position each recognizes that the disruption of these conditions is a danger for the liberty of all. . . . To restrain liberty of conscience at the boundary, however inexact, of the state's interest in public order is a limit derived from the principle of the common interest, that is, the interest of the representative equal citizen. . . .
>
> Furthermore, liberty of conscience is to be limited only when there is a reasonable expectation that not doing so will damage the public order which the government should maintain. This expectation must be based on evidence and ways of reasoning acceptable to all. . . . Now this reliance on what can be established and known by everyone is itself founded on the principles of justice. It implies no particular metaphysical doctrine or theory of knowledge. For this criteria appeals to what everyone can accept. It represents an agreement to limit liberty only by reference to a common knowledge and understanding of the world. Adopting this standard does not infringe upon anyone's equal freedom. . . . (26), pp. 212–213.

Rawls's theory poses in new terminology the old question of the limits of legitimate constraint. The self-interest of equal individuals is transformed by a compact into the common interest. The common interest is defined by generally accepted criteria and modes of reasoning which are also used to determine when constraint should be imposed. This determination is no easier to make than the determination of "clear and present danger." The Supreme Court has argued and reargued the facts that comprise danger and has rarely reached agreement. Given the experience of the Court and the depths of the splits on the question, it seems unlikely that a society would achieve consensus as Rawls's model postulates or that liberty of conscience based on the original compact would serve for long as a control on behavior.

A different approach to First Amendment questions based on linguistic principles also fails to provide protection for the individual from the expanding claims of government. In fact, the "Note" in the *Harvard Law Review* specifically claims that it does not seek the protection of particular speeches; rather it seeks to preserve the overall quality of freedom of speech (24) p. 374. The strength and attraction of First Amendment symbols suggests that widespread agreement already exists on preservation of the quality of freedom in general, and that the problem lies in applying that protection to specific actions. The "Note" offers an elegant analysis which justifies ignoring the contradictions of application and provides a rationale which facilitates the legitimation of government constraints on specific expression.

This brief survey of philosophical defenses of freedom of expression suggests that changes in the climate of opinion since the eighteenth century have played havoc with the assumptions that underlie the First Amendment. The shift from the individualistic model based on natural rights has not been systematically or comprehensively analyzed, in part because the symbolic and value aspects of the model are embedded in the American consciousness. Analyses which assume the shift to a collectivist model or gloss over the implications may claim to conform to the values of liberal society and afford protection of individual rights, but they prove inadequate to the task [cf. Scanlan (28), pp. 224–226].

The claim that the First Amendment is absolute is the last-ditch effort to extend protection to the full range of individual expression. Typically, such claims either omit reference to natural rights or use natural rights arguments as ritual to attract support. In consequence, First Amendment rights, although presented as absolutes, appear to be arbitrary demands which contradict common-sense understanding of the need for security and protection. The common-sense appraisal of the exigencies of any specific conflict too often seems more compelling than arbitrary claims to First Amendment guarantees [cf. *Berns* (4) pp. 151–157). The tenuous character of the claim of absoluteness thus undermines efforts to afford full protection to expression and magnifies the ambiguities of the prescriptions derived from the First Amendment.

THE RATIONALITY OF LAW AND THE PASSION OF DISSENT

Common-sense resistance to toleration of dissent is mitigated by the tendency to submit First Amendment questions to the courts for resolution.

> . . . legal symbols are used to persuade those involved in the conflict that it makes sense to think of the problem at hand in terms of rights and obligations—thus tapping that latent sensibility to the need for rules and, at the same time, framing the issue in readily comprehensible fashion. Lurking behind the appeal to everyone's common sense, however, is the machinery of government . . . which can produce an authoritative determination of the controlling rule. The underlying purpose of the debate is to channel dispute into established institutions [Scheingold (29), p. 50].

Whether divisive issues can be shaped to fit into established channels for resolution is always problematic. The conflict of competing ideas might escalate and pose a threat to the existing distribution of power in society. Thomas Jefferson in his first Inaugural Address claimed that the American Republic was based on a sacred principle: "That though the will of the majority is in all cases to prevail, that will to be rightful must be reasonable; that the minority possess their equal rights, which equal law must protect, and to violate would be oppression." This statement of principle, which continues to serve as a succinct summary of American values, assumed that

> every difference of opinion is not a difference of principle. We have called by different names brethren of the same principle. We are all Republicans, we are all Federalists. If there are any among us who would wish to dissolve the Union or change its republican form, let them stand undisturbed as monuments of the safety with which error of opinion may be tolerated where reason is left free to combat it [Jefferson (14) pp. 378–379].

When all are brethren of the same principle, there is little to fear from the clash of ideas in the marketplace. Jefferson's statement established American priorities, but the conditions under which the statement becomes operative imply that dissent must stay within bounds and only offer a limited challenge to established institutions.[5] There remains the possibility of a different response if conditions change.

Tolerance is more difficult to maintain when a challenge in existing institutions is perceived. The various debates on the court and in American history over striking the correct balance between liberty and authority illustrate the difficulties of deciding the priorities of competing claims.

These debates make explicit a variety of reservations concerning the effects of freedom of speech. The salience and action potential of the reservations depend upon an empirical assessment of the intensity and threat of the challenge, which is never merely an observation but an observation shaped by the fears, interests, and ambiguous wants of the observer.

The contrast between the communal assessment of political needs and objectives and the dissenter's demand for justice or a "New Jerusalem" intensifies societal reservations concerning the effects of free speech. The career of Eugene V. Debs serves as an example. Speaking on December 10,1905, he claimed

> . . . I am one of those who believe that the day is near at hand when we shall have one great revolutionary economic organization, and one great revolutionary political party of the working class. . . .
>
> This great body will sweep into power and seize the reins of government; take possession of industry in the name of the working class . . . and then the working class in control of industry, will operate it for the benefit of all. . . . Every man will work. . . , not as a slave, but as a free man, and he will express himself in his work and work with joy. Then the badge of labor will be the only badge of aristocracy. The industrial dungeon will become a temple of science. The working class will be free, and all humanity disenthralled [Tussey, (32), p. 144].

Debs was not allowed to stand as a monument of the "safety with which error of opinion may be tolerated where reason is left free to combat it." He was harassed; he was jailed several times and, while in prison in 1920, he ran as the Socialist Party candidate for President, and received more than 900,000 votes. The prison sentence was affirmed by the Supreme Court in a decision which raised serious questions as to what the First Amendment and the "clear and present danger" test could have meant at that time [Kalven (16) pp. 235–237]. Although the Debs decision is no longer good law, it serves as a reminder of the strength of the antipathy to political dissent and suggests the source of repressive responses to dissent.

The example of Debs also illustrates the discrepancy between an individual's existential position and the taken-for-granted conceptions of the larger community. R. D. Laing in his analysis of schizophrenia suggested a model of what happens in the individual case.

> A "truth" about his (the patient's) "existential position" is lived out. What is "existentially" true is lived as "really" true. Undoubtedly most people take to be "really" true only what has to do with grammar and the natural world. A man says he is dead but he is alive. But the truth is that he is dead. He expresses it perhaps in the only way common (i.e. the communal) sense allows him. He means that he is "really" and quite "literally" dead, not merely symbolically or "in a sense" or "as it were," and is seriously bent on

communicating his truth. The price, however, to be paid for transvaluating the communal truth in this manner is to be mad for the only real death we recognize is biological death (18), pp. 37–38.

Laing's model deals with individual manifestations of alienation from common-sense understandings of reality. In the same way, the perspective of the political dissenter differs radically from the common sense understandings of the political process, and the cost to a political dissenter of asserting a radical existential position may be equally high. Howard Zinn claimed that "those who have subjected the Bill of Rights to severe test have often ended up in concentration camps or jails. . . . Radicals and extremists were so small a minority that they could be safely put away without any nationwide burst of outrage" (36), p. 224; cf. Goldman (13), pp. 239–264.

The dissenter, who publicly challenges official explanations of political realities, offers alternatives, and seeks to put his ideas into the competition of the marketplace, must communicate with and mobilize others. This process activates the perception of threat in those who have a stake in communal values. At this point, none of the participants is likely to realize that time will upset many fighting faiths or that the ultimate good desired is better reached by free trade in ideas.

Lawrence's study of the relation between procedural norms and tolerance analyzes public willingness to permit demonstrations and petitions by a variety of groups on a variety of issues. His data are reproduced as Table 2.

Demonstrations are a more immediate threat than petitioning, and the public responds accordingly. It is less threatening if neighbors demonstrate about crime or pollution than if black militants or radical students do so;

Table 2. Percentage Permitting Demonstrating and Petitioning on Various Issues and by Various Groups[a]

	Demonstrate (percent)	Petition (percent)
Because they were concerned about crime in their community	80.7	94.6
By a group of your neighbors	80.7	94.6
To ask the government to stop a factory from polluting the air	79.5	93.2
By a group of radical students	59.9	71.9
By a group of black militants	60.7	69.0
Calling for the legalization of marijuana	41.3	52.0
Calling for the government to make sure that blacks can buy and rent homes in white neighborhoods (whites only)	55.2	69.9

[a]*Source:* David G. Lawrence (19), p. 88.

and the favorable percentage varies accordingly. The tolerant percentage is far higher than could be anticipated from the studies of Stouffer or Prothro and Grigg [Lawrence (19) p. 88] and this could be reason for optimism; the spread of education might increase the tolerant majority.

For purposes of this essay, however, the significant point is the variation in tolerance by issues and groups, a variation which can be explained by the relative threat of particular groups and issues. The attempt to bring about a fundamental reorientation of a communal truth remains a high risk and high stakes game. The scope and extent of the challenge increases the perception of threat and transforms the perception of dissent. Dissenters are likely to be perceived as extremists who reject the rules of democratic society, and Edward Shils described the product of this transformation.

> An extremist group is an alienated group. . . . It cannot share that sense of affinity to persons or attachment to the institutions which confine political conflicts to peaceful solutions. . . . The ideological extremists (of the left and right)—all extremists are inevitably ideological—because of their isolation from the world, feel menaced by unknown dangers. The paranoiac tendencies which are closely associated with their apocalyptic and aggressive outlook make them think that the ordinary world, from which their devotion to the ideal cuts them off is not normal at all; . . .[6]

Dissent is likely to appear as a clear and present danger to segments of the public and may arouse latent fears and loyalties. In this circumstance, affirmation of enduring political verities may generate proclamations of tolerance for dissent or increase allegiance to a threatened political system. The actual response is not predictable from the rhetoric, practices, or constitutional values of American politics, for the response depends in large part on the perception of threat. If threat is salient, protest is likely to be viewed as a challenge to "a way of life" and the cost of the fight for change is escalated accordingly.

A comparison of Shils's description of extremists with Laing's description of the schizophrenic rejection of communal truth illustrates the point more strongly. In the political description, the sympathy that creates understanding is lacking and the lack is predictable. When dissenters challenge an established way of life, they appear to reject the rules of society. Primordial concerns about security and the need for the reassurance of rules are asserted and may result in rejection of the literal interpretation of the First Amendment. This complex mix of fear, interest and a sprinkling of constitutional values is the origin of reservations concerning the impact of free speech on the lawful and pressing purposes of government.

The clear and present danger test was a device for keeping this fundamental conflict within the bounds of established traditions and institutions.

From the perspective of this essay, the significance of the test lies in its utility for containment and routinization of conflict. It could be seen as a device to extend the area of freedom to its farthest point or, equally persuasively, could be decried as illegitimate constraint on individual expression and a violation of constitutional imperative. In either case, conflict was kept within traditional bounds and the discrepancy between ideal and practice was explained and minimized.

The "clear and present danger" test has been criticized primarily by liberal jurists and scholars who discuss in detail the difficulties of its application and its adequacy as a complete constitutional solvent [Strong, (31), pp. 44–45]. Linde attacked the legitimacy of the test when he pointed out that in the case of the Smith Act, judicial deference to legislative assessment of the dangers of sedition produced historical anomalies and inadequate solutions. His criticism shows the dangers of bowing to exigency when First Amendment guarantees are at stake.

> Against this kaleidoscope of history, what was the legislative judgment that would deserve deference for its assessment of the danger from revolutionary speech? From conception to application, the Smith Act spans the whole spectrum of changing radicalism in this century. A prescription against internal revolutionary advocacy—designed as an answer to 19th century anarchy, first applied locally against disciples of Leninism at the time of the Russian Revolution, transferred intact into federal law at the end of a bitter but largely peaceful economic crisis—was found constitutional in punishing the organization of the Communist Party immediately after World War II, because of the exigencies of foreign policy in the years of the Cold War that followed (21) pp. 1176–1177.

Strong approaches the problem differently and makes a plea for development of "a new and meaningful role for the 'clear and present danger' test." However, widespread criticism of the impact of the test on free speech has diminished its utility. A universally applicable constitutional rule to take the place of the "clear and present danger" test has yet to be formulated. Instead, the doctrines of overbreadth and vagueness, derived from the requirement of due process, have been used to protect speech from certain chilling effects of government restraint. Adoption of rules about overbreadth and vagueness mollifies liberal fears about encroachment by government on the domain of the First Amendment. However, these tests fail to provide an amelioration of the conflict between dissent and the commonsense perception that dissent challenges "a way of life."

Just as philosophic defenses of freedom of expression fail to secure individual rights when collectivist assumptions predominate, so judicial decisions fail to reconcile permanently the classic conflict of liberal values with primordial fears and concerns for security. The decisions of particular cases reinforce contradictory perceptions of the conflict which persist and put a firm, unyielding standard of interpretation beyond reach. Instead, there is the fluctuation of decisions between opposing poles and the ad hoc balancing of constitutional imperatives. The result is varying degrees of satisfaction about the implications of any decision for the preservation of cherished values.

CONCLUSION

Identification of the strength and pervasiveness of contradictory cognitions defines the boundaries of the controversy over the First Amendment. Despite the erosion of their philosophical underpinnings, the values of liberalism, especially the stress on individual rights, are deeply embedded in the American consciousness and serve as barriers against shifts to collective assumptions. The values endure, regardless of whether and how circumstances change, and regardless of whether particular actions stand in opposition. The First Amendment is a pervasive and persuasive symbol of American dedication to freedom of expression as the first value of liberalism.

The primordial fears—concern about security, about rules, about the maintenance of a way of life as well as the common sense perception of threat and challenge—are just as deeply embedded in consciousness. These fears mark the other pole of a continuing relationship. The specific response to dissent is shaped according to perceptions of the priorities of national security, internal security, indifference or an openness to change.

Individual rights have been and are violated, and such lapses are criticized in Supreme Court dissents and by segments of the public. At times, the needs of "national security" are overlooked and such lapses are criticized with equal severity. The continuing argument erects a buffer against crisis and uncertainty and masks the dilemma of efforts to apply the guarantees of the Amendment to individual dissenters.

The development of judicial procedures and rhetoric serves to moderate the passions generated by dissent and to fill the void created by the erosion of belief in natural rights. As long as elites and the public assume that the First Amendment serves the purposes for which it was written, judicial decisions and official rhetoric strengthen routinely believed interpretations. Dissent appears to have a sanctioned place in the hierarchy of American values. Although there is resistance to the theory expressed in Abrams v. U.S., "that the ultimate good desired is better reached by free trade in ideas—that the best test of truth is the power of the thought to get itself accepted in the competition of the market. . . ." (33) p. 630, it can be overlooked or relegated to the background. Education increases tolerance, the extent of tolerance has been shown to have increased dramatically between 1954 and 1974, and a larger, more tolerant majority may be waiting in the wings.

But the response to dissent remains problematic. Dissent introduces elements of uncertainty into the political process and the guarantees of the First Amendment do not always provide a reliable guide to official behavior. Formal guarantees offer reassurances about the purposes of government, but they cannot petrify political action or control the psychological and sociological determinants of action. Attempts to apply the prescriptions of the First Amendment to hard cases activate latent fears and concerns, and violations of individual rights occur. Thus the cost of dissent is as integral a part of American politics as the guarantees of the First Amendment. Yet when an illiberal response to dissent emerges, it appears as an aberration or is explained away by contemporary exigencies, and the dilemma posed by equally valid opposing values is minimized.

Although the relationship between the Amendment and the exigencies of the times is pervaded with tension, it provides the framework which contains the conflict over opposing values. In other words, the disparity between liberal ideals and the realities of an imperfect world are mitigated by the rhetoric and precedents which surround the Amendment. Sanctioned by American ideals and intertwined with American history, the symbols and rhetoric cushion the import of dissent and assimilate new challenges to a familiar process. As the arguments take the same well-worn paths, opposing value assumptions fall into "natural" linkages and legitimacy is provided for the entire spectrum of argument.

The historical accretion of ways and means to cope with dissent offsets the threat of escalation. Official recognition of divergent expectations sets the stage for the ensuing subtle and not so subtle adjustments to the fears and concerns of the historical period. The repetition of familiar arguments strengthens and reinforces public belief in the necessity and legitimacy of striking a balance between competing imperatives, and the symbols of the First Amendment retain their tenacious hold on public assumptions. In this way, a controlled social setting, supported by official rhetoric, judicial precedents and the rituals of American politics, facilitates the containment of conflict.

The respective imperatives reflect persisting differences concerning the hierarchy of values, persisting ambiguities about facts and persisting conflicts of interest. The conflicts cannot be resolved, but as this essay suggests, their import for society can be mitigated. Insofar as the particular conflict fits traditional assessments of the dichotomies and traditional objectives continue to serve as sought-after ideals, a fluctuating balance between liberal values and primordial concerns develops. Sharply divergent expectations are modified and the ambiguities of belief and perception which are the source of the controversy over the Amendment are muted.

Legal precedent, terminology and ritual surround the controversy, soften the impact of passion and help to maintain a complex interrelationship of divergent beliefs and perceptions. Conveying the appropriate reassurances, this evocation of pervasive traditions contributes to the viability of the polity.

FOOTNOTES

1. I am indebted to Murray Edelman for this suggestion.
2. Zechariah Chaffee, Jr., *Free Speech in the United States* (Cambridge Mass.: Harvard University Press, 1941); David G. Barnum, *The Problem of Public Order and the Public Forum in Anglo-American Civil Liberties* (unpublished Ph.D. thesis, Stanford, 1974); Thomas I. Emerson, *The System of Freedom of Expression* (New York: Vintage Books, 1970); Harry Kalven, Jr., "The Concept of the Public Forum: Cox v. Louisiana," 1965 *The Supreme Court Review*, 1; Hans A. Linde, "'Clear and Present Danger' Reexamined: Dissonance in the Brandenburg Concerto," *Stanford Law Review* 22 (June 1970): 1162; and Alexander Meiklejohn, *Free Speech and Its Relationship to Self Government* (New York: Harper and Brothers, 1948).
3. See for example Carl A. Auerbach, "The Communist Control Act of 1954," *University of Chicago Law Review* 23 (Winter 1956): 2, 173; Walter Berns, *Freedom, Virtue and the First Amendment* (Chicago: Henry Regnery, 1965); Robert H. Bork, "Neutral Principles and Some First Amendment Problems," *Indiana Law Journal* 47 (Fall 1971):1; and John H. Wigmore, "Abrams v. U.S.: Freedom of Speech and Freedom of Thuggery in War-time and Peace-Time," *Illinois Law Review* 14 (March 1920): 539.
4. See for example Zechariah Chaffee, Jr., "Review of Meiklejohn's 'Free Speech and its Relation to Self Government'" 62 *Harvard Law Review* (1949): 891, 901, where Chaffee suggested that the alternative to the clear and present danger test "was no immunity at all in the face of legislation. Any danger, any tendency in speech to produce bad acts, no matter how remote, would suffice to validate a repressive statute, . . ." See also Alexander M. Bickel, "From 'Sullivan' to the Pentagon Papers," *Commentary* 54 (November 1972): 59–60, where Bickel sugests that there is more liberty before the scope of legitimate constraint is defined, regardless of whether the definition expands the scope of freedom of expression.
5. W. Cody Wilson, "Belief in Freedom of Speech and Press," *Journal of Social Issues* 31 (Spring 1975): 2, 74, asserts that "Indeed a majority of the adult population of the United States rejects the free exercise of speech and press when it is directed at criticism of popular basic dogma. A majority does appear, on the other hand, to support a somewhat restricted freedom of communication in the political-social arena as long as the communication does not attack what seem to be basic tenets of the system."
6. Quoted in Seymour Martin Lipset (22), p. 374.

REFERENCES

1. Auerbach, Carl A., "The Communist Control Act of 1954," *University of Chicago Law Review* 23 (Winter 1956): 2, 173.
2. Barnum, David G., *The Problem of Public Order and the Public Forum in Anglo-American Civil Liberties,* unpublished Ph.D. thesis, Stanford, 1974.
3. Berger, Peter, and Thomas Luckman, *The Social Construction of Reality,* Doubleday, New York (1966).

4. Berns, Walter, *Freedom, Virgue and the First Amendment,* Henry Regnery, Chicago (1965).
5. Bickel, Alexander M., "From Sullivan to the Pentagon Papers," *Commentary* 54 (November 1972): 5, 60–67.
6. Black, Hugo, "Justice Black and First Amendment 'Absolutes': A Public Interview," *New York University Law Review* 37 (June 1962): 4, 549.
7. Bork, Robert H., "Neutral Principles and Some First Amendment Problems," *Indiana Law Journal* 47 (Fall 1971): 1.
8. Chaffee, Jr., Zechariah, *Free Speech in the United States,* Harvard University Press, Cambridge, Mass. (1941).
9. ———, "Review of Meiklejohn's "Free Speech and Its Relation to Self Government,'" *Harvard Law Review* 62 (1949): 891.
10. Edelman, Murray, *Politics as Symbolic Action,* Markham Publishing Co. Chicago (1971).
11. Emerson, Thomas I., *The System of Freedom of Expression,* Vintage Books, New York (1970).
12. Erskine, Hazel, and Richard L. Siegel, "Civil Liberties and the American Public," *Journal of Social Issues* 31 (Spring 1975): 2, 13–29.
13. Goldman, Harvey, ed., *American Radicals,* Monthly Review Press, New York (1957).
14. Jefferson, Thomas, "First Inaugural Address," in Alpheus Mason, ed., *Free Government in the Making,* 3rd ed., Oxford University Press, New York (1965) pp. 377–380.
15. Kalven, Jr., Harry, "The Concept of the Public Forum: Cox v. Louisiana," *The Supreme Court Review* (1965): 1.
16. ———, "Ernst Freund and the First Amendment Tradition," *University of Chicago Law Review* 40 (Winter 1973): 2, 235.
17. Kammen, Michael, *People of Paradox,* Knopf, New York (1972).
18. Laing, R. D., *The Divided Self,* Pelican Books, Harmondsworth (1965).
19. Lawrence, David G., "Procedural Norms and Tolerance: A Reassessment," *American Political Science Review* 70 (March 1976): 1, 80–100.
20. Lee, Richard Henry, "Letter From the Federal Farmer," in Forrest McDonald, ed., *Empire and Nation,* Prentice-Hall, Englewood Cliffs, N.J.: (1962).
21. Linde, Hans A., "'Clear and Present Danger' Reexamined: Dissonance in the Brandenburg Concerto," *Stanford Law Review* 22 (June 1970): 1162.
22. Lipset, Seymour Martin, "The Sources of the 'Radical Right,'" in Daniel Bell (ed.), *The Radical Right,* Doubleday-Anchor, New York (1964).
23. Meiklejohn, Alexander, *Free Speech and Its Relationship to Self Government,* Harper and Bros., New York, (1948).
24. "Notes: The Speech and Press Clause of the First Amendment as Ordinary Language," 87 *Harvard Law Review* (1973): 374.
25. Prothro, James W. and Grigg, Charles M., "Fundamental Principles of Democracy: Bases of Agreement and Disagreement," in C. F. Cnudde and D. E. Neubauer (eds.), *Empirical Democratic Theory,* Markham, Chicago (1969).
26. Rawls, John, *A Theory of Justice,* Belknap Press, Cambridge, Mass. (1971).
27. Rothman, Rozann, "Stability and Change in a Legal Order: The Impact of Ambiguity," *Ethics* 83 (October 1972): 37–50.
28. Scanlan, Thomas, "A Theory of Free Expression," *Philosophy and Public Affairs* 1 (Winter 1972): 2, 204–226.
29. Scheingold, Stuart A., *The Politics of Rights: Lawyers, Public Policy and Political Change,* Yale University Press, New Haven (1974).
30. Simon, Rita J., *Public Opinion in America: 1936–1970,* Rand McNally, Chicago (1974).

31. Strong, Frank R., "Fifty Years of 'Clear and Present Danger': From Schenck to Brandenburg—And Beyond," *The Supreme Court Review* 41 (1969).
32. Tussey, Jean Y., (ed.), *Eugene V. Debs Speaks,* Pathfinder Press, New York (1970).
33. Wigmore, John H., "Abrams v. U.S.: Freedom of Speech and Freedom of Thuggery in War-Time and Peace-Time," *Illinois Law Review* 14 (March 1920): 539.
34. Wilson, W. Cody, "Belief in Freedom of Speech and Press," *Journal of Social Issues* 31 (Spring 1975): 2.
35. Wolff, Robert Paul, *The Poverty of Liberalism,* Beacon Press, Boston (1968).
36. Zinn, Howard, SNCC: *The New Abolitionists,* Beacon Press, Boston (1964).

PUBLIC SUPPORT FOR CIVIL
LIBERTIES IN ISRAEL AND THE
UNITED STATES*

Rita J. Simon, UNIVERSITY OF ILLINOIS

David Barnum, UNIVERSITY OF ILLINOIS

INTRODUCTION

There are widely varying and strong opinions about support for civil liberties in Israel. Israelis themselves have repeatedly charged that a substantial body of law permits or legitimizes serious violations of individual rights and supports among Israelis an attitude of disregard and insensitivity to basic civil liberties. Outside Israel, even greater scrutiny has focused on the way in which Israel protects the rights of its minorities and insures the free expression of dissenting opinion. A major purpose of this research was

*The authors wish to acknowledge the assistance of Jean Henry in the preparation of the tables and the analysis of the data. Funds for the American survey were supplied by the Program in Law and Society at the University of Illinois. The help is gratefully acknowledged.

Research in Law and Sociology—Vol. 1, 1978, pages 81–100.

to find out the extent to which public opinion in Israel is supportive of and sensitive to issues involving civil liberties.[1]

A similar and perhaps even stronger tradition of concern about public attitudes toward civil liberties exists in the United States, dating back at least to Samuel Stouffer's 1955 study of American attitudes toward communists and other unpopular minorities or dissenters (Stouffer, *Communism, Conformity and Civil Liberties*, 1955). This article will update some of Stouffer's findings and compare American and Israeli attitudinal support for civil liberties in a variety of areas. In addition, we will compare the state of public opinion to the state of the law on civil liberties matters in the United States and Israel. Public opinion does not always coincide with the state of the law in either country, and it should be instructive to juxtapose and compare the two.

The protection of basic civil liberties in Israel is not formally embodied in a constitutional framework. In 1949, the first Parliament entertained, but rejected, the idea of drafting a constitution to insure civil liberties; instead it instructed a Constitutional Law and Judicial Committee to draft and present basic laws which would eventually form a constitution. Such laws were expected to articulate the fundamental powers of state institutions and define the relationship of the state to the individual.

This procedure for progressively accepting a set of basic laws rather than originally drafting a complete document was adopted to avoid impasses in regard to certain issues which would necessarily have been considered in an all-encompassing document, particularly the status of individual civil liberties. Under conditions in which the dominant national concern was the security of the state, and the establishment of unifying communal institutions, it did not seem likely that agreement could be reached on how to embody the rights of the individual in a constitutional document. Disagreement focused not only on the problem of defining the status of religion, but also on other functional freedoms such as the right of free expression and the right of privacy. While such rights had been detailed in the Jewish Agency's initiated Draft Constitution which was submitted to the then governing Provisional Council, the committee could not reach consensus and the idea of a detailed document was dropped. The step-by-step drafting of basic laws which took the place of the formal constitution led to the enactment of four bills, none of them directly touching on individual civil liberties.

The absence of a constitution or of any similar authoritative declaration of individual civil liberties has produced recurrent public and parliamentary debate about how to establish a stronger legal basis for the protection of such liberties. Attempts were made at drafting a constitution or bill of rights in 1962 and again in 1964. Unsuccessful attempts were also made to repeal legislation still in force from the British Mandatory Period that

permits arrests, searches, seizures, and censorship in a broadly discretionary manner (particularly the Defense Emergency Regulation of 1945).
Most recently debate in the Parliament centered on enactment of a proposal for a basic law on the Rights of the Individual and the Citizen. This
latter proposal, which has been in committee for four years, has come
under strong attack for being too weak and thus is opposed by members of
parliament who, in principle, favor a basic law of civil liberties.

The fact that a formal constitution has not been adopted in Israel and that
no basic laws have been enacted in the field of individual civil liberties leads
to the question: to what extent is the public aware of, and how much does it
support, civil liberties? Given the lack of any authoritative statement of
principles, and given the special security conditions in Israel which sometimes require substantial incursions into the privacy of the individual, one
might expect a low awareness of and value for certain basic principles of
individual civil liberties among the Israeli public.

At the same time, opinion surveys conducted in the United States have
frequently revealed a substantial ignorance of civil liberties principles and a
substantial lack of support for the basic rights of others among Americans,
despite the prominent character of our Bill of Rights protections and the
widespread publicity that surrounds many decisions of the United States
Supreme Court. Public opinion about civil liberties clearly is often quite
independent of the nature and extent of civil liberties protections and
infringements. The findings from national surveys conducted in 1975 both
in Israel and in the United States should help clarify the relationship
between public attitudes and the formal status of civil liberties in the two
countries.

SAMPLE AND DESIGN

The questions contained in the Israeli survey were included in the weekly
public opinion poll that is conducted on a regular basis by the Israel
Institute for Applied Social Research.[2] They are personal interviews conducted by the Institute's field staff in the respondent's home. The target
population in these surveys is a random sample of 530 adults who live in the
four major urban areas: Jerusalem, Haifa, Tel Aviv, and Beersheva.[3]

The American survey was conducted by phone in the fall of 1975 by the
National Family Opinion Incorporated. The sample frame was composed
of respondents who live all over the United States. The questions in the
American survey were limited to matters pertaining to civil liberties and
were not part of any larger ongoing survey. Five hundred people participated in the American survey.

The first group of questions asked: (Israeli version)

How suspicious would you be of a citizen's loyalty to Israel if that person who lives in Israel engaged in the following behavior. . . .

American version:

I would like you to tell me if you think you would be very suspicious, somewhat suspicious, hardly suspicious, or not at all suspicious of a citizen's loyalty to the United States if that person. . . .

The distribution of responses to the two surveys are reported in Tables 1 and 2.

Commenting first on the Israeli data, note that the five items described in Table 1 may be divided into two categories: one category concerns Arabs, the other concerns the right of citizens to criticize the state or its institutions. On the latter, the responses show that a large majority of the Israeli public (between 63 and 80 percent) approve and support the right of citizens to criticize their country and to speak out against its institutional characteristics.

Toleration for criticism is at a lower level, however, when the behavior concerns either the status of Israeli Arabs or the appropriate response of

Table 1.   Degree of Suspicion About Various Expressions of Opinion in Israel

	Degree of Suspicion					
Expression of Opinion	Very suspicious	Somewhat suspicious	Hardly suspicious	Not at all suspicious	Don't know	Total
	(Percent)					
1. Goes around talking against religion	2	4	6	80	8	100 (530)
2. Claims that Israeli Arabs are discriminated against	5	13	16	58	9	100 (530)
3. Says that he favors direct talks with representatives of the PLO	19	16	15	40	10	100 (530)
4. Is a teacher who tells his students that there are many things wrong in Israel	6	11	12	63	8	100 (530)
5. Argues in favor of establishing a Palestinian state on the West Bank	22	17	13	39	9	100 (530)

Table 2. Degree of Suspicion About Various Expressions of Opinion in the United States

Expression of Opinion	Degree of Suspicion					
	Very suspicious	Somewhat suspicious	Hardly suspicious	Not at all suspicious	Don't know	Total
			(Percent)			
1. Goes around talking against religion	37	27	10	24	2	100 (500)
2. Claims that blacks are discriminated against	13	28	20	36	3	100 (500)
3. Says he favors admission to U.N. for both North and South Vietnam	20	29	14	29	8	100 (500)
4. Refuses to sign oath of loyalty to the U.S.	62	25	5	6	2	100 (500)
5. Is against imprisonment of radical groups for property crimes	66	25	4	4	1	100 (500)
6. Goes around criticizing conditions in this country	22	25	20	32	1	100 (500)
7. Is teacher who tells his students there are many things wrong in the U.S.	26	24	18	30	2	100 (500)
8. Is against imprisonment of radical groups for crimes against persons	75	17	4	3	1	100 (500)

the government to the claims and aspirations of the Palestinians. On the matter of discrimination against Israeli Arabs, though there is some drop in tolerance, most people support the right to express criticism. Only 34 percent indicate that they are even slightly suspicious. But when the issue concerns negotiations with the PLO (Palestine Liberation Organization), and the advocacy of a Palestinian state, suspicion of loyalty grows and we see significantly lower toleration for criticism. But even here it is worth noting that only about 20 percent of those questioned were "very suspicious," while about 40 percent answered that they were "not at all suspicious" of someone who says that he favors direct talks with representatives of the PLO or who argues in favor of establishing a Palestine state on the West Bank.

One way to assess the meaning of the results in Table 1 is to compare them against the level of support that these policies have received by the

Israeli public. In response to a national survey in July 1974, 80 percent of the public said that they were against the establishment of a Palestinian state on the West Bank (which might be compared with the 52 percent from our survey who expressed some degree of suspicion of persons who take this view) and 71 percent of the public was against talks with Palestinians at Geneva (which could be compared with 50 percent from our survey who expressed some degree of suspicion of a person who takes this view). Thus, in two instances which touch on critical issues of national interest, we find a significantly higher degree of support for the right of expression (represented by a lack of suspicion about the loyalty of that person) than we do actual support for the policy. Without making a judgment as to whether we should expect this level to be higher or lower, we see suggested an awareness of the integrity of differing political positions in regard to sensitive political questions.

Shifting now to the responses on the American survey, we note that all of the items save the third one deal with domestic issues. The behaviors about which most of the respondents were very suspicious concerned defense of radical groups who committed crimes either against individuals or property and of persons who refused to sign a loyalty oath. The behaviors that evoked much less suspicion concerned persons who claimed that blacks are discriminated against and persons who criticize conditions in the United States.

The reasons for the lesser degrees of suspicion for such behavior are not obvious. Plausible arguments could be made for explaining the responses on grounds that of course blacks are discriminated against, and of course there are conditions that need improving and therefore criticism of such matters is perceived by most people as being within the realm of loyal behavior. On the other hand, one could interpret the responses as meaning that the issues involved are nonthreatening perhaps because the criticism has so little basis in fact. The fact that the responses to the teacher and the talking against religions items evoke comparable although slightly higher levels of suspicion suggests that a sizable minority of Americans view such behavior as being within the purview of "helpful and loyal criticism" and not seriously threatening to the body politic. The responses to the items about admission to the United Nations of Vietnam reflect the division that existed about the war itself. Probably the 43 percent who were "not at all" or "hardly suspicious" of such advocacy had been opposed to the United States' continued participation in the war.

Four of the items in Table 2 appeared for the first time in the national survey of civil liberties conducted by Samuel Stouffer in 1955. We remember that the early and mid-fifties were marked by widespread fear of internal subversion, suspicion of disloyalty, and emphasis on political conformity. Laws were passed such as the Internal Security Act of 1950 to insure such conformity. We note, however, that the comparisons between the 1955 and the 1975 responses shown in Table 3 indicate that tolerance for political deviance has neither increased nor declined across the board. It has remained closely tied to particular substantive issues.

In the 1950s the public's response could be interpreted as reflecting the collective insecurity and fear that pervaded much of the political atmosphere of the country during that period. But the 1975 responses show that Americans are no less suspicious today than they were during that "special period." Indeed, on the item about religion they seem to be even more suspicious. Some might place the blame today on Watergate. But perhaps the responses should be interpreted to mean that even during stable periods, when fear about internal subversion is not especially intense, Americans still do not have much tolerance for expressions of political deviance.

On the matter of religion, for example, the results of the earlier and later surveys suggest that anyone who is outspokenly or stubbornly unreligious or antireligious in American society is apt to become the object of substantial community suspicion. In 1975, 65 percent of the respondents indicated that they would be either very suspicious or somewhat suspicious of the loyalty of a person who "goes around talking against religion."

Table 3. Degree of Suspicion About Various Expressions of Opinion in the United States in 1955 and 1975

Expression of Opinion and Year	Degree of Suspicion				
	Very suspicious	Somewhat suspicious	Hardly suspicious	Not at all suspicious	Don't know
1. Goes around talking against religion			(percent)		
1955[a]	16		28	53	3
1975	37	27	10	24	2
2. Refuses to sign an oath of loyalty to the U.S.					
1955	63		26	8	3
1975	62	25	5	6	2
3. Goes around criticizing conditions in this country					
1955	15		28	52	5
1975	22	25	20	32	1
4. Teacher who tells his students there are many things wrong in the U.S.					
1955	34		32	30	4
1975	26	24	18	30	2

[a]In the survey conducted in 1955, the categories were: great, slight, none, don't know.

Fifty percent of the respondents are also suspicious of a teacher who "tells his students that there are many things wrong in America," as indicated by the polls in 1975. In addition to these results, McClosky (in his 1964 study of attitudes toward civil liberties) found that 56.7 percent of the general electorate agreed with the proposition that "Freedom does not give anyone the right to teach foreign ideas in our schools" (McClosky, "Consensus and Ideology in American Politics," 58 *APSR* 361, 367, 1964).

The issue of the right of a teacher to be critical of American society in the classroom has never been fully aired in the Supreme Court.[4] However, at least two prominent lower court cases have explored the problem. In one, an art teacher—Susan Russo—was dismissed for her silent refusal, on grounds of conscience, to participate in her school's daily flag-salute ceremony (Lang, "A Reporter at Large: Love of Country," *The New Yorker,* July 30, 1973). In the other, an eleventh-grade English teacher—Charles James—was discharged for wearing a black armband in class to protest the Vietnam war (Harris, "Annals of Law: A Scrap of Black Cloth," *The New Yorker,* June 17 and 24, 1974, August 18, 1975). The Court of Appeals for the Second Circuit ordered reinstatement of both teachers, on the ground that their constitutional rights of freedom of speech had been violated by their dismissals (Russo v. Central School District, 469 F.2d 623, 1972; James v. Board of Education, 461 F.2d 566, 1972).

In both cases, the court acknowledged the specially sensitive position occupied by a teacher, with great authority over pupils, but could not accede to the Board of Education's request—as expressed to the court in the *James* case—to be able to control the content of a teacher's speech in the classroom. "More than a decade of Supreme Court precedent leaves no doubt," according to the Court of Appeals, "that we cannot countenance school authorities arbitrarily censoring a teacher's speech merely because they do not agree with the teacher's political philosophies of learning" (461 F.2d at 573).

Comparison of the Israeli and American responses to the two "tolerance" items common to both surveys (a person who talks against religion and a teacher who tells his students there are many things wrong in the United States) indicates that Israelis are more tolerant of critical opinion about internal affairs than are Americans. This is a surprising result, considering that the conditions in Israel today, and indeed since the nation's birth, seem particularly conducive to an emphasis on conformity in political thinking and to a lack of tolerance for critical viewpoints. Yet, relative to the American responses, the Israeli public shows a high degree of support for the right of criticism and freedom of expression.

The next series of items asked the Israeli and American publics to consider the extent to which they believe in such civil liberties as the right of privacy, freedom of movement, and the right of organized dissent. Shown below are the specific items and the response choices; following that, we have arranged the responses in tabular form.

Do you approve or disapprove of the police tapping the telephones of citizens who belong to political groups that are on. . . .
(Israeli choices)
———the far right, and religious groups that oppose the state
———approve only for groups that are on the far left and the far right
———approve only for religious groups that oppose the state
———approve only for groups that are on the far left
———approve only for groups that are on the far left and for religious groups that oppose the state
———disapprove of the police tapping the phones of any of the above
———do not have an opinion
(American choices)
———the far left
———the far right
———militant ethnic, religious, or racial groups

The next four items in the series followed the same format. They asked about:

———opening mail of persons who belong. . . .
———limiting the movement within the country of persons who belong. . . .
———preventing any of the following groups from holding public demonstration. . . .

Looking first at the Israeli responses, we note that the single most important result in Table 4 is that on four out of the five issues, more people disapproved of police interference than approved. The only reversal occurred on the matter of police surveillance. On that issue, more people supported such action for all of the political groups in question. We also see that more people expressed disapproval of interference with political demonstrations and limitations of movement within the country, than for the tapping of phones or the opening of mail. But looking at the range of responses for all five items, the modal one consistently demonstrates a higher degree of respect for the right of privacy and support for freedom of movement and expression than for police interference and limitations on those rights.

A second important finding from the data in Table 4 is the distinction that the public makes among the various groups. To the extent that the public distinguishes between groups (between 17 and 32 percent of the

Table 4. Attitudes Toward Police Practices Concerning Invasion of Privacy and Right to Demonstrate in Israel

Police Practices in Israel	Disapprove of such action for all groups	Approve of such action for all groups	Approve only for leftist groups	Approve only for rightist groups	Approve only for leftist and rightist groups	Approve only for religious groups	Other answers	No opinion	Total
				(percent)					
30. Tapping of telephones	43	20	11	—	5	2	3	11	100 (530)
31. Opening of mail	45	20	10	1	5	1	6	12	100 (530)
32. Placing people under surveillance	26	31	15	1	6	1	9	11	100 (530)
33. Placing limitations on movements within the country	50	15	9	—	5	1	6	14	100 (530)
34. Preventing such groups from holding public demonstrations	56	14	7	—	3	1	6	13	100 (530)

respondents made different judgments about the various groups) it is more willing to have the police interfere with leftist groups than it is to have them interfere with groups that are on the right, or religious groups.

Again, it is difficult to make an absolute judgment about the level of response. But we do see that, on the one hand, more people disapprove than approve of the police tapping telephones, opening mail, limiting personal movement, or preventing public demonstrations, while on the other hand, existing Israeli legislation provides a broad legal basis for the execution of each of these activities by administrative bodies which are essentially free from public scrutiny or judicial review.[5]

The responses of the American public described in Table 5 shows that they did not distinguish at all by type of group but made greater distinctions than did the Israeli public about the practice involved.

When the 1975 responses to the issue of telephone taps are compared against responses made at an earlier time the differences suggest that the American public was shaken by Watergate. For example, in 1954 Stouffer reported that 65 percent thought it was legitimate for the government to tap private telephones as long as the purpose was to gather evidence against communists. In 1969 a Gallup poll showed that 43 percent disapproved of wiretapping in principle, but in the fall of 1972, Harris reported that 75 percent believed that wiretapping and spying under the excuse of national security is a serious threat to people's privacy.

On the whole the opinions reported here are both "in step" and "out of step" with actual police and governmental policies in the five areas. For example, the police cannot impose any limitations on the internal movement of American citizens. The closest that actual policy comes to coinciding with the view of some 36 to 38 percent of the respondents is that in the past the government has, unsuccessfully, attempted to limit the foreign travel of Communist Party members (Aptheker v. Secretary of State, 378 U.S. 500, 1964). More recently, legal disputes have arisen over the constitutionality of foreign and domestic travel restrictions placed upon individuals as a condition of their parole from prison. Refusal of the United States Board of Parole to grant permission to Fathers Philip and Daniel Berrigan to travel to Hanoi was upheld by a Federal Court of Appeals in 1974 [Berrigan v. Sigler, 499 F.2d 514 (D.C. Cir. 1974), affirming 358 F. Supp. 130, D.D.C. 1973]. On the other hand, a Board of Parole decision to refuse permission to released Rosenberg co-defendant Morton Sobell to travel to Washington (from New York) for antiwar demonstrations and to Los Angeles for a speaking engagement was overturned by a Federal District Court on First Amendment grounds in 1971 (Sobell v. Reed, 327 F. Supp. 1294, S.D.N.Y. 1971).

The Federal "Anti-Riot" Act of 1968—which prohibits traveling interstate with intent to incite a riot and thereafter "perform[ing] any overt

Table 5. Attitudes Toward Police Practices Concerning Invasion of Privacy and Right to Demonstrate in the United States

Police Practices in the United States	Disapprove of such action for all groups	Approve of such action for all groups	Approve only for leftist groups	Approve only for rightist groups	Approve only for leftist and rightist groups	Approve only for religious groups	Don't know	Total
				(percent)				
Tapping of telephones	69	24	24	24	24	23	6	
Opening of mail	80	14	14	14	14	16	5	
Placing people under surveillance	17	76	78	76	76	76	6	
Placing limitations on movements within the country	53	37	38	36	37	36	9	
Preventing such groups from holding public demonstrations	70	23	24	23	23	24	6	

act for [the] purpose of inciting a riot" (18 U.S.C. ##2101-2)—is also regarded by some as a form of internal travel restriction (or at least inhibition). However, even in its broadest and—to libertarians and radicals—most objectionable interpretation, it does not authorize the government to limit travel before the fact.[6]

At the opposite extreme, public opinion may be very close to the mark in expressing widespread approval of the power of police to place groups and group members "under surveillance." If we focus for a moment on "physical surveillance"—that is, infiltration of groups, use of informers, photographing of demonstrators, and so forth, as opposed to use of mail covers and electronic surveillance—then both in law and in practice control of surveillance, or even accurate knowledge of its extent, is exceedingly tenuous. In the words of one set of commentators, "the use of informers, in contrast to national security electronic surveillance, is a somewhat informal, large-scale activity, traditionally engaged in at low levels of the law enforcement bureaucracy, and often resulting in no identifiable government action against a citizen. The imposition of effective judicial sanctions against the misuse of informers could be extremely difficult. Therefore, the argument as to the effective control of informers must be directed at least as much to the executive branch as to the courts." (Note, "Developments in the Law—the National Security Interest and Civil Liberties," 85 *Harv. L. Rev.*, 1130, 1245-6, 1972.)

The most recent executive action to limit surveillance activities on the part of U.S. government foreign intelligence agencies was President Ford's Executive Order of Feb. 18, 1976, which prohibited—subject to some exceptions—physical surveillance "directed against a United States person"; electronic surveillance to intercept communication; unconsented physical searches within the United States; opening of mail; examination of federal tax returns; "infiltration or undisclosed participation within the United States in any organization for the purpose of reporting on or influencing its activities or numbers"; and generally "collection of information, however acquired, concerning the domestic activities of United States persons" (*New York Times*, February 19, 1976). It remains to be seen what actual effect the order will have. In any case, of course, it applies only to Federal foreign intelligence agencies—such as the Central Intelligence Agency, the National Security Agency, and the Defense Intelligence Agency—and not to the Federal Bureau of Investigation or state or local police agencies.[7]

Supreme Court involvement—or noninvolvement—in the problem of physical surveillance and use of informers has taken two forms. In one line of cases, the Court has thus far rejected claims that a Fourth Amendment warrant requirement should apply to use of informers, as it does to use of wiretaps and bugging devices (Katz v. United States, 389 U.S. 347, 1967).

Proceeding on the theory that "the Fourth Amendment [does not] protect a wrongdoer's misplaced belief that a person to whom he voluntarily confides his wrongdoing will not reveal it" (Hoffa v. United States, 385 U.S. 293, 302, 1966), and that "the risk of being overheard by an eavesdropper or betrayed by an informer . . . is the kind of risk we necessarily assume whenever we speak" (*ibid.* at 303, quoting Brennan, J., dissenting in Lopez v. United States, 373 U.S. 427, 465, 1963), the Court's most recent ruling on the subject has upheld the admissibility of evidence obtained—without a warrant—by means of a radio transmitter concealed on the person of a government informer. "If the law gives no protection to the wrongdoer whose trusted accomplice is or becomes a police agent," reasoned Justice White for a plurality of the Court, "neither should it protect him when the same agent has recorded or transmitted the conversations which are later offered in evidence to prove the State's case" (United States v. White. 401 U.S. 745, 752, 1971).

The present status of wiretapping and bugging is that, theoretically, none should occur in the absence of a warrant obtained from a judge.[8] In all of this it must be remembered, of course, that the debatable issue has been the necessity of a warrant, not the legitimacy or constitutionality of electronic surveillance itself. While the Justice Department—according to Attorney General Levi—authorized *warrantless* national security wiretaps on 148 persons in 1974 (*New York Times,* June 25, 1975) a total of 728 "interceptions" in twenty-four jurisdictions were *judically authorized* in the same year. According to figures made public by the Administrative Office of the United States Courts, these interceptions enabled agents to overhear more than 40,000 people engaged in some 590,000 "private" conversations, mostly in gambling and narcotics cases (*New York Times,* Mar. 3, 1975).

Government surveillance may also take the form of "mail covers"—that is, examining the outside of envelopes—or of opening mail.[9] Current postal regulations apparently authorize the Postal Inspector to order mail covers when requested to do so "by any law enforcement agency to protect the national security (524 F. 2d at 873). Moreover, current law, according to President Ford, "permits the opening of United States mail, under proper judicial safeguards, in the conduct of criminal investigations ("Message to Congress," *New York Times,* Feb. 19, 1976).

Finally, we note that some 70 percent of the American respondents disapprove of allowing the police to prevent various groups from holding public meetings. In American law, of course, the police could not constitutionally base a decision to prevent a group from holding a public meeting merely on the identity of the group. Although the law in this area is not as fully developed as in other areas of American civil liberties policy,[10] the police would at least need very specific information about the likelihood of violence or other unlawful activity occurring in connection with the meeting before they could justifiably move to prevent its being held.

RESPONDENT STATUS AND ATTITUDES TOWARD CIVIL LIBERTIES

We did find some noticeable and significant differences on these issues among various categories of people within Israeli and American society. The relationship between education and pro–civil liberties sentiments has been cited by Stouffer, McClosky, Lawrence, and other researchers who have surveyed attitudes toward civil liberties among various groups in American society.[11] As shown in Tables 6 and 7 we found that the more educated the respondent the more likely he or she was to favor freedom of expression, right of dissent, and limitations on police activities. For example, the proportion of respondents within homogeneous educational categories who answered they would not be at all suspicious of the behavior described in Tables 1–2 shows a consistent pro–civil liberties trend among respondents with college degrees.[12]

We also found that the more educated the respondent the more likely he or she was to disapprove of police action.

The Israeli survey found that men were consistently, but only slightly, more supportive of freedom of expression and right of privacy than were women. The differences between men and women were never more than 12 percent, and usually they ranged between four and eight per cent. The American findings are less consistent. There was no pattern that indicated men were more or less supportive of civil liberties and for each item the difference between men and women was small and not significant. For

Table 6. Level of Education by Percentage Not At All Suspicious of Various Political Expressions in Israel[a]

Education	Percent not at all suspicious Items				
	1	2	3	4	5
8th grade (127)	65	46	27	46	24
9–10 grade (103)	75	59	44	64	39
High school diploma (109)	84	62	50	61	43
Some college (103)	87	63	43	75	48
College degree (68)	94	65	43	79	49

[a]X^2 for Education by suspicion of various political expressions: $X^2$16 d.f. (.95) = 21.0; X^2 = 24.8, 13.8, 12.7, 20.9, 48.5.

Table 7. Level of Education by Percentage Not at All Suspicious of Various Political Expressions in the United States[a]

Percent not at all suspicious

Education	Items							
	1	2	3	4	5	6	7	8
Grade school	17	18	27	7		24	10	0
High school	20	34	30	5		27	26	3
College	32	45	34	9		42	42	3

[a]X^2 signif at .01.

example, in the percentage disapproving of police actions, the American data looked like this: Men: 75, 81, 16, 63, 72; Women: 78, 88, 17, 53, 78. The Israeli data showed the following: Men: 45, 47, 25, 53, 58; Women: 42, 43, 26, 48, 55.

"Age" followed much the same pattern as sex. On the Israeli survey there was a small but consistent difference in responses such that the under 30 respondents were less likely to be suspicious of the opinions described in Table 1 than were persons in the older age categories. The "under 30" group were also slightly less likely to favor invasions of privacy by the police. The American data showed, as it did for sex, a less consistent pattern. Contrary to previous studies, we did not find the youngest respondents more supportive of civil liberties; nor did we find significant differences among any of the age categories. Respondents under 35 were less likely to be suspicious of persons who talk about religion and who say blacks are discriminated against; but more suspicious of teachers who say there are many things wrong in American society. On the Police Practices items, older respondents (55+) were less disapproving of preventing public

Table 8. Level of Education by Percentage Disapprove of Certain Police Activities in Israel[a]

Police activities for items 6–10

Education	Items				
	6	7	8	9	10
8th grade and less	33	34	14	28	33
9–11 grade	34	38	28	50	56
High school diploma	50	51	32	54	59
Some college	47	47	24	61	68
College degree	64	67	39	72	76

[a]The X^2 was calculated only for the "Approve" and "Disapprove for all groups" cells because the N was too small in many of the other cells. Types of police activities by education: $X^2$4 d.f. (.95) = 9.5; X^2 = 14.6, 14.5, 11.1, 17.5, 22.6.

Table 9.   Level of Education by Percentage Disapprove of Certain
Police Activities in the United States

Education	Wiretapping	Opening of mail	Surveillance	Limiting movement	Preventing demonstrations
Grade school	68	74		56	62
High school	70	80		52	71
College	83	90		72	82

meetings than younger respondents (66 vs 84 percent) but showed no greater approval for any of the other practices.

The last item in both surveys tapped the dimension of public attitudes or respect toward law in general. It posed this problem:

There are different views on the question of how one should observe the laws. Please tell me which of the following opinions match your own most closely.

	Israeli	American
	(percent)	
Laws should always be obeyed even if we think they are wrong	37	16
Laws considered wrong should be obeyed, but one should work to change them	53	83
Laws should be disobeyed when they are considered wrong	10	1

Slightly more than one-third of the Israeli public believe in obedience for the sake of obedience in contrast to less than 20 percent of the Americans. But ten percent of the Israelis in contrast to one percent of the American respondents believe that each person should decide for himself whether to obey or disobey a national law. The majority (53 percent) of Israelis, and almost all Americans (83 percent) support a system that grants legitimacy to the law but recognizes that laws can and should be changed if they are considered wrong.

Compared with responses in European countries (see below) in which this same item was included on national surveys, we see that the Americans as well as the Israelis are less likely to favor obeying laws that they think are wrong. The American responses, especially, differ greatly from the Europeans. It is interesting that the Polish and Dutch responses are closer to each other than either is to the West German responses.

Nationality	Percent believe the law should always be obeyed even when we think it is wrong
Americans	16
Israelis	37
Poles	45
Dutch	47
West Germans	66

CONCLUDING REMARKS

Commenting first on the Israeli data, although we are wary of making conclusive judgments on the basis of one survey, the findings do suggest that there is a high degree of awareness and respect for fundamental individual civil liberties among the Israeli public. More specifically, the data indicate that there is a high degree of tolerance for criticism of social conditions, a consciousness of the need to respect politically deviant viewpoints, a preference for limiting police activity in favor of private rights, and marked support for involvement of judicial processes where an individual's rights are limited.

We have indicated that in several important instances Israeli public opinion shows a greater desire to protect individual rights than is reflected in existing legislation. Considering the circumstances in which there is no formal constitutional statement of individual civil liberties, existing legislation that permits substantial incursions into individual civil liberties, and objective security conditions that require restrictions on individual freedoms, the level of expressed belief in individual liberties and freedoms appears high.

These limited conclusions, however, raise other questions. For example, the degree of disparity between the existing legal norms and the attitudes expressed by the Israeli public suggests that the issue of civil liberties may not be an important one to most Israelis. Illustrative of this point is the irony that, on the one hand, we found in the question about obedience to law an expressed "belief" that people should "work to change laws considered wrong"; but on the other hand, the law itself is evidence that, for whatever reason, Israelis have not provided for a legal structure which reflects their attitudes and beliefs in civil liberties.

The American responses tell us two important facts. One, that many of the attitudes and beliefs expressed in the 1950s during the era of McCarthyism and the "cold war" were not atypical. In comparing them with responses to the same or comparable items twenty years later, during a period of "detente" with the Soviet Union and internal quiescence, the American public appears no more supportive of or tolerant toward political deviance than it did during the earlier period which was considered one of unusual tension and fear.

Secondly, the results indicate that the American public expresses less support for civil liberties issues than are guaranteed under the constitution and federal statutes. Such results might suggest that if those liberties were not protected from recall or revision by enormously complicated mechanisms, they might indeed be in jeopardy. But on the other hand, and especially given the stability of popular sentiment, another interpretation that can be made of these results is that the American public feels freer than publics in many other democratic societies that lack written constitutions guaranteeing civil liberties, to express intolerant and repressive sentiments about civil liberties because it understands implicitly that the right of free speech and dissent will not be seriously endangered by such, perhaps, largely "expressive" opinions.

Finally, comparison of the Israeli and American responses indicates greater tolerance and support for civil liberties on the part of the Israelis. But it is important to remember that Israeli responses "matter more" because constitutional guarantees are lacking in the Israeli system and therefore laws limiting civil liberties are much more responsive to public sentiment since the range of actions available to the parliament is much greater under the Israeli system.

FOOTNOTES

1. To the best of the authors' knowledge, these data are based on the first national survey ever conducted in Israel on the issue of civil liberties.

2. The Institute for Applied Social Research is a major survey agency comparable in the United States to the Harris or Gallup polls. Members of Parliament, the Israeli press, and government agencies frequently cite their findings. Various government agencies also commission surveys on pertinent topics that are conducted by the Israeli Institute for Applied Social Research. The Institute states that its sample is a national one and that the results obtained generalize to Israeli society as a whole, just as the typical sample of 1,500 respondents in American surveys generalize to American public opinion on most issues.

3. Approximately 85 percent of the Israeli population live in urban settlements and two-thirds live in the four cities in which the survey was conducted.

4. But see generally Note, "Developments in the Law—Academic Freedom," *Harv. L. Rev.* 81 (1968): 1045.

5. See *Defense Emergency Regulations,* 1945: chapter 95: mail censorship permitted; chapters 109–111: restrictions on personal movement made by military commander or police officer; *Police Ordinance,* 1971, chapter 84: prohibitions of gatherings made by police officer. Note also that there is no legislation prohibiting or restricting wiretapping, although there is a proposal which is now being debated in Knesset.

6. See, e.g., United States v. Dellinger, 472 F.2d 348 (7th Cir. 1972).

7. Separate guidelines governing the F.B.I. to be released by the Attorney General in 1976.

8. See Katz v. United States, 389 U.S. 347 (1967); Omnibus Crime Control and Safe Streets Act of 1968, Title III, 802, 18 U.S.C. ##2510-20 (1970); United States v. District Court, 407 U.S. 297 (1972). The Ford Administration proposed legislation in 1976 to make virtually all electronic surveillance, including that of foreign nationals living in the United States, subject to the warrant requirement of the Fourth Amendment. See *New York Times,* March 17, 1976.

9. See, e.g., Paton v. La Prade, 524 F.2d 862 (3rd Cir. 1975), vacating and remanding Paton v. La Prade, 382 F. Supp. 1118 (D.N.J. 1974).

10. For a thorough exploration of the legal and practical issues involved in controlling public demonstrations, see Blasi, "Prior Restraints on Demonstration," 68 *Mich. L. Rev.* 68 (1970): 1482.

11. Stouffer, *op cit.,* 1957, McClosky, "Consensus and Ideology in American Politics" 58, APSR 361 (1964), Erskine and Siegel, "Civil Liberties and the American Public," *The Journal of Social Issues,* Vol. 31, No. 2 (1976): 13.

12. We also found that the more educated respondents were more likely to have an opinion on these issues than were the less educated respondents. The "no opinion" percentages among the grade school category were between 16 and 18; among respondents who had completed college the proportions ranged from one to nine.

DETERRENCE, PENAL POLICY, AND THE SOCIOLOGY OF LAW

Jack P. Gibbs, UNIVERSITY OF ARIZONA

The recent revival of interest in the deterrence doctrine originated largely outside the sociology of law, notably in criminology and economics [see surveys by Zimring and Hawkins (24); Gibbs (8)]. That locus is unfortunate because criminologists and economists commonly write as though the *empirical validity* of the doctrine is the only question. On the contrary, there are several other crucial questions, and all of them should be central for the sociology of law.

IDENTIFYING THE GOALS OF PENAL POLICY

In their survey of the deterrence literature, Zimring and Hawkins (24) emphasize Morris's conclusion (12), p. 631, that deterrence is a "primary and essential postulate" in all but one of the world's criminal law systems.

Research in Law and Sociology—Vol. 1, 1978, pages 101–114.

Morris can point to all manner of official statements about penal policy as being consistent with his conclusion; nonetheless, one must surely wonder about the validity of those statements. In particular, it is difficult to judge the extent to which criminal statutes and enforcement practices are really consistent with official statements about penal policy. The alternative, inferring penal policy from criminal statutes and enforcement practices, is not only difficult but also extremely questionable.

Even assuming that the severity of statutory penalties can be assessed objectively, it hardly follows that deterrence is a goal of penal policy if the penalties are severe. Retribution is an alternative goal of penal policy, and legislators or social critics [e.g., van den Haag (19)] who favor the retributive doctrine advocate severe criminal sanctions. As for general statements of penal policy in a criminal code (or any official document), they may not apply to all statutes in the code, especially when those statutes are products of legislative action over several generations. In such a case, an assessment of legislative intent is difficult, and there are even doubts about assessing the intent of contemporaneous enactments. The point is not just that the expressed opinions of legislators about deterrence, retribution, or rehabilitation are one thing, while their votes on particular proposed criminal statutes may be quite another; additionally, assuming that the opinions of legislators could be solicited in a defensible manner, there is no assurance whatever of consensus in those opinions. The possibility of marked dissensus creates a conceptual problem, as one does not think of a penal policy in terms like, say, .41 deterrence, .33 retributive, and .26 rehabilitative.

Any attempt to identify the penal policy of a particular legal system (or jurisdiction) would be incomplete if it did not go beyond general official statements, particular statutes, and legislative intent to a consideration of those agency rules and procedural laws that supposedly govern the activities of officials in matters unrelated to sentencing. However, such "administrative norms" do not clearly reflect an identifiable penal policy any more than do the substantive statutes of criminal law, and it often happens that there are startling gaps in these norms. The most conspicuous gap in U.S. jurisdictions is the paucity of written prescriptions and proscriptions pertaining to prosecutorial discretion, "plea bargaining" in particular. Of course, that very paucity in itself could be construed as a policy, but what is the goal of minimizing statutory restraints on prosecutorial discretion? It may appear that the supposed policy promotes greater certainty of legal punishment; yet, even so, that consequence could be a latent rather than a manifest function of penal policy. Moreover, even if maximizing the certainty of legal punishments is a penal policy goal, one latent function of plea bargaining may be a reduction in the certainty of *severe* punishments (i.e., those which defendants seek to avoid through bargaining).

The problem is not just the prevalence of unwritten administrative norms, the operating rules of agencies in particular. Not even written administrative norms reveal penal policy, and only rarely are they accompanied by policy statements. Intent is again relevant, but the problems in inferring it are even more difficult than in the case of substantive laws. Whatever the methodology of inferring the intent of administrative norms, it must be applied to diverse officials (e.g., high-ranking police officers and members of parole boards). Given such a diversity of officials, consensus as to the goals of penal policy becomes even more unlikely; and to the extent that dissensus is "structural" (e.g., the police overwhelmingly view the goal of law enforcement as deterrence but members of parole boards emphasize rehabilitation), then one can rightly speak of inconsistent penal policies.

Needless to say, numerous scholars would question the idea of identifying penal policy by reference to statutes, administrative norms, or other official statements. Their argument is, of course, that such matters have no necessary bearing on "law in action"; and the argument extends to the declaration that penal policy lies in *actual reactions* of legal officials to allegations of crimes, commencing with the police and extending to the actions of parole or probation officers. That argument is consistent with legal realism in that it tacitly belittles normative considerations, but it is questionable nonetheless. If one *infers* penal policy from the actual behavior of legal officials, then it is difficult to see how penal policy and that behavior could diverge. Similarly, if penal policy goals are inferred from the ostensible *outcomes* of actions taken by legal officials, how could one possibly conclude that the goals are not being realized? Then consider the problems entailed in making inferences about penal policy goals from actual sentences. If a judge sentences an individual to the maximum term of imprisonment rather than to the minimum, that sentence is no less indicative of a retributive penal policy than of a deterrent policy. Indeed, appearances to the contrary, not even a probated sentence is irrefutable evidence of a rehabilitative penal policy.

All such inferences are debatable primarily because contending doctrines pertaining to the goals of penal policy do not differ in all respects. Conventional versions of the deterrence doctrine do not reject a gradation in the severity of legal punishments; rather, they simply call for a severity sufficient to deter individuals from the type of offense in question, and the very notion of "exemplary" punishment presumes judicial discretion. Similarly, retributivists are content to prescribe a severity of punishment that corresponds to the seriousness of the offense; and even though retributivists traditionally appear ambivalent about or hostile to judicial discretion, mandatory sentences are not absolutely essential for a retributive penal policy. Hence, there does not appear to be any truly defensible way to distinguish retribution and deterrence as goals of penal policy by reference to the severity of penalties (actual or statutory) or to provisions for discretion in sentencing.

Practical Import.

All of the foregoing reduces to one question: What is the appropriate methodology for identifying the goals of penal policy? A more specific version of the question is: What is the appropriate methodology for determining the extent to which deterrence is a goal of penal policy? Whatever version of the question, those who have training in the sociology of law are suited to attempt an answer, and the answer is not provided by an enumeration of the possible *aims* of punishment [Walker (20)].

Some social scientists may look on the methodological question as trivial, the argument being that it has no practical import or bearing on genuine societal problems. In reply to that argument, Diogenes could find an honest man more readily than he could identify an American who is content with what he or she takes to be U.S. penal policy. To be sure, the citizenry's discontent is commonly expressed in lamentations over the "crime problem," but that problem is commonly attributed to real or imagined penal policies. Moreover, during the past decade billions of state and federal dollars have been spent on special programs pertaining to law enforcement or criminal justice, and critics of those massive expenditures point to evidence that the increase in the crime rate was not even checked [e.g., Wilson (23)]. Yet most of the critics blithely assume that the money was spent with a view to reducing crime. It may appear that crime prevention is the obvious goal of any penal policy, but crime prevention is not the goal of a purely retributive penal policy. For that matter, one would be hard pressed to demonstrate that the *goal* of probation is crime prevention, let alone that the goal is realized.

Questions about penal policy have not been treated as central by those governmental agencies (e.g., LEAA) that supposedly were created to "do something about the crime problem." Rather, those agencies have given direct support (largely "hardware") to local or regional law enforcement organizations and funded research *as though the penal policies of U.S. jurisdictions are obvious*. They are not obvious by any means, and that point takes on significance in light of recent denials by some LEAA officials that the primary mission of the agency is the reduction of crime. They evidently now regard that mission as "unrealistic," but that characterization is singularly uninformative. It would be more informative to say something like this: The incidence of crime in the United States cannot be reduced substantially without a change in penal policy from such-and-such to such-and-such. Yet a statement in that form is not really meaningful without some defensible way to identify current penal policy and to identify the statutory and procedural changes in criminal law (including parole and custodial practices) that would be necessary to pursue some other policy.

At present, most critics of the American criminal justice system appear to be saying little more than this: It isn't working. That cryptic complaint suggests that no goal of penal policy is being realized. Yet critics are prone to assume that there is only one penal policy, and they commonly disagree in their characterizations of that policy. For example, whereas Menninger (11) characterized the criminal justice system as barbaric vengeance, van den Haag (19) castigated it as excessively lenient. Since Menninger advocates the medical model of penology and van den Haag is an avowed retributivist, their divergent criticisms of the criminal justice system are hardly surprising. Even so, the magnitude of the divergence is telling.

Although critics of the U.S. criminal justice system speak as though the system is governed by a definite, coherent penal policy, the system actually appears to be an ungoverned mishmash. One question posed for the sociology of law is: When can one rightly speak of a legal system as having no particular penal policy?

CONCERN WITH SOCIAL ORDER

While sociologists are not likely to question the significance of penal policy, there is no further consensus on the subject. Durkheim (4, 5) and his fellow functionalists view penal practices as both reflecting and maintaining social solidarity; but conflict theorists (especially Marxists) view penal practices as instruments by which a dominant class controls exploited classes, largely by intimidating or incapacitating dissidents. Thus, members of both schools stress the role of legal punishments in social order, but the two schools differ in their interpretations of that role.

Since a concern with "larger" questions (especially those about social order) is a tradition in the sociology of law, it is surprising that in recent decades the practitioners have done so little in the way of comparative studies of penal practices. Inattention by Durkheim's disciples is all the more surprising. The few studies on Durkheim's theory of law [e.g., Schwartz and Miller (15); and Spitzer (16)] cast grave doubts on its validity; but no large number of Durkheim's followers have attempted to refute those findings, nor to modify the theory in light of the findings.

Since Durkheim was supremely indifferent to the political character of criminal laws, his theory virtually ignores the coercive features of a penal system and related conflicts of interests. Conflict and coercion are central in the Marxist theory of social order, but Marxists have done very little in the way of deriving testable propositions from that theory. To illustrate, if the penal system is used by an economically dominant class to control exploited classes, then members of the dominant class should exhibit greater acceptance of prevailing penal practices. Stating the proposition more briefly, whatever the penal practices may be, members of the dominant class are more inclined to accept them. But Marxist sociologists show no inclination for research to test that proposition; and as long as they are determined to invoke "false class-consciousness," the findings would not alter their opinions (e.g., what would otherwise be negative evidence could be attributed to false class-consciousness).

Still another line of relevant research has been discontinued. The general idea, best exemplified by the work of Rusche and Kirchheimer (14) is that penal policies change so as to be consistent with trends in the labor market (e.g., banishment becomes a penal practice when the labor market is glutted, and imprisonment becomes the practice when the demand for labor exceeds the supply). Rusche and Kirchheimer's work was not truly systematic research, and the evidence they reported for their Marxist perspective was very limited; but their investigation was a step in a commendable direction. Today, the only concern with penal policy from the Marxist perspective is found in the literature of so-called "critical criminology" [e.g., Taylor, et al., (18)], and that literature rarely goes beyond exhortations to the formulation of testable propositions.

THE VALIDITY OF THE DETERRENCE DOCTRINE

Although largely unrecognized, recent attempts to assess the validity of the deterrence doctrine do bear on both the Durkheimian and the Marxist theory of criminal law. Durkheim (4, 5) was very much concerned with the sociological significance of legal punishments, but he did not argue that deterrence is the manifest or latent function of severe punishments. To the contrary, he belittled the utilitarian instrumental quality of criminal law to the point of virtually rejecting the deterrence doctrine. Hence, evidence that severe punishments do deter crime also would be evidence that Durkheim's assertions about the functions of legal punishments are incomplete at best.

The secret scandal of the Marxist theory of criminal law is that it tacitly attributes validity to the deterrence doctrine. That attribution can best be grasped by contemplating a question: How can legal punishments be used as a repressive instrument by a dominant class if the threat of punishment does not deter? It would be curious to reply that legal punishments are not really necessary to control dissidents, and that argument would cast doubt on Marxist ideas about the origin of criminal law. A more cogent but still not compelling argument is either (1) legal punishments deter dissidents but not apolitical criminals or (2) legal punishments prevent crimes but not through deterrence. The first argument grants validity to the deterrence doctrine; yet there is no rationale for it, and evidence to support the argument will not be forthcoming if Marxists remain indifferent to deterrence research. There is a rationale for the second alternative argument, as punishments may prevent crimes by nine ways other than deterrence [Gibbs (8)]. However, Marxist writers commonly stress the intimidating character of criminal law, and intimidation is a central notion in the deterrence doctrine. The general point, however, is that advocates of the Marxist theory of criminal law cannot pretend that the theory is unrelated to the deterrence doctrine, let alone contrary to the doctrine. Yet none of the so-called critical criminologists emphasizes the importance of deterrence research *in connection with Marxist theory* [the word deterrence does not appear in the subject index of Taylor, *et al.* (18)], and one [Quinney (13), p. 415] goes so far as to castigate the revival of deterrence research.

Evidential Problems.

Although sociologists of law may refrain from assessing the validity of the deterrence doctrine, they can scarcely ignore a condition that makes the assessment difficult and debatable. That condition has been alluded to previously—the distinct possibility that legal punishments prevent crimes independently of deterrence, and hence what investigators have construed as evidence of deterrence is most disputable. To illustrate, suppose someone demonstrates an inverse statistical relation (i.e., a negative correlation) between the auto theft rate and the objective certainty of imprisonment for that type of crime. While that relation could reflect deterrence (i.e., omission of crimes out of fear of *punishment*), it may reflect only incapacitation (auto thieves do not thrive in prison).

As far as the sociology of law is concerned, incapacitation and other possible preventive mechanisms are hardly less important than deterrence. That is the case because the function of law is perhaps the central subject for the discipline, and in the case of criminal law it is a gross oversimplification to speak blithely of "control of behavior" without stipulating specific mechanisms. The point is no less significant when speaking of the goals of penal policy. To speak of crime prevention as a goal of penal policy is virtually meaningless without identifying the preventive mechanisms (e.g., deterrence, incapacitation, normative validation) that are contemplated by those who make penal policy. It may well be that some of the mechanisms are little more than logical possibilities, meaning that those who make penal policy are either ignorant of the mechanisms or have no faith in them. There is very little systematic knowledge about the "strategies" contemplated by policy makers, let alone a theory on the subject; accordingly, one illustrative conjecture must suffice. If those who make penal policy rarely rely on incapacitation as the primary preventive mechanism, one possible explanation would be that substantial incapacitation can be realized without an enormous monetary cost only through capital punishment, banishment, or very harsh conditions of incarceration.

Despite the importance of incapacitation as an evidential problem in deterrence research (i.e., what appears to be a manifestation of deterrence may reflect only the incapacitation of potential recidivists), no sociologist is likely to think of incapacitation as a truly significant factor in social order. Yet that is not the case for certain other possible preventive mechanisms of legal punishment, normative validation in particular. The idea is that legal punishments of a type of act may generate and/or maintain the social (moral) condemnation of the act. Durkheim has made the most forcible argument for the importance of the idea (though without using a systematic terminology to describe it), and James Stephens [quoted in Zimring and Hawkins (24), p. 80] succinctly clarified the idea in this observation: "The fact that men are hanged for murder is one great reason why murder is considered so dreadful a crime."

Unfortunately, neither Durkheim nor Stephens provided systematic evidence of normative validation, and even today the importance of the idea is conjectural. There is evidence that punishment looms large in childrens' conception of law [Tapp and Kohlberg (17)], but that evidence does not speak to the central question: How much does the experience of legal punishments contribute to the social (moral) condemnation of crime? Few studies on that question have been conducted [see, e.g., Walker and Argyle (21)], and the findings hardly support the idea of normative validation; but the design and scope of those studies left much to be desired. Since the relation between law and morality is a central subject for the sociology of law, the paucity of sophisticated research on normative validation is puzzling.

DETERRENCE AND DUE PROCESS

In renewing research on the deterrence doctrine, criminologists and economists have ignored an issue that is no less controversial than the validity of the doctrine. The issue is the allegation that the deterrence doctrine justifies, condones, or is conducive to the punishment of innocent individuals. Briefly, if publicizing punishments furthers *general* deterrence by increasing the perceived certainty of punishment, then to that end the guilt or innocence of those punished is irrelevant. Be that as it may, surely it is not difficult to imagine how unrestrained attempts to increase the certainty of punishment for crimes could lead to flagrant violations of due process in law enforcement (e.g., illegal searches, entrapments, coerced confessions).

Philosophers have been more sensitive to the issue than have criminologists or economists, but the related debates in philosophy have not been constructive [see Grupp (9); Ezorsky (6)]. Utilitarians have resorted to logomachy in defending the deterrence doctrine, arguing that innocent individuals cannot be "legally" punished (i.e., it is logically impossible). As one utilitarian has argued, it may not make sense to say, "I am punishing you for something you did not do"; but as a critic has replied, it does make sense to say, "He was punished for something he did not do." In any case, a convict who knows that he is serving time on a bum rap could not be other than bemused (to put it mildly) if informed that his imprisonment is not a legal punishment.

The debate among philosophers has been unconstructive largely because the issue has not been treated as an empirical question. Specifically, to what extent is there a direct relation among jurisdictions between the objective certainty of punishment (e.g., imprisonment) and violations of due process? To illustrate, Gibbs (7) estimated that the objective certainty of imprisonment for criminal homicide was about .87 in Utah, (*circa* 1960), over three times greater than the estimate for South Carolina. Hence the question: Were violations of due process in homicide cases appreciably greater in Utah than in South Carolina?

The larger question is much broader than the foregoing illustration suggests. Specifically, what is the empirical relation between deterrence as a penal policy goal and adherence to the principle of due process? Scholars trained in the sociology of law should be drawn to that question, and the answer could have a real impact on penal policy. Until the promotion of deterrence is shown to be incompatible with accepted principles of justice, the deterrence doctrine will appear to be an attractively simple strategy to reduce crime.

Other Questions.

Recent research findings suggest that for some types of crimes the objective certainty of punishment varies a great deal among jurisdictions [e.g., Logan (10)]. That variation poses a question for the sociology of law; and it is a question that criminologists have not considered in assessing the deterrence doctrine. In those assessments the focus is on the hypothesized consequences of variation in certainty rather than the cause of that variation; however, the deterrence doctrine has no particular policy implications if properties of legal punishment, such as its objective certainty, cannot be manipulated.

Only one major property of legal punishments, their *presumptive* severity can be manipulated readily by legislators [Gibbs (8)]; and hence it is not surprising that legislators are preoccupied with the magnitude of statutory penalties. Indeed, with a view to furthering deterrence in a direct way, legislators can do little more than increase the presumptive severity of statutory penalties, the length of imprisonment or the amount of fines. Certainly there is no obvious way that legislators can increase the objective certainty of punishment, especially if they are determined to maintain due process in law enforcement. So we arrive at another question for the sociology of law: What changes in law enforcement practices would be necessary to increase the objective certainty of punishment?

Some sociologists may find the pursuit of such questions distasteful, viewing the requisite research as promoting repressive penal policies [see, e.g., Quinney (13), p. 415]. However, again, the deterrence doctrine will appear to be an attractively simple solution of a problem until *unanticipated* costs are demonstrated. Even if policy makers do not reckon due process violations as a cost, they are surely sensitive to monetary costs; and it could be that the monetary cost of a substantial increase in the objective certainty of punishment would stagger even the most ardent proponent of law and order. In any event, from the viewpoint of the sociology of law, the empirical validity of the deterrence doctrine is by no means the only issue and perhaps not even the most significant issue.

COGNITIVE ASPECTS OF LEGAL PHENOMENA

Although there is considerable agreement among both sociologists and jurisprudents that questions about the functions of law are central, the significance of that consensus hinges on a hoary debate over the *social* importance of law. Stating one argument briefly, laws are obeyed only to the extent that they are consistent with extralegal norms; as such, law does not play a major role in the maintenance of social order or in the promotion of social change. The counterargument encompasses three theses: 1) the threat of legal punishments, backed by organized coercion, is sufficient for a small minority to govern; 2) the validating or reinforcing relation between legal and extralegal norms is *reciprocal;* and 3) in a pluralistic, complex society law is essential for social order and the only effective means for promoting social change.

The contending arguments will be resolved (if at all) only by focusing sociology of law research on specific empirical questions. Rather than continue to entertain all-too-general traditional questions (e.g., What role does law play in the maintenance of social order?), researchers should ask: To what extent do members of the public at large have accurate knowledge of criminal law? The question is important to the extent that one accepts the following proposition: If the public's knowledge of the law is grossly inaccurate, law plays a negligible role in maintaining social order and promoting social change.

The proposition cannot be clarified readily, and at this point only two complexities are recognized. First, not even absolutely accurate public knowledge of some facet of law would be compelling evidence of the importance of that facet, because there may be no behavioral consequence of legal ignorance if laws merely reflect extralegal norms or values. Second, while evidence can be brought to bear on the proposition, it is difficult to imagine any finding that would warrant a generalization to all social units (including legal systems) or all facets and types of law.

The very complexity of the proposition may account for the paucity of studies on the subject [e.g., Beutel (1); Cohen, *et al.* (3); Williams and Hall (22)], but it could be that investigators view research on "public knowledge of the law" as a pedestrian enterprise. Moreover, even if it is recognized that such research bears directly on the hoary debate over the social importance of law, it may appear that the debate itself is academic. Yet the debate would have immediate policy implications if the related research were focused on public knowledge of criminal law, for the findings would be relevant in assessing the deterrence doctrine. Indeed, the findings could be especially strategic because deterrence research has virtually ignored *cognitive* variables. The only reservation about the prescribed focus is that the findings would be restricted to criminal law, and it may well be that public knowledge of other types of law (e.g., tort, contract) is substantially less accurate (for that matter, the relative social importance of the various types of law is disputable).

Cognitive Questions and Deterrence.

At first glance, it may appear that the deterrence doctrine assumes absolutely accurate knowledge of criminal law on the part of those who contemplate criminal acts, the argument being that an individual cannot be deterred by a *particular* law unless he or she "knows" of that law. Yet that view of the deterrence doctrine is most disputable if only because it ignores the possible impact of the criminal law system as a whole.

In the renewal of deterrence research over the past decade, only one study has treated public knowledge of the criminal law as the central consideration [California Assembly Committee on Criminal Procedure (2)]. The investigators found that a negligible proportion of a sample of California residents had accurate knowledge of the statutory penalties for any one of various types of crime. In interpreting that finding, the investigators created the impression that it somehow invalidates the deterrence doctrine. To the contrary, it could be that numerous individuals are deterred by the belief that the act being contemplated is a *crime of some type* and therefore subject to *some kind of legal punishment,* which is to suggest that the specific statutory penalties for particular types of crime may play a minor role in deterrence. In any event, the absolute accuracy of public knowledge of statutory penalties is one thing, while relative accuracy is quite another. To illustrate the distinction, if an individual is asked to stipulate the maximum statutory imprisonment term for several types of felonies, each of those stipulations may be wrong and hence inaccurate in an absolute sense; even so, there could be a perfect positive correlation between the terms stipulated by the individual and those stipulated in the criminal code as the maximum term, in which case the individual's knowledge would be *relatively* accurate. The point takes on significance in contemplating one of the propositions ostensibly implied by the deterrence doctrine—that the *rate* for a type of crime varies inversely with the presumptive severity of punishment for that type of crime (e.g., if the maximum statutory imprisonment term is ten years for crime A but only five for B, then the A rate will be less than the B rate). Absolutely accurate knowledge of statutory penalties is *not* necessary for the relation asserted in the proposition to hold.

The distinction between absolutely accurate and relatively accurate knowledge of statutory penalties complicates an assessment of the deterrence doctrine, and it is complicated even more by recognition that "knowledge of the law" encompasses more than statutory penalties. It also encompasses the enforcement of criminal law, notably the perceived certainty of particular types of legal reactions (e.g., arrest, conviction, imprisonment) to alleged instances of particular types of crime. The perceived certainty of punishment is a central variable in the deterrence doctrine, but only recently have deterrence investigators attempted to incorporate that variable in their research.

Even if an individual knows the statutory penalties for a type of crime and perceives those penalties as being both fairly certain and severe, his or her conception of that type of crime may differ sharply from that of the police and prosecutors. To illustrate, what legal officials would construe as aggravated assault may be thought of by a private citizen as nothing more than the legal "protection of private property"; if so, whatever the citizen's beliefs about legal punishments for aggravated assault, those beliefs will not deter that citizen from acts that he or she views as legal. Hence, we arrive at a question: Given descriptions of particular acts that were subsequently labeled by the police as instances of particular types of crime, on reading those descriptions how much would members of the public agree with the police as to those labels? The question may appear to be exotic or academic, but the validity of the deterrence doctrine could depend in large part on the amount of agreement between legal officials and the public as regards conceptions of crimes. Unfortunately, however, deterrence investigators have yet to consider conceptions of crimes as a variable.

The foregoing observations constitute a list of the ways in which deterrence research has been incomplete, and some scholars may regard the completion of that research as scarcely relevant for the sociology of law. However, whereas tests of the deterrence doctrine take the criminal law and the various cognitive properties of it as "givens," there is every reason to suppose that the accuracy of public knowledge of criminal law (including conceptions of criminal acts) varies from one social unit to the next and historically. Apart from the validity of the deterrence doctrine, that variation poses a question for the sociology of law. The variation may or may not reflect a contrast in penal policies; in any case, there are social units (Anglo-American jurisdictions in particular) where *as a matter of penal policy* governmental agencies do very little to further public knowledge of criminal law. Why that is the case should be treated as a central question for the sociology of law and one hardly less significant than the validity of the deterrence doctrine itself.

REFERENCES

1. Beutel, Frederick K., *Some Potentialities of Experimental Jurisprudence as a New Branch of Social Science* (Lincoln, Nebraska: University of Nebraska Press, 1957), 440 pp.
2. California Assembly Committee on Criminal Procedure, *Deterrent Effects of Criminal Sanctions* (Sacramento, California: Assembly of the State of California, 1968), 124 mimeographed pp.
3. Cohen, Julius, *et al., Parental Authority: The Community and the Law* (New Brunswick, New Jersey: Rutgers University Press, 1958), 301 pp.
4. Durkheim, Emile, *The Division of Labor in Society* (New York: Free Press, 1949), 439 pp.
5. ———, "Two Laws of Penal Evolution," trans. by Maureen Mileski, in Russell Sage Program in Law and Social Science, Working Paper #7, Yale Law School, 1973, 41 mimeographed pp.
6. Ezorsky, Gertrude (ed.), *Philosophical Perspectives on Punishment* (Albany, New York: State University of New York Press, 1972), 377 pp.
7. Gibbs, Jack P., "Crime, Punishment, and Deterrence," *Social Science Quarterly*, Vol. 48 (March, 1968), pp. 515–530.
8. ———, *Crime, Punishment, and Deterrence* (New York: Elsevier, 1975) 259 pp.
9. Grupp, Stanley E. (ed.), *Theories of Punishment*, (Bloomington, Indiana: Indiana University Press, 1971), 401 pp.
10. Logan, Charles H., "General Deterrent Effects of Imprisonment," *Social Forces*, Vol. 51 (September, 1972), pp. 64–73.
11. Menninger, Karl, *The Crime of Punishment* (New York: Viking Press, 1966), 305 pp.
12. Morris, Norval, "Impediments to Penal Reform," *University of Chicago Law Review*, Vol. 33 (Summer, 1966), pp. 627–656.

13. Quinney, Richard, in "Symposium on Wilson's *Thinking About Crime,*" *Contemporary Sociology,* Vol. 5 (July, 1976), pp. 414–418.
14. Rusche, Georg and Otto Kirchheimer, *Punishment and Social Structure,* (New York: Russell and Russell, 1939), 268 pp.
15. Schwartz, Richard D. and James C. Miller, "Legal Evolution and Societal Complexity," *American Journal of Sociology,* Vol. 70 (September, 1964), pp. 159–169.
16. Spitzer, Steven, "Punishment and Social Organization: A Study of Durkheim's Theory of Penal Evolution," *Law and Society Review,* Vol. 9 (Summer, 1975), pp. 613–635.
17. Tapp, June L. and Lawrence Kohlberg, "Developing Senses of Law and Legal Justice," *Journal of Social Issues,* Vol. 27 (No. 2, 1971), pp. 65–91.
18. Taylor, Ian, *et al.* (eds.), *Critical Criminology* (London: Routledge and Kegan Paul, 1975), 268 pp.
19. van den Haag, Ernest, *Punishing Criminals* (New York: Basic Books, 1975), 283 pp.
20. Walker, Nigel, "Aims of Punishments," pp. 48–65 in Leon Radzinowicz and Marvin E. Wolfgang (eds.), *Crime and Justice,* Vol. 2, *The Criminal in the Arms of the Law* (New York: Basic Books, 1971), 703 pp.
21. ———, and Michael Argyle, "Does the Law Affect Moral Judgments?", *British Journal of Criminology,* Vol. 4 (October, 1964), pp. 570–581.
22. Williams, Martha and Jay Hall, "Knowledge of the Law in Texas: Socioeconomic and Ethnic Differences," *Law and Society Review,* Vol. 7 (Fall, 1972) pp. 99–118.
23. Wilson, James Q., *Thinking About Crime* (New York: Basic Books, 1975), 231 pp.
24. Zimring, Franklin E. and Gordon J. Hawkins, *Deterrence: The Legal Threat in Crime Control* (Chicago: University of Chicago Press, 1973), 376 pp.

THE POLITICAL ECONOMY OF SMACK: OPIATES, CAPITALISM AND LAW*

William J. Chambliss, UNIVERSITY OF DELAWARE

The law may be hallowed but it does not exist in a vacuum. That much sociologists and lawyers have come to agree upon. But agreement ends on precisely what it is in the social milieu of law that determines its content and shape. For longer than we should be happy to admit the embarrassingly simplistic view that the law reflected customs and norms dominated sociological reasoning. Conflict has now replaced consensus as the prevailing perspective within which the law is analyzed.

*There is no way to adequately express my indebtedness and gratitude to Paul Takagi of the University of California. He generously shared ideas and information which he gathered in his own research. He read the manuscript on two occasions and commented fully and insightfully. The paper has benefited immeasurably from his help. Also Gerald Turkel, Alan Block, and Lisa Stearns read the manuscript and made many valuable suggestions. I am indebted to all of these people for their help and commitment.

Research in Law and Sociology—Vol. 1, 1978, pages 115–141.

What type of conflcit? And how much does that view tell us? More often than not conflict analyses focus on the events taking place within a particular nation-state. Thus it is that people today are studying the dynamics of the lawmaking process in Austria to see how the changes in abortion laws have come about in recent years. Others are studying the process of lawmaking vis-à-vis women's rights in the United States and Denmark.

An important point is missed, however, in these studies of law creation. Austria, Denmark, the United States, and England are not separate entities developing in their own particular way. It is far more significant that abortion laws are being changed throughout the Western capitalist world than what the specific quality and character of the process of change in Austria is. Put differently: we often lose sight of the fact that basic changes in law are a reflection of qualitative and quantitative changes in the political economy of a historical period and *not* simply the forces within a particular country. By way of explicating this, and also in the hope of developing a model of rule creation useful for analyzing law from a macro-political economic perspective, I will focus upon the development of legislation and law enforcement practices with respect to opium and its derivatives (especially heroin).

My tack, however, will not be to start with the law and attempt to explain changes in it by reference to other historical forces. Rather, I shall begin with an analysis of opium as a product in the capitalist economic system and show, I hope convincingly, that it was the fact that opium became a product from which capitalism could profit that was the most important force behind the legislation and enforcement of laws relating to these drugs.

THE MAGIC PLANT

Opium is a plant which grows abundantly in warm climates at very high altitudes. Such unusual ecology is not found everywhere—it is found in that chain of mountains that extends from Turkey through Iran, India, China, and Southeast Asia. Opium is a plant which requires a very high investment in labor for its slow maturation. In addition to its unique ecology, this stretch of mountains also contains a very large number of people who live at a low standard and provide an abundant source of cheap agricultural labor.[1] Thus this strip of land has had for centuries a corner on the world's supply of opium comparable to the corner held by the Middle East on the world's supply of oil.

Someone discovered that the juice that oozes from the opium poppy can be taken internally with some highly desirable effects, the most important of which was, in the early days, relief of pain. In areas of the world where medicine was (and is) not readily available and many debilitating diseases (such as tuberculosis, leprosy, and the more common diarrhea and tooth-ache) abound, an easily grown product that can relieve the pain of these diseases is most welcome.

So far as we know, Turkish traders were the first people to introduce opium to the rest of the world. In their search for exchangeable commodities, the Turks carried opium into India, China, and Southeast Asia. This was taking place in the eighth and ninth centuries. All indications are, however, that the trade in opium was small and relatively inconsequential. A full-fledged market in opium was not introduced into South Asia until the emergence of capitalism and its attendant search for labor, profits, and markets.

THE EUROPEAN WAY

As capitalism emerged from the ashes of feudalism in Europe, the newly formed economic necessities pushed nations and capitalists in tandem to scour the world for new markets and products. Italy, Spain, and Portugal were at the forefront of this exploration and search for profits.

In the 1500s the Portuguese arrived in Asia with crews searching for goods to take back to Europe and for markets where items from Europe could be sold. At the time, the economies of the Asian nations were self-contained. There was some trade and a minimal amount of emigration among the Chinese who emigrated to neighboring lands. But commerce between the countries was limited.

Europe had little to offer Asia. While Asia had spices, tea, silk, and pottery which could turn a handsome profit on the European market, Europe had only silver or gold that interested the Asians. The purchasing of commodities such as silk and tea with silver and gold soon became unpopular with European governments, however, as it was apparent that the value of silver and gold was rising while the commodities purchased were consumed.

When the Portuguese began setting up small enclaves on Asian shores, they also moved to control the sea traffic through plunder and piracy. In the course of plundering Asian vessels, the more military, powerful Portuguese ships discovered that there was a small but already established trade in opium, at the time used primarily for medical purpose. Asian ships from Singapore and Bangkok carried opium to Indonesia, China, and other Asian ports where they traded it for other commodities. The trade was small and sufficiently local so that opium use was rare and relatively inconsequential.

The Portuguese traders, however, were quick to realize that for at least a small part of their trade they could use opium instead of gold and silver.

They first crushed the Asian traders and ran their vessels out of the seas. Then they began purchasing opium from Turkish and Indian traders, trading the opium in turn for spices and tea and so forth which they could sell profitably in Europe.

For the next three hundred years, European powers fought over Asian colonies, with the Dutch gaining the upper hand in Indonesia and much of Southeast Asia. During this period the colonial powers expanded into the interior of Asia, colonizing territories to varying degrees. Increasingly the European colonizers turned to the opium trade as a source of income to pay for the military excursions and as a way of obtaining purchasing power for the spices, tea, silk, and pottery they sought [Koh (20), pp. 51–52; Scott (35); Alexander (1); Lubbock (23].

Opium dens began appearing in the major cities of Asia [Koh (20), p. 52]. India gradually replaced Turkey as the main opium-growing area. India's opium was produced mainly by the British East India Company, a private company which had been given almost total political and economic control over the Indian colony by the British government. The British East India Company, through its representatives in Asia and local colonial governments, encouraged and expanded opium addiction throughout Asia and especially among the huge Chinese population. In the early years, the Chinese government, fraught with its own internal political problems and struggling to throw off the yoke of feudalism, paid scant attention to the growing spate of opium smoking. By the middle of the nineteenth century China came to realize that it was trading away its precious metals (silver especially) as well as its silks and tea for opium [Owen (31); Fairbanks (12)]. As Europe had tried to do earlier, China sought to stem the outflow of silver by curtailing the importation of opium. The Manchu rulers announced a stringent anti-opium policy with the explicit intention of stopping British and American traders. At the time, Whampoa was the major port through which opium flowed.[2] In 1839 the Manchu rulers appointed one Commissioner Lin to the task of stopping opium importation. Although the basic issue was the outflow of silver, Lin approached the problem moralistically and argued that it was a ". . . class of evil foreigner that makes opium and brings it for sale, tempting fools to destroy themselves" [Haley, (15), p. 29].

Lin demanded the right to inspect all incoming vessels and to confiscate any opium found thereon. The American traders complied with this demand; the British traders refused. Meanwhile one of the principal companies working under a franchise from the British East India Company began a lobbying campaign in the English Parliament to support its right to trade opium in China [Johnson (18); Stelle (38)].

The debate in Parliament was short-lived. The Prime Minister at the time, Palmerston, authorized the British fleet to seize Whampoa, Canton, and other major ports along the Chinese coast. Thus began the infamous Opium War between China and Great Britain which lasted from 1839 to 1842. In the end the superior naval power of Britain brought the Manchu dynasty a most humiliating defeat. The terms of settlement after the war indicate the extent to which the British had subjugated the Chinese government:

1. Great Britain was given possession of Hong Kong.

2. British traders were given completely open access to five Chinese ports (including Canton).

3. The Chinese agreed to pay $21 million in reparation for opium that had been seized and destroyed by Commissioner Lin prior to the war.

4. British traders would henceforth be subject *only* to British, not Chinese, laws when conflicts occurred.

5. Smuggling was outlawed but opium was not specifically mentioned in the agreements. The responsibility for enforcing laws against smuggling was placed in the hands of the smugglers (the British), not the persons smuggled against (the Chinese).

Several years after the end of the war a British consul in Shanghai seized three opium ships flying the British flag. He was subsequently removed from his post and transferred to India [Wu (43)].

After the 1839–1842 war, opium remained illegal by Chinese law although in effect the British East India Company and its affiliates had a free hand to import and distribute opium in at least five Chinese ports besides Hong Kong.

Opium smuggling entered new heights. The fastest ships available, mainly British, but also American and Indian, transported opium from Calcutta to the Chinese ports. These cargoes were moved to opium storeships lying outside each treaty port. Opium was sold over the side of the ship to Chinese smugglers or sent on small lorchas (coastal ships) to agreed-upon locations on the mainland [Johnson (18)].

For the next fourteen years the opium trade flourished. However, in 1856 the Chinese commissioner of Canton seized a British-registered (but Chinese-owned) lorcha, the *Arrow*. There followed a second war between China and Great Britain which ended much the same as the first, except this time Britain was able to demand and get from the defeated Chinese the legalization of opium smoking and trading. The Chinese, however, did reserve the right to impose a tax on all opium imported: a decision which, paradoxically, would be a major factor in the decline of opium trading by the end of the nineteenth century.

The immediate consequence of China's legalization of opium was to vastly increase the potential and actual market. Now British traders could bring to bear all their skills and imagination to spread the opium habit to the interior of China. The market was truly overwhelming and couched in the nicest of terms when the head of one of the major opium-trading companies noted that opium was a "comfort to the hard-working Chinese" [Owen, (31), p. 243].

Legalization, however, planted the seed that would eventually destroy the profits and the British opium monopoly. For with legalization came (a) taxes and (b) the legal right of Chinese farmers to grow their own opium. Competition would shortly ruin the hard-won right to import opium from India into China.

From 1850 onward, however, British capitalism in China flourished in large part on the profits and labor advantages from the opium traffic. By the end of the nineteenth century it was often said that China had become a nation of opium smokers.

The growing and expanding Industrial Revolution in Europe increased Europe's demand for markets and raw materials. Southeast Asia became a major pawn in the political economy of Europe's capitalist development. Burma was occupied and became British Burma; Malaysia became a British colony and Thailand fell under Britain's "sphere of influence." Laos, Vietnam, and Cambodia were brought together politically under French rule and were named "French Indochina." The Netherlands colonized Indonesia, Britain had possession of Hong Kong, and China was formally independent but in effect had a status similar to that of other British "protectorates."

OPIATE OF THE MASSES

Labor was a major problem for the colonizers of Asia. Still thoroughly in the grip of feudalism, the inhabitants of Southeast Asia were little inclined to move to the plantations of foreigners growing rubber, sugar, cotton, jute, and hemp. And the labor force in Singapore, Hong Kong, Saigon, or Bangkok were disinclined to work on the docks at hard labor. Yet the demand for cheap labor was great. A famine in South China, the Tai Ping Rebellion, and the drain of silver by the opium traffic combined to provide a convenient solution. The population that had moved out of other provinces concentrated in the Kwantung area in the south of China from which they began soon to emigrate to other cities of South Asia.

As the population of China's southern provinces reached a point of saturation, people began emigrating by the thousands. Some went as far away as the United States where they provided hordes of cheap labor for the railroads. Most, however, went to the nearby cities of Southeast Asia where they were employed as laborers on the docks. By 1910 there were over 100,000 Chinese in Saigon, 200,000 in Bangkok, and smaller numbers in every other major city in the area [Purcell (32, pp. 58, 215].

Not all of the Chinese migration was, however, voluntary. Chinese "coolies" were an important source of profit for traders. And there is evidence that many of the Chinese who were brought to the United States and other parts of America were kidnapped and sold into indentured service. in Cuba, for example, many of the Chinese laborers who were interviewed about the circumstances surrounding their leaving China insisted that they did not leave voluntarily but were kidnapped [The Cuba Commission (9)].[3] The same is true of many Chinese who were brought to the United States.

The Chinese brought with them the opium-smoking habits which had been so meticulously encouraged by British merchants and traders. The colonial governments were quick to recognize the value to them of encouraging the opium smoking of the Chinese laborers. Profits were substantial and an opium-addicted labor force was magnanimously compliant. In every major city of Southeast Asia from Rangoon to Saigon, colonial and local governments developed opium dens. The opium trade was carefully, albeit corruptly, organized and controlled by an unholy alliance between colonial officials, local governments, and a new class of entrepreneurs who were given government franchises to import and sell opium. Opium sales provided 40–50 percent of the income of colonial governments [McCoy (27), p. 63; Wen (42), pp. 52–75]. Opium profits helped finance the railways, canals, roads, and government buildings as well as the comfortable living conditions of colonial bureaucrats.

From time to time local governments resisted the expanding opium trade. King Rama II of Thailand decreed a ban on opium trading in 1811, and in 1839 the death penalty was instituted for traffickers [Skinner (37) pp. 118–119]. Unfortunately for King Rama II, British merchant ships which carried opium to the ports were beyond his control. When a British captain was arrested, the British government rumbled its warships, and the local government quickly released the opium smuggler. In 1852, King Mongkut of Thailand succumbed to British pressure and created an opium monopoly under Thai government control and leased the monopoly to a wealthy Chinese merchant [Skinner (37) p. 119]. The king also established franchises in gambling, lottery, and prostitution. Opium became the mainstay of the government revenues. It was simultaneously the main thread on which the working class hung and was ensnared into providing labor for the European trade with these nations. It was opium, not religion, that was the opiate of the masses in Southeast Asia. By the 1940s there were in Indochina (Cambodia, Laos, and Vietnam) over 2,500 opium dens providing 45 percent of all tax revenues and an immeasurable percentage of the unclaimed salaries of both local and colonial government officials [McCoy (27) p. 76].

The Chinese immigrants into Southeast Asia and the United States were not, of course, the sole or perhaps even the principal market for opium. Opium smoking quickly spread to indigent American and Asian populations. The spread was encouraged by the same political and economic forces that had provided the impetus for its growth in China earlier.

AGRI-OPIUM BUSINESS

British traders were joined in the late 1700s by American ships and merchants. However, the Jay treaty signed in 1794 prohibited American merchants from dealing in commodities under British control. The profits from opium were, however, too appealing to be turned down, and American merchants therefore began to introduce into China opium grown in Turkey—returning us, in some symbolically diabolical way, to the first opium route of the eighth century.

The American trade was less than that of its British competitors, but it was nonetheless large, profitable, and important for the development of U.S. capitalism. In the years 1816, 1817, and 1818 there was an annual volume of 672,900 pounds of opium handled by U.S. merchants [Dulles (10); Latourette (21)]. This volume of opium, according to the historians Latourette and Dulles, formed the capital which was basic to the growth of industrialization in New England [Dulles (10); Latourette (21)]. The profits from opium trading were invested in the textile mills in Massachusetts and other New England states following the introduction of the power loom in 1814. Thus the neat paradox that opium helped create a labor force for capitalist expansion in Asia and America and the profits from the opium provided the capital for the development of the factory system in New England.[4]

From the period 1830–1860 (the period of the two opium wars) American clipper ships, sometimes referred to as Opium Clippers, competed successfully with the British in the opium market. But when the British introduced the steamship, U.S. merchants lost their competitive advantage and the British once again dominated the trade.

This change was combined with the fact that the treaty of 1856 had set the stage for the emergence of Chinese competition in the growth and distribution of opium. Chinese farmers discovered that the high mountains of South China were amenable to opium growing. Since the profits from opium were higher, there was a rather rapid transformation of the agricultural products in many mountain regions of China first, and later other parts of Southeast Asia. By the late 1800s, "British and American mercantile firms, seeking more profit from other goods, slowly withdrew from opium trade" [Johnson (18) p. 18; Owen (31) p. 260]. The British continued active trading until World War I; but the total trade in opium that had once been the mainstay of American and British mercantile operations in Asia had declined gradually from the late 1800s.

The production of opium spread to the high mountain plateaus of neighboring countries. The border states of Laos and Burma and Thailand quickly shifted from traditional crops to opium as the profits from opium (as well as the pleasures of local consumption) became increasingly apparent. Britain's loss of revenues was a boom for the impoverished hill tribes of Southeast Asia. World War I all but stopped the competition from British and American traders carrying Indian and Turkish opium, thus bringing down the curtain on the Asian opium drama begun some four hundred years before when the first Portuguese ships of war pirated opium from the small trading vessels that were then supplying a tiny market.

Between 1914 and 1940 the opium monopolies in Indochina (controlled first by the French, then by the Japanese colonial government) sought new, closer, and more dependable sources of opium and found them among the Meo tribes of Laos. Indochina's opium production leaped from 7.5 tons in 1940 to 60.6 tons by 1944 [McCoy (27), p. 65–68]. Similar leaps and changes occurred somewhat later in the other countries—Thailand and Burma—that now comprise the Golden Triangle. When the Chinese Liberation Army emerged victorious in 1949 the supply of opium from China disappeared. This further stimulated opium growing in the Golden Triangle.

As was the case in the early years of colonizing Southeast Asia, opium smoking and trafficking were encouraged and stimulated by both local and colonial governments. Addiction provided profits for the governments and kept at least the addicted segment of the labor force dependent on their employers. With the emergence of subterranean warfare conducted by colonial government intelligence units, the opium trade came to supply a new link in the armament of the colonial nations. France especially used the opium trade as a source of revenues to finance its clandestine intelligence operations in Vietnam, Cambodia, and Laos. The wedge provided by the opium trade was two-pronged: first there was money earned that paid for government administrative costs; and second, the opium trade was a carrot offered to those hill tribes and local leaders who would support the French struggle against the communists.

When the United States took over from France the management of Indochina, it also inherited the link between military control and opium in these countries. It was necessary and indeed highly expedient to adopt the French policy of encouraging friendly tribesmen to grow and traffic in narcotics (opium) in return for fighting the communists.

America's Central Intelligence Agency thus became a major trafficker in the international narcotics industry [McCoy 27)].

EYEWITNESS TESTIMONY

There is trouble at Long Cheng, the secret Central Intelligence Agency military base in north Laos. Meo guerilla leaders are demanding full operational control over the dozen or so aircraft that work daily from this 5,000-foot paved runway in the middle of nowhere. The Americans resist, knowing only too well what the implications of giving in would be. They hassle. Everybody, of course, knows the stakes in this little game. Everybody knows that the Meo have their own ideas as to how these flying machines can be put to efficient use. It's there for everybody to see: the neat, banana-leaf-wrapped cubes of raw opium stacked neatly alongside the runway, not quite a hundred yards from the air-conditioned shack from which Agency officers command a clear view of the entire area. In the end, General Vang Pao, commander of the Meo army, has his way. The Americans who are supporting this army might regret the small loss of operational control. But the war must go on. Anyway, even if the Meo rack up all the planes, more can always be brought in. The time is 1967.

An American refugee-relief worker visits a Meo village atop a 4,500-foot mountain just north of the Plain of Jars. Having come to discuss local food and medical problems, he is given a walking tour of the area. Of particular interest to him is a sizable patch of unripe poppies growing on the side of a hill just up from the village. It is opium, he is told. Soon it will be harvested. Then "we will sell it to the General [Vang Pao]." It represents a bit of cash; they will receive about $5 a pound. "You Americans don't pay us very much," he is told. The time is 1967.

A Lao Air Force C47 transport taxies to the head of the dirt airfield at Ban Houei Sai, a small town in the extreme northwest corner of the country. As the engines shut down, a Lao army truck pulls up beside the main door of the plane. Quickly, the soldiers manning the vehicle begin tossing small packages up to the receiving crew members. An American, observing from a distance, asks a native employee to get a closer look. He reports back directly: opium, about 500 pounds of the stuff, is being placed on board. He also says that the commander of the Laotian Regular Army, General Ouan Rathikun, has come in with the flight and is supervising the operation.

North of the Ban Houei Sai, on the Lao side of the Mekong River near the Burmese border, is a cluster of opium "cookers" in which the raw product is reduced, in this case to a morphine base. They belong to Chao La, a Yao tribal leader and CIA guerilla commander. For months, an American badgers Chao La for permission to visit the site. Finally he does. Not operational at the time, the apparatus evokes images of a bootleg still in the backwoods of Kentucky. The opium processed here comes in from Burma and Yunan, contacts having been made by Chao La's intelligence network that, funded and supplied by the CIA, works undercover in these areas. The time is 1968.

These foregoing accounts have not been conjured up from my imagination. They are factual incidents, and I am the American mentioned in three of the examples. And they shouldn't be viewed as isolated events, but rather as a mere sampling of just how deeply the trafficking of opium runs as a central and integral part of the Laotian power structure.

The object of bringing these facts into the open is twofold. First, to show that opium trafficking was rampant in these areas when I was there. And second, to state my belief that the American Embassy, together with other agencies nominally working under its auspices, not only knew what was going on but was fully aware that it was in no small way conducted by the manipulation of U.S. aid earmarked for other purposes. I don't make this charge lightly. It was common knowledge to every field worker in the north. Talked about, but only on an informal basis, the opium question was subordinated to the primary needs and objectives of U.S. policy.

The utter ruthlessness of this tactical methodology is important to bear in mind. It mattered not what ancillary problems were created by our presence. Not, that is, so long as the Meo leadership could keep their wards in the boondocks fighting and dying in the name of, for these unfortunates anyway, some nebulous cause. If for the Americans this meant, as it did, increasing the potential reward, or quite literally, payoffs, to the Meo leadership in the form of a carte blanche to exploit U.S.-supplied airplanes and communications gear to the end of greatly streamlining opium operations, well, that was the price to be paid. In time, the arrangement became increasingly mercenary. Dealing on such contractual terms perhaps made it easier to rationalize away the other half of Laotian reality: that hundreds of thousands of natives had been caught up in an American war of attrition, and that the essence—the very lifeforce—of an entire people had been horribly scarred, if not fatally extinguished.

The war in Laos has always been depicted as only a "holding operation"; merely a place to buy time for our supposed allies, to allow them a period of grace in which to mobilize. Thus, with a second line of defense established, the fate of this beleaguered kingdom could be left to the whim of fate. For the generals, Ouan and Vang Pao, and for the rest of their cronies, there has been time to prepare for the inevitable day of abandonment by their benefactors. For them, enough opium has been grown, enough heroin processed from it and sold on the streets of Saigon to American G.I.'s and in the back alleys of New York City, so that the generals' future portends surfeit, not destitution. The tragedy in Laos is that of the poor—the Meo soldier, his family, and the rest of the conglomerate Lao society who have long been bombed, shot at, burned, uprooted, and who must now, in stark confusion, ponder the enormous catastrophe that has befallen them.

The Americans ultimately will go home; the creators and engineers of the Laos operation will be duly complimented on a job well done. For them there will be high-ranking appointments, and general promotions all around.

But for the great bulk of the American people, who must one day come to realize the crimes that have been committed in the false name of national honor, for them, there can only be shame.

Ronald J. Rickenbach
East Hampton, N.Y.

From *Harper's Magazine*, October 1972, pp. 120–121

Until very recently, the governments of Thailand, Laos and South Vietnam have been as dependent on the opium trade as they were at the end of the nineteenth century. The profits are immense. The former head of Thailand's police department is alleged to have put over $600 million into European banks before he was forced to resign (*Bangkok Post,* 1973a). More recently the three Kitchihoun family members who ruled Thailand's military dictatorship from 1964 to 1973 amassed over $200 million worth of property in Thailand in that short period of time and an unknown fortune stashed in secret foreign banks (*Bangkok Post,* 1973b). Much of this fortune derived from their share of profits from the opium trade. The South Vietnamese governments from Diem to Thieu profited immensely as well. In Laos, General Ouane openly admits that without the huge traffic in opium between his country and Saigon, which he controlled, Laos could not have survived economically (*Bangkok Post,* 1973c). No wonder then that the United States provided the planes and the military equipment that enabled General Ouane to ship Laotian hill tribe opium to Saigon, where it was processed into heroin and either sold to American G.I.'s in Vietnam or shipped back to the United States—sometimes in the coffins of American soldiers [McCoy (27)].

OUANE: OPIUM CARRIER FOR KMT

General Ouane Rathikone, former Supreme Commander of the Laotian Armed Forces, is transporting narcotics on contract for the Kuomintang and the Shan State Army (SSA).
by Kalthorn Sermkase

He made the disclosure during an exclusive interview at his Houei Sai headquarters on the Laotian border with Chiang Khong District of Chiang Rai.

General Ouane, who has often been accused of drug trafficking, said he used a fleet of C47 and Avro aircraft to transport the shipments to Saigon and Hong Kong.

But he added: "I am only responsible for transporting. I am not a narcotics dealer. What happens to the narcotics after they get to their destinations is not my business."

He said that the KMT or Chinese Irregular Forces (CIF) "prefer gold and M16 ammunition to paper money for their opium and heroin. They will also barter for rice, salt and sugar."

I had crossed the Mekong to see him when I heard that he was making an annual visit to his sawmill at Ban Kwan in Houei San. Ban Kwan in Laos, with Ban Sop Luak in Thailand and Ban Tao Thun in Burma, is where the Golden Triangle starts.

Asked whether he would give up his business of transporting narcotics, Gen. Ouane said: "I have to take care of 200 followers."

Asked if he had an airport behind his sawmill, he said: "There is a ricefield but it can be used for landing small aircraft."

He also disclosed that he held the concession to forests along the Mekong border. "I export the timber to Thailand," he said.

Gen. Ouane, who is now an MP for Luang Prabang, met me, wearing a cream-coloured sweater, at the army headquarters in Houei Sai. When I raised the matter of "opium," he became excited.

"The Americans are selfish. They are trying to get the Laotian Assembly to outlaw the opium trade. Europeans started the opium business in the seventeenth century and this cannot stop in just one or two years," he said.

"About 50,000 hill tribe people depend upon poppy cultivation, producing between 50–60 tons a year. What do we do with them? Let them become Communists?"

"The United States has threatened to cut off aid if Laos does not stop opium planting. But they give us only $1.2 million a year to help the hill tribes give up opium," Gen. Ouane said.

"However, the money has been used as expenses for 20 American experts who needed good houses, air-conditioned cars, Polaris water. Nothing is left for the hill-tribes."

He also accused the Central Intelligence Agency (CIA) of destroying four heroin plants in Laos.

The Bangkok Post
November 27, 1973

Opium traffic still plays an important part in capitalism's political economy. In Southeast Asia the Shan tribesmen with their own independent armies, the KMT (Chinese Nationalist Army) and the Laotian Armed Forces, were, until the Cambodian Revolution, three principal sources of transporting and marketing opium from the hill tribe growers in the Golden Triangle to the middlemen who oversee its passage to the laboratories in Bangkok and Hong Kong. These three groups—the Shan, the KMT and the Laotian Armed Forces—were supported by arms and technical assistance from the United States because they were believed to be serving U.S. interests by providing a wedge against the communist liberation armies in Burma, Laos, Cambodia, and Thailand.

Another parallel between opium use today and the historical roots of opium smoking in Asia is its function as both an expression and a suppressor of social conflicts. In Vietnam the widespread use of heroin by the American Army may have reduced the overt expression of rebellion so often commented on as a characteristic of the people fighting in that war without public sanction. Heroin in the ghettos of America's large cities may also serve the same purpose it did among the Chinese laborers of the late nineteenth century: immobilizing a segment of discontented laborers who might otherwise more openly fight against the oppression and despair of their position at the bottom of the scale in a class society.

OPIUM AND HEROIN IN THE UNITED STATES

The use of opium and heroin in the United States must be understood in the same general terms that have been applied to understanding its Asian background. The first major influx of opium smokers came when the Chinese came to the West Coast of America as coolies working in the gold and silver mines and building the railroads that would connect the Eastern manufacturing centers with the Western frontier.

Conditions of work for the Chinese immigrants were abominable. The workers were brought without families, were forced to labor long hours under the worst physical conditions imaginable and with little relief. Opium smoking was a way of lulling the psychological pain of the arduous conditions. It was also an extremely effective way of reducing the pain of physical illness for which medical care was practically nonexistent.

From the point of view of the employers, the laborer's opium smoking was a blessing. The employers, by controlling the importation and distribution of opium, made a profit from selling it to the workers. Furthermore, the threat of withdrawing the supply of opium kept many potential labor complaints from becoming a serious threat to the employer.

It was in this social situation that opium smoking began a slow but steady growth throughout the American working class, especially in the West, where the work was often unbelievably demanding, where there were few families in the mines and cities and where even "women for hire" were difficult to come by. In the late 1800s when opium was legally imported and sold, the annual importation into the United States exceeded 500,000 pounds. The market was supplied by normal business channels. Opium was still coming into San Francisco and some had begun to find its way East to Chicago and New York. Opium dens have been reported as far south as New Orleans and as far north as Montreal during the early 1900s.

The following are estimates of the amount of opium imported into the United States (most of it legally) during 1860–1900:

Years	Opium imported (in pounds)
1860–1869	110,305
1870–1879	192,602
1880–1889	328,392
1890–1899	513,070

By the 1880s, mining and railroad building began to decline in the West. Thus the need for cheap labor such as had been supplied by Chinese immigrants declined as well. The U.S. government became concerned over the growing number of immigrants entering the United States who were rapidly becoming a burden rather than an economic asset. An envoy thus was dispatched from Washington to China with the mission of gaining Chinese cooperation in reducing immigration to the United States. China was willing, it turned out, providing the United States would in turn take steps to reduce the opium being brought into China by American ships. The United States agreed—the opium business was substantial for a small group of shipowners, but as we have seen, the market inside China was rapidly declining, and in any case the lion's share of the market was controlled by the British. The United States then passed the first anti-opium legislation in the world: a statute at large passed in 1886 making it illegal to trade in opium.[5]

Thus, by the beginning of the twentieth century the opium trade and traffic had shifted.substantially. Southeast Asia was still a major market, as was China. The supply of opium, however, had begun to shift from India to Turkey to sources closer to home: mainly South China and the Golden Triangle. Turkey and India were still producing opium which was shipped to Europe and the United States. Opium dens were run and organized by the governments of China and Southeast Asia and the profits from these enterprises served to support not only local governments but colonial governments as well. The United States had become a market of some importance for opium from Turkey, India, and Southeast Asia. Probably the major routes were for morphine to be manufactured in Europe, out of opium grown in India and Turkey, to the United States and throughout Europe. Opium in its raw form was being smuggled into the United States from Southeast Asia.

As the Asian opium trade became less profitable for Europeans, anti-opium legislation began to appear in most Western countries. A series of International Opium Conferences (Shanghai in 1909; The Hague during 1911–1914; and Geneva in 1924) were the consequence of the changing economic realities which helped spread anti-opium sentiment and subsequent legislation.

In 1898 a German pharmaceutical company, Bayer, began distributing a patented product called heroin, which, the manufacturer claimed, was a nonaddictive drug with the same medical value as opium, without the undesirable side effects.

The United States in 1914 passed the Harrison Act which made it illegal to trade in opium or its derivatives (heroin included) without registering with the U.S. government and paying a small tax. As a result of bureaucratic maneuvering (particularly the careful selection of cases for appeal) the Federal Bureau of Narcotics succeeded in getting a series of court decisions (especially in the U.S. Supreme Court decision Behrman vs. the U.S.) which made it illegal for doctors to prescribe morphine, opium, or heroin to anyone who was an addict [Lindesmith (22)].

World War I interrupted the traffic in opium. This provided increased incentive to grow the poppy in China and Southeast Asia, as trade routes with India and Turkey were now totally severed; it also interfered somewhat with the opium traffic to the United States. Nonetheless, enough opium and heroin were imported throughout the war to supply a stable addict population. World War I also inadvertently opened up connections with Turkish and Middle Eastern opium sources.

It is not clear from the records how the opium and heroin business was organized after World War I. It seems likely that from 1918 to 1940 the opium-heroin business was a highly competitive one run by local merchants making special arrangements with merchant seamen and mercantiles. There is evidence that in the twenties the New York trade was concentrated around some (but not all) of the same people (such as Arnold Rothstein and Frank Erickson) who were major organizers of the business in illegal whiskey [Gosch and Hammer (14)]. In San Francisco, an underworld figure known as "Black Tony" was a central organizer of the opium-heroin trade.

> We all worked for the Narcotics Syndicate in San Francisco which at that time was run
> by Black Tony. It was a pretty big operation even then. The Syndicate used to get its
> morphine from Germany and its opium from China. The morphine came in through
> New York and was handled by the local narcotic wholesalers. Then it was shipped to
> the West Coast [King (19) pp. 5–6].

Through connections with the Hearst newspaper chain, "Black Tony" used delivery boys and street-corner paper sellers to distribute opium and heroin to his customers. Interestingly, this same pattern appeared in Chicago about this time [Gosch and Hammer (14)].

By 1938 the heroin business in the United States had become one of the nation's larger industries. Senator John Coffee estimated that the sale of heroin at this time exceeded $1 billion annually [Congressional Reports (40)]. We know less than we should about the organization of this industry and the extent to which it was monopolized. There is some evidence, however, that by the close of the 1930s Vito Genovese had managed to gain control over some of the heroin business through working agreements with people in Italy and France [Gosch and Hammer (14)]. Genovese may have worked closely with John Erickson, a Scandinavian who had inherited the illegal business empire of Arnold Rothstein when the latter was murdered in 1928.

World War II interrupted a great many things, including the smooth flow of morphine and heroin from Europe to the United States and of opium from Asia. According to Alfred McCoy, the addict population in the United States declined to such an extent that following World War II the "heroin problem" had become quite manageable [McCoy (27) pp. 30–57].

The affluence of the fifties created unprecedented demand by the consuming American public for everything from ballpoint pens to refrigerators. The living and working conditions for many Americans created an unprecedented demand for narcotics as well. The iron law of capitalism is that where there is a demand there will be a supplier, if the profit is high enough. Suppliers emerged throughout the United States but especially in the largest cities where living conditions and political forces combined to make the demand and distribution of heroin manageable.

Prohibition had produced a large number of businessmen with the knowledge and the capital capable of organizing international cartels for the production, shipment, and distribution of illegal goods. Meyer Lansky, Vito Genovese, and Joe Adonis had established a network of business and political contracts throughout Europe, Latin America, and the Caribbean that made the importation of illegal commodities highly profitable.

These businessmen and their associates had very large profits from gambling and real estate investments made during the 1930s and 1940s [U.S. Congress (39)]. Capital was of course essential. Lansky is reported to have taken $20 million to France in the 1950s to gain a monopoly on the heroin produced in Marseille: heroin which was manufactured from opium base that came mainly from Turkey via the Middle East. The success of Lansky's mission was such that thereafter Turkey and Marseille became the major suppliers of America's illegal opiates:

Although it is difficult to probe the inner workings of such a clandestine business . . . there is reason to believe that Meyer Lansky's 1949–1950 European tour was instrumental in promoting Marseille's heroin industry. After leaving Switzerland (where he had set up Swiss Bank accounts to take care of money transfers) Lansky traveled through France, where he met with high-ranking Corsican syndicate leaders on the Riviera and in Paris. After lengthy discussions, Lansky and the Corsicans are reported to have arrived at some sort of agreement concerning the international heroin traffic. . . . In future years, U.S. narcotics experts were to estimate that the majority of America's heroin supply was being manufactured in Marseille [McCoy (27), pp. 28–29].[6]

Our knowledge about the inner workings of the heroin industry is sketchy. We can safely conclude, however, that the profits from opium and heroin were growing at a rate that would have made even the growth rate of General Motors and International Business Machines seem modest. The average heroin addict in the United States in the early 1970s was spending $30,000 a year on heroin [Brown and Silverman (2)].[7] While this is a very high figure, it is noteworthy that it is an average based upon the fact that not all heroin addicts are "street people." Many addicts are wealthy professional and business people who no doubt pay considerably higher prices for their "shit" than do the people in the ghettos and the slums.

Accepting, for the sake of argument, this average expenditure per addict enables us to also estimate the gross volume of business from heroin. If, as most experts agree, there are at least one million addicts in the United States, then this means that the annual gross sale of heroin in the United States today exceeds $30 billion [DuPont and Greene (11)]. Some sense of the importance of this industry to the national economy is gleaned from the fact that this would make the heroin industry comparable in gross volume of business to the largest corporations in the United States: in 1970 General Motors, Exxon, IBM, ITT, and a half dozen other of the largest multinational corporations in the world had a gross volume of business of *less than* $30 billion a year [Council of Economic Researches, (8)].[8] Indeed, there were only twenty countries in the world with a Gross National Product in excess of the gross volume of business of the heroin industry in the United States. (See Table 1.)

The heroin industry is a highly competitive one. That Meyer Lansky or Vito Genovese or Joe Adonis might gain a competitive advantage does not mean they could do this without a struggle. Nor does it mean that their monopoly position is unassailable. There is evidence that the heroin industry is currently undergoing a substantial upheaval brought about by the emergence in the late 1960s of competitive forces with substantial political influence. To understand this, the latest chapter in the political economy of heroin, we must digress slightly.

The development of the state in the modern world is such that virtually every aspect of economic life is influenced by decisions of the state. Laws, regulations, government contracts, licenses—what the lawyer Charles Reich has called "The New Property" [Reich (33), pp. 765–782]—are the life substance of most industries in the capitalist world. Illegal businesses, including the business of heroin, are no exception. State and government cooperation, especially the cooperation of those agencies responsible for regulating the industry, is an essential ingredient for protecting profits and maintaining monopolistic advantages. State cooperation, in turn, depends upon being able to influence those political leaders who most directly affect the industry.

Throughout the period from 1930 to 1960 the major corporate executives who owned and managed the heroin industry in the United States were well represented by key people in state and federal government. The heroin industry had grown up during the heyday of the Democratic Party—quite predictably, their ties and allegiance to the Democrats were stronger than their connection with politicians in the Republican Party.

Table 1. Gross National Products of countries and net sales of companies interspersed: by rank, 1970*

Rank	Country or Company	GNP or sales (billion $)	Rank	Country or Company	GNP or sales (billion $)
1	United States	974.0	26	Pakistan	17.9
2	Soviet Union	485.7	27	South Africa	17.8
3	Japan	196.7	28	American Telephone and Telegraph[2]	17.0
4	West Germany	184.8			
5	France	146.3	29	Standard Oil (N.J.)[2]	16.6
6	People's Republic of China	121.0	30	Denmark	15.8
7	United Kingdom	116.3	31	Ford Motor[2]	15.0
8	Italy	91.7	32	Indonesia	14.0
9	Canada	78.0	33	Austria	13.7
10	India	52.5	34	Bulgaria	11.7
11	Poland	46.0	35	Norway	11.2
12	Brazil	40.4	36	Royal Dutch Shell[2]	10.8
13	East Germany	39.6	37	Venezuela	10.3
14	Mexico	33.2	38	Finland	10.2
15	Australia	32.9	39	Iran	10.1
16	Spain	32.5	40	Philippines	9.8
17	Czechoslovakia	32.5	41	Sears Roebuck[2]	9.3
18	Sweden	31.5	42	Greece	9.2
19	Netherlands	31.3	43	Korea, South	8.9
20	Belgium	25.0	44	General Electric[2]	8.7
21	Romania	24.4	45	Turkey	8.7
22	Argentina	23.9	46	Chile	8.4
23	Switzerland	20.6	47	International Business Machines[1]	7.5
24	General Motors[2]	18.8	48	Mobil Oil[2]	7.3
25	Yugoslavia	18.5	49	Colombia	7.1
			50	Chrysler[2]	7.0

[1]indicates company
[2]indicates American company
*Council of Economic Researches, Guide to Corporations: A Social Perspective, Chicago: Swallow Press, 1974.

But the hegemony of the Democratic Party was undermined in the 1960s. Even old established labor union ties, such as that between the Teamsters and the Democrats, began to show signs of wearing thin as Jimmy Hoffa was put in prison at the insistence of a Democratic-controlled Attorney General's office [Sheridan (36)] and the Teamsters subsequently shifted their allegiance from the Democrats to the Republicans (*New York Times,* 1972).

TEAMSTERS UNION PLANS TO SHIFT TO LAW FIRM WITH TIE TO NIXON

By WALTER RUGABER

WASHINGTON, Dec. 8—The Teamsters Union plans to transfer its legal business from a law firm identified with the Democrats to one that is soon to be appointed by one of President Nixon's leading political advisers.

The union plans to drop Williams, Connolly & Califano, whose leading members include Edward Bennett Williams, the well-known criminal lawyer, and Joseph A. Califano, Jr., former counsel to the Democratic National Committee.

It will be represented instead by Morin, Dickstein, Shapiro & Galligan, a firm to which Charles W. Colson, who is now a special counsel to the President, is expected to move early next year.

The change, involving legal fees that union sources put at about $10,000 a year, was regarded by some as further evidence of the close political ties that have developed between the Teamsters Union hierarcy and the Nixon White House.

Frank E. Fitzsimmons, president of the International Brotherhood of Teamsters, is one of Mr. Nixon's principal labor supporters. He remained on the Pay Board, for example, when other union leaders resigned in protest against Administration economic policies.

Mr. Colson has served as the President's liaison with labor. Earlier this year he proposed that the President commute the prison sentence of James R. Hoffa, the former Teamsters Union chief. Hoffa was subsequently released.

Williams, Connolly & Califano, a Washington firm, represents the Democrats in a civil suit that the party filed against leading Republican figures in connection with the break-in and bugging of the Democratic National Headquarters in the Watergate complex here.

Mr. Williams and Mr. Califano took part personally in pressing the Democrats' suit, which is still pending. This is thought to have angered Mr. Fitzsimmons, and some observers advanced it as a major reason for the union's shift in the law firm. Other observers disagreed, but a union source acknowledged that Mr. Fitzsimmons was probably unhappy with the firm's pursuit of the case, which was embarrassing to the President during his re-election campaign.

"But I doubt it was the reason he [Mr. Fitzsimmons] made the move," the source said. "He developed a close relationship with Colson while he was at the White House, and it just made sense to have him as [the Teamsters] lawyer."

The union official also pointed out that the Williams firm had been retained originally while Hoffa was president of the Teamsters Union and that a reason for the change might be a desire by Mr. Fitzsimmons to choose his own lawyer.

Nine of the sources disputed the political significance of the union's move. The timing of it raised a question since Mr. Colson is not expected to leave the White House until March 1.

However, Henry Cashen, a member of Mr. Colson's staff who is familiar with labor matters, is also expected to join Morin, Dickstein, Shapiro & Galligan, a Washington firm, and could handle the union account before Mr. Colson arrives.

Aside from confirming the planned shift, neither of the firms involved nor Mr. Colson or the Teamsters Union had any official comment. Mr. Fitzsimmons was reported to be abroad and could not be reached.

The New York Times, December 9, 1972

The emergence of Richard Nixon as a political force of substance posed a threat to the established monopoly in the heroin industry greater than any experienced since the 1930s. The Nixon Administration adopted policies which were clearly inimical to the interest of the established monopoly. First and perhaps most importantly, heretofore unheard of pressure was brought on Turkey to curtail its production of opium. At the threat of dissolving the massive allocation of Foreign Aid, the Nixon Administration forced Turkey to enforce its long-existing laws restricting the growth of opium. Secondly, the Bureau of Dangerous Drugs (formerly the Federal Bureau of Narcotics) was expanded and given sustantial encouragement to curtail the heroin traffic from Latin America and France—an importation route established and largely controlled by Meyer Lansky and his associates [Clark and Horrock, (5)].

The anti-heroin war begun by President Nixon and his associates might have reduced the amount of heroin coming into the United States save for one small thing: at the same time that effective programs to reduce the flow of heroin from Turkey and Marseille were being implemented, the supply of heroin from Southeast Asia was increasing by leaps and bounds. From 1968 to 1972 the amount of heroin coming from Turkey declined by almost 50 percent. The amount of heroin consumed in the United States supplied by Southeast Asian sources increased by 20–30 percent [U.S. Congress, (41)]. Whereas in the mid 1960s it was estimated that over 95 percent of America's heroin was from Turkey, by 1971 it was estimated that less than 50 percent was coming from Turkey [McCoy (27) pp, 52–67].

In 1968 Santo Trafficante, Jr., took a trip to Southeast Asia, visiting Bangkok, Thailand, Singapore, and Saigon [McCoy (27) pp. 29, 52–67]. This trip was to establish agreements between Southeast Asian producers and distributors for the importation of heroin into the United States. Santo Trafficante, Jr., is a Florida-based financier and organizer of illegal businesses whose roots in organized crime were inherited from his father. For almost twenty years he shared an uneasy alliance with Meyer Lansky. The roots of their competition go deep and began in the late 1950s when, at a crucial meeting in Florida, Santo Trafficante, Jr., agreed under threat of death to arrange for the murder of his close personal friend, Anastasia, allowing Lansky and his associates an opportunity to murder their chief competitor [Messick, (29), pp. 209–215; Cook (7); Gosch and Hammer, (14)].

Following Anastasia's murder, Lansky and Trafficante cooperated in investments in Cuba, the Bahamas, Florida, and the heroin trade. Trafficante also had close financial and business ties, however, with Lansky competitors: among them Bebe Rebozo [Sale (34); Messick, (29)].

A number of events suggest that the 1968 trip of Trafficante was connected with an attempt to reduce Lansky's control of the heroin monopoly. The major organizer of the opium and heroin traffic in Southeast Asia was a Chinese businessman from Laos by the name of Huu Tin Heng, who organized the *Chiu Chow* Syndicate [McCoy (28)]. Huu was, among other things, the Laotian manager of the Pepsi-Cola Company. The president of Pepsi-Cola has been one of Richard Nixon's long-time and most important friends and financial supporters (Lurie, 1972; Mazo and Hess, 1968). In return, Pepsi-Cola has received substantial help from Nixon, such as monopoly franchises in foreign countries, including a franchise on the Soviet Union market [Sale (34) p. 1].

Following Nixon's election as President, a campaign to expose and eliminate "organized crime syndicates" throughout the United States was widely publicized. In fact the campaign was only directed at selected syndicates in cities where their support was inimical to Nixon and his Republican associates [Chambliss (4)]. One city where this was the case was Seattle, Washington, where a Nixon-appointed U.S. attorney successfully spearheaded a campaign that exposed a criminal syndicate involving over fifty of the city's police and political leaders. It was subsequent to this "clean-up" of Seattle's "mafia" that Seattle became a major import center for heroin in the United States: heroin coming from Southeast Asia, from the Chiu Chow connection, and in direct competition with Meyer Lansky's European connection. No wonder, then, that Meyer Lansky had over a quarter of a million dollars in campaign contributions for Hubert Humphrey in 1968 in an attempt to stop Nixon, nor that Lansky had gone to Washington State and offered to finance the gubernatorial campaign of the Democratic candidate in an effort to unseat the Republican governor who was an ally of Richard Nixon. Both Humphrey and the Democratic gubernatorial candidate lost, and the Southeast Asian–Seattle heroin route opened up.

Seattle was the only American city where the *Chiu-Chow* syndicates had been able to dominate the narcotics supply. After the abolition of Turkish cultivation in 1971 deprived the dominant Montreal Corsican syndicates of their sources, Vancouver's Chinese dealers increased their imports from Hong Kong and were soon supplying Canada's 9000 to 16,000 addicts with 80 percent of their heroin needs. Vancouver's Chinese began distributing to neighboring Seattle and Southeast Asian heroin jumped from 12 percent of the city's identifiable seizures in 1972 to 40 percent in 1973 [McCoy, (28)].

The Narcotics Bureau's arrests and seizures of heroin from Europe were increasing at a dramatic rate. In 1968 the Federal Bureau of Narcotics was transferred from the Treasury Department (where it had been established at its inception) to the Justice Department. Dr. John Ingersoll was appointed head of the new bureau, which was renamed the Bureau of Narcotics and Dangerous Drugs.

In 1968 and 1969 the total seizures of illegal heroin coming into the United States were under 200 pounds. However, the reorganization resulted in the most effective attack on the international heroin traffickers ever put together by the U.S. government. By the end of 1970 the government had seized almost three times as much heroin as during the preceding years (over 600 pounds). And in 1971 the increase in the number of seizures was over 1,600 pounds. (Browning (3) p. 164). In 1972 the combination of the efforts of Customs and the Bureau of Dangerous Drugs resulted in the seizure of *2,700 pounds* of heroin, almost fifteen times as much heroin as had been seized only four years before.

By 1972 the Nixon Administration had seriously disrupted the established monopoly. Furthermore, the emerging control over the Southeast Asian supply was getting firmly established. At this point the Attorney General and the President proposed yet another reorganization of the narcotics enforcement process. The reorganization culminated in the formation of the Drug Enforcement Administration. The seizure of heroin immediately plummeted to 900 pounds in 1973, and in 1974 it fell to less than 600 pounds. Dr. John Ingersoll resigned his post as head of the bureau and accused the Nixon Administration of interfering with the agency [Browning, (3), p. 164].

Watergate, and a series of scandals, undermined Richard Nixon's political power and he resigned the presidency. With his resignation went the shift from European to Southeast Asian heroin. Seattle's importation of heroin began to decline almost immediately. Dr. Robert L. Dupont, Gerald Ford's Presidential Adviser on Drug Abuse Prevention, in testimony before Congress, wondered: "Why hasn't Southeast Asian heroin come more to the United States than it has?" [U.S. Congress (4)].

Other officials have wondered why Seattle, posed as it was to become the major heroin port of the United States, lost some of its momentum following Nixon's resignation.

The answer, I would suggest, is that with the demise of the Nixon Administration the old established monopoly of Lansky and his associates were able to re-establish their ties and their routes. Trafficante and Rebozo will not have resigned quietly, and indeed there is evidence that in Corsica, France, Amsterdam, and Southeast Asia there is at this moment considerable overt conflict and fighting for control of the international traffic in heroin. Southeast Asian producers have rapidly increased the market for, and their control over, heroin distribution throughout Europe, as one Drug Enforcement Administration officer put it, "from Spain's Costa del Sol to Oslo" [McCoy (28)].

And within the United States the competition is fierce. Turkey is producing opium again. Marseille is once again going at full stream, and the routes through Latin America and Mexico are wide open. Seizures of incoming heroin are down, and while competition is intense the supply is steady.

At the moment there is "chaos in the industry." Southeast Asia has become an unreliable source of opium. Laos, Cambodia, and Vietnam are no longer the distribution and processing centers they were while the American Army was fighting its infamous war. There is still, nonetheless, a large growing area of Burma, Laos, and Thailand where magnificent poppies are produced. There is also a well-worn and heavily used route through Thailand and Burma to heroin factories in Hong Kong. And there are traffickers in the United States—among them Santo Trafficante, Jr.—who are connected with the production and shipping of heroin from Asia. These people are not giving up their control or their profits easily, simply because "their man in the White House" has moved to San Clemente. There is open warfare in Corsica as different elements vie for monopolistic control over the distribution and processing of heroin. There is warfare among competing groups of middlemen in Latin America and Europe (Amsterdam has emerged as a major transfer point for heroin from

Europe to the United States, and Chinese merchants involved in the trade are killing each other—literally). And in the United States the battle for control is taking the form of marshaling political assistance from friendly government politicians as well as eliminating competition wherever and whenever possible. The end is not in sight, but the tendency to monopoly is strong. No one, least of all the police and cooperating politicians, want the war to continue. They, as well as the most powerful executives in the industry, are doing everything possible to bring order into the industry and re-establish a smooth-working monopoly. Exactly who will control the business when the present crisis ends is at the moment problematic. What is not problematic, however, is the state of this industry: it will continue to thrive, to expand, to reap large profits and to support large numbers of law enforcement people, politicians and specialists in illegal business.

The heroin industry is a mainstay of the political economy of much of the capitalist world and it shall not be eliminated any more readily than will the automobile, banking or construction industries.

CONCLUSION

For the user, drugs represent a source of relief from the pains of living: be they physical, as in tuberculosis and leprosy, or mental, as in anguish and ennui. For the seller they represent a source of profit and the satisfaction of "doing business." For the politician they solve some pressing problems: like how to keep some of the unemployed masses happy. For the academic they represent an endless source of data for theorizing.

These and other uses, are at the root of "the drug problem." Given the alarming amount of attention devoted to the subject, one might think that yet another way of analyzing it would be unnecessary. Yet there may be some merit in looking at the historical development of drugs from the perspective of a political economy of law: that is, a look at the political and economic forces that have shaped the laws governing the manufacture, distribution, sale, and technology of the drug industry.

The starting point for this analysis is capitalism as an economic system. Not a particular capitalist nation-state. But capitalism. For it has been the moving force behind the development of the market in drugs, legal and illegal. Inextricably linked to capitalism are various political forms: colonial government, electoral politics, and the emergence of the state, which have also played critical roles.

Opium and its derivatives are particularly interesting because of their intense hold and their long history. The opiates also have a certain smack of intrigue which heightens the joy of investigation while depressing the spirit of humanity. It is not a particularly happy scene but it is nonetheless informative. In the end we can only hope that knowledge will lead to liberation from opiates in all their forms.

FOOTNOTES

1. Paul Takagi writes: ". . . an important reason why opium is found in the areas you specified is because of the supply of a cheap labor force. Opium was cultivated in the United States during the nineteenth century. The morphine content did reach the desired level, around 14 percent, but the cost of labor made the experiment prohibitive. I once calculated the average yield per acre and it comes to around eight pounds. The description of how it is harvested and the amount of time available to do the harvesting gave me the impression that it takes a huge amount of labor. For opium growing in the United States see: Consular Reports, No. 86, Vol. 24, 1887, p. 357; see also *Hunt's Merchants Magazine*, "The Production of Opium in Alabama," 1856, p. 249; and Stephen Holder, "Opium Industry in America," *Scientific American*, 1898, p. 147.

2. Paul Takagi writes: "I have the impression that Whampoa was the international settlement and the 'thieve's den of China' at this time."

3. I am indebted to Paul Takagi for pointing this out to me. He also writes: "Professor Ling Chi Wang at UC-Berkeley says that there are Chinese documents showing that many Chinese who came to the United States were also shanghaied. Robert Schwendinger of San Francisco who is interested in maritime history mentioned to me that he has data from the logs of ship captains indicating the shanghaiing of Chinese workers."

4. Paul Takagi pointed this out to me.

5. Paul Takagi brought this statute to my attention in a letter.

6. See also Alvin Moscow, *The Merchants of Heroin*, Dial Press, New York (1968).

7. For estimates of prices paid by street addicts see Robert A. Gordon and William E. McAuliffe, *American Journal of Sociology*, January 1974.

8. *Fortune Magazine* also publishes an annual review of the profits of America's 500 largest corporations.

REFERENCES

1. Alexander, R. *Narcotics in India and South Asia*, Unwin Brothers, London (1930).
2. Brown, George F., Jr., and Lester R. Silverman, The Retail Price of Heroin: Estimation and Applications, The Drug Abuse Council, Inc., Washington, D.C.: (May 1973).
3. Browning, Frank, An American Gestapo, *Playboy*, February 1976, p. 164.
4. Chambliss, William J., *The Crime Cabal*, forthcoming.
5. Clark, Evert, and Nicholas Horrock, *Contrabandista*, Praeger, New York (1973).
6. Consular Reports, No. 86, Vol 24, 1887, p. 357.
7. Cook, Fred J., *Mafia*, Fawcett, Greenwich, Conn. (1973).
8. to Corporation: A Social Perspective, Swallow Press, Chicago (1974).
9. Cuba Commission. "Report of the Commission Sent to Cuba to Ascertain the Condition of Chinese Coolies in Cuba," *The Cuba-Commission*, The Imperial Customs Press, Shanghai (1876).
10. Dulles, Foster R., *The Old China Trade*, Library Editions, New York (1930).
11. DuPont, Robert L., and Mark H. Greene, "The Dynamics of a Heroin Addiction Epidemic," *Science*, August 24, 1973.
12. Fairbanks, John K., *Trade and Diplomacy on the China Coast*, Harvard University Press, Cambridge, Mass. (1953).

13. Gordon, Robert A., and William E. McAuliffe, *American Journal of Sociology*, January 1974.
14. Gosch, Martin A., and Richard Hammer, *The Last Testament of Lucky Luciano*, Dell, New York (1974).
15. Haley, Arthur, *The Opium War Through Chinese Eyes*, Allen and Unwin, London (1959).
16. Holder, Stephen, "Opium Industry in America," *Scientific American* (1898), p. 147.
17. *Hunt's Merchants Magazine*, "The Production of Opium in Alabama," 1856.
18. Johnson, Bruce, "No Opium Policy Which Is Morally Wrong Can be Politically Right," unpublished manuscript, 1975.
19. King, Harry, *Box Man: A Professional Thief's Journey*, Harper and Row, New York (1971).
20. Koh, T. T. B., "Drug Use in Singapore," *International Journal of Criminology and Penology*, 2, February 1, 1974.
21. Latourette, Kenneth Scott, *The History of Early Relations Between the United States and China 1784–1844*, Yale University Press, New Haven (1971).
22. Lindesmith, Alfred R., *The Addict and the Law*, Indiana University Press, Bloomington (1969).
23. Lubbock, Basil, *The Opium Clippers*, Brown, Son and Ferguson, Glasgow (1933).
24. Lurie, Leonard, *The Running of Richard Nixon*, Coward, McCann and Geoghegan, New York (1972).
25. *The Opium Trail: Heroin and Imperialism*, Free Press, New York (1972).
26. Mazo, Earl, and Stephen Hess, *Nixon*, Harper and Row, New York (1968).
27. McCoy, Alfred W., *The Politics of Heroin in Southeast Asia*, Harper and Row, New York (1972).
28. ———, "Report from the Golden Triangle," unpublished paper, 1976.
29. Messick, Hank, *Lansky*, Medallion Books, Berkeley, Cal. (1971).
30. Moscow, Alvin, *The Merchants of Heroin*, The Dial Press, New York (1968).
31. Owen, David, *British Opium Policy in China and India*, Yale University Press, New Haven, (1934).
32. Purcell, Victor, *The Chinese in Southeast Asia*, Oxford University Press, London (1951).
33. Reich, Charles, "The New Property," Yale Law Journal 63 (1964), pp. 765–782.
34. Sale, Kirkpatrick, "The World Behind Watergate," *New York Review of Books* May 3, 1973.
35. Scott, J. M., *The White Poppy: A History of Opium*, Heineman, London (1969).
36. Sheridan, Walter, *The Fall and Rise of Jimmy Hoffa*, Saturday Review Press, New York (1972).
37. Skinner, G. William, *Chinese Society in Thailand: An Analytical History*, Cornell University Press, Ithaca, N.Y. (1957).
38. Stelle, Clarkson, *Americans and the China Opium Trade in the 19th Century*, unpublished Ph.D. dissertation, Department of History, University of Chicago, 1938.
39. U.S. Congress, *Organized Crime and Illicit Traffic in Narcotics*, Washington, D.C., Senate Committee on Government Operations, 88th Congress, 1964.
40. *U.S. Congressional Reports*, 1938.
41. U.S. Congress, Committee on International Relations, "Proposal to Control Opium from the Golden Triangle and Terminate the Shan Opium Trade," Government Printing Office, Washington, (1975), p. 91.
42. Wen, U. Cheng, "Opium in the Straits Settlements 1867–1910," *Journal of Southeast Asian History*, March 1961, pp. 52–75.
43. Wu, Wen-Tsao, *The Chinese Question in British Opinion and Action*, Academy Press, New York (1928).

ASCRIPTIONS OF DANGEROUSNESS: THE EYE (AND AGE, SEX, EDUCATION, LOCATION, AND POLITICS) OF THE BEHOLDER

John Monahan, UNIVERSITY OF CALIFORNIA–IRVINE

Gloria L. Hood, UNIVERSITY OF CALIFORNIA–IRVINE

Throughout recorded history, and in all known cultures, people have engaged in the process of ferreting out those among them who were dangerous and in need of confinement for the safety of the majority [Dershowitz (3, 4)]. Blackstone himself, author of the libertarian credo "It is better that ten guilty persons escape than that one innocent suffer" held that "preventive justice is upon every principle of reason, of humanity, and of sound policy, preferable in all respects to punishing justice" and that confinement was justified "without any crime actually committed by the party, but arising only from a probable suspicion that some crime is intended or likely to happen" [quoted in Dershowitz (3) p. 26]. Benjamin Franklin successfully argued for the creation of the first mental hospital in the colonies by asserting that the mentally ill were a dangerous class and

Research in Law and Sociology—Vol. 1, 1978, pages 143–151.

therefore subject to preventive confinement. In his petition before the Pennsylvania Assembly he set forth the claim:

> That with the numbers of people, the number of persons distempered in mind and deprived of their rational faculties, has greatly increased in this province; that some of them going at large are a terror to their neighbors, who are daily apprehensive of the violences they may commit [quoted in Deutsch (5), p. 24; see also Monahan & Geis (16)].

Such concern for the identification and confinement of persons believed to be dangerous characterizes much of contemporary criminal and "mental health" law. Indeed, the president of the National Council on Crime and Delinquency has called the identification of persons who reliably can be predicted to engage in dangerous acts "the greatest unresolved problem the criminal justice system faces" [Rector 18, p. 186]. It has also been referred to as "the paramount consideration in the law-mental health system" [Stone (24), p. 25].

There are seven major stages in the criminal justice and mental health systems where an assessment of dangerousness currently can be performed [Shah, (21)]: (1) Decisions regarding the granting of bail to persons accused of crimes, and the level of bail to be set; (2) decisions to waive to adult courts juveniles charged with serious crimes; (3) decisions concerning the sentencing of convicted persons with respect to probation or imprisonment; (4) decisions of whether to invoke special civil proceedings for handling "sexual psychopaths," "defective delinquents," and the like; (5) decisions about the involuntary commitment of persons considered to be mentally ill and a danger to self or others; (6) decisions regarding special legal proceedings or sentencing options for "habitual" or "dangerous" offenders; and (7) decisions of when to release from confinement incarcerated offenders and persons involuntarily committed to mental hospitals. The assessments of dangerousness made at each of these stages are justified as a legitimate prerogative of the police power of the state to protect its citizens [*Harvard Law Review* (8), pp. 1190–1406].

The focus of this paper will be on the definitions of dangerousness—the ascriptions of danger to behaviors—which are the concern of the criminal justice or mental health system. Predictions of dangerousness necessarily presuppose a class of behaviors which serve as a criterion. To predict *who* will be dangerous, we must first have a clear notion of *what* dangerousness is.

At first glance, the definitional issue appears to be an exceedingly simple one: a number of behaviors judged to be unusually harmful to society, and whose occurrence is subject to verification by the judicial process, are by consensus placed in the class of "dangerous." This, indeed, is the tack taken by the F.B.I. in compiling its *Uniform Crime Reports*. Dangerous or violent crimes comprise a class, the members of which are (a) murder, (b) rape, (c) robbery and (d) aggravated assault.

Most legal and mental health definitions of dangerousness, however, fall far short of such precision. Some definitions include destruction of property as well as injury to persons, others include thoughts as well as overt acts. Some courts have ruled that a propensity to commit *any* crime makes one sufficiently dangerous to confine, even if that crime is writing bad checks. Some commitment statutes have defined "dangerous acts" as those which cause "trouble" or "inconvenience" in the community, and others have not defined the acts at all, while still mandating the detention of those who perform them [see Harvard Law Review (8); Monahan (12); and Shah (22) for a review of these definitional vagaries]. One's hopes for a precise legal definition of dangerous acts are not raised by the knowledge that the term "dangerous" derives from a thirteenth-century word meaning "difficult to deal with or please" [Steadman (23)].

Courts have made several attempts in recent years to reduce the ambiguity inherent in concepts of dangerousness [Shah, (22)]. In Millard v. Cameron (9), an indecent exposure case, the U.S. Court of Appeals ruled that "dangerous conduct [must] be not merely repulsive or repugnant but must have a serious effect on the viewer." In Cross v. Harris (1) the same court stated that without a more elaborated judicial framework

> 'dangerous' could readily become a term of art describing anyone whom we would, all things considered, prefer not to encounter on the streets. We did not suppose that Congress had used 'dangerous' in any such Pickwickian sense. Rather, we supposed that Congress intended the courts to refine the unavoidably vague concept of 'dangerousness' on a case-by-case basis, in the traditional common-law fashion (p. 1099).

This investigation will consider how jurors rate various behaviors as to their dangerousness, and how those ratings vary as a function of significant characteristics of the jurors. Jurors were chosen as subjects (rather than judges, psychiatrists, police officers, or parole board members) for two reasons: (1) jurors may *directly* determine what is dangerous, as a finding of fact, in several stages of the legal process (e.g., stages 4, 5, and 6, above); and (2) as representatives of the general citizenry, jurors may *indirectly* determine what is dangerous by establishing the community sentiments and tolerance levels in the context of which other decision-makers (judges, psychiatrists, etc.) make their own ascriptions of danger. Variations in ascriptions of dangerousness as a function of characteristics of persons making the ascription is the topic of the investigation since the charge is frequently made that danger is in "the eye of the beholder" and reflects social and personal value preferences as much as objective estimates of anticipated physical or emotional harm [e.g., Szasz (25); Miller (10); Sarbin (19); and Shah (22)]. To the extent that these biases in the ascription of danger can be assessed through research (rather than merely charged or assumed), steps to remedy those biases or to more narrowly construe the concept of danger may be facilitated [cf. Dershowitz (2); von Hirsch (26)].

METHOD

Legal, criminological, mental health, and popular literature were culled for references to various acts as "dangerous." A list was constructed of the twenty-five items which most frequently appeared to be designated as such. The items were put in a survey format, with respondents asked to answer the question "How dangerous is a person who commits the act?" Each item was rated on five-point scale from "not at all" dangerous to "very" dangerous.

Subjects were taken from the public-information jury rolls in two California counties—San Francisco and Orange. These two areas were chosen to represent the geographic extremes of the political continuum of California, with San Francisco being one of the most liberal counties in the state and Orange being among the most conservative.

One hundred randomly selected jurors in each county were sent a cover letter asking their cooperation in completing a "Criminal Justice Survey." The anonymous survey with an attached sheet requesting data on several background variables (sex, age, educational level and position on the political spectrum) and a stamped return envelope were enclosed.

Responses were received from ninety-seven persons which (excluding nine surveys returned due to a lack of forwarding address) constituted a response rate of 51 percent).

RESULTS

Table 1 presents the 25 items, the mean rating of each on the five-point scale of dangerousness, and the resulting ranking.

Table 2 presents the analysis of the total dangerousness scores (i.e., the scores for all 25 items) by subject variables. Significant effects are found for each of the five comparisons: the older half of the sample ranked the items as more dangerous than did the younger half, females more than males, those without a college degree more than those with a college

Table 1. Mean dangerousness ratings and standard deviations of all surveyed acts

Rank	Act	Mean Rating	S.D.
1	Commits murder	4.82	.52
2	Commits forcible rape	4.78	.65
3	Commits armed robbery	4.70	.63
4	Is a drunk driver	4.48	.80
5	Sells heroin	4.44	1.02
6	Physically abuses his or her children	4.40	.81
7	Commits aggravated assault	4.07	1.11
8	Manufactures unsafe cars	3.98	1.30
9	Uses heroin	3.93	1.67
10	Is a house burglar	3.80	1.04
11	Operates a factory which pollutes the air or water	3.35	1.41
12	Is a store burglar	3.34	1.07
13	Is a car thief	3.06	1.09
14	Sells marijuana	2.88	1.50
15	Engages in corporate price-fixing	2.59	1.42
16	Embezzles from his or her company	2.57	1.21
17	Makes illegal campaign contributions	2.14	1.23
18	Sells pornography	2.13	1.34
19	Has been a patient in a mental hospital	2.10	1.08
20	Is a prostitute	1.72	1.02
21	Uses marijuana	1.68	1.04
22	Is a homosexual	1.60	.99
23	Reads pornography	1.51	.95
24	Is seeing a psychiatrist or psychologist	1.48	.82
25	Illegally gambles	1.45	.83

Table 2. Analysis of total dangerousness scores by subject variables

Variable	Groups	Mean	F^1
Age	Younger[2]	3.01	1.69*
	Older[3]	3.09	
Sex	Male	2.99	1.67*
	Female	3.14	
Educational level	College degree	2.96	1.61*
	No college degree	3.16	
County of residence	San Francisco County	2.98	2.74**
	Orange County	3.13	
Political position	Liberal	2.92	1.61*
	Conservative	3.20	

[1]Computed from Hotellings T^2 (Overall & Klett, 1972); *df*, 25, 71
[2]Median age = 30 years
[3]Median age = 55 years
*$p < .07$
**$p < .01$

degree, persons residing in Orange County more than those residing in San Francisco, and persons describing themselves as "very" or "fairly" conservative in political matters more than those describing themselves as "very" or "fairly" liberal.

An analysis of subject differences by individual items is also informative. A complete presentation of the 25 items by the five-subject variables would be unwieldly. Therefore, we shall restrict ourselves to reporting those differences which achieved statistical significance.

Older persons believed that selling marijuana was more dangerous than did younger people (t = 3.26, df = 97, p < .01). They also believed that operating a factory which pollutes the air or water was less dangerous than did younger people (t = 2.80, df = 97, p <.01).

Gambling was rated as more dangerous by women than by men (t = 2.04, df = 84, p < .05), as was physically abusing children (t = 2.23, df = 88, p < .05), and drunk driving (t = 1.99, df = 97, p < .05).

Persons who have not graduated from college, compared with those who have, give higher dangerousness ratings to former mental patients (t = 2.62, df = 89, p < .05), embezzlers (t = 2.63, df = 96, p < .01), homosexuals (t = 2.24, df = 95, p < .05) and people who use marijuana (t = 2.06, df = 96, p < .05).

Residents of Orange County, California, perceived several acts to be more dangerous than did residents of San Francisco County: car theft (t = 2.69, df = 97, p < .01), reading pornography (t = 2.24, df = 96, p < .05), selling pornography (t = 3.81, df = 95, p < .01), homosexuality (t = 2.70, df = 96, p <.01) and selling marijuana (t = 3.61, df = 95, p < .01). Residents of San Francisco County, however, perceived both making illegal campaign contributions (t = 2.37, df = 89, p < .05) and operating a factory which pollutes the air or water (t = 2.08, df = 97, p < .05) as more dangerous than did those who reside in Orange County.

Finally, self-defined conservatives rated several items as more dangerous than did self-defined liberals: being a prostitute (t = 2.75, df = 54, p < .01), a car thief (t = 2.96, df = 64, p < .01), a homosexual (t = 2.81, df = 56, p < .01), and persons who sell marijuana (t = 3.68, df = 66, p < .01), or pornography (t = 2.24, df = 66, p < .05).

CONCLUSIONS

The three acts rated most dangerous by the subjects in this sample were among the four F.B.I. "violent index crimes," *viz*, murder, rape, and robbery. The fourth index crime, aggravated assault, was ranked seventh in dangerousness, behind drunk driving, sale of heroin, and child abuse. While the high ranking of heroin sale as dangerous is probably related to the belief that heroin is implicated in a variety of other crimes (e.g., robbery to maintain a habit), rather than to its dangerousness per se in affecting people's health, it is somewhat surprising that drunk driving and child abuse ranked as high as they did in terms of public perception of their danger. The law has been notoriously lax in punishing drink drivers, despite the overwhelming data on the havoc they cause [Shah (20)]. Perhaps people are beginning to ascribe to drunk driving the danger that actually is presented by the act. Child abuse has likewise received scant attention by the law, which vacillates between treating it as a criminal or a mental health problem. Again, the danger perceived in child abuse by the subjects of this study is disproportional to the current legal treatment of the behavior.

The consumer movement appears to have made modest inroads in affecting public perceptions of dangerousness. Subjects in this study ranked the manufacture of unsafe cars as more dangerous than heroin use or house burglary; likewise, the operation of a factory which pollutes the air or water was rated as more dangerous than store burglary or car theft (cf. Geis and Monahan (7); Monahan, Novaco and Geis (17).

With the above notation, the rankings of the dangerousness of the various acts generally proceeds in three stages: (1) acts which result in injury to persons (ranked high in danger); (2) acts which result in the illegal appropriation of property or money (ranked medium in danger); and (3) acts which result in harm (if any) only to the person performing them (ranked low in danger).

The variations in the ascription of dangerousness by age, sex, educational level, county of residence, and political position support the position that social values play a substantial role in determining what shall be considered dangerous. In the determination of whether a given person was sufficiently dangerous to be preventively confined in a mental hospital, jail, or prison, it might make a great deal of difference whether the persons making that determination were young, liberal, college-educated males from San Francisco or older, conservative, noncollege-educated females from Orange County. The existence of such variation in the ascription of dangerousness as we have found here would argue in support of judicial and legislative efforts to specify more precisely the kinds of behavior so harmful that their perpetrators—more usually, their predicted perpetrators—should be confined, and to reduce the arbitrariness involved when the very definition of the harms we wish to avoid is held to be a matter of discretion.

Data such as those presented here also have important implications for future research on the topic of dangerousness. The specification of certain behaviors as dangerous for research purposes has been done primarily to study the validity of clinical or actuarial predictions of dangerousness with the common finding that dangerous behavior is vastly overpredicted, regardless of the method of prediction [Monahan (11); Monahan & Cummings (14, 15)]. The fact that definitions of dangerousness vary across age, sex, educational, regional, and political groups suggests two modifications to improve the conduct of future prediction research.

(1) *Multiple definitions of dangerous behavior should be used in assessing the validity of prediction efforts.* With definitions of dangerous behavior varying as widely as they do, it is impossible to compare the results of studies employing different definitions of the criterion event. Rather than seek one agreed-upon definition of dangerous behavior (which, given the nature of researchers, would be fruitless in any event), several hierarchical definitions could be constructed and simultaneously applied to the data, with policy makers and other researchers left to choose the most "appropriate" definition, based upon their own social values.

(2) In research on clinical predictions of dangerous behavior (e.g., predictions by psychiatrists and psychologists), the data presented here underlie *the necessity to achieve a consistency between the "working definitions" of dangerous behavior used by the persons making the predictions and the "research definitions" used by the follow-up researchers.* If a psychiatrist considers house burglary (ranked tenth in dangerousness in this study) to be a sufficiently dangerous behavior to justify detention to prevent its occurrence, and if the follow-up researcher is limiting his or her definition of dangerousness to those items ranked ninth or higher, it would not be surprising that overprediction would be reported. Rather than overprediction, however, this would more properly be a case of unsynchronized definitions. Even if the predictions were perfectly accurate—if those predicted to burgle houses actually committed burglary—the follow-up researcher, using a less inclusive definition of dangerousness, would report them as false positives. The two ways in which this inconsistency could be resolved are to match the follow-up criteria to the working definitions used by the clinicians predicting violence, or to provide the clinicians with the definitions to be used in the follow-up studies and have them predict to those definitions. Given the need for consistency across different prediction studies, as well as within each prediction study, the latter alternative would appear preferable [Monahan (13)].

REFERENCES

1. Cross v. Harris, 418 F. 2d, 1095 (1969).
2. Dershowitz, A., "Preventive confinement: A suggested framework for constitutional analysis," *Texas Law Review* 51, (1973): 1277–1324.
3. Dershowitz, A., "The origins of preventive confinement in Anglo-American law. Part I: The English experience," *University of Cincinnati Law Review* 43 (1974): 1–60.

4. ———, "The origins of preventive confinement in Anglo-American Law. Part II: The American experience," *University of Cincinnati Law Review* 43 (1974): 781–846.
5. Deutsch, A., *The mentally ill in America,* (2nd ed.), Columbia University Press, New York (1949).
6. "Developments in the law: Civil commitment of the mentally ill," *Harvard Law Review* 87 (1974): 1190–1406.
7. Geis, G., and J. Monahan, "The social ecology of violence," in T. Lickona (ed.) *Moral development and behavior,* Holt, Rinehart, & Winston, New York (1976), pp. 342–356.
8. *Harvard Law Review,* "Note," 87, (1974): 1190–1406.
9. Millard v. Cameron, 373 F. 2d 468 (1966).
10. Miller, K., *Managing madness: The case against civil commitment,* The Free Press, New York (1976).
11. Monahan, J., "The prediction of violence," in D. Chappell and J. Monahan (eds.), *Violence and Criminal Justice,* Lexington Books, Lexington, Mass. (1975), pp. 15–31.
12. ———, "The prevention of violence," in J. Monahan (ed.), *Community Mental Health and the Criminal Justice System,* Pergamon Press, New York (1976), pp. 13–34.
13. ———, "The prediction of violent criminal behavior: A methodological critique and prospectus," in Mutual Research Council (ed.), *Deterrence and Incapacitation.* National Academy of Sciences, Washington, D.C., in press.
14. ———, and L. Cummings, "The prediction of dangerousness as a function of its perceived consequences," *Journal of Criminal Justice* 2 (1975): 239–242.
15. ———, and L. Cummings, "Social policy implications of the inability to predict violence," *Journal of Social Issues* 31 (1976): 153–164.
16. ———, and G. Geis, "Controlling 'dangerous' people," *Annals of the American Academy of Political and Social Science* 423 (1976): 142–151.
17. ———, R. Novaco, and G. Geis, "Corporate violence: Research strategies for community psychology," in T. Sarbin (ed.), *Community Psychology and Criminal Justice,* Human Sciences Press, New York, in press.
18. Rector, M., "Who Are the Dangerous?" *Bulletin of the American Academy of Psychiatry and Law* 1 (1973): 197–198.
19. Sarbin, T., "The dangerous individual: An outcome of social identity transformations," *British Journal of Criminology* (July 1967): 285–295.
20. Shah, S., "Some interactions of law and mental health in the handling of social deviance," *Catholic University Law Review* 23 (1974): 674–719.
21. ———, "Dangerousness: A paradigm for exploring some issues in law and psychology. The David Levine Invited Address, American Psychological Association, Washington, D.C., September 5, 1976. (a)
22. ———, "Dangerousness: Some definitional, conceptual, and public policy issues," in B. Sales (ed.) *Perspectives in law and psychology,* Spectrum, New York, in press.
23. Steadman, H., "Some Evidence of the Inadequacy of the Concept and Determination of Dangerousness in Law and Psychiatry, *Journal of Psychiatry and Law,* (Winter 1973): 906–926.
24. Stone, A., *Mental health and Law: A system in transition,* Government Printing Office, Washington, D.C. (1975).
25. Szasz, T., *Law, liberty, and psychiatry,* Macmillan, New York (1963).
26. Von Hirsch, A., "Prediction of Criminal Conduct and Preventive Confinement of Convicted Persons," *Buffalo Law Review* 21 (1972): 717–758.

LAW AND SOCIAL STATUS IN COLONIAL NEW HAVEN, 1639–1665*

M. P. Baumgartner, YALE UNIVERSITY

Law is unevenly distributed in social life. There is, for example, variation in the degree to which individuals invoke the law or are summoned to appear before it, the risks of conviction and of punishment which they run, and the nature of penalties to which they are subject. It has often been suggested that social status is a major predictor of variation of this kind [see, e.g., Carlin *et al.* (8); Chambliss and Seidman (9); Quinney (30); Black (5)]. Most relevant evidence for this claim, however, derives from a limited number of modern societies, and there is a need to evaluate its broader applicability [but see, e.g., Rusche and Kirchheimer (31);

*I would like to thank Donald Black for advice at each stage of the research reported here, Rita J. Simon for comments on an earlier draft of the paper, and the New Haven Colony Historical Society for assistance in the location of the data upon which the study is based.

Research in Law and Sociology—Vol. 1, 1978, pages 153–174.

Garnsey (16); Samaha (32)]. With this end in view, the following is an historical study: It begins with a brief description of seventeenth-century New Haven and its legal system, and then examines the relationship between aspects of law and social status in a colonial court.

THE NEW HAVEN COMMUNITY AND ITS LAW

New Haven was settled in 1638 by a group of English Puritans. A year later, a civil government was established, and, in 1643, the town was joined by several others to form the short-lived Colony of New Haven. In 1665, only a little more than two decades after its formation, the Colony was absorbed into neighboring Connecticut and the town of New Haven entered the jurisdiction of that government. The population of the town ranged from about 800 persons at the time of settlement to a few thousand by 1665 [Atwater (1), pp. 154, 75]. Within this population, there was considerable diversity. Some individuals were much wealthier than others: The richest 25 percent of the town in the early 1640s controlled 70 percent of the wealth, while the poorest quarter owned but one percent [Shumway (33), p. 31]. Some held title to land and had access to property and services communally owned, while others did not. Some were engaged in more prestigious occupations than others, being professionals or merchants rather than farmers, craftsmen, or, lowest of all, common laborers or servants [see Calder (6); Chapter 8; Shumway (33), p. 26]. In addition, some citizens were distinguished by membership in New Haven's Congregational Church and some by political enfranchisement, or freemanship. Finally, some were married and had families while others were single or childless, an important distinction in a community which held marriage and parenthood in high esteem.

New Haven had a reputation for moral stringency, even among other Puritan communities. Social control was exercised by several agents, only one of which was the town court whose records are analyzed below. Family control by the male heads of households, for instance, was strong [see Morgan (25)]. In matters between families, informal sanctions such as gossip, reprimands, and ostracism were routine. Finally, for church members, there was the additional social control of the church itself, including formal sanctions of censure and excommunication [see generally Oberholzer (28)]. Each of these types of control drained potential cases from the court, though little can be known about how many this involved.

The laws of New Haven, like those of other New England colonies, were "a syncretization of biblical precedent and a complex English heritage" [Haskins (21), p. xi]. Although not codified until 1656, in substance they proscribed violent crimes and crimes against property as well as a large array of morals offenses. In civil matters, damages were required for such wrongs as defamation, neglect, endangerment, and failure to repay debt, among others. In addition, there was a large body of ordinances. Generally, then, the scope of law in New Haven was broad.

The present study is based upon the records of the New Haven Particular Court, or Town Court, a court of first instance. Before 1643, when the town consolidated with several others to form the New Haven Colony, this court heard all cases, whether serious or trivial. Thereafter, capital cases and civil cases involving extremely large sums of money were removed from its jurisdiction and channeled to superior courts. The court consisted of a pre-eminent magistrate and four deputies, all equally responsible for the settlement of cases. Their decisions were subject to appeal only in civil affairs. [For an overview of the court system, see generally Levermore (23)]. In matters of procedure, the court was very informal. Trial by jury was unavailable, as were attorneys in the modern sense of paid, professional advocates. Magistrates assumed a prosecutorial stance, questioning witnesses, and, frequently, expressing moral judgments at any stage of the hearing. Standards of relevancy in testimony were broad [see Townshend (40), p. 221], and accused persons might even be convicted and sentenced on the spot for long-past offenses incidentally revealed during their trials for other misdeeds. In all of these regards, the New Haven court exhibited patterns common to the courts of many tribal and other intimate communities [see, e.g., Cohn (10); Gluckman (18); Fallers (14); Nader (26)].

THE COURT RECORDS

The present study analyzes the social characteristics, the issues, and the outcomes in the cases heard before the New Haven Town Court between the years 1639 and 1665. It excludes from consideration routine ordinance violations and estate cases, cases involving juveniles, and the few capital cases heard before 1643, prior to their becoming the concern of higher courts. Since cases involving strangers are subject to separate analysis at the end of this paper, all major generalizations apply to court actions in relation to town citizens. Beginning with the first records of the court, this study concludes with the 1665 absorption of the Colony of New Haven into Connecticut. It is important to end the study with that event, since the merger involved the adoption of Connecticut law, which differed substantively and procedurally from that of New Haven.

Most previous work on early New England law has centered on statute and procedure, especially as these compared to English law of the same period [see, e.g., Goebel (19); Haskins (20; 21)]. By contrast, this study deals with the New Haven court as an agency of social control in the ongoing life of the town, addressing itself specifically to variation in complaints, outcomes in civil and criminal matters, and the nature and severity of sanctions administered. It explains this variation with the social status of the participants, as measured by various features of their location in the social life of the community. An index of social status is used which includes information on two broad aspects of status—vertical location and radial location. Vertical location refers to rank or position in a system of inequality, and radial location to integration into group life [see Black (5), pp. 16–21, 48–49]. For this study, rank is measured by land ownership, sex, and the mode of address accorded an individual, which was determined by his wealth and occupation ("mister" being the highest term of respect, "goodman" an intermediate one, and no honorific title at all an indication of lowest status). Integration is measured by whether or not a person was a church member, a freeman, a spouse, or a parent, and by the number of his children. Since women were rarely landed proprietors and never freemen, their status is measured by that of their family heads on these two attributes, whereas, for all other matters, they are treated independently. Citizens who were of high status on more than half of these dimensions are considered of composite, or overall, high status. Those remaining are of composite low status. For instance, to take extremes, a landowning man referred to as "mister" who belonged to the church, had taken the freeman's oath, and was the head of a large family would be of composite high status, while an unmarried female servant accorded no title of respect and without church membership would be of low status. In addition, citizens who were of high status on any of these dimensions, other than sex, are classified as of partially high status and those high on none, again other than sex, as of completely low status. In the following pages, "high status" and "low status" refer to the composite measures; partially high and completely low status are specified as such.

The court records have been transcribed, edited, and published by Hoadly [Town of New Haven (37)]; Colony of New Haven (11) and Dexter [Town of New Haven (38; 39)]. The summaries of the cases which they contain vary in length, detail, and style with time and with court recorders and outline the parties, issues, proceedings, and outcomes of the cases. In addition, compilations and histories of early New Haven provided relevant, often crucial, supplementary material on the social backgrounds of litigants, which are usually not adequately described in the court records. Especially helpful were the genealogical work of Jacobus (22) and work on church membership by Dexter (13).

ISSUES

During the years 1639–1665, 389 cases involving adult New Haven residents—excluding ordinance and estate matters—entered the town court. The issues in these cases are outlined in Table 1.

Of the total, 38 percent were civil and 62 percent criminal. As in modern courts [see, e.g., Wanner (41), p. 437], most civil suits were brought over a small number of issues. Moreover, as is also true today (41), the most frequent civil complaint in colonial New Haven was debt. Next most frequent was damage inflicted by negligence, overwhelmingly property damage. A standard case in this category might involve the destruction of crops by a neighbor's animals, usually hogs, negligently allowed to roam the fields, or it might involve neglect by cowherds resulting in the loss or

Table 1. Percentage of Cases Brought before the New Haven Town Court, 1639–1665.

	Civil cases	Criminal cases	All cases	Number
CIVIL CASES			38	
Debt	30		12	(45)
Negligence	22		8	(33)
Defamation	17		6	(25)
Breach of contract	10		4	(15)
Miscellaneous	11		4	(16)
Not ascertainable	9		4	(14)
CRIMINAL CASES			62	
Crimes against individuals		35		
Contempt of authority		17	11	(41)
Theft		14	8	(33)
Miscellaneous		4	2	(9)
Morals offenses		45		
Drunkenness		14	9	(34)
Lying		8	5	(20)
Fornication		7	4	(16)
Filthy dalliance		5	3	(12)
Lewdness		7	4	(17)
Swearing		1	1	(3)
Sabbath-breaking		3	2	(7)
Crimes against the public		9		
Disturbing the peace		5	3	(12)
Violation of public duty		1	1	(3)
Miscellaneous		3	2	(7)
General misconduct		11		
All general misconduct		11	7	(27)
Total percent	99	100 100	100 100	
Total cases	(148)	(241) (241)	(389) (389)	(389)

maiming of cattle. Nearly as common as negligence complaints were those charging defamation, while suits for breach of contract were less frequent. Beyond these, a small number of civil cases dealt with miscellaneous issues such as boundary disputes, inheritance disputes, and claims for injuries deliberately inflicted through assault.

There was more variety in the crimes. All criminal matters may be broken down into four categories—offenses against individuals (about a third of total crimes), morals offenses (the largest group at half the total), offenses against the public (a tenth of all crimes), and, finally, general misconduct or nuisance cases (also a tenth of the total). It is interesting to observe the high frequency of morals offense charges, in keeping with the Puritans' reputation for moral stringency. It might be noted that, in general, the distribution of crime was similar to that found in Massachusetts courts of the time [see Powers (29), pp. 404–408].

The large categories of crime may be further broken down. For instance, of offenses against individuals, about half were cases of contempt of authority, including contempt of court. It was true in New Haven as elsewhere in New England that "the official sense of dignity was so punctilious and pragmatical that the magistrates could not bear the slightest criticism" [Weeden (42), p. 79]. "The court was extremely sensitive as to any criticism of its decisions" [Townshend, (40), p. 225]. Next to the authority of the court itself, that of masters in relation to servants was most frequently upheld. Finally, most remaining crimes against individuals were thefts.

Morals offenses covered a wide spectrum of misbehavior, with drunkenness complaints the most numerous, followed by lying, fornication, filthy dalliance (other consensual heterosexual behavior outside of marriage), and lewdness (other illicit sexual behavior). As a general category, in fact, sex offenses were even more common than drunkenness, comprising about a fifth of all criminal cases that appeared before the court, though trials for adultery and bestiality (both capital crimes) generally took place in higher tribunals. In addition, there were small numbers of swearing and Sabbath-breaking cases.

Offenses against the public also took various forms in colonial New Haven, including disturbance of the peace, violation of public duty, and other like delicts. Lastly, there were crimes of general misconduct. Rather than being on trial for the commission of one or two easily described misdeeds, persons accused in this category were found innocent or guilty of a series of annoying acts which together constituted their misbehavior. These were the persons "not fitt to live in the Plantation," since they did not "behave themselves well and righteously amonge their neighbours" [Town of New Haven (38), p. 285]. They were brought into court, for instance, because their children were improperly reared, or because they entertained servants too often, or for "endeavoring to make discord among neighbors," one of the offenses for which Goodwife Bailey was held accountable:

> For her makeing differenc amonge neighbours, she one time came to Goodwife Merri-
> mans, and said Thomas Barnes hath killed many duckes, and intimated that it was not
> kindely done that he gave her none: Goodwife Merriman said, she looked for none;
> then she went to Goodwife Barnes, and intimated to her that Goodwife Merriman was
> troubled that her husband killed so many ducks and gave her none, and the like
> carriage she used betwixt Goodman Barnes and some other of his neighbours about
> some porke wch Thom Barnes had killed [Town of New Haven (38), p. 245].

Offenses of this sort are most likely to be prosecuted in intimate communities. Moreover, it has been observed that people in some societies who commit such offenses and gain reputations as undesirables run high risks of being accused of witchcraft. This applies, for example, to patterns of witchcraft accusation among various tribal people [see, e.g., Wilson (43), p. 104] as well as in seventeenth-century England [Thomas (36), pp. 526–534) and parts of Puritan New England [Demos (12)]. Goodwife Bailey herself, accused of causing dissension among neighbors, was told that she was "very suspitious in poynt of witchcraft. . . ." [Town of New Haven (38), p. 245]. By no means was witchcraft the only possible charge against offenders of this type, however; many were processed as public nuisances of a more conventional type. In Puritan New Haven, good citizenship was an ideal tended by the court as worthy of enforcement in its own right.

THE PARTIES

It is often difficult to tell from the court records which private citizen, if any, complained about a defendant on trial. In a community as small as New Haven, news of misbehavior diffused quickly throughout the town, making a particular complainant superfluous in many instances. This applied, however, only to crimes, since the magistrates took no initiative in civil cases and did not act unless the wronged party demanded redress. In addition, some complaints, both civil and criminal, are lost to history through omissions in the records.

A striking pattern in the cases is the extent to which the court served New Haven's elite. Thus, most identifiable criminal complainants—over three-fourths—were of high status. Although the full significance of this finding cannot be known without information on who was most likely to be victimized, it should be noted that persons of high status comprised only a minority of the total population. On the other hand, the overwhelming majority of criminal defendants were of low status. Similarly, the majority of civil cases for which the complainant is known were initiated by plaintiffs of high status, whereas less than half the civil defendants were high in standing. Comparable differentials in modern society are often partly explained by varying access to and attitudes toward quality lawyers across the classes [see, e.g., Smith (34); Carlin and Howard (7)], but this pattern prevailed in colonial New Haven despite a complete absence of lawyers.

It is also possible to describe the direction of complaints in social space, that is, to describe them as passing from one social location, such as a status, to another [Black (5), pp. 21–24, 49–54]. In the present context there are four possible categories of direction: a high-status citizen against a low-status citizen, a high-status citizen against another high-status citizen, a low-status citizen against another low-status citizen, and a low-status citizen against a high-status citizen. It has been proposed that downward complaints (from a high social position against a person lower in social standing) are more likely than upward complaints in all legal systems (5), and this was true in colonial New Haven (see Table 2).

By far the most common criminal complaint in the New Haven court, representing almost three-fourths of the cases, was that in which a person of high status brought a person of low status to court. Next most frequent were complaints made by low-status citizens against other low-status persons. Equally unlikely were criminal complaints made by either high- or low-status persons against high-status people. In civil matters, most complaints were downward. Slightly fewer in number were complaints passing between two high-status citizens, followed closely by those between two persons of low status. Least frequent were those made by low-status citizens against those of higher social standing than themselves.

Table 2.   Percentage of Cases According to Type of Complaint, by Status of Complainant and Defendant, in the New Haven Town Court, 1639–1665.

Direction of complaint by status	Type of complaint		
	Criminal	Civil	Total
Low against low	18	25	22
Low against high	5	14	10
High against low	71	33	51
High against high	6	28	17
Total percent	100	100	100
Total cases	(103)	(112)	(215)

Since many differences of law are differences of style rather than quantity [see generally Black (5), pp. 4–6], other features of the New Haven cases might be noted as well. For instance, most high-status citizens brought to court were accused of civil wrongs, while most low-status defendants were on trial for crimes (again, see Table 2). At the same time, complainants of high standing usually complained about crimes, but low-status persons, when they complained at all, were more likely to be plaintiffs in civil suits. In terms of direction, the vast majority of complaints made by high-status citizens against others of high status were for civil wrongs, as were those made by low-status individuals against those above them. By contrast, complaints by low-status people against others of their standing were about equally civil and criminal, and most of those brought by high-status citizens against those below them were for crimes. In modern society, high-status persons are more subject to civil law and low-status persons to criminal law [Sutherland (35)], and the patterns of complaint in the colonial New Haven court reveal a similar correlation.

The greater willingness of both high- and low-status persons to complain against high-status defendants in civil cases may reflect differentials in the commission of offense in the community, or it may reflect differentials in the likelihood of a complaint of one type or the other given a similar rate of offense. Which of these explanations is the better, or whether the patterns result from a combination of both factors, could be revealed only by knowledge of the type and amount of victimization in New Haven, irrespective of the court statistics. In any event, however, this does not affect the fundamental social reality revealed by these findings: The civil type of law, compensatory in its style, was more likely to be brought to bear against persons of high status in New Haven than was criminal law, which was disproportionately applied to persons of low social standing. This affinity between the penal style of law and persons of low status, on the one hand, and other less punitive styles and those of high status, on the other, will be seen to have been of great importance in other workings of the New Haven court as well.

LITIGIOUSNESS

The significance of the likelihood that a plaintiff or complainant would be of high status becomes more vivid when an examination of repeat complainants is made. Although some persons have concluded that the early New Englander was a litigious person [e.g., Powers (29), p. 43], it is not clear what the empirical grounding for this assertion is. Nevertheless, it is possible to describe degrees of litigiousness within the New Haven population itself. Of those who used the court at all during the years 1639–

1665, most used it only once. A fourth of the total number of complainants brought two complaints, while about a fifth were responsible for the initiation of three or more cases. The latter group accounted for nearly half of all the complaints received by the court. In addition, a fourth of this group, comprising only 5 percent of all complainants, brought five or more complaints each. They were thus responsible for a fifth of all instances of accusation.

It is clear that the repeat accuser made a large part of the business which the court was called upon to handle. For purposes of the following analysis, all persons who brought three or more cases are considered litigious. In addition, any citizen who brought the same ratio of complaints in relation to his residence in New Haven as did a man who lived there for the entire period 1639–1665 and made three accusations is also considered such in this analysis. That is, if a man averaged one or more complaints every nine years, he was, for these purposes. litigious. This insures that the category of litigiousness is more than an artifact of length of residence.

By this definition, there were 41 litigious people who used the court during the period in question. Since the likelihood of a complaint increased with social status (pages 159–160), it is not surprising that a disproportionate number of litigious people were of higher status [compare, more generally, Galanter (15)]. Over three-fourths of the litigious people in New Haven were of composite high status, and the rest of low standing. In addition, all were of partially high status. In other words, no one without some characteristics of the upper strata was a frequent user of the court.

It might be noted that, in particular, litigiousness in New Haven varied with occupation. Among those litigious people whose work can be determined, the least numerous were ministers and farmers at 7 and 10 percent of the total. This constitutes overrepresentation for ministers and decided underrepresentation for farmers. Next were craftsmen, comprising slightly less than a third of all litigious people. By far the most prominent users of the court were the merchants, greatly overrepresented at half the total. Beyond this, some of the litigious nonmerchants were involved in trade to a degree; some dabbled in it while retaining primary commitment to a craft, while at least one of the litigious farmers had been a London merchant before coming to New Haven. It should be observed that wealth differences alone cannot account for this pattern, since farmers in New Haven were wealthier than the more litigious craftsmen [Shumway (33), p. 30]. Moreover, farmers and craftsmen were not so low in social standing that status could be a sufficient explanation. A person's occupation was independently associated with his use of law in colonial New Haven.

THE COURT'S WILLINGNESS TO SETTLE DISPUTES

It should never be assumed that law is available to all who call upon it for help. Thus, although the New Haven Town Court always honored criminal complaints, many civil complaints were turned away: ". . . the Court itself seemed anxious that disputes should be settled, if possible, out of court" [Levermore (23), p. 143]. "Every possible attempt was made to have parties settle out of Court. They were frequently enjoined by the Court to do so. . . ." [Townshend (40), p. 222]. For example,

> An action was entered by Allen Ball against Jeremiah Whitnell and Jeremiah Johnson for the loss of a cow of his the last Spring, as he conceives by their neglect who kept the heard that day and the Court heard sundrie debates on both sides, and understanding that they had before bine upon some treaty to put it to arbytration, advised them thereunto, to wch they all agreed. . . . [Town of New Haven (38), p. 327].

Or, more succinctly, "A difference betwixt Mr. Craine and Captain Turner refered to bro: Gilbert and bro: Newman to arbitrate" [Town of New Haven (37), p. 41]. Sometimes, the court merely "advised them to agree it themselves" [(37), p. 403]. The major difficulty in this course of action was delay; one plaintiff appeared before the court and explained that in two years the arbitrators had not been able to settle his claim. The court asked him to give arbitration another chance [Town of New Haven (38), p. 230].

Differences in the court's willingness to handle civil suits may be understood as a differential in the amount of law involved across the cases. What predicts lawsuits should therefore predict the court's willingness to hear cases. Thus, it might be expected that the third of all civil cases submitted to outside arbitration would contain a disproportionate number of disputes between low-status parties. But this was not the case: Although high-status persons were more likely to invoke the law, the court was more likely actually to settle the disputes of low-status citizens. In other words, the pattern of referral to outside arbitration was not the same as the pattern of complaint (see Table 3).

Specifically, the court refused to settle over a third of the cases involving two parties of high status. The proportion of disputes between people of unequal status, one high and one low, referred to extralegal arbitration was similar, but the situation for cases brought by two disputants of low social status was different. The court was significantly more willing to hear the arguments and settle the quarrels of two persons of low standing, with only 16 percent of such cases turned aside by the court. To summarize this differently, the court made judgment on the issues presented to it in 64 percent of the civil cases involving two high-status persons, 62 percent of

Table 3.   Percentage of Civil Cases According to Status of Parties,
by Response of Court, in the New Haven Town Court,
1639–1665.

Response of court	Status of parties			
	Low	Mixed	High	Total
Referral	16	38	36	32
Court settlement	84	62	64	68
Total percent	100	100	100	100
Total cases	(32)	(58)	(39)	(129)

those involving two persons of mixed rank, and 84 percent of the cases involving parties of low social standing. There are several possible explanations of this pattern.

It appears, for one thing, that law increases as other social control decreases [Black (4), p. 1108]. This means, for instance, that law is more active in the lives of persons subject to comparatively few alternative means of social control. Since high status in New Haven is itself partly defined by church membership and participation in family life, the quantity of other social control available in these contexts was necessarily greater for higher-status people. Hence, the hesitancy of the court to involve itself in the affairs of persons of high social standing may have been a response to the greater access to other means of dispute settlement which they had.

Another possible explanation may lie in the social relationship between citizens and legal officials in New Haven, since this varied with the status of the citizens. Magistrates in colonial New Haven were always of high status, and so were socially closer to the disputants of high position who appeared before them than to those of low status. Judge and high-status litigant were more likely to be intermarried, to share an occupation, to sit near each other at church services, and to socialize. Together they might steer the course of municipal affairs at town meetings and vote on candidates for admission to the church. In sum, there was little social distance between them. Since law is less likely among intimates than among persons more distant from each other [Black (3), p. 740], the magistrates may have drawn back from cases involving their high-status associates. If this explanation has merit, high-status people in contemporary societies should not be as likely to have their cases turned away by legal agencies, since they no longer have such rich relational ties to most legal agents.

DECISIONS IN CIVIL CASES

The status of participants in civil suits predicts other features of their handling in the New Haven court as well. In their decisions, magistrates had two broad options available to them. They could decide against one or the other of the litigants in the suit, declaring him the loser and supporting his opponent, or they could hand down a compromise decision, finding both parties partially right and granting neither of them full victory. An instance of such compromise occurred when Thomas Powell accused John Punderson of causing the death of one of his cows:

> Thomas Powell declared that John Ponderson (sic) was warned to keepe cows wth the keeper one day, and he attended it so farr as to goe forth wth them in ye morning, but it rained and he returned home and fell to his occasions, and though aboute one a clock it left raining, yet he went not againe to attend his worke in preserving the cattell, so as the heard came home he had a cow swamped, wch was the occasion of her death [Town of New Haven (38), p. 314].

John Punderson countered that the cow was weak and that this was really to blame for her fate. The court decided that plaintiff and defendant were "to beare the loss betwixt them,"

> . . . and so the cow was to be prised by indifferent men chosen betwixt them, who knew the cow the morning she went out, and what was made of her by hide, tallo, or otherwise, being deduckted, the pure neat loss is to be equally divided (38), p. 314.

Of the cases settled by the court, about three-fourths ended with winners declared and the rest with a compromise decision. Considering all civil cases, however, including those sent to outside arbitrators, about half involved the selection of a winner and 15 percent a compromise. As with the court's refusal to handle certain cases, so its willingness to define a winner varied with the social status of the parties (see Table 4).

It was much more likely to seek a compromise if both disputants were of the same status than if they were of mixed status. Thus, of the cases which it settled between two high-status litigants, over a third involved compromise and the rest the selection of a winner. The likelihood of compromise was about the same when the parties were both of low social standing. Between people of different status, however, compromise was far less likely, with only 8 percent of the cases ending in this way. Moreover, the court's greater reluctance to compromise mixed-status cases applied whether the complaint was upward or downward. This is consistent with the suggestion

Table 4.   Percentage of Civil Cases According to Status of Parties,
by Outcome, in the New Haven Town Court, 1639–1665.

Outcome	Status of Parties			
	Low	Mixed	High	Total
Compromise	30	8	36	23
Winner/loser	70	92	64	77
Total percent	100	100	100	100
Total cases	(27)	(36)	(25)	(88)

that conciliation is more likely among equals than among people of different rank [Black (5), p. 30].

Social variables predict not only whether and how a case is handled but also who wins. For instance, it has been proposed that downward complainants are more likely to win than are upward complainants [Black (5), p. 22–23]. Thus, in colonial New Haven, over four-fifths of the winners in all mixed cases were of high status. Downward complaints ended with decisions in favor of the plaintiff 91 percent of the time, whereas the plaintiff won only half of the 8 cases in which a lower-ranking citizen complained about his superior.

In sum, the status of participants in civil suits affected the judicial process in several ways. Persons of high status were more likely than those of low status to be referred to outside arbitration, whatever the status of their adversaries. Disputes between persons of different status more often ended with the declaration of a winner and a loser than did disputes between equals, which were more likely to end with a compromise. Finally, when winners were selected in mixed cases, they were more likely to be of high status than of low status. Overall, these patterns reveal that high-status persons were more immune to law than were those of lower social position.

DECISIONS IN CRIMINAL CASES

The New Haven court was a difficult one in which to win an acquittal of criminal charges: 90 percent of all criminal cases resulted in guilty verdicts, with another 5 percent referred to a higher court. Only 5 percent ended with a verdict of not guilty, and, furthermore, this was often reluctantly given. It should be noted that in modern America most defendants are convicted as well, with about 90 percent bargaining a plea of guilty in return for a lowered charge or penalty [Newman (27)]. In colonial New Haven, however, there were no bargains of this kind, and every criminal complaint was given a full hearing.

As in civil cases, differences in the status of the parties predict outcomes in the criminal cases. Acquittal is a type of victory for the defendant, and high-status people were more often acquitted than were those lower in standing. In fact, the chance of acquittal was some five times as great for a defendant of high social position as for a low-status person (see Table 5). It is also possible to provide another kind of comparison by social status through dividing the criminal defendants into persons of partially high status and those without any characteristics of the elite. This results in a similar, though less extreme, finding (again, see Table 5).

Although the defendant's status by itself predicts his fate in criminal cases, the direction of the criminal complaint, when it can be ascertained, predicts this all the more strikingly. Of those cases in which the complaint issued from a high-status person against a low-status defendant, only one

Table 5.   Percentage of Criminal Cases According to Status of Defendant, by Outcome, in the New Haven Town Court, 1639–1665.

Outcome	Status of defendant		
	Composite low	Composite high	Total
Acquittal	3	15	4
Referral to higher court	5	5	5
Conviction	92	80	90
Total percent	100	100	99
Total cases	(208)	(20)	(228)

Outcome	Status of defendant		
	Completely low	Partially high	Total
Acquittal	3	8	4
Referral to higher court	3	12	5
Conviction	95	80	91
Total percent	101	100	100
Total cases	(153)	(65)	(218)

percent—a single case—ended in acquittal, with 7 percent referred to a higher court and the rest resulting in conviction. This contrasts with the outcomes of cases in which both complainant and accused were of low standing, where 11 percent of the defendants were acquitted, 5 percent referred to a higher court, and 84 percent convicted. As noted earlier, few low-status people complained about those above them. High-status people were accused by those of low status in only five instances; in addition, they were complained of by other high-status people only six times. Of the high-status defendants accused by others equal in standing, all were found guilty. Of those complained against by low-status people, however, three were acquitted, one was sent to a higher court, and only one was convicted. Hence, there were three times as many acquittals in five complaints made by low-status people against those of high status as there were in 73 complaints in the opposite direction.

High-status people were thus very successful in their complaints, whatever the status of their opponents, and, overall, they were more likely to be acquitted than were those beneath them in the status hierarchy. As in the civil cases, then, here too high status conferred an advantage in court.

CRIMINAL SANCTIONS

Sanctions meted out to the guilty also vary with social status [see Rusche and Kirchheimer (31]. Since there were only a few defendants of composite high status tried for crimes in the New Haven court, variations are examined in the sentences of those of completely low and partially high status. These comparisons are made on the basis of a proportionately matched sample of crimes committed by the two ranks. A sample of this kind, containing equal percentages of a variety of crimes for both statuses, serves to hold offense constant in the absence of a sufficient number of cases of any one crime to permit separate analysis.

In New Haven, both the nature of the sanction and its severity differed with the social standing of the convicted. Every type of sanction was different across the strata (see Table 6).

Thus, although punishments of humiliation were not very common in the sample (or, for that matter, in the court at all), when they appeared they were applied to persons of low social standing. No one of partially high status was sentenced to the stocks or to wear locks or halters, for instance, but this happened to about a tenth of the completely low-status defendants. In addition, miscellaneous penalties, such as temporary imprisonment, the posting of peace bonds, and simple multiple restitution for cases of theft, came to a fifth of the sanctions of the higher-status defendants in the sample but did not appear in the punishments of the completely low in status.

Table 6.   Percentage of Matched Sample of Crimes Resulting in Sanction According to Status of Offender, by Type of Sanction, in the New Haven Town Court, 1639–1665.

Type of sanction	Status of offender		
	Completely low	Partially high	Total
Admonition	6	0	5
Humiliation	8	0	5
Corporal punishment	49	20	40
Fine	37	60	44
Miscellaneous	0	20	6
Total percent	100	100	100
Total cases	(63)	(30)	(93)

Admonition alone was given to lower-status persons upon a few occasions, but never to the higher-status people.

As in Massachusetts courts of the time [Powers (29), p. 415], however, the two major sanctions in the New Haven court were fine and corporal punishment: 35 percent of the sanctions administered to all defendants for all crimes were fines and 41 percent were corporal punishments, sometimes combined with fines as well. These varied with status, too, so that whippings were disproportionately inflicted upon those of completely low status and fines more often exacted of the partially high-status people. Magistrates used their considerable discretion in such a way that the likelihood of whipping decreased as rank increased. Specifically, in the matched sample analyzed here, fines accounted for 60 percent of the sanctions given the partially high-status defendants, but only about a third of those given to people of completely low standing. Correspondingly, exactly a fifth of the higher-status citizens received corporal punishment, compared to half of the lower-status ones. Since higher-status persons in New Haven were also less likely to be tried in the first place for crimes which usually elicited corporal punishment, such as morals offenses of all kinds, they were extremely unlikely to receive that sanction. For lower-status persons, the situation was reversed, and whipping was especially likely for them.

Although the style of punishment varied with status, so that physical sanctions were favored for the lowly and fines for more substantial citizens, this was not a simple matter of differential severity. Whether punished corporally or fined, higher-status citizens received more severe degrees of their sanctions. For example, the whippings that partially high-status people did receive for the crimes they committed in the sample were more likely to be designated by the magistrates as "severe." Unlike at least some Massachusetts courts [Powers (29), p. 415], the New Haven court did not specify a certain number of lashes when sentencing, though the law decreed that forty was a maximum. The court did, however, distinguish between whipping and severe whipping. For the group of identical crimes, four of the six whippings given partially high-status defendants were designated severe, while only a third of the 31 inflicted upon completely low-status people were so labeled. Fines also became heavier with rank, though the greater ability of high-status people to afford large fines makes difficult any comparison of the actual deprivation inflicted by monetary penalties on the different statuses. Fines of £1 or less constituted 61 percent of all higher-status persons' penalties, but 83 percent of those given lower-rank defendants. A tenth of the fines of those of higher social standing were greater than £5, while none of the ones demanded of their social inferiors was so high. Finally, and aside from the matched sample under analysis, it should be noted that although no one of composite high status ever received corporal punishment in the New Haven court, the fines which members of this group received were heavier than those demanded of people only partially high in social standing. In sum, the style and severity of sanction fell unevenly across the New Haven citizenry in court.

STRANGERS

In addition to the cases involving only New Haven residents, 33 involved strangers. For this purpose, a stranger is any individual, whether Dutch, English, French, or Indian, who did not reside in the New Haven Colony. (Cases involving residents of the Colony from towns other than New Haven are not considered here or elsewhere in this study.) In the nature of the case, strangers were persons of extremely low radial status, or integration. However well-integrated they might have been in their own home towns, they were at a great distance from the center of New Haven's social life. Beyond this, certain aspects of their vertical status at home, such as land ownerwhip, were less relevant in New Haven. They occupied a far different social position from that of either high- or low-status persons who lived in the town and participated in its daily activities. In this, they were like strangers in all times and places.

In other respects, however, the condition of strangers varies from one society or community to another. In pre-Norman England and in some African kingdoms, for example, strangers in the realm were under the direct protection of the king or chief [Maitland (24), pp. 305ff.; Gluckman (17), p. 216], and thus enjoyed a special status. On the other hand, legal harshness toward strangers has been reported in some rural and primitive social settings [see, e.g., Beidelman (2)]. In New Haven, the court reacted to outsiders in the former fashion, extending certain privileges to them. Despite their low integration, strangers received treatment in the court similar to that received by genuinely high-status natives. They were even, in some regards, treated more like high-status people than were the actual high-status citizens themselves. This was true, however, primarily in their dispositions. When it came to accepting their disputes for settlement, the court related to them in a fashion similar to that used for low-status New Haven residents. It accepted all of these cases, referring none to extralegal modes of control such as arbitration.

Much like the higher strata of New Haven, strangers won nearly all of the lawsuits in which they were involved—six of the seven that they brought against New Haven citizens and two of the four that residents brought against them. Hence, New Haveners stood in relation to strangers as parties of lower status did to those of higher status in disputes among themselves. Further, like stratified disputes, those between strangers and New Haven residents were more likely to be settled with the declaration of a winner than the issuance of a compromise. In fact, there were no compromises in any of the 11 suits involving townsmen and outsiders.

The acquittal rate for the 20 criminal cases with foreign defendants was higher than that for any group of New Haven residents. As mentioned previously, completely low-status persons were acquitted less than 3 percent of the time, people of partially high status 8 percent of the time, and those of composite high standing 15 percent of the time. Strangers, by contrast, were acquitted in 25 percent of their trials. Even when convicted and sentenced, they received treatment like that accorded natives of high standing. Thus, over half of the punishments inflicted upon strangers were fines, but less than a third were corporal punishments. These percentages are similar to those for persons of partially high status in New Haven. In addition, such whippings as were received by strangers, like those given higher-status New Haven citizens, were often severe, with two of the four they received so specified by the court. Their fines tended to be large as well.

Finally, there were two instances of criminal complaint brought by strangers against New Haveners, both of which issued from Indians and both of which were successful. The special concern of the court with the treatment of outsiders is shown in the handling of a white settler accused by an Indian of stealing venison he had killed. The magistrates were harsh, explaining their severity with the nature of the victim, in that the settler

had done it to an indian, & to a poore indian, & when himselfe had noe need of it & soe often denieing it etc. Whereby he makes the English & their Religion odious to the heathen & thereby hardens them [Town of New Haven (39), p. 77].

SUMMARY

The main findings of this study may be summarized in the following generalizations. First, in colonial New Haven high-status citizens initiated a disproportionate number of legal cases, both civil and criminal, while low-status citizens were more likely than their high-status neighbors to have complaints brought against them. The most frequent complaint involved a high-status complainant and a low-status defendant; the least frequent was the reverse. Beyond this, the most litigious people were of high status, and merchants were most litigious of all.

In civil disputes, cases involving at least one high-status individual were more likely than those involving two low-status parties to be referred to outside arbitration. When the court did decide a civil case, disputes between equals of any status were more likely than disputes between persons of different status to end with compromise, and when it selected a winner in the context of a mixed-status dispute, the high-status party was likely to win. In criminal cases, the chance of acquittal increased with status. In regard to sanctions, high-status citizens were more likely to be fined, low-status citizens to receive corporal punishment. When given corporal punishment, however, high-status citizens were more likely to have their whippings designated severe; their fines were also heavier, though not necessarily greater deprivations. Finally, the New Haven court treated strangers in a manner similar to that usually accorded those of high status.

In several ways, then, law varied with social status in colonial New Haven. This provides some corroboration for claims that similar patterns occur in every legal system. More studies are needed, however, before such general propositions will be established beyond question.

REFERENCES

1. Atwater, Edward E., *History of the Colony of New Haven to Its Absorption into Connecticut,* Private Printing, New Haven (1881).
2. Beidelman, T. O., "Intertribal Tensions in Some Local Government Courts in Colonial Tanganyika: II," *Journal of African Law* 11 (Spring 1967): 27–45.
3. Black, Donald, "Production of Crime Rates," *American Sociological Review* 35 (August 1970): 733–748.
4. ———, "The Social Organization of Arrest," *Stanford Law Review* 23 (June 1971): 1087–1111.
5. ———, *The Behavior of Law,* Academic Press, New York (1976).
6. Calder, Isabel MacBeath, *The New Haven Colony,* Yale University Press, New Haven (1934).
7. Carlin, Jerome E., and Jan Howard, "Legal Representation and Class Justice," *UCLA Law Review* 12 (January 1965): 381–437.
8. ———, ———, and Sheldon L. Messinger, "Civil Justice and the Poor: Issues for Sociological Research," *Law and Society Review* 1 (November 1966): 9–89.

9. Chambliss, William J., and Robert B. Seidman, *Law, Order, and Power*, Addison-Wesley Publishing Company, Reading (1971).

10. Cohn, Bernard S., "Some Notes on Law and Change in North India," *Economic Development and Cultural Change* 8 (October 1959): 79–93.

11. Colony of New Haven, *Records of the Colony or Jurisdiction of New Haven from May, 1653 to the Union: Together with the New Haven Code of 1656.* Transcribed and edited in accordance with a resolution of the General Assembly of Connecticut by Charles J. Hoadly. Case, Lockwood and Company, Hartford (1858).

12. Demos, John, "Underlying Themes in the Witchcraft of Seventeenth-Century New England," *American Historical Review* 75 (June 1970): 1311–1326.

13. Dexter, Franklin Bowditch (compiler), *Historical Catalogue of the Members of the First Church of Christ in New Haven, Connecticut (Center Church): A.D. 1639–1914.* Private Printing, New Haven (1914).

14. Fallers, Lloyd A., *Law without Precedent: Legal Ideas in Action in the Courts of Colonial Busoga*, University of Chicago Press, Chicago (1969).

15. Galanter, Marc, "Why the 'Haves' Come Out Ahead: Speculations on the Limits of Legal Change," *Law and Society Review* 9 (Fall 1974): 95–160.

16. Garnsey, Peter, "Legal Privilege in the Roman Empire," *Past and Present: A Journal of Historical Studies* 41 (December 1968): 3–24.

17. Gluckman, Max, *The Ideas in Barotse Jurisprudence*, Manchester University Press, Manchester (1965).

18. ———, *The Judicial Process among the Barotse of Northern Rhodesia*, (2nd edition; 1st edition, 1955), Manchester University Press, Manchester (1967).

19. Goebel, Julius, Jr., "King's Law and Local Custom in Seventeenth Century New England," *Columbia Law Review* 31 (March 1931): 416–448.

20. Haskins, George Lee, "The Beginnings of Partible Inheritance in the American Colonies," *Yale Law Journal* 51 (June 1942): 1280–1315.

21. ———, *Law and Authority in Early Massachusetts: A Study in Tradition and Design*, (2nd edition; 1st edition, 1960), Archon Books, Hamden (1968).

22. Jacobus, Donald Lines, *Families of Ancient New Haven*, Genealogical Publishing Company, Baltimore (1974); originally published as *New Haven Genealogical Magazine* 1–8 (1922–1932).

23. Levermore, Charles H., *The Republic of New Haven: A History of Municipal Evolution*, Johns Hopkins University Press, Baltimore (1886).

24. Maitland, Frederic William, "The Early History of Malice Aforethought," pp. 304–328 in *The Collected Papers of Frederic William Maitland*, Cambridge University Press, Cambridge (1883).

25. Morgan, Edmund S., *The Puritan Family: Religion and Domestic Relations in Seventeenth-Century New England* (2nd edition; 1st edition, 1944), Harper and Row, New York (1966).

26. Nader, Laura, "Styles of Court Procedure: To Make the Balance," pp. 69–91 in L. Nader (ed.), *Law in Culture and Society*, Aldine Publishing Company, Chicago (1969).

27. Newman, Donald J., "Pleading Guilty for Considerations: A Study of Bargain Justice," *Journal of Criminal Law, Criminology, and Police Science* 46 (March–April 1956): 780–790.

28. Oberholzer, Emil, *Delinquent Saints: Disciplinary Action in the Early Congregational Churches of Massachusetts*, Columbia University Press, New York (1956).

29. Powers, Edwin, *Crime and Punishment in Early Massachusetts, 1620–1692: A Documentary History*, Beacon Press, Boston (1966).

30. Quinney, Richard, *Critique of Legal Order: Crime Control in Capitalist Society*. Little, Brown, Boston (1974).

31. Rusche, Georg, and Otto Kirchheimer, *Punishment and Social Structure*, Russell & Russell, New York (1968).
32. Samaha, Joel, *Law and Order in Historical Perspective: The Case of Elizabethan Essex*, Academic Press, New York (1974).
33. Shumway, Floyd Mallory, *Early New Haven and Its Leadership*, Unpublished Doctoral Dissertation, Department of Political Science, Columbia University (1968).
34. Smith, Reginald Heber, *Justice and the Poor: A Study of the Present Denial of Justice to the Poor and of the Agencies Making More Equal Their Position Before the Law, with Particular Reference to Legal Aid Work in the United States*, The Carnegie Foundation for the Advancement of Teaching, Bulletin 13, New York (1919).
35. Sutherland, Edwin H., "White-collar criminality," *American Sociological Review* 5 (February 1940): 1–12.
36. Thomas, Keith, *Religion and the Decline of Magic*, Charles Scribners' Sons, New York (1971).
37. Town of New Haven, *Records of the Colony and Planatation of New Haven from 1638 to 1649*. Transcribed and edited in accordance with a resolution of the General Assembly of Connecticut by Charles J. Hoadly, Case, Tiffany, and Company, Hartford (1857).
38. ———, *Ancient Town Records, Vol. I: New Haven Town Records 1649–1662*. Edited by Franklin Bowditch Dexter for the New Haven Colony Historical Society. Printed for the Society, New Haven (1917).
39. ———, *Ancient Town Records, Vol. 2: New Haven Town Records 1662–1684*. Edited by Franklin Bowditch Dexter for the New Haven Colony Historical Society. Printed for the Society, New Haven (1919).
40. Townshend, Henry H., "Judicial Administration in New Haven Colony Before the Charter of 1662," *Connecticut Bar Journal* 24 (June 1950): 210–234.
41. Wanner, Craig, "The Public Ordering of Private Relations. Part One: Initiating Civil Cases in Urban Trial Courts," *Law and Society Review* 8 (Spring 1974): 421–440.
42. Weeden, William B., *Economic and Social History of New England. Vol. I: 1620–1789*, Houghton Mifflin, Boston (1891).
43. Wilson, Monica, *Good Company: A Study of Nyakyusa Age-Villages*. Beacon Press, Boston (1963).

JUSTICE, VALUES AND SOCIAL SCIENCE: UNEXAMINED PREMISES[1]

Edward Seidman, UNIVERSITY OF ILLINOIS AT

URBANA–CHAMPAIGN

Reviewing contemporary social science research literature and participating in recent meetings and discussions of social policy with regard to law and criminal justice, I have experienced a gnawing feeling of discomfort and disillusionment. As I have attempted to pin down the source of my emotional reaction, I have come to recognize that most of the research and theorizing perpetuates the status quo. Specifically, it seems to do little more than reify existing legal and criminal justice policies, practices, and inherent values. Often the process is both insidious and unwitting. This paper is an initial effort to understand the nature of that process by unraveling its intertwining elements.

To begin, the process itself will be more clearly explicated through the use of several intriguing notions developed by other writers [Mitroff and

Research in Law and Sociology—Vol. 1, 1978, pages 175–200.

Turoff (22); Watzlawick *et al.* (34)] which separately and together provide a metaperspective to understand the selection and formulation of the "wrong" problem. I shall refer to such problem selection and definition as an *error of conceptualization*. In the second section, the determinants or unexamined premises facilitating the selection and formulation of the "wrong" problem will be analyzed. In the third and final section, an initial set of guidelines will be put forth as an attempt to move social scientists toward awareness of the multitude of pathways available to us even at the point of problem selection and definition. I hope this will stimulate development of a more refined set of guidelines that will eventually force us to make our choices more wittingly.

In an effort to concretely demonstrate the points discussed in each of the following sections, I will employ two contemporary areas of legal and criminal justice research—behavior modification and social indicators. A third fully encapsulated example concerning juvenile delinquency is presented later in the paper to highlight and further clarify the issues, processes, consequences, and alternatives being discussed (see Table 1). I have chosen these examples both for the diversity of their content and because I have some familiarity with them. Their selection is not meant to cast aspersions on investigations of the particular type they exemplify, any more than numerous others which I have not chosen as examples of which I am uninformed. One important thesis of this paper is that if one were to critically examine the bulk of research on law and criminal justice in the ways being discussed here, the identification of unwitting errors of conceptualization would be seen to occur frequently.

PROBLEM SELECTION, FORMULATION AND ITS CONSEQUENCES

At the most general level, one salient set of intended goals and objectives for social scientists engaged in law and criminal justice research is the enhancement of social welfare, equity and justice. The major thesis put forth for examination is that while this set of objectives may ostensibly represent the *intended* outcomes, more often than not the functional result is quite the opposite. A number of writers, for example Runkel and McGrath (27), have conceived of the scientific process as akin to the process of problem solving. Based on this notion, the alternatives at each successive choice point in the scientific enterprise following problem selection and definition (i.e., design, operational plan, observations, and so on) are increasingly curtailed. Since the manner in which an issue is addressed is seriously circumscribed by its initial selection and formulation [Caplan and Nelson (4); Mitroff and Turoff (22); Rappaport (26);

Sjoberg & Miller (33)], the focus of this paper is on that first step. As Caplan and Nelson have so aptly stated:

> The social scientist who becomes "relevant" seldom questions already established problem definitions, or the wisdom behind the process that leads to the identification of so-called social problems. Nor does he question whose ends are served by the entire definitional process and by his participation in that process. Instead he waits in the wings until the problems have been selected for attention. Only then does he become involved, as if accepting as given that (a) whatever becomes identified publicly as a social problem is a genuine problem, derived from universally recognized truths; and (b) the problem is of such priority that it deserves attention over other problems that go unattended or unrecognized (4), pp. 206–207.

Those who formulate research and social policy in criminal justice are not immune from the influences described by Caplan and Nelson. Blumberg has recently delineated twelve properties which he sees as characteristic of modern criminology. Among these, one and its corollary are of particular interest in this context:

> Criminologists recognize that they constitute an interest group that seeks access to funds, resources, and official patronage of the very groups they wish to study, and that a price will be exacted for this institutional respectability. As a corollary . . . they recognize that they have a vested interest to some degree in existing social arrangements in that they share some of the benefits along with the police, prison, parole, probation, and other crime control functionaries (1), p. 31.

What Blumberg (1) makes clear is that the values and goals of the parenting criminal justice organizations contribute a great deal to the selection and definition of a problem, even before the criminologist enters the picture. What I am suggesting is that the social scientist in collaboration with representatives of the judicial or crime control organizations agree, often unwittingly and usually for unexpressed reasons, to solve some problem before they have considered if it is the "right" problem. This situation increases the likelihood that the scientist will, almost before realizing it, select the "wrong" problem. Mitroff and Turoff (22) have aptly titled this mistake an *error of the third kind* or E_{III}. They discuss E_{III} as an error of conceptualization, one of the most important errors associated with the problem-solving process.

From what at first appears to be a dramatically different perspective (i.e., psychotherapy and behavior change), Watzlawick, *et al.* (34) utilize several mathematical theorems to understand the solution of the "wrong" problem.[2] Following their lead let me present a classical illustration.

Figure 1.   Nine-dot problem[1]

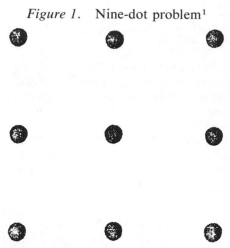

[1]*Source:* Watzlawick, *et al.* (34), p. 25.

Above you will find an arrangement of nine dots. Your task is to connect the nine dots with four straight lines without lifting the pencil from the paper. If you have never done it before, try it.

> Almost everybody who first tries to solve this problem introduces as part of his problem solving an assumption which makes the solution impossible. The assumption is that the dots compose a square and that the solution must be found *within* that square, a self-imposed condition which the instructions do not contain. His failure, therefore, does not lie in the impossibility of the task, but in his attempted solution. Having now created the problem, it does not matter in the least which combination of four lines he now tries, and in what order; he always finishes with at least one unconnected dot (34), p. 25.

Whether through the self-imposed or implicit acceptance of the premise that the nine dots compose a square, the problem solver is inhibited from examining this very salient premise. Thus, the problem solver has accepted and addresses the "wrong" problem. There is no way out of this bind until one alters or questions what appears to be the "given." Ignoring, failing to accept, or changing the assumption that the nine dots need compose a square might lead one to the solution presented in Figure 2.

Solutions which accept implicit but unnecessary assumptions are referred to as *first-order change* and are derived from the mathematical Theory of Groups. This refers to change that can occur within a system that itself stays invariant. But as we have seen in the nine-dot problem, the solution cannot be found within the system as it first appears. *One*

Figure 2. The solution of the nine-dot problem[1]

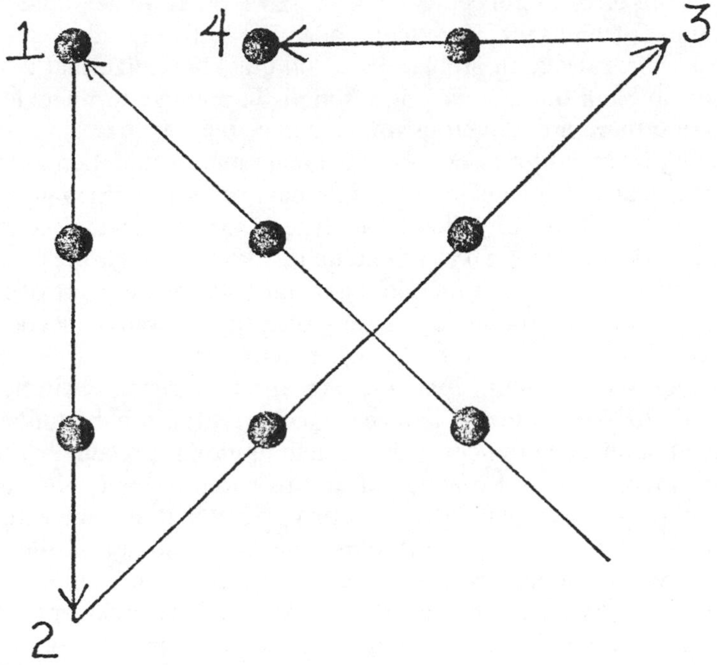

[1]*Source:* Watzlawick, *et al.* (34), p. 27.

*must instead ask what the rules, assumptions, or premises of the game
are. Now seen from outside the system, the solution requires a change of
the premises, rules, or assumptions governing the system as a whole.* This
is referred to as *second-order change*, derived from the mathematical
Theory of Logical Types. The Theory of Logical Types is not concerned
with what goes on inside a class, i.e., between its members (dots), but
gives us a frame for considering the relationship between member and
class and the peculiar metamorphosis which is in the nature of shifts from
one logical level to the next higher. These authors go on to point out that if
we accept this basic distinction between the two theories, it follows that
there are two different types of change: one that occurs within a given
system which itself remains unchanged, and one whose occurrence
changes the system itself, i.e., the body of rules governing the system's
structure. The rhetoric of most policy studies suggests that criminal justice policy analyses should be aimed at second- not first-order change.
This requires that the social policy analyst step outside the system. When
the distinction between member and class is obscured or ignored, an *error
of logical typing* is committed. Consequently, the attempt might be to
solve the "wrong" problem (e.g., a first- versus a second-order solution).

Let us refer to this error of logical typing or error of the third kind more simply as an error of conceptualization. If we try to understand the precise nature of an error of conceptualization with regard to a legal or criminal justice research problem, we will quickly realize that unlike the nine-dot problem there is no single simplistic premise to uncover or expose. Here there are numerous unexamined rules, values, and premises originating from multiple sources that create and/or maintain an error of conceptualization. Several important domains of unexamined premises or determinants will be more closely analyzed in the following section. But first, let us return to the areas of exemplification noted earlier in order to illustrate what is meant at the most general level by an error of conceptualization and how the understanding of a first- versus a second-order solution helps to clarify the nature of such an error.

Behavior modification, conducted in either a penal institution or a community-based setting, is avowedly aimed at the rehabilitation of the convicted or alleged offender. While rehabilitation is presumably the goal of those involved in the practice of and research on behavior modification, the society as a whole views our correctional system with mixed objectives. Some see its primary objective as punishment, others deterrence or rehabilitation, and still others as varying combinations of these attributes. Rehabilitation implies the reshaping of the prisoner to live and work independently in the community on his/her return, without repeated criminal offenses. The focus of change is seen as the individual offender. Furthermore, it follows logically from the prior statement that the individual is implicitly assumed to be the source of the problem—criminal activity. Centuries of theorizing and decades of research have neither definitively confirmed nor refuted this implicit, philosophical and value-based premise, nor should we realistically expect it to. In any case, the implicit assumption of either a rehabilitative, punishment, or deterrent view is the same; that is, crime is viewed as caused by individual "deviants." The functional outcome of this view can only be more of the same, or a first-order solution in which new techniques are employed to attain old ends—social control—more effectively [Davidson and Seidman (6)]. (For example, even within a correctional facility it is not uncommon that behavior modification research and practice are only conducted on the most recalcitrant inmates.) Thus, behavior modification and other therapeutically oriented schools of research and practice have and continue to function as "benign" agents of social control. Functionally, they agree with the often implicit premise that the individual is the source of the problem; this is the error of conceptualization. Parenthetically, it is particularly paradoxical that behavior modification research functionally treats the individual as the source of the difficulty and as the focus of change, since it is theoretically based on an environmental conception of human behavior.

Without a struggle to break out of our usual modes of thinking and acting, it is quite difficult to understand how or why this might not be the problem to address (as the square seemed to be in the nine-dot problem). If we were to ask whether there are other conceptualizations possible regarding the rules, assumptions, or premises of criminal activity, we are on the road to developing different conceptualizations, including, perhaps, one that addresses the "right" problem. As I see it, the intended outcome of policy-oriented research should be an alteration of the social system itself. Attempting to change individual "deviants" helps maintain the social system in an unchanged fashion; it is a first-order change. If one were to step outside the system and look, as Watzlawick, *et al*. (34) imply, at the relationship between the identified target group of individual "deviants" and the larger society, instead of exclusively within the group of so-called deviants, a novel conceptualization might become apparent. This could lead to a second-order change. A specific example of such a reformulation will be presented in the final section.

As a second specific example, consider the research on social indicators. The ostensible goal of social indicators research is to improve the quality of life of individuals and the social well-being of the community. Researchers in this area generally seek to understand the effects of various types of public investment upon the latter objectives. Social indicators research, as it pertains to the area of law and criminal justice, has public safety, a euphemism for crime control, as its major goal. When we move to the actual use of this research for social policy formulation, the objective of establishing an optimal relationship between public safety and expenditures overshadows the more diffuse and general objectives. Herein lies the fundamental unexamined premise and consequently an error of conceptualization. Striving for the optimal point of maximization, if successful, guarantees the long-run maintenance of homeostasis and the status quo. Such a negative feedback mechanism insures only within system variations (first-order changes), simultaneously precluding change of the system itself. No significantly new answers are likely to occur from framing the question based on the rule of optimal maximization. Again, in the final section a reformulated conception will be presented.

While the specific errors of conceptualization identified in each of the preceding examples differ somewhat, they can each be culled from an analysis of the unexamined premises, assumptions, values or rules. On occasion, these premises receive some attention but it appears to be only pro forma consideration; they are rarely seriously questioned or challenged. One negative long-range consequence common to both areas is that the process of continually investigating each area based on the pre-existing problem formulation reifies that endeavor and the error of conceptualization in particular. In this society, that usually serves to preclude the investigation of alternative conceptualizations.

DETERMINANTS FACILITATING AN ERROR OF CONCEPTUALIZATION

What are the assumptions, rules, premises, and/or antecedents that lead to an error of conceptualization, and make it difficult to recognize such an error in the field of criminal justice policy analysis? Two key sources of the error of conceptualization have been highlighted by Caplan and Nelson (4) in an article primarily addressed to the discipline of psychology, but which is equally applicable to other disciplines.

> By investigating a social problem in terms given him, a *mutually beneficial exchange relationship* is established: the researcher is rewarded both materially and in terms of prestige (in addition to remaining a "proper member of the group") by using the tools of his trade; while on the other side of the exchange, officialdom stands to have its preferred interpretation buttressed by the respectability of "scientific data" (4), p. 206.

This quotation highlights the mutual interdependence of two determinants—the researcher and officialdom (i.e., the parenting agency of the social policy research)—involved in an error of conceptualization. In addition, two other determinants need consideration: the dominant values of our society and constituents (or recipients) of criminal justice policies (or programs). The researcher will be considered more broadly under the subheading of *Social Science*. These four major determinants will be presented in the following order: dominant societal values, officialdom, social science, and constituents. Despite the obvious fact that the determinants are mutually interrelated and causal, they are presented separately for ease of explication. The discrete and sequential structure of this presentation should not obscure these interrelationships.

Dominant Societal Values

Sjoberg (31) has noted that social scientists have too often accepted the power structure's definition of what is right and what is wrong. Both social science and officialdom naturally embody this value system in their daily functioning. Consequently, these societal values constrain the problem formulation. For example, the notion of individual motivation and responsibility has always been a cherished, dominant, and pervasive value in this society. It is at the root of our legal and constitutional structures. It has led to what Caplan and Nelson (4) and Ryan (28) among others have referred to as a person-centered causal attribution bias or "victim blaming" ideology. This refers to the tendency to find individuals responsible for their own problems, despite the antecedent and contextual economic, social, and political factors. This is part of a larger set of social processes in which our institutions work toward the socialization of almost everyone to a "single standard," and those who fail to behave in conformity with the norm are labeled as deviant [Rappaport (26); Ryan (28)]. As we shall see, neither the scientist, decision maker, nor anyone else is immune from these values and biases.

In addition to the tendency toward victim blaming, the dominant cultural groups in Western society hold in high esteem the value of pragmatism and rationality with regard to personal, organizational, and institutional functioning. This is accomplished by a quantitative supply-and-demand orientation with a tendency to convert cultural, social, and psychological considerations into monetary values.

As indicated in the earlier discussion of behavior modification in corrections, the premise that the individual is not only the culprit, but also the proper focus of change, is central to research and practice in the area. As expressed by the man on the street, it reads, "I did it the hard way (i.e., worked, did not steal) and made it . . ." If one is only minimally familiar with behavior modification research, its pragmatism should be apparent. In many token economy programs "good" behavior is rewarded by tokens having direct monetary purchasing power.

While superficially the premise of individual responsibility seems less apparent in the social indicators research, one need only recall that a goal of such policy research is to more effectively control crime via increased police power, hardware, etc. The pragmatism, quantitative supply-and-demand orientation, and conversion of social and psychological factors into monetary values by such research is based to a large extent on economic models and needs no further elaboration. These illustrations have crystallized how the dominant societal values substantially determine and curtail the selection and formulation of social science research problems.

Officialdom

The stated goals and values of an organization established for the enhancement of criminal justice usually have to do with improving human and social welfare, equity, etc. This goal may be expressed in attempts to adequately or efficiently achieve certain program objectives; but it is implicitly assumed that the attainment of such objectives would in no way bring the death of that agency. This is not hard to understand, in that entertainment of such a possibility threatens the very administrators who have, to say the least, a vested interested in maintaining their jobs, status, and power. The question of how an agency can attain its lofty objectives usually means, "How can we more adequately or efficiently, by doing what we already know how to do, attain these objectives and maintain, or better yet increase, the quantity and quality of our jobs, status, and power?"

Any organization will find it inordinately difficult to change, if change implies an alteration in the nature of its role relationship with clients or constituents [Fairweather (8); Watzlawick, et al. (34)]. A change in role relationship means a change in the ongoing pattern of transactions; thus, if one party consistently made the decisions and the other party conformed, an altered role relationship would result if they now alternately shared the decision-making role. An analysis of the functioning of any social system from a general system's theory perspective would lead us to a similar recognition [Buckley (2, 3)]. In this way, a hidden agenda severely constrains the scope of the particular problem formulation, from the point of view of agency officials. Consequently, a second-order solution, one which. requires a shift in relationships, will not be logical or feasible from their point of view. Parenthetically, we cannot ignore the fact that this publicly funded organization may only be interested in collaborating with the social scientist to "improve" their functioning in order to appease or, more specifically, to get the funding source "off their back." This also enables the organization to appear "accountable," to have its preferred mode of operation buttressed by the respectability of scientific data.

Beyond the question of vested self-interest, there is a second more subtle factor which contributes to an error of conceptualization. Most program managers and decision makers, as indicated above, hold to the dominant cultural theme of attributing responsibility to individuals. The acceptance of person-blame explanations for deviance tends to turn the program managers away from a social policy which looks outside the individual and focuses on the social system. This, then, interacts with their own vested interests to allow first-order change and prohibit second-order change.

Most individuals receiving correctional services have endured a powerless role, in terms of access to and availability of material and psychological resources, for most of their life. Placement in a behavior modification program maintains the representatives of authority in a position of dominance and concomitantly keeps the prisoner in his/her place, that is, down, but more systematically and effectively. It is not unlikely that such programs reinforce, as opposed to change, the already powerless feelings and actions which may lead the person to further criminal activity. The unfortunate consequence of this process is that the victims are again blamed and with greater vehemence—"See how bad they are; we invested all this money . . . ; just lock 'em up." The system remains invariant since role relationships between different social statuses remain unchanged.

Aside from providing officialdom with increased control, power and easier jobs, their involvement in avowedly rehabilitative programs make them appear committed to the rehabilitation of offenders and their successful return to the community. Returning prisoners to the community in any substantial number would jeopardize the very jobs of these employees. This unlikely desire has occasionally been exposed for what it is when the intention to close such an institution has been made public. In such instances the political and economic issues maintaining the institution raise their "head" and guarantee the institution's continued existence. Thus a continual influx of prisoners is essential. The result must be first- rather than second-order change.

For the salient institutional structures, research on social indicators permits them the luxury of appearing accountable, being concerned about the improvement of human welfare, and requires little additional effort on their part. Often, the outcome of such research is not unlikely to be demonstrative of their need for additional resources to "control crime."

In summary, we have seen how the self-interests, threat of altered role relationships, and dominant societal values converge to severely restrict the research questions an agency is willing to collaboratively address.

Social Science

The social scientists themselves are no less immune, nor value-free, than the program managers or policy makers [for one discussion of this see Gouldner (12)]. They often share the same person-centered causal attribution biases, as well as a concern with their own vested interests. More often than not, they accept as given the premise that individual performance is a function of individual motivation and responsibility. In fact, the outcomes of many research investigations have, implicitly or explicitly, given credence and scientific respectability to such biases among the lay public, program managers, and politicians, precisely because of the assumptions inherent in problem definition. That is, the assumptions inherent in the social scientist's definition of a particular problem cause one to structure the question in a fashion that frequently leads to a verification of those inherent biases—victim blaming. Thus, as Green (14) has indicated, officialdom's "sponsorship can only emphasize the existing tendency in the social sciences to concentrate attention on the personality structures of the least influential of all constituents" (p. 18).

At this point it would be helpful to recall the behavior modification and social indicator illustrations of how the dominant societal values of pragmatism, rationality, quantitative supply-and-demand orientation, and tendency to convert cultural, social and psychological consideration into monetary values are accepted by the social scientist and consequently constrain problem selection and formulation.

What additional factors interact with these societal values to further constrain the definition of problems addressed by the social scientist? Several major factors can be culled from what Moore (24) has called the "research organization set" in her discussion of sociological research on minorities. Two of these factors are the funding agency and university administration constraints, and what we shall call "paradigm" constraint.

Funding agency constraint. Most funding exists through some governmental agency. "It seems obvious that if social science is to have a practical short-run application, a given research problem must be defined in terms which are familiar to public officials" [Green (14) p. 15]. In fact, Galliher and McCartney (9) have recently demonstrated how funding patterns have affected the use of certain research strategies and methods as well as the emphasis on individuals in the sociological literature on juvenile delinquency. Moore and Nay (25) provide similar documentation for research in the social sciences more broadly conceived. A special issue of the *Annals of the American Academy of Political and Social Science* was devoted to an extensive discussion of this general topic entitled, "Social Science and the Federal Government" [Lyons (16)]. It is not difficult to imagine the ramifications of governmental funding patterns on formulating problems of study by social scientists. For example, at the technical level one may accept governmental statistics, definitions, and categories of criminal behavior. This is precisely what has occurred with regard to social indicators research with such government agencies as the Law Enforcement Assistance Administration requesting scientists to make use of the data banks they have compiled, e.g., victimization surveys and Uniform Crime Reports, for policy analysis. Results of such investigations can only support inherent biases, already existing in their definitions and categories of criminal behavior. As long as we allow funding agencies to determine the type and formulation of research problems we address, we are bound to continue making errors of conceptualization.

University administration constraint. Moore (24) indicates that the academic researcher is constrained by the administration's demand that one publish, acquire large grants, and "avoid generating controversy that would 'offend' the nonuniversity public" (p. 69). Anyone remotely associated with academia knows the salience and potency of these issues.

For example, funding agencies and universities have, until recently, been supporting and encouraging behavior modification research. It was held in considerable esteem throughout the 1960s and early 1970s. It also provided the investigator with a captive population over which one had a great deal of control, mimicking the rigor of the idealized experimental laboratory situation and at the same time being "relevant" by presumably improving social well-being. Such a course produced numerous publications (in fact, the creation of many new journals) and a resultant increase in academic status and prestige for these scientists, individually and collectively.

The social indicators movement seems to be following a similar course in terms of growth, funding, and prestige, although it began much later.

Paradigm constraints. Perhaps the most difficult of all constraints on problem formulation for the social scientist to recognize are those rooted in the scientific models subscribed to by most contemporary social scientists. Maruyama (20) delineates the structures of reasoning, or as he labels them, "paradigms" that lie beneath different cultures, professions and disciplines. Scientists and others seem unaware of these structures of reasoning. Maruyama explicates a dimension of paradigms ranging from a unidirectional causal paradigm to a mutual causal paradigm. The unidirectional causal paradigm is essentially a traditional "cause"-and-"effect" model. This paradigm appears to be uncritically employed most often by social scientists in an apparent attempt to emulate the physical sciences. It is heavily based on a classificational logic. The assumptions of this classificational logic are:

1. The universe consists of material substances (and in some cases also of power substances).
2. These substances persist in time.
3. They obey the law of identity and the law of mutual exclusiveness, except that the power substance may penetrate into things.
4. The substances are classifiable into mutually exclusive categories. The classification is unambiguous. The categories persist in time and space. (The categories are believed to be uniformly and universally valid.)
5. Categories may be divided into subcategories, and categories may be combined into supercategories. Thus, categories are a hierarchy.
6. The categories can be constructed a priori, i.e., they can preexist before the things are to be put into them. They have their reality independent from things, and higher than things. [Maruyama (19), p. 136].

From a different perspective, Watzlawick, *et al.* (34) have commented on the negative consequences of such classificational logic:

For instance, the handling of many fundamental social problems—e.g., poverty, aging, crime—is customarily approached by separating these difficulties as entities unto themselves, as almost diagnostic categories, referring to essentially quite disparate problems and requiring very different solutions. The next step then is to create enormous physical and administrative structures and whole industries of expertise, producing increased incompetence in ever vaster numbers of individuals. We see this as a basically counterproductive approach to such social needs, an approach that requires a massive deviant population to support the raison d'etre of these monolithic agencies and departments (p. 159).

A major, but subtle, reason why behavior modification issues have been readily addressed is that the formulation of the problem is consistent with most social scientists' underlying theoretical framework—a unidirectional causal model. Since behavior modification research sees the environmental contingencies as causing an individual's behavior, it meshes well with a unidirectional causal framework. Furthermore, the usual behaviors monitored are consistent with the classificational logic assumptions delineated above. Finally, behavior modification has itself become an industry, with its own conventions, professional and paraprofessional training programs, journals, degrees, certificates, etc. Consequently, we can expect more and more problems to be framed as in need of behavior modification, perpetuating errors of conceptualization.

Coming from a different, but somewhat similar, vantage point, Mitroff and Turoff (22) describe how different methodoligies stem from different philosophical premises or inquiring systems [Churchman (5)]. These different inquiring systems (e.g., Lockean, Leibnitzian, Kantian, Hegelian) may be ill-suited to the conceptualization of a particular problem, but are employed without a thorough analysis of their fit and concomitant constraints on problem definition, methodology and outcome.

The indices employed in the Unified Crime Report are frequently employed in social indicators research on public safety. Included in this research are categories regarding specific kinds of crime and related public expenditures for personnel, hardware, etc. The specific nature of these indices is consistent with the statements by Maruyama (19) concerning classificational logic. What enters the equation are a small number of very select variables. While passing reference may be given to the inadequacy and unreliability of such measures, they nevertheless appear to be enthusiastically employed. The employment of such static, hierarchical and mutually exclusive indices demands and is well suited to a unidirectional causal paradigm. This traditional cause and effect model restricts the possibility of novel conceptualizations of research problems. A novel set of indices and assessment devices that defy the simplistic classificational logic would have to be developed if, for example, we intended to build our research on the assumptions of a mutual causal paradigm. Questioning this body of research as performed will not be easily heard, because it possesses all the prestigious elegance and trappings of mathematics and science. Nevertheless, if we seek solutions other than more or less public expenditures for one method of crime control over another, we need to select and formulate problems differently; that is, based on different premises, scientific and otherwise.

Caplan and Nelson (4) have again cogently stated the issue:

> If social scientists choose to be morally indifferent social bookkeepers and leave the selection of indicators and their use in the hands of others, then, to use Biderman's (1966) term, social "vindicators" would be a better name for such measures. If our apprehensions are confirmed, these vindicators will take the form of person-blame data collected for the poltiical mangement of guilt and culpability (p. 207).

Unfortunately, such research has the additional face value and congruence with the dominant value structure in this country: they are pragmatic, accounting-like, and so on.

Integration. To buck the tide of the societal, funding agency, university and discipline-based underlying rules, premises, pressures and assumptions described above would seriously jeopardize an individual investigator's understandable striving for academic and material success. Nevertheless, not to at least question them forces the researcher into a number of predetermined actions which are taken for granted, and may inhibit desirable social changes. This is not meant to imply that most researchers do not also exhibit a genuine quest for knowledge, but rather that social scientific activities have multiple determinants, not all of which are encompassed by the search for "truth." Furthermore, all of these determinants commingle in a complex fashion with those of the host organization to form a mutually beneficial exchange relationship. The frequent but unwitting consequence may be an error of conceptualization or the investigation of the "wrong" problem. Paradoxically, the "real" problem goes unaltered and is, in fact, often perpetuated. Successive phases in the research process are subject to similar determinants, but the selection and formulation of the problem is most critical.

Unfortunately, the social scientist's acceptance of preselected and preformulated research problems adds credibility and legitimation to the values inherent in such conceptualizations. Individually and collectively social scientists must take a much more active role in the process of problem selection and formulation, and institute mechanisms—to the largest extent possible—to maximize diversity in the conceptualization of research problems.

Constituents or Recipients

It may appear from the analysis to this point that one major determinant has been omitted—the constituents or clients of the judicial or criminal justice policy/program. This is not an oversight. They are often ignored or exert little if any pressure on the formulation of the problem and are most often themselves labeled as the problem. Since the ostensible goal is the constituents' welfare or the clients' rehabilitation, would it not make sense to incorporate their views into problem selection and definition in a central fashion? We shall return to this later.

MECHANISMS FOR VALUE CONFLICT GENERATION

Having followed the line of reasoning presented to this point, the reader may feel quite powerless in dealing with the multitude of forces and pressures impinging upon selection and formulation of a research problem. The convergent values inherent in many of these determinants make it quite difficult for the social scientist to address a research problem other than one to which the answers will most likely perpetuate the status quo, rather than to foster an increase in justice and human welfare.

Given this situation, how can the social scientist cope, that is, how can one more effectively select, define, and address research problems, the potential answers to which have a greater possibility of enhancing justice, equity, and social welfare? Obviously, there is no simple answer. In some ultimate sense what is required for social scientists, individually and collectively, is a heightened level of consciousness and responsibility which transcends personal and social pressures and needs. The fact that few of us, if any, are such "superpersons" necessitates a set of guidelines, for what I am referring to as value conflict generating mechanisms, to minimize the likelihood of our falling into these "traps." This tentative set of guidelines is offered in the hope that it will make it more difficult to unwittingly select, conceptualize, and address the "wrong" problem. Nevertheless, each scientist *must not* shirk his indiviudal responsibility in actively seeking to achieve the essential message conveyed by these guidelines through yielding to the omnipresent personal, social, and organizational constraints and pressures.

The precursor to any actual steps needs to be what Maruyama (20) has called *demonopolarization*. Monopolarization is the tendency of persons, particularly of Western heritage, to develop a dependency on *one* right theory, *one* truth, etc. [Maruyama (17)]. Consequently, demonopolarization is necessary, that is, we have to become aware that there are other ways of thinking. Similarly, Johnson has discussed the importance of including criticism per se as a formal step in public policy evaluation. He defines criticism as including "both the examination and advocacy of alternative policies, based upon alternative outcomes," and goes on to state that "Doing criticism means exposing the implicit values that guide our research and recognizing that research which precludes implications for alternative policy choices is not worth doing." Sjoberg (31), pp. 90–91, further suggests that ". . . criticism alone will not advance the cause of human dignity. We must formulate research orientations that emphasize the development of alternative structural arrangements that transcend some of the difficulties inherent in the present-day social order" (p. 45).

To begin in this direction, it is useful to return to the metaperspective offered throughout this paper, i.e., the notions regarding first- versus second-order change. In the examples presented earlier, despite the often expressed intent of the social policies they represent, the problem selected, formulated and addressed could only lead to solutions of a first-order nature, in that the solution was sought given the extant rules of the game. It is precisely the rules of the game which need to be seriously questioned as a precondition to further action. As was apparent with the nine-dot problem presented earlier, failing to question the implicit rules precluded solution of the real problem; and only through a reconceptualization of the rules and premises could a second-order solution be discovered. The way most people approach the nine-dot problem is analogous to the social scientists addressing legal, judicial, and criminal justice issues by accepting the problems as defined, with all their inherent values, and without questioning the appropriateness of the problem definition per se, or its selection. Given the pressures against questioning our most basic premises, how might we proceed?

Watzlawick, *et al.* (34) suggest that the major means of extricating ourselves from this bind is a *reframing of the question*. To reframe means to place the "facts" within an alternative conceptual framework. While the "facts" should fit equally well, their new context should change the entire meaning attributed to the situation (i.e., its underlying premises), and therefore its consequences. An important key to this reframing is to look at the pattern of transactions or relationships *between* levels, e.g., group, organization, institution, that represent the rules governing the game [Seidman (30)]. To stay within a level accepts the premises or the rules of the game as they exist.

Let us concretize the process of reframing by returning to the behavior modification example. The goal is to rehabilitate individual offenders, based on the premise that they are the source of the problem and the proper focus of change. However, the social scientist's acceptance of this premise, along with the notion that these individuals need to be taught to conform to the culturally valued norm, is unlikely to lead to anything but a reification of age-old values and conceptions, and as a social policy this approach does little to curb crime, or for that matter to alter the behavior of individuals once released from the control of the therapeutic agents. At best, this is a first-order solution in that it only leads to within group changes (differential changes within the group of "deviants"). If one were to try to reframe the question one might begin by looking at the relationship *between* these identified groups of "deviants" and the organizations and institutions with which they must interact [Seidman (30)]. These transactions are characterized by their one-up, one-down (or powerful, powerless) nature with regard to access and availability of environmental resources [Davidson and Rapp (6)]. From this perspective the research problem to be addressed might be conceptualized as the alteration of a relatively stable pattern of transactions between employment opportunities and a high-risk crime group (i.e., a group having a high probability of being apprehended for criminal activities). Interventions, if successful, would be expected to increase the variability in the existing pattern of transactions where members of the high-risk crime group have repeatedly failed to be given access to jobs, or at least to jobs associated with a modicum of dignity, respect, and financial renumeration. However, such a reformulation of the problem requires the development and measurement of indices reflecting the pattern and nature of these transactions and mutually interdependent factors. Formulating the problem in this fashion will lead to the development of new interventions and social policies.

In dealing with a population of "hard-core" youth, all of whom had been "given up" on by existing social service agencies, Goldenberg (11) reframed, both at the conceptual and action levels, the rehabilitation or treatment issue. He developed an autonomous alternative residential setting. A direct attempt was made to alter the one-up, one-down pattern of relationships which characterizes the daily transactions in superficially similar correctional facilities. Goldenberg (11) characterizes this as a function of a vertical organizational structure. Seeing this as a central problem, he reframed the issue and developed a program emphasizing a horizontal organizational structure as a vehicle to facilitate the "growth" of staff as well as clients. It was a genuine collaborative venture in which residents and staff were all directly and equitably involved in all aspects of life in the setting, including decision making. Thus, the aim was precisely an alteration of the nature and pattern of transactions between "treater" and "treated." The richness and excitement conveyed in *Build me a mountain* can only be captured by reading the detailed descriptions and examples provided by Goldenberg (11). While the venture seemed to be successful by traditional criteria, Goldenberg failed to measure or develop assessment devices reflecting the pattern and nature of the transactions.

Sjoberg and Cain (32) describe what they term "countersystem analysis" which can similarly produce a significant reformulation of the research problem to be addressed. The countersystem analysis is described as a form of dialectical reasoning in which the existing social order (or social structure) is negated and a logical alternative is suggested. Pertaining to the behavior modification example, one could negate the need for rehabilitation and postulate an alternative of the need to accept and reward, via material and psychological resources, diverse personal and social competencies, and not simply attempt to standardize all to a single culturally-valued norm of the dominant society [Rappaport (26)]. One can easily imagine the potentially diverse consequences resulting from the latter problem formulation as opposed to the one originally posed.

How can we reframe the research question pertaining to our second example, that is, social indicators research on public safety? You will recall that the fundamental unexamined premise or error of conceptualization depicted was the objective of establishing an optimal relationship between public safety and expenditures. Striving to accomplish this objective was viewed as simply perpetuating the existing homeostatic balance. Consequently, reframing or negating this implicit premise should lead the social policy analyst to question its utility and suggest an alternative formulation. One such alternative premise might be to disrupt the homeostatic balance or equilibrium. To change the system, deviation-amplifying positive feedback mechanisms must be employed (Maruyama, 1968). Only through such deviation-amplification, as contrasted with negative feedback, can the calibration of the system itself be eventually altered. Thus a different system with a new equilibrium could be created.

In a further attempt to concretize the issues discussed in this paper— the error of conceptualization, its consequences and determinants, and a reframing of the unexamined premise(s)—a self-contained example concerning juvenile delinquency research (and based heavily on the writing of Schur, 1973) is portrayed in Table 1. Hopefully, this will help the reader in thinking about other illustrations, for example, diversion and incompetency to stand trial.

In order to put these metaperspectives in their appropriate context, I must state emphatically that questions resulting from a reframing or negation of the original problem have no greater priority on truth or justice than those traditionally posed, despite an implicit preference of the author. What is imperative is that we *examine the premises underlying the selection and formulation of research problems, generate alternative conceptualizations, evaluate each empirically, and thoroughly examine their respective intended and unintended social consequences.*

Thus, we are led to the posing of a set of dialectical mechanisms that force the generation and examination of value conflicts. In order to do this systematically I shall borrow, adapt and add to a set of guidelines suggested by Mitroff and Blankenship (21) with regard to the conceptualization of large-scale social experiments.

1. *At least two "radically distinct" philosophical models must be brought to bear on the formulation of any potential research problem.*

Table 1. Conceptualizations of Delinquency and Their Consequences[1]

Issue	(A) Individual treatment	(B) Liberal reform	(C) Radical nonintervention	Comments
Facts	Youth violating societal rules. Oftentimes, the rules violated are those that apply solely to youth, i.e., status offenses.			These are not mutually exclusive. They also represent a historical progression from A to C.
Social science orientation	(A) Individual treatment	(B) Liberal reform	(C) Radical nonintervention	
Basic underlying assumption (conceptualization)	Offenders are *different* from nonoffenders and differences are assumed to be a function of *individual* variables.	Offenders are *different* from nonoffenders, but differences are assumed to result from *social conditions* to which they've been exposed.	*Reactions* to certain behaviors largely determine their social meaning (i.e., "deviance") and consequences (i.e. further rule-violations).	Orientation C's frustration with the lack of efficacy of orientation A and B's policies led them to reframe the basic underlying research problem (or error of conceptualization) of A and B. A and B are basically similar because of the common assumption or concern with differences. A and B are heavily influenced by dominant societal values.
Favored research methodology and focus	Comparison samples of delinquent and nondelinquent youth matched on demographic and other social variables. Thus, social system variables are held constant and *personological-like factors are free to vary* (∴ the focus).	Comparison of rate of rule violations in different social classes, neighborhood settings, group and subcultural contexts. In a sense, holds constant individual variability, leaving *social and cultural variables free to vary* (© the focus).	Self-reports, observations, and legal analyses focused upon *pattern of inter-actions between* "deviants" and social control agents.	In A and B one or the other is the focus (individual or social system variables) while the focus of orientation C is on the pattern of interactions between the two. Reframed conceptualization of C leads to a different methodology and focus.

Issue				Comments
Facts	Youth violating societal rules. Oftentimes, the rules violated are those that apply solely to youth, i.e., status offenses.			
Social science orientation	(A) Individual treatment	(B) Liberal reform	(C) Radical nonintervention	These are ideal types; they are not mutually exclusive. They also represent a historical progression from A to C.
Implicit causal perspective	*Unidirectional causality;* individual difference variables, by the nature of methodology employed, are "set up" to be the cause of rule-violating behavior.	*Unidirectional causality;* environmental or social parameters, by the nature of methodology employed, are "set up" to be the cause of rule-violating behavior.	*Mutual causality;* patterns of interactions, by the nature of methodology employed, is "set up" to be cause of rule-violating behavior.	A and B's causal perspective is similar in attempting to emulate the physical sciences. The reframed conceptualization of C implies a different causal model than A and B.
Social policies created (or implied)	*Treatment and rehabilitation of "deviants";* agents of social control must act on behalf of the violators' "best" interests.	*Treatment and rehabilitation of "deviants",* with increased attention to social factors and causes.	*Narrowed scope of juvenile court jurisdiction.* Decriminalization of status offenses. Treatment only on a voluntary basis.	Social policies stem directly from prior issues.
Long-range effect on the "facts"	Increased numbers viewed as "deviant" and in need of treatment or rehabilitation. Problem has reached crisis proportion.	Increased numbers viewed as "deviant" and need for social reform is emphasized. However, functionally is translated to increased services. Problem has reached crisis proportion.	Increased tolerance of diversity. Fewer individuals viewed as problematical.	The manner in which C reframed the basic assumption of A and B leads to drastically different long-range consequences.

[1]*Source:* This table is adapted from Table 1 (p. 20) of Schur (29).

What is implied here are two philosophical systems like a unidirectional causal paradigm, i.e., a traditional cause and effect model, versus a mutually interdependent causal paradigm [Maruyama (20)], or a Leibnitzian inquiring system, i.e., an abstract formal, mathematical or logical system versus a Hegelian inquiring system, i.e., a conflictual system [Churchman (5)]. Additionally, two less formal philosophical models, previously discussed, can be employed. A first- versus second-order formulation [Watzlawick, *et al.,* (34), 1974], as well as the system and counter-system conception [i.e., negation; Sjoberg & Cain (32)], can be brought to bear on problem selection and definition, as previously exemplified.

2. *At least two radically distinct disciplines must be brought to bear. . . .*

This point is also supported by Johnson (15), who states, "The internal standards of a discipline are inadequate guidelines for making research choices and encourage perpetuation of fraudulent academic claims on scarce societal resources" (p. 77). Mitroff and Blankenship (21) go so far as to suggest that these must not simply be two diverse social science disciplines, but, for example, a behavioral and physical science. Two different behavioral science disciplines alone would still view the problem primarily in behavioral and human terms. "Both are valid; each is required" (p. 345).

3. *At least two "radically distinct" kinds of conceptualizers must be brought to bear. . . .*

As Johnson (15) has pointed out everyone, including the self- or other-appointed critic, is in a sense trapped within his own conceptual framework. What is most frequently needed here is someone who formulates problems contrary to the traditional expectancies of mainstream social science. Such mavericks or critics are often viewed with disdain and go unrewarded by their own disciplines. We really need to cultivate a group of persons who are able to walk with only one foot in our camp. This remains a major challenge for each discipline, university, funding agency, etc.

Mitroff and Blankenship (21) indicate a much narrower interpretation of this guideline. They are referring to conceptualizers with convergent versus divergent cognitive styles. Mechanisms number one, two and three are obviously not mutually exclusive and derive primarily from our discussion of the social science constraints.

One likely consequence of the actualization of this mechanism is what Maruyama (20) has called transpection, the process of getting into the head of the other, and secondly, letting the other person transpect one's own paradigm.

4. *The constituents, participants, or the ultimate beneficiaries or vic-*

tims of the research endeavor must be incorporated into the selection and formulation of the research problem.

Those people whom the research is presumed to benefit in the short or long run can no longer be excluded or incorporated in only a token fashion if research is to be truly meaningful and beneficial to them. They may have a dramatically different conceptualization. These individuals rightfully deserve a major role of influence in problem selection and formulation. The ultimate value of research must be with "the human population on whom policy consequences are perpetrated" [Johnson (15)]. In another context Goulet (13) has indicated that our "subjects" must actively define the ground rules by which they are studied. While this is a threatening and uncomfortable position for the social scientist to enter, it is nevertheless crucial. It may curtail some potentially fruitful research, along with reducing the number of trivial studies, but in the long run I am confident that it will benefit the populations whose welfare is central as well as benefitting our mutual relationships. Viable mechanisms for the genuine incorporation of these populations, i.e., with decision-making power and not of a token nature, need to be developed. This guideline derives primarily from our discussion of the fact that the constituents (or recipients) of social policies (or programs) are rarely, if ever, a meaningful determinant in the selection and formulation of social policy research questions.

5. *Autonomy from the organizations and institutions we evaluate and/or serve should be maximized.*

While complete independence is not feasible in many instances, Glaser (10) has pointed out that autonomy is critical not only for the increased theoretical grounding of criminal justice research, but also with regard to the unadulterated release of potential findings. The development of such autonomy would hopefully increase the diversity of problem selection and formualtion. This suggestion is derived primarily from the discussion of officialdom as a determinant and other funding constraints on social science research.

Even if all these conflict generating mechanisms were implemented, there is obviously no assurance that problems would not be conceptualized in such a way that their results would not simply perpetuate, directly or indirectly, what is. Furthermore, the guidelines may be viewed as impractical. However, the point to be emphasized is that we should not ignore or sidestep their importance because they are not foolproof or practical. Rather, we must, individually or collectively, strive to actualize as much as is possible for the ultimate benefit of society and the quality of knowledge. At a minimum, they should make us more aware and cautious of the "traps" in problem selection and formulation.

Several closing comments seem warranted. While this paper emphasizes an examination of the unexamined premises and their determinants with regard to problem selection and conceptualization, it should be recalled that this is primarily because the initial stage in the process is viewed as the most influential. However, similar concerns could be raised about each successive choice point in the research process. The mechanisms for generating value conflict can and should be applied at each successive choice point, although the phase of problem selection and formulation remains most essential.

The general issues and guidelines discussed in this paper are applicable to other areas of social science research—education, mental health, public welfare, etc.—even though the paper is addressed to scientists interested in social policy research with regard to law and criminal justice. Furthermore, I am not only referring to applied research, but also to what is often called "basic" research with direct or indirect implications for the development of social policy. The traps in such research are even more subtle and potentially dangerous.

FOOTNOTES

1. The author expresses his gratitude to Philip L. Berck, Guy Desaulniers, James Lamiell, Thom Moore, Julian Rappaport, Ronald Roesch, Evelyn N. Seidman and Rita J. Simon for their helpful comments on an earlier draft of this manuscript. I am especially grateful to Thom Moore for continually suggesting pertinent references. This work was supported in part from Grant #MH 22336 from the National Institute of Mental Health.

2. For a more detailed explanation of these mathematical theorems, the interested reader is referred to their exciting book, *Change: Principles of problem formation and problem resolution*.

REFERENCES

1. Blumberg, A. S. (ed.), *Current Perspectives on Criminal Behavior,* Alfred A. Knopf, Inc., New York (1974).
2. Buckley, W., *Social and Modern Systems Theory,* Prentice-Hall, Englewood Cliffs, N.J. (1967).
3. ——— (ed.), *Modern Systems Research for the Behavioral Scientist: A sourcebook,* Aldine, Chicago (1968).
4. Caplan, N., and Nelson, S. D., "On Being Useful: The Nature and Consequences of Psychological Research on Social Problems," *American Psychologist* 28 (1973): 199–211.
5. Churchman, C. W., *The Design of Inquiring Systems,* Basic Books, New York (1971).
6. Davidson, W. S., and Rapp, C., Child Advocacy in the Justice System, *Social Work* 21 (1976): 225–232.
7. ———, and Seidman, E., "Studies of Behavior Modification and Juvenile Delinquency: A Review, Methodological Critique, and Social Perspective," *Psychological Bulletin* 81, (1974): 998–1011.

 8. Fairweather, G. W., *Social change: The Challenge to Survival,* General Learning Press, Morristown, N.J. (1972).
 9. Galliher, J. F. and McCartney, J. L., "The Influence of Funding Agencies on Juvenile Delinquency Research," in *Social Problems* 21 (1973), pp. 77–90.
10. Glaser, D., "Remedies for the Key Deficiency in Criminal Justice Evaluation Research". *Journal of Research in Crime and Delinquency,* 1974, *11,* 144–154.
11. Goldenberg, I. I., *Build me a Mountain.* MIT Press, Cambridge, Mass. (1971).
12. Gouldner, A. W., "Anti-Minotaur: The Myth of a Value-free Sociology," in W. G. Bennis, K. D. Benne, and R. Chin (eds.), *The Planning of change,* Holt, Rinehart & Winston, Inc., New York (1969).
13. Goulet, D., "An ethical model for the study of values," *Harvard Educational Review* 41 (1971): pp. 205–227.
14. Green, P., The Obligations of American Social Scientists," in *The Annals* 394, the American Academy of Political and Social Science (1971): 13–27.
15. Johnson, R. W., "Research objectives for policy analysis," in K. M. Dolbeare (ed.), *Public policy evaluation,* Sage Publications, Beverly Hills, Calif.: (1975).
16. Lyons, G. M. (ed.), "Social science and the federal government," in *the Annals 394* (The American Academy of Political and Social Science), 1971, 1–120.
17. Maruyama, M., "Monopolarization, family, and individuality" *Psychiatric Quarterly* 40 (1966), pp. 133–149.
18. ———, "The Second Cybernetics: Deviation Amplifying Mutual Causal Processes," in W. Buckley (ed.), *Modern systems research for the behavioral scientist: A sourcebook.* Aldine, Chicago (1968).
19. ———, M., Cultural, Social and Psychological Considerations in the Planning of Public Works. *Technological Forecasting and Social Change* 5 135–143, 1973.
20. ———, Paradigms and communication, *Technological Forecasting and Social Change,* 1974, *6,* 3–32.
21. Mitroff, I. I., and Blankenship, L. V., "On the Methodology of the Holistic Experiment: An Approach to the Conceptualization of Large-Scale Social Experiments," *Technological Forecasting and Social Change* 4 (1973), pp. 339–353.
22. ———, and Turoff, M., "Technological Forecasting and Assessment: Science and/or Mythology," *Technical Forecasting and Social Change,* 1973, *5,* 113–134.
23. ———, and ———, "On measuring the Conceptual Errors in Large Scale Social Experiments: The Future as Decision," *Technological Forecasting and Social Change* 6 (1974), pp. 389–402.
24. Moore, J. W., "Social Constraints on Sociological Knowledge: Academics and Research Concerning Minorities," *Social Problems, 21,* (1973): 65–77.
25. Moore, T., and Nay, W. R., "Control of Freedom in Social Research," unpublished manuscript, University of Illinois, 1977.
26. Rappaport, J., *Community Psychology: Values, Research and Action,* Holt, Rinehart & Winston, New York (1977).
27. Runkel, P. J., and McGrath, J. E., *Research on Human Behavior: A Systematic Guide to Method,* Holt, Rinehart & Winston, New York, 1972.
28. Ryan, W., *Blaming the victim,* Vintage Books, New York (1971).
29. Schur, E. M. *Radical Non-intervention: Rethinking the Delinquency Problem.* Prentice-Hall, Englewood Cliffs, N.J.: 1973.
30. Seidman, E. "Steps Toward the Development of Useful Social and Public Policies," paper presented at interdisciplinary seminar on "Public policy in industrialized countries," Urbana, IL, 1976.
31. Sjoberg, G., "Politics, Ethics and Evaluation Research," in M. Guttentag & E. L. Struening (eds.), *Handbook of Evaluation Research,* Vol. 2, Beverly Hills, Calif.: Sage Publications, 1975.

32. —————, & Cain, L. D., Jr. Negative Values, Countersystem models, and the Analysis of Social Systems, in H. Turk and R. L. Simpson (eds.), *Institutions and Social Exchange: The Sociologies of Talcott Parsons and George C. Homans*. Bobbs-Merrill, Indianapolis, 1971.

33. —————, and Miller P. J., Social Research on Bureaucracy: Limitations and Opportunities," *Social Problems,* 21, (1973) 129–143.

34. Watzlawick, P., Weakland, J. H. and Fisch, R., *Change: Principles of Problem Formulation and Problem Resolution,* Norton, New York 1974.

CAUSAL ANALYSIS AND THE LEGAL PROCESS*

Stuart Nagel, UNIVERSITY OF ILLINOIS

Marian Neef, UNIVERSITY OF ILLINOIS

The purpose of this article is to demonstrate in a simple manner some basic concepts and methods for determining the existence of causal relations in the legal process. By legal process we mean the making and applying of law by legislatures, courts and administrative agencies. By causal analysis in this context, we mean attempting to account for why outputs vary in the legal process by looking to variations in the inputs. A causal analysis can be considered completed when there is no other input item that will substantially change the nature of the relations between (a) the output variation

*Thanks are owed to the Ford Foundation Public Policy Committee, the LEAA National Institute of Law Enforcement and Criminal Justice, and the University of Illinois Law and Society Program for financing aspects of the larger study on which this paper is based, although none of them is responsible for the ideas advocated here.

Research in Law and Sociology—Vol. 1, 1978, pages 201–227.

being explained and (b) the input variations being used as the basis of the causal explanation.

The above concept of causal analysis, however, is too abstract to be very meaningful. In order to give it clearer meaning, this article will provide a series of examples to illustrate three different types of causal analysis. The first type includes situations where the relation between an input variable and an output variable is shown to be noncausal by controlling for a third variable. The second type includes situations where one input variable cannot by itself cause the output to change, but requires a certain second input variable acting in joint causation. A third type is the reciprocal causation situation where the input causes the output, but the output has feedback causation on the input. Like the basic concept of causal analysis, these classifications take on clearer meaning when concrete examples are presented.

Before proceeding to discuss different ways one could explain variation on an output variable, we should clarify that we are seeking generalizations concerning relations between types of inputs and types of outputs. In other words, we are not discussing the causes of a specific incident like the death of murder victim John Doe, or the skidding of Peter Roe's car at a certain intersection on a certain day. That kind of causation is very much a part of legal analysis in specific cases, rather than a part of a social science analysis designed to explain variation across cases or across other legal phenomena. Seeking the proximate cause in a specific criminal or personal injury case may also differ from our concern for causal generalizations, in that proximate cause determination often involves normative judgments of blameworthiness, rather than just empirical relations. Likewise, empirical causation in criminal and personal injury cases may emphasize medical analysis of the cause of death or an automotive engineering analysis concerning the defectiveness of a car's antiskidding qualities, rather than a social science subject matter that emphasizes interaction among people or individual psychological characteristics.[1]

I.   CO-EFFECTS AND INTERVENING VARIABLE CAUSATION

In order to understand better co-effects or intervening variable causation, the concept of noncausal relation should be clarified. A noncausal relation is a relation between an input variable and an output variable in which the relation disappears or substantially changes when one takes into consideration a third or intervening variable. The input variable (or variable being predicted from) can be symbolized X; the output variable (or variable being predicted to) can be symbolized Y; and the intervening variable can be symbolized as Z, Z_1, or Z_2, depending on how many intervening variables there are. A variable is a characteristic of a person, place, or thing in which differences can occur on the characteristic as with the ages of people, the per capita incomes of places, or whether the prosecutor or defendant won in various criminal cases. Some characteristics, such as age, allow for many categories, and others, such as the winner in criminal cases, tend to allow only for two categories, although age can be collapsed into young and old (or above and below some average) and one can talk in terms of degrees of victory in criminal cases. This article will emphasize dichotomized variables for simplicity of presentation, although recognizing that dichotomizing sometimes loses useful information.

Relations can often be understood more clearly through the use of symbols and arrow diagrams. Thus, the arrow diagrams in Figure 1 provide some symbolic examples of co-effects causation and intervening variable causation. An arrow from one variable to another indicates that the first variable is hypothesized or alleged to cause the second variable to increase when the first variable increases (a plus relation), or to cause the second

Figure 1. Arrow diagrams to illustrate co-effects and intervening variable causation.

A. Co-effects causation

B. Intervening variable causation

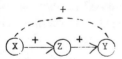 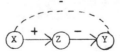 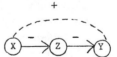

Meaning of symbols:

X = Input variable or variable being predicted from.
Y = Output variable or variable being predicted to.
Z = A third variable that is believed to explain the relation between X and Y.

variable to decrease when the first variable increases (a minus relation). A broken line from one variable to another indicates that the first variable is hypothesized as having at least a partly noncausal relation with the second variable so that they increase or decrease together (a plus relation) or in opposite directions (a minus relation) due to their relations with a third variable. In the absence of the Z variable, the broken line relation between X and Y might be zero, plus, or minus.

In a co-effects situation, the input variable X bears a noncausal relation with the output variable Y because they are both effects of a third variable Z, or are somehow otherwise related to one or more other variables. In an intervening variable situation, the input variable X bears a noncausal relation with the output variable Y, because X causes Z which in turn causes Y, rather than due to a more direct relation between X and Y. These two kinds of causation are treated together because as will be seen shortly, the methods are almost identical for analyzing whether one or the other is present.

Relations can also often be understood more clearly through the use of four-cell tables which show the percentage of persons, places, or things that are high on the input variable and also high on the output variable, and the percentage of persons, places, or things which are low on the input variable but high on the output variable. Table 1 provides a concrete illustration using state supreme court justices serving in 1955 as an example. The input variable is being a Democrat rather than a Republican on a bipartisan state supreme court. The output variable is being above the average of one's court with regard to the percentage of times one decided in favor of the employee rather than the employer in employee injury cases. The intervening variable or variable of which those two variables are believed to be co-effects is having a liberal attitude as measured by a mailed questionnaire.[2]

The basic relation in Table 1 shows that being a Democratic judge on a bipartisan state supreme court tends to correspond to having a pro-employee decisional propensity. More specifically, 68 percent of the Democratic judges had such a propensity whereas only 35 percent of the Republican judges did so. The difference between those two percentages is a good measure of the degree of relationship or slope between the two variables. It means that if one goes from being a Republican (scored 0) to being a Democrat (scored 1), then the data would predict that such a judge would move up $+.33$ from .35 to .68 from being pro-employer (scored 0) to being pro-employee (scored 1). This relation can be expressed by the simple equation $Y = .35 + .33(X)$ where Y refers to being pro-employer or pro-employee and X refers to being a Republican or a Democrat.[3]

In doing a causal analysis to determine whether the alleged Z variable is at least partly responsible for the relation between the input X variable and

Table 1. Four-cell tables to illustrate co-effects or intervening variable causation

A. The basic relation between X and Y

	Republican	Democrat		
Pro-employee	12 (35%)	19 (68%)	31	$b_1 = +.33$
Pro-employer	22 (65%)	9 (32%)	31	
	34	28	62 judges	

B. Checking the relation between Z and X and between Z and Y (the Positive Test)

	Conservative	Liberal		
Democrat	8 (25%)	20 (67%)	28	$b_2 = +.42$
Republican	24 (75%)	10 (33%)	34	
	32	30	62 judges	

All conservatives

	Conservative	Liberal		
Pro-employee	9 (28%)	22 (73%)	31	$b_3 = +.45$
Pro-employer	23 (72%)	8 (27%)	31	
	32	30	62 judges	

C. Checking the relation between X and Y holding Z constant (the Negative Test)

	Republican	Democrat		
Pro-employee	6 (25%)	3 (38%)	9	$b_4 = +.13$
Pro-employer	18 (75%)	5 (62%)	23	
	24	8	32 judges	

All conservatives

	Republican	Democrat		
Pro-employee	6 (60%)	16 (80%)	22	$b_5 = +.20$
Pro-employer	4 (40%)	4 (20%)	8	
	10	20	30 judges	

All liberals

Note: If perfect co-effects present, then $b_1 \sim \pm1.00$, $b_2 \sim \pm1.00$, $b_3 \sim \pm1.00$, $b_4 \sim 0$, and $b_5 \sim 0$.

the output Y variable, it is logical to follow a two-step process. The positive step or test says if Z is the cause of the relation between X and Y, then Z should bear a relationship to X and a relation to Y in conformity to one of the arrow diagrams shown in Figure 1 such as the first diagram under 1A. Both parts of this test are passed in Table 1B where being a liberal has a +.42 slope with being a Democrat, and where being a liberal has a +.45 slope with being pro-employee. The negative step or test says if Z is the cause of the relation between X and Y, then that relation goes toward zero when one deals separately with entities that are low on Z and separately with entities that are high on Z, thereby negating Z or holding Z constant. Both parts of this test are passed in Table 1C, where being a Democrat has a much lower relation with being pro-employee (than the original +.33) when all the judges analyzed are conservatives, and where being a Democrat has a much lower relation with being pro-employee (than the +.33) when all the judges analyzed are liberals. If either part of the positive test or either part of the negative test had failed, then one would either have to look for another explanatory Z variable or at least tentatively conclude that there is a causal relation between X and Y.[4]

The reason the relation between being a Democrat and being pro-employee did not go to perfect zero in either part of Table 1C is because liberalism apparently does not account for all of that relation, especially since the variables may have been imperfectly measured.[5] Some of that relation may involve a more direct kind of causation between party and propensity in that by being a Democrat one tends to come in contact more with people who are pro-employee, thereby reinforcing one's pro-employee propensities. There may also be some direct causation between being pro-employee and choosing to be a Democrat since Democrats are perceived as being supportive of that value. Some of that relation may also be attributable to another Z variable, such as urbanism, in the sense that living in an urban area where so many people are Democrats is likely to cause one to be a Democrat, and living in an urban area where unions are strong causes one more likely to be pro-employee. Even if the relation in both parts of Table 1C did go to zero, this would only establish a noncausal relation between being a Democrat and being pro-employee. It would not necessarily establish that liberalism is causally responsible, since being liberal and being a Democrat might be co-effects of some additional variable like urbanism that we have not yet tabulated. If, however, no additional variable makes sense in that role, then we could tentatively conclude that a causal relation is present between being a liberal and being a Democrat.

One could have more faith that the relation between being a Democrat and being pro-employee is a causal relation rather than a noncausal co-effects relation if the researcher could randomly assign some judges to be

Democrats and some judges to be Republicans. Such randomization would eliminate the relation between being a liberal and being a Democrat. In other words, by randomly assigning judges to political parties, the proportion of liberals who are Democrats would be about the same as the proportion of conservatives who are Democrats. Stated differently, the proportion of Democrats who are liberals would be about the same as the proportion of Republicans who are liberals. Such randomization, however, is impossible to obtain since the judges themselves, not the researcher, determines which judges are Democrats and which are Republicans. Through self-selection rather than randomization, the liberal judges are more likely to call themselves Democrats, and the conservative judges are more likely to call themselves Republicans.

There are other variations on this basic type of causal analysis such as where one hypothesizes that controlling for a Z variable will cause the initial relation between X and Y to become negative if it were positive to begin with, or positive if it were negative, rather than just disappear toward zero. For example, OEO legal services agencies have a negative relation between the evaluation scores they have received (Y) and the amount of money they spent for routine case handling (X) rather than law reform activities.[6] That negative relation exists in spite of the fact that case handling dollars and law reform dollars tend to increase together as co-effects of an increased budget. The negative relation may be due to the fact that intense community dissatisfaction (Z_1) causes increased legal services expenditures including routine case handling (X), but community dissatisfaction may also produce low evaluation scores (Y), thereby causing X and Y to have a negative relation when they otherwise would have a positive one. Likewise, the negative relation may be due to the fact that increased legal services expenditures including routine case handling (X) may result in rising expectations and heightened goals (Z_2), but heightened goals produce low evaluation or satisfaction scores (Y) since satisfaction is a function of goals minus achievement. If data could be obtained on Z_1 and Z_2 as it has been on X and Y, then those causal models could be tested in a manner similar to that used in Table 1.

The methodology shown in Table 1 applies in either the co-effects situation or the intervening variable situation as depicted in Figure 1. To determine which of those related models best fits a set of actual data, one has to either have data over time or have some knowledge as to whether Z precedes X in time (as in the co-effects situation) or whether X precedes Z in time (as in the intervening variable situation). Over time data are often especially helpful in causal analysis because disruptive Z variables are more likely to be held constant when making comparisons on Y before and after a change on X in one place, than is the case if one compares two places at one point in time, one of which is high on X and one of which is low. With over time data, one can change the arrow diagrams and tables to talk in terms of the relation between a change in X and a change in Y rather than just the relation between X and Y. The time element also is part of the basic definition of causation in that one can define a causal relation between X and Y as existing when (1) X precedes Y in time, (2) X and Y tend to vary together or in opposite directions, and (3) no third Z variable being held constant destroys or substantially changes the relation between X and Y.[7]

II.   JOINT CAUSATION AND CO-CAUSATION

Another common kind of causation in the legal process involves joint causation situations where one input variable by itself is not likely to cause the output variable to change substantially, but instead requires a second input variable interacting with it. Figure 2 provides some arrow diagrams illustrating two common kinds of joint causation. One situation involves two input variables that together are necessary and sufficient for the output variable to substantially increase, but that separately have little effect. Their joint causal relation is shown in the arrow diagram by the curved line which links them to the causal arrow. This situation is contrasted with a co-causation model where each input variable by itself is capable of having a substantial effect on the output variable, but the two input variables together have no greater effect than the sum of their separate effects.

The joint causation situation with two input variables is illustrated with data in Table 2. The data consist of questionnaire responses from a nationwide sample of 61 usable attorneys in 1970. The output variable involved asking them "Have you ever defended an unpopular client where an acceptance of the case could have damaged your career?" to which 45 percent or 27 lawyers responded "Yes." The first input variable involved asking them whether they agreed that "Lawyers should be encouraged to represent the unpopular client," to which 82 percent or 50 lawyers responded "Yes." The second input variable involved asking them "Is your legal practice primarily business and corporate?" to which 29 percent or 18 lawyers responded "Yes."[8]

In Table 2, the relation between having a favorable attitude and representing unpopular clients is almost zero. Likewise, the relation between having favorable opportunities as reflected by having a relatively favorable legal specialty (i.e., other than a business or corporate specialty) is also almost zero. However, when one compares in Table 2B lawyers who have both favorable attitudes and opportunities with lawyers who lack one or the other, then the relation with representing unpopular clients

Figure 2. Arrow diagrams to illustrate joint causation.

A. Two input variables

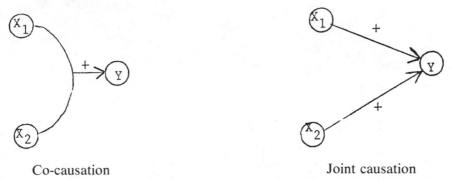

Co-causation   Joint causation

B. One input variable and one control variable

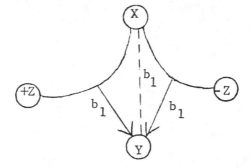

Meaning of new symbols:

+Z = Relating X to Y where all entities are in the affirmative category on Z.
−Z = Relating X to Y where all entities are in the negative category on Z.
b = The slope or degree of relation between X and Y.

becomes quite substantial. If Table 2B had involved a degree of relation only slightly higher than the +.10, the +.08, or the sum of the two relations from Table 2, then a co-causation relation might be present or at least a co-predictive relation, but not a joint causation relation. To have a joint causation relation with two input variables, their interactive combined causal impact has to be in effect greater than the sum of the parts.

Table 2. Four-cell tables to illustrate joint causation with two input variables

A. The input variables separately have little effect

Attitudes

	Unfavorable attitudes	Favorable attitudes	
Represented unpopular clients	4 (36%)	23 (46%)	27
Did not represent	7 (64%)	27 (54%)	34
	11	50	61 lawyers

$b_1 = +.10$

Opportunities

	Unfavorable specialty	Favorable specialty	
Represented unpopular clients	7 (39%)	20 (47%)	27
Did not represent	11 (61%)	23 (53%)	34
	18	43	61 lawyers

$b_2 = +.08$

B. The input variables jointly have a substantial effect

Attitudes and opportunities

	Not both favorable	Both favorable	
Represented unpopular clients	2 (10%)	25 (63%)	27
Did not represent	19 (90%)	15 (37%)	34
	21	40	61 lawyers

$b_3 = +.53$

Note: If perfect joint causation present with two input variables, then $b_1 \sim 0$, $b_2 \sim 0$, and $b_3 \sim \pm 1.00$.

For further detail, Table 2B could have been shown with four columns instead of two columns. The four columns would read, (a) unfavorable attitudes and unfavorable specialty, (b) favorable attitudes and unfavorable specialty, (c) unfavorable attitudes and favorable specialty, and (d) favorable attitudes and favorable specialty. If there were a perfect joint causation relation between attitudes and opportunities on the one hand and representing unpopular clients on the other, then 0 percent of the category (a) lawyers would have represented unpopular clients, 0 percent of the category (b) lawyers, and 0 percent of the category (c) lawyers, but 100 percent of the category (d) lawyers. Table 2B does not show a perfect joint causation, but about as close as one might expect to get given the imperfections in measuring the variables, the relevance of other variables and the somewhat small samples of lawyers involved.

The same four columns approach could be used with a co-causation relation. If the co-causation relation were perfect, then b_1 in Table 2 would be plus or minus 1.00, and b_2 would also be plus or minus 1.00. Zero percent of the category (a) lawyers would then be likely to represent the unpopular, and 100 percent of the category (d) lawyers would be likely to do so. One hundred percent of the category (b) and (c) lawyers would represent the unpopular if both the input variables were sufficient conditions to generate representation but not necessary conditions. However, 0 percent of the category (b) and (c) lawyers would represent the unpopular if both the input variables were necessary conditions but not sufficient conditions. It is impossible for two input variables to both be necessary and sufficient conditions even if they both have perfect co-varying relations with the output variable. About 50 percent of the lawyers in category (b) and in category (c) would be likely to represent the unpopular if the input variables are just good correlates of the output variable, but neither one is separately a necessary or a sufficient condition for representing the unpopular, although they might jointly constitute a necessary and sufficient condition if perfect or near-perfect joint causation were present.[9]

A second common joint causation situation involves one input variable and one control variable as indicated in Figure 2B and in Table 3. The data consist of a nationwide sample of felonious assault and grand larceny cases for 1962 in which the defendant was convicted. The input variable shown is race, and the output variable is whether the convicted defendant was jailed or instead granted probation or suspended sentence. The initial Table 3A shows a small positive relation (+.16) between being a black rather than a white convicted defendant and receiving a jail sentence rather than probation. If, however, we control for the type of crime by separating the original table into an assault table, then the relation between being black and being jailed almost becomes negative (+.05). Likewise, if we control for the type of crime by separating the original table

Table 3. Four-cell tables to illustrate joint causation with one input variable and one control variable

A. The basic relation between X and Y

	Whites	Blacks	
Jailed	336 (54%)	301 (70%)	637
Probation	288 (46%)	128 (30%)	416
	624	429	1053 convicted defendants

$b_1 = +.16$

B. Checking the relation between X and Y holding Z constant

	Whites	Blacks	
Jailed	141 (62%)	155 (67%)	296
Probation	86 (38%)	77 (33%)	163
	227	232	459

All assault crimes

$b_2 = +.05$

	Whites	Blacks	
Jailed	195 (49%)	146 (74%)	341
Probation	202 (51%)	51 (26%)	253
	397	197	594

All larceny crimes

$b_3 = +.25$

Note: If perfect joint causation present with one input variable and one control variable, then $b_1 \sim 0$, $b_2 \sim -1.00$, and $b_3 \sim +1.00$.

into a larceny table, then the relation becomes substantially positive (+.25). In other words, when race or being black (X) is jointly combined or interacts with being an assault defendant (−Z), the original relation drops, possibly because assault crimes tend to be more intraracial than larceny. When, however, race or being black (X) is jointly combined with being a larceny defendant (+Z), the original relation rises, possibly because larceny crimes tend to be more interracial than assault.[10]

Joint causation with two input variables or with one input variable and one control variable can be expressed in terms of simple equations. With two input variables, we have the equation $Y = .36 + .10(X_1)$ for the data in Table 2A1, and the equation $Y = .39 + .08(X_2)$ for Table 2A2. The equation expressing the relation in Table 2B is $Y = .10 + .53 (X_3)$ where X_3 is X_1 times X_2. In other words, if either X_1 is 0 or X_2 is 0, then that third equation would predict that Y would be a low .10. If, however, both X_1 and X_2 are scored 1, then that third equation would predict that Y would be a high .63. With one input variable and one control variable, we have the equation $Y = .54 + .16(X)$ for the relation between being jailed and being black in Table 3A. That initial equation, however, becomes $Y = .62 + .05(X)$ when all cases are 0 on Z, and it becomes $Y = .49 + .25(X)$ when all cases are 1 on Z. Expressing those relations in terms of equations is a useful kind of shorthand over the more detailed tabular approach although each of these equations merely involves transcribing two key numbers from the corresponding four-cell table, namely the initial percentage expressed as a decimal and the slope of the relation.[11]

III.   RECIPROCAL CAUSATION

A third common kind of causation in the legal process is reciprocal causation where one variable has an impact on a second variable and that second variable has a feedback effect on the first variable. This is a common legal process model by virtue of the fact that it symbolizes the law and society relationship whereby law has an impact on shaping society, and society in turn has a reciprocal impact on shaping the law. Scholars in the field of sociology of law frequently discuss whether social behavior is more influential on social norms than social norms are on social behavior.

Although the reciprocal relation between law and behavior is often discussed, it is not so often measured, partly because the methodology for separating the impact effect from the feedback effect is not so well understood. One can illustrate that methodology by working with the relation between divorce law and divorce rates following the lead in this area of political scientist Gillian Dean.[12] Figure 3 provides arrow diagrams illustrating reciprocal causation both in a general symbolic way and using the

Figure 3.   Arrow diagrams to illustrate reciprocal causation.

A. Symbolically

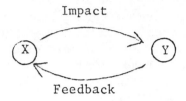

B. Using the impact of divorce laws on divorce rates as an example (also showing the basic slopes among the relevant variables)

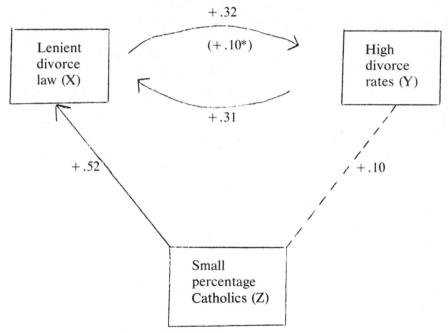

*The slope of predicted X to Y rather than actual X to Y.

divorce subject matter as an illustrative example. Table 4 provides the four-cell tables which clarify the slopes which are shown in Figure 3.

All the subtables in Table 4 are based on 47 states rather than 50 states because data were unavailable for Alaska and Hawaii and because Nevada was excluded due to its atypical nature as a state specializing in divorces for short-term residents. Divorce rates refer to divorces per 1,000 married women as of 1960 according to the U.S. Public Health Service statistics. A

Table 4. Four-cell tables to illustrate reciprocal causation

A. The basic relation between X and Y, and between Y and X

Divorce law

	Severe	Lenient	
High divorce rates	7 (35%)	18 (67%)	25
Low	13 (65%)	9 (33%)	22
	20	27	47 states

$b_1 = +.32$

Divorce rate

	Low	High	
Lenient divorce law	9 (41%)	18 (72%)	27
Severe	13 (59%)	7 (28%)	20
	22	25	47 states

$b_2 = +.31$

B. The relation between Z and X, and between Z and Y

Percent Catholics

	Large	Small	
Lenient divorce law	6 (29%)	21 (81%)	27
Severe	15 (71%)	5 (19%)	20
	21	26	47 states

$b_3 = +.52$

Percent Catholics

	Large	Small	
High divorce rates	10 (48%)	15 (58%)	25
Low	11 (52%)	11 (42%)	22
	21	26	47 states

$b_4 = +.10$

C. The relation between predicted X and actual Y (where X is predicted from Z)

Predicted divorce law

	Severe	Lenient	
High divorce rates	10 (48%)	15 (58%)	25
Low	11 (52%)	11 (42%)	22
	21	26	47 states

$b_5 = +.10$

Note: If perfect reciprocal causation present, then $b_1 = +1.00$, $b_2 = +1.00$, $b_3 = 0$, $b_4 = 0$, and $b_5 = 0$.

high divorce rate means above the national average for the 47 states, and a low divorce rate means below the national average. Divorce law leniency refers to the results of a questionnaire by Gillian Dean directed to law professors teaching family law in all 47 states asking them a number of questions designed to position each state on a divorce law leniency index.

Lenient states are those that are above the national average on that index, and severe states are those that are below.

Table 4A1 indicates that if a state moves from being a severe to a lenient state, then it is likely to move up on the divorce rate scale from a score of .35 to a score of .67 for a slope or marginal increase of +.32. Table 4A2 indicates that if a state moves from being a low divorce rate state to being a high one, then it is likely to move up on the divorce law leniency scale from a score of .41 to a score of .72 for a slope of +.31. Those two tables might lead one to believe that divorce law has about the same impact on divorce rates as divorce rates have on divorce law. Such a conclusion, however, might be false by virtue of the possible fact (as indicated in the arrow diagram of Figure 3) that divorce rates have a causal effect on divorce law which may explain much of the +.32 relation from divorce law to divorce rates. In other words, if X is believed to cause Y, and Y is also believed to cause X, then any slope obtained by trying to predict Y from X may really be circular like trying to predict Y from Y.

What we need is a way of determining the effect of X or divorce law on Y or divorce rates while somehow controlling for the feedback effect of Y on X. To be more specific, we need a method that will tell us how much of the variation on Y can be predicted by the pure variation on X. In this context, the pure variation on X refers to the variation on X that is not attributable to Y, but instead is attributable only to a third variable in the model which we have labeled Z. In this substantive context, a meaningful third variable is the smallness of the percentage of Catholics in each of the 47 states being used in Table 4. A small percentage is one that is below the national average of the 47 states, and a large percentage is one above the national average as of 1960.

There are a number of reasons why the percent of Catholics in each state is a good Z variable for filtering out the feedback effect of divorce rates on divorce law in relating divorce law to divorce rates. First, as shown in Table 4B1, the smallness of the percentage of Catholics in a state has a high +.52 relation with the leniency of divorce law. This probably indicates that legislators in Catholic states are reluctant to make their divorce laws more lenient for fear of losing many votes. This means that percent Catholics is capable of generating a substantial amount of variation in the leniency of divorce law separate from the feedback effect from divorce rates. Second, as shown in Table 4B2, the percentage of Catholics in a state has almost a zero relation with divorce rates. This probably indicates that Catholics have divorce rates close to the national average, or they tend to live in states where other groups live who have above average divorce rates which offset the lower Catholic divorce rates. It also means that divorce rates cannot influence leniency of divorce law through percent Catholics since that relation is so low. Third, if a state adopts lenient divorce laws, that does not cause Catholics to move away from there or to move toward severe divorce law states. Thus, since X does not cause Z, the feedback effect of Y on X cannot feed into Z through X and then indirectly back on X again. In other words, percent Catholics is a variable that is independent, or exogenous, from the causal influence of the two reciprocal variables which are partly dependent, or endogenous, on each other.

In Table 4C, we predict divorce rates not from divorce law but rather from predicted divorce law. By predicted divorce law in this context, we mean the score a state would be expected to receive in view of the percent of Catholics in the state and in view of the fact that Table 4B1 shows a relation between divorce law and percent Catholics that may be expressed by the equation $X = .29 + .52(Z)$. The Z variable can take the value 0 if the state has a large percentage of Catholics, and the value 1 if the state has a small percentage of Catholics. Thus, there are 21 states that score 0 on Z, and their predicted X score would be .29 which leads to a prediction that they would have relatively severe divorce laws. Likewise, there are 26 states that score 1 on Z, and their predicted X score would be .81 which leads to a prediction that they would have relatively lenient divorce laws. Table 4C thus shows 21 states in the column of states with divorce laws that are predicted to be severe from their Catholic percentages, and 26 states in the lenient prediction column. Of the 21 severe predicted states, 48 percent had high divorce rates, whereas of the 26 lenient predicted states, 58 percent had high divorce rates for a slope difference of +.10. Predicting a divorce law score for each state from its percent Catholic score can be considered a first-stage prediction, and then predicting a divorce rate score for each state from its predicted divorce law score can be considered a second-stage prediction.

The +.10 slope tells us the relation between variation in divorce laws and variation in divorce rates where the only variation in divorce laws is due to variables or a variable other than divorce rates. In other words, if a state moves or varies from a severe predicted state to a lenient predicted state, then it is likely to move up on the divorce rate scale from a score of .48 to a score of .58 for a slope or marginal rate of +.10. That +.10 is substantially less than the +.32 before we controlled for the feedback effect of divorce rates changes on divorce law changes. That +.10 may, however, still indicate that there is some causal impact effect of divorce laws on divorce rates separate from the feedback effect although not much of a causal impact effect. Apparently, variation in divorce rate from state to state is much more influenced by variables other than divorce law. These variables may especially include income, education, and urbanism levels.

In the above example, we analyzed the causal impact of leniency in divorce laws (X) on the highness of divorce rates (Y), filtering out the feedback effect of divorce rates on divorce laws. We could likewise analyze the impact of Y on X, filtering out the feedback effect of X on Y. Doing so would involve finding a Z variable like median educational level for each state for use in predicting divorce rates. We would then use predicted divorce rates to predict divorce law scores. The slope of that relation could then be compared with the +.10 slope going in the other direction. Doing so reveals that divorce rates have about twice the impact on divorce law in this context as divorce laws have on divorce rates. Perhaps in general, social behavior may have more influence on shaping legal rules than legal rules have on shaping social behavior.[13]

An alternative approach to analyzing reciprocal causation involves obtaining data over a period of time rather than at one point in time as shown in Figure 4. If we find in a given state or set of states that divorce rates were going down or were level before the divorce law became more lenient, but that they rose afterwards, then this indicates the law has more of a causal

Figure 4. Diagrams to illustrate reciprocal causation
(with data at more than one point in time)

A. Interrupted time series (multiple time points)

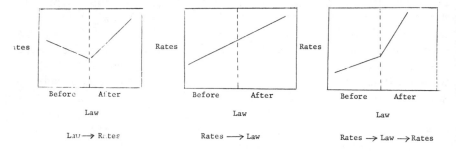

B. Cross-lagged panel analysis (two points in time)

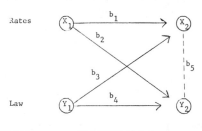

Rates → Law if $r_{x_1 y_2 \cdot y_1}$ is greater than $r_{y_1 x_2 \cdot x_1}$

(where $r_{x_1 y_2 \cdot y_1}$ means relation between X_1 and Y_2 holding Y_1 constant)

Rates → Law if b_1 times $b_2 = b_5$, more so than b_3 times b_4

force on the rates than otherwise (as in Figure 4A1). If on the other hand we find that divorce rates were going up before the divorce law became lenient and they continued upward at about the same projection, then this indicates that the rates are probably having more of an influence on the law then vice versa (as in Figure 4A2). If, however, the rates are going up before the legal change, but even more up after the legal change, that would tend to indicate the rates influence the law, and the law in turn influences the rates (as in Figure 4A3). In that time series situation, though it is more difficult to determine the relative degrees of influence as compared to the two-stage prediction method with either one-point-in-time scores or change scores. Nevertheless, both approaches usefully supplement each other.[14]

If data can be obtained for divorce rates at two points in time (e.g., X_1 at 1950 and X_2 at 1970) and for divorce law at two points in time (Y_1 at 1950 and Y_2 at 1970), then one can determine in which direction the reciprocal causation is greater by using what is known as cross-lagged panel analysis. That approach basically involves testing whether the relation between the X_1 rates and the subsequent Y_2 law is greater or less than the relation between the Y_1 law and the subsequent X_2 rates as shown in Figure 4B.[15]

IV. INTEGRATING DIVERSE FORMS OF CAUSATION

Legal process phenomena usually involve a combination of diverse forms of causation. For example, suppose we are trying to explain why some criminal cases involve short sentences and others involve long sentences. We might partly do so by hypothesizing that the short-sentence cases are more likely to be associated with Democratic judges and the long-sentence cases with Republican judges. We might, however, recognize that party affiliation is probably not likely to directly cause sentence differences, but rather may be a co-effect along with sentence differences of a liberalism attitude. We might also hypothesize that short sentences are disproportionately received by white defendants and long sentences are disproportionately received by black defendants, but especially when we only use theft crimes rather than assault crimes, since theft crimes tend to be more interracial than assault crimes are. We might further hypothesize that committing a misdemeanor rather than a felony causes one to be more likely to receive a short sentence rather than a long sentence, but that receiving only a short sentence may have a feedback effect causing the further committing of misdemeanors or other crimes which would not be so likely to happen if a long sentence had been given.

In the above example, we have one output variable, namely, sentence length, that we are trying to explain the variation on through causal analysis. The analysis includes a co-effects relation with regard to judicial characteristics, a joint causation relation with regard to the defendant's characteristics, and reciprocal causation with regard to the nature of the crime. We could add an intervening variable causation by hypothesizing that urbanism indirectly causes short sentences by causing liberalism, which in turn causes short sentences. We could also add a direct co-cause that does not involve any of the other types of causation by hypothesizing that having hired counsel leads to shorter sentences than having a public defender if the severity of the crime is held constant, although we could insert an intervening variable like greater resources and lesser backlog available to hired counsel. Other examples could be given of other causal variables related to each other in a variety of ways. Those relations in a complex causal model, however, all tend to reduce the subparts of the model which deal with co-effects, joint causation, reciprocal causation, intervening variables, or direct co-causation.

Causal models can be made more complex not only by combining different types of causation into one model, but also by increasing the number of variables wtihin each sub-model. For example, a co-effects relation can involve more than two variables that relate to each other because they are all co-effects of one or more outside variables. Likewise, more than two variables can have a joint causal relation or a nonjoint co-causal relation with another variable. A reciprocal or a circular relation can also involve more than two variables where, for example, X_1 causes X_2 which causes X_3 which causes X_1. However, neither the types of causation nor the basic causal analysis methodology changes when the number of variables increases.

Often in looking for causes, researchers tend to only think mechanically in terms of a list of co-causes, each of which relates directly by way of a one-way arrow to the output variable being explained. With a little more imagination, other forms of causation could be hypothesized and tested for. One could also determine how much of the total variation on the output variable is explained by each separate subpart of the model taken alone or added incrementally to the other parts of the model. The main goal, however, is not so much to compare different causal explanations, but rather to find the combination of causal explanations that will meaningfully explain the greatest percent of the total variation on the output variable in terms of the data and the common sense of what is already known about related matters. That kind of explanatory causal analysis makes sense to strive for, regardless whether one is attempting to explain the outcomes of cases, the behavior of judges or attorneys, the treatment of defendants, the effects of regulatory laws, or other legal matters. That kind of explanatory causal analysis can also be achieved if legal researchers will make more of an effort to understand the causal methods involved and to apply those methods to obtaining a better understanding of the legal process.

FOOTNOTES

1. For further detail on the general methodology of causal analysis, see Zeisel (25); and Blalock (1). More specialized and advanced treatments are cited elsewhere in this chapter. For a more substantive orientation on social causation, see MacIver (14). No book or article seems to have been written dealing with the oveall determination of explanatory causal generalizations in the legal process as contrasted to determining causation in specific cases. A classic of the latter type is Green (10).

2. The basic data shown in Table 1 comes from Nagel (16). The questionnaire data is discussed in Nagel (17). There were, however, not enough questionnaire respondents to position all 62 judges on party affiliation, decisional propensity, and liberalism. Therefore, the data in sections B and C of Table 1 is partly hypothetical although consistent with the overall patterns of those judges who did respond.

3. The percentage of Democratic judges who are pro-employee may be higher than the percentage of Republican judges who are pro-employee because Democrats have traditionally tended to empathize more with the working class and with minority ethnic groups. The percentage of Democratic judges who are pro-employee is not 100 percent, however, and the percentage of Republican judges who are pro-employee is not zero percent because: (1) party choice is frequently determined by considerations other than the similarity between one's values and those of the party he has chosen, such as the party of his relatives or friends; (2) a person may have average Democratic or Republican values on most issues, making him a Democrat or a Republican, but not necessarily be like an average Democrat or Republican on attitudes toward all employer-employee conflicts; and (3) two judges may have the same value systems and thus possibly be of the same party, but one of the two judges may hold his values with a greater intensity and may frequently dissent without being joined by his less vigorous associate of the same party.

4. Instead of comparing Democrats and Republicans on being pro-employee first with all conservatives and then with all liberals, there are two related approaches one could use to test whether the relation between being a Democrat and being pro-employee is caused by a liberalism variable. One approach involves determining whether b_6 goes close to zero where b_6 is defined as $(b_1 - b_2 \cdot b_2)/\sqrt{(1 - b_2^2)(1 - b_3^2)}$ which equals $(.33 - .42 \cdot .45)/(1 - .42^2)(1 - .45^2)$, which in turn equals .17. That figure is not zero, but it is substantially less than the original b_1 b_2 of .33. This method, known as partial correlation, tells us the approximate relation between being a Democrat and being pro-employee adjusting for liberalism, but it has the disadvantage of not truly holding liberalism constant the way we do in Table 1C, assuming liberalism is a meaningful dichotomous or binary variable. It has the advantage, though, of not requiring dichotomous variables and of not requiring that each column in Table 1C involve a substantial number so that the percentages will be meaningful. As the formula indicates, the partial correlation coefficient or b_6 relates positively to the original b_1 relation, but inversely to the b_2 and b_3 relations.

The second alternative approach involves determining whether b_7 equals b_1 where b_7 is defined as b_2 times b_3, which equals .42 times .45, which in turn equals .19. That figure is not a .33, but it is substantially higher than zero in the direction toward .33. This method, known as path analysis, in effect says that if b_2 and b_3 were 1.00, then our arrow diagram would predict that b_1 would be 1.00. The b_7 or predicted b_1 is 1.00 discounted by the extent to which b_2 and b_3 are proportionally less than 1.00. In other words, b_1 is predicted to be 1.00(.42)(.45). Both of these alternative approaches normally use correlation coefficients rather than slopes, but correlation coefficients are closely approximated by slopes when one is working with a four-cell table, especially if the ratio between the row totals roughly equals the ratio between the column totals. Technically speaking, a correlation coefficient shows the percentage of the variation on Y which is accounted for by X, and a slope shows the number of units that Y changes when X changes one unit.

5. In order to concentrate on the causal analysis, this article does not discuss in detail problems relating to reliability of measurement and generalizing from samples. For further detail on those matters, see Guilford and Fruchter (11); Blalock (1); and Caulcott (6).

6. Data dealing with the relation between evaluation scores of OEO Legal Services agencies and how they allocate their funds between routine case handling and law reform activities is analyzed in Nagel (19).

7. For further detail on co-efficients and intervening causation, see Simon (23), and Campbell and Stanley (5).

8. For further detail concerning this data, see Nagel et al. (20). The data presented here slightly exaggerate the joint causation relation beyond the data presented in that aritcle in order to more clearly distinguish joint causation from co-causation. Doing so, however, may result in some inconsistencies across the subtables of Table 2.

9. The possible interaction between the certainty of being caught and the severity of punishment as determinants of crime occurrence represents another important legal process situation which some researchers have claimed is an example of joint causation. For example, Tittle (24) in effect says that crime rates for various places will be high if either certainty or severity is low, but crime rates will be low if, and only if, both certainty and severity are high. Kritzer (13), however, presents data which tend to refute the joint causation relation and instead shows that crime rates, severity, and certainty vary together because they are co-effects of cultural variables like region, education, and urbanism.

10. For further detail concerning this data, see Nagel (18). Cases not containing information on race, type of sentence, and type of crime were ignored in developing Table 3 from the data.

11. For further detail on joint causation, see Blalock (1), pp. 308–309 (one input variable and one control variable), at pp. 463–464 (two input variables), and at pp. 337–347, 463–464, and 483–489 (miscellaneous related matters).

12. Dean (7,8). The data presented in Table 4 are consistent with Dean's general findings as presented in those two papers, but do not reflect her data in detail since her data are not presented in four-cell tables.

13. For further discussion of reciprocal causation and of the methodology of separating the impact effect from the feedback effect, see Miller (15), and Fowler and Lineberry (9).

The slope of Y predicted from X may be substantially different in magnitude from the slope of X predicted from Y depending on the relation between the spread on the Y variable and the spread on the X variable. There is no way, however, that those two slopes can be opposite in sign. This shows that merely reversing the direction of the regression analysis cannot get at reciprocal causation because sometimes reciprocal causation does involve relations that are opposite in sign. For example, an increase in capital punishment may decrease the murder rate over a set of places or time points. However, if there is an increase in the murder rate, this is likely to result in an increase in the use of capital punishment. There is thus a negative slope in one causal direction, and a positive slope in the other.

Analyzing reciprocal causation not only indicates which way the causation is stronger and how much stronger, but it may also indicate whether there is any causation in both directions. In other words, one may find from the analysis that although Y is highly predictable from X, the predictability is due to Y causing X, not to X causing Y, and not to X and Y causing each other. That kind of analysis has important policy implications with regard to such matters as does antidiscrimination legislation cause a reduction in discrimination, or does a reduction in discrimination cause antidiscrimination legislation? Likewise, does marijuana decriminalization cause an increase in the use of marijuana, or does an increase in the use of marijuana cause marijuana decriminalization, or both, or neither?

14. For further detail on analyzing time series that are subjected to the interruption of a legal change, see Campbell and Ross (4), and Ross et al. (22).

A fourth graph could have been shown in Figure 4A where neither a change in the law causes a change in the rates, nor does a change in the rates cause a change in the law. Such a graph might involve a horizontal line indicating that although the law changed, the rates did not, and since there was no change in the rates, a change in the rates could not have been responsible for a change in the law. Such a graph could also involve a negatively sloping line. If the slope is constant, then the change in the law is not having an effect on the rates. If to attribute a decrease in divorce rates (as cause) to a change in the law that goes from severe before to lenient after (as effect). Likewise, a negative sloping line could not be responsible for a change in the law since it would be difficult to attribute a decrease in the divorce rates as an effect (meaning people are becoming less tolerant of divorce) to a change in the law as a cause that goes from severe before to lenient after.

15. There are two frequent forms that the cross-lagged panel approach takes. One form involves comparing (1) the partial correlation between the alleged cuase X_1 and the alleged effect Y_2 holding constant the previous Y_1, and (2) the partial correlation between the alleged cause Y_1 and the alleged effect X_2 holding constant the previous X_1. If partial correlation 1 is greater than partial correlation 2, then rates have a greater effect on law than vice versa, but if partial correlation 2 is greater, then law has a greater effect on rates than vice versa. The partial correlation coefficients are calculated in a manner like that described in note 4 above.

The other form of CLPA involves comparing whether b_1 times b_2 comes closer to equaling b_5 than b_3 times b_4 does, where (1) b_1 is the slope between X_1 and X_2; (2) b_2 is the slope between X_1 and Y_2; (3) b_3 is the slope between Y_1 and X_2; (4) b_4 is the slope between Y_1 and Y_2; and (5) b_5 is the slope between X_2 and Y_2. What we are in effect saying is that X_2 and Y_2 are co-effects of either X_1 (i.e., rates at an earlier point in time) or Y_1 (i.e., law at an earlier point in time). If the X_1 rates are the stronger cause, then the method of path analysis discussed in note 4 above says that b_1 times b_2 will more closely approximate b_5 than b_3 times b_4 will, but not if law is the stronger cause.

For further detail on cross-lagged panel analysis, see Heise (12), and Pelz and Andrews (21).

REFERENCES

1. Blalock, Hubert, *Causal Inferences in Nonexperimental Research,* University of North Carolina Press, Chapel Hill, N.C. (1964).
2. ———, *Causal Models in the Social Sciences,* Aldine, Chicago (1971), pp. 295–373.
3. ———, *Social Statistics,* McGraw-Hill, New York (1972).
4. Campbell, Donald, and Laurence Ross, "The Connecticut Crackdown on Speeding: Time Series Data and Quasi-Experimental Analysis," *Law and Society Review* 3, (1968), pp. 33–53.
5. ———, and Julian Stanley, "Experimental and Quasi-Experimental Designs for Research on Teaching," in N. L. Gage (ed.), *Handbook of Research on Teaching,* Rand McNally, Chicago (1973), pp. 171–246.
6. Caulcott, Evelyn, *Significance Tests,* Routledge & Kegan Paul, London (1973).
7. Dean, Gillian, "Divorce Policy and Divorce: An Empirical Study," unpublished paper, Vanderbilt University, 1973.
8. ———, "Impact and Feedback Effects: Divorce Policy and Divorce in the American States," unpublished paper, Vanderbilt University, 1975.
9. Fowler, Edmund, and Robert Lineberry, "Comparative Policy Analysis and the Problem of Reciprocal Causation," in Craig Liske *et al., Comparative Public Policy: Issues, Theories, and Methods,* Sage-Halsted-Wiley, New York (1975).

10. Green, Leon, *The Theory of Proximate Cause,* Vernon Law Book Co., Kansas City (1929).
11. Guilford, J. P., and Benjamin Fruchter, *Fundamental Statistics in Psychology and Education,* McGraw-Hill, New York (1973), pp. 120–171, 396–460.
12. Heise, David, "Causal Inference from Panel Data," in Edgar Borgatta and George Bornstedt (eds.), *Sociological Methodology,* Jossey-Bass, San Francisco (1970).
13. Kritzer, Michael, "Sanctions and Deviance," *Justicia* 3 (1975): 18–28.
14. MacIver, Robert, *Social Causation,* Harper and Row, New York (1964).
15. Miller, Alden, "Logic of Causal Analysis: From Experimental to Non-experimental Designs," in H. Blalock (ed.), *Causal Models in the Social Sciences,* Aldine, Chicago (1971), pp. 273–294.
16. Nagel, Stuart, "Political Party Affiliation and Judges' Decisions," *American Political Science Review* 4 (1961): 843–850.
17. ———, "Off-the-Bench Judicial Attitudes," in Glendon Schubert (ed.), *Judicial Decision-Making,* Free Press, New York (1963), pp. 229–254.
18. ———, *The Legal Process from a Behavioral Perspective,* Dorsey, Homewood, Ill. (1969).
19. ———, *Minimizing Costs and Maximizing Benefits in Providing Legal Services to the Poor,* Sage, Beverly Hills, Calif. (1973).
20. ———: Anthony Champagne; and Marian Neef, "Attorney Attitudes toward the Unpopular and the Poor," in S. Nagel, *Improving the Legal Process: Effects of Alternatives,* Lexington-Health, Lexington, Mass. (1975), pp. 81–115.
21. Pelz, Donald, and F. M. Andrews, "Detecting Causal Priorities in Panel Study Data," *American Sociological Review* 29 (1964), pp. 836–848.
22. Ross, Lawrence; Donald Campbell, and Gene Glass, "Determining the Social Effects of a Legal Reform: The British Breathalyser Crackdown of 1967," in S. Nagel (ed.), *Law and Social Change,* Sage, Beverly Hills, Calif. (1970), pp. 15–32.
23. Simon, Herbert, "Spurious Correlation: A Causal Interpretation," *Journal of the American Statistical Association* 49 (1954): 457–479.
24. Tittle, Charles, "Crime Rates and Legal Sanctions," *Social Problems* 16 (1969): pp. 409–423.
25. Zeisel, Hans, *Say It with Figures,* Harper and Row, New York (1968), pp. 109–240.

APPENDIX: SUMMARY OF SOME MAJOR PRINCIPLES IN CAUSAL ANALYSIS

This Appendix pulls together on a more abstract level the major causal analysis principles which are illustrated in the chapter with law and society examples from judicial decision making, attorney-client relations, comparisons across litigants, and reciprocal relations between law and society. By seeing the principles on a more abstract level, their interrelations and generalizability are further clarified. This Appendix also briefly refers to some important general matters which did not seem appropriate to discuss in the text given the emphasis on concrete legal process illustrations.

I. BASIC SYMBOLS

1. B_{YX} = The slope of the relation between dependent variable Y and independent variable X.
   a. In causal analysis, these slopes generally involve working with standardized scores on the variables, although unstandardized scores can also produce meaningful results especially where the variables are dichotomized and there is thus little difference between the two kinds of slopes.
   b. If only two variables are involved, correlation coefficients (r) can be used as a substitute for these slopes since $B_{YX} = r_{YX}$ in bivariate relations.
2. $B_{YX.z}$ = The slope of the XY relation holding a third or Z variable constant. If the Z is preceded by a − or +, this refers to partitioning the sample into those that are in the negative category on Z and those in the positive category.
3. High = A slope that is high relative to the other slopes that are part of the causal analysis.
4. Low = A slope that is low relative to the other slopes that are part of the causal analysis.
5. X→Y = The presence of variable X causes variable Y to be present or absent, or changes in variable X cause changes in variable Y.
6. X---Y = Variable X covaries with variable Y in the same or in opposite directions, but they do not have a causal relation.

II. THE GENERAL DEFINITION OF CAUSATION

There is a causal relation between variable X and variable Y if:

1. X precedes Y in time, or the alleged causal changes in X precede in time the alleged effect changes in Y.
2. X substantially co-varies with Y either in the same direction or in opposite directions. How much covariation or degree of correlation constitutes substantial covariation depends on the relative costs of making an error of concluding there is a causal relation when there is none versus making an error of concluding there is no causal relation when there really is one.
3. No Z variable can be controlled for that will substantially change the covariation.
   a. How much change constitutes substantial change depends on the same criterion as mentioned above.
   b. When one stops looking for additional Z variables depends on the cost of doing additional research and the likely benefits in light of what is already known about the relation between the proposed Z variables and the XY relation.

III. CO-EFFECTS AND INTERVENING VARIABLE CAUSATION
A. Definitions
1. Co-effects models: X---Y. $Z{\rightarrow}X$. $Z{\rightarrow}Y$.
2. Intervening variable model: X---Y. $X{\rightarrow}Z$. $Z{\rightarrow}Y$.
B. Conditions to satisfy
1. The original relations: B_{YX} = high. B_{XZ} = high. B_{YZ} = high.
2. Partitioning the sample: $B_{YX.-Z}$ = low. $B_{YX.+Z}$ = low.
3. Multivariate relations: $B_{YX.Z}$ = low. $B_{YZ.X}$ = high.
4. Path analysis: B_{ZX} times B_{ZY} equals B_{YX}.
5. Whether the co-effects model or intervening model applies depends on the known temporal order of the variables.

IV. JOINT CAUSATION
A. Definitions
1. Two input variables: $(X_1$ and $X_2){\rightarrow}Y$, but not $X_1{\rightarrow}Y$ or $X_2{\rightarrow}Y$
2. One input variable and one control variable: $X{\rightarrow}$middling Y. $X{\rightarrow}$low or negative Y, when all entities are $-Z$. $X{\rightarrow}$high or positive Y, when all entities are $+Z$.
3. Co-causation: $X_1{\rightarrow}Y$. $X_2{\rightarrow}Y$.
B. Conditions to satisfy
1. Two input variables:
a. Changing the measurement: B_{YX1} = low. B_{YX2} = low. $B_{YX'}$ = high, where X' is a variable such that one has to be plus on both X_1 and X_2 in order to be plus on X'.
b. Multivariate relations: $B_{YX1.X2X3}$ = low. $B_{YX2.X1X3}$ = low. $B_{YX3.X1X2}$ = high, where X_3 is the product of X_1 and X_2.
2. One input variable and one control variable:
a. Partitioning the sample: B_{YX} = middling. $B_{YX.-Z}$ = low. $B_{YX.+Z}$ = high.
b. Multivariate relations: $B_{YX.Z}$ and $B_{YZ.X}$ tell us nothing relevant to this model.
3. Co-causation: B_{YX1} = high. B_{YX2} = high. B_{YX3} = low.

V. RECIPROCAL CAUSATION
A. Definition: $X{\rightarrow}Y$. $Y{\rightarrow}X$.
B. Conditions for establishing which way the causation is greater:
1. The original relations: B_{YX} = high. B_{XY} = high.
2. One point in time data: B_{XZ1} = high. B_{YZ1} = low. B_{YZ2} = high. B_{XZ2} = low. $X{\rightarrow}Y$ more than $Y{\rightarrow}X$ if B_{YXp} is greater than B_{XYp}, where X_p is the value of X predicted from Z_1 and Y_p is the value of Y predicted from Z_2.

3. Two points in time data:
   a. Multivariate relations: X causes Y more than Y causes X if $B_{Y2X1.Y1}$ is greater than $B_{X2Y1.X1}$.
   b. Path analysis: X causes Y more than Y causes X if B_{X2X1} times B_{Y2X1} equals B_{Y2X2} more so than B_{X2Y1} times B_{Y2Y1} equals B_{Y2X2}.
4. Multiple time points with interrupted time series (where Y is a continuous variable and X is a dichotomous variable changing once over time)
   a. X causes Y if B_{YX} substantially changes direction or degree when X changes from minus to plus, provided the other causation essentials are present.
   b. Y causes X if B_{YX} does not change direction or degree when X changes from minus to plus, provided as above.
   c. Y causes X which in turn causes Y if B_{YX} goes up before X changes and up more after X changes, or if B_{YX} goes down before X changes and goes down more after X changes, provided as above.
5. To establish reciprocal causation rather than which way the causation is greater, both X→Y and Y→X must satisfy the general definition of causation under II.

SCHOOL DESEGREGATION AND SOCIAL SCIENCE: THE VIRGINIA EXPERIENCE

Adolph H. Grundman, METROPOLITAN STATE

COLLEGE—DENVER

On May 17, 1954, the United States Supreme Court in *Brown v. Board of Education* declared that segregated schools were inherently unequal. In so deciding, the Supreme Court directed a fatal blow to the legal superstructure which subordinated American Negroes to the level of second-class citizens. The Court itself recognized that the issue raised in *Brown v. Board of Education* had revolutionary implications from the Southern perspective. As a result, the Court heard two arguments and postponed fashioning an implementation decree until May 31, 1955 (349 U.S. 294).

This cautious approach was followed in an effort to prepare the South for the decision and to fashion a strategy which would gain the unanimous endorsement of the Court [Kluger (21), p. 667–746]. In many ways Chief Justice Earl Warren's opinion demonstrated a sensitivity for the issue

Research in Law and Sociology—Vol. 1, 1978, pages 229–250.

before the Court and the country. His opinion rejected the rhetoric of a radical reformer by omitting any moral condemnation of the South. In part, Warren's opinion made a simple appeal to all Americans that this country had changed in significant ways since the passage of the Fourteenth Amendment (1868) and the Court's holding in *Plessy v. Ferguson* (1896). By 1954 America's investment in public education alone stood as evidence of a fundamental change in its values and history. Moreover, there was abundant proof that blacks benefited from public education since many blacks "had achieved outstanding success in the arts and sciences as well as in the business and professional world" (*Brown v. Board of Education* (9), p. 490). Finally, and most controversially, Warren concluded that the state of psychological knowledge no longer supported the *Plessy* dictum (9), p. 494.

The *Brown* decision, it is too easily forgotten, came at a moment when there was a remarkable consensus about our institutions and among our social scientists about the psychology and sociology of race relations. Today, at a time when America has apparently reached its limits of Court-ordered desegregation, it is clear that this consensus no longer exists and that its disruption has played an important role in drawing lines beyond which the Supreme Court will not go.[1] The purpose of this paper is to focus on one element of the 1954 consensus: the almost unanimous agreement among social scientists that there was a positive relationship between segregation and Negro economic inequality, underachievement in education, and low self-esteem. Using Virginia as a test case, research demonstrates that social science findings evolved into an ambiguous justification for ordering desegregation and that its sheer complexity as evidence led to opinions that were not convincing from the perspective of social science.[2]

In *Brown* I, Warren wrote that segregated schools generated "a feeling of inferiority" among black children which was "unlikely ever to be undone." As a result segregated schools were "inherently unequal." To justify this assertion Warren cited a portion of the Kansas three-judge district court's opinion which acknowledged that segregation was educationally and psychologically harmful, but found Topeka schools otherwise equal and constitutional under the *Plessy* doctrine. Warren followed this citation with the famous footnote eleven, which listed seven studies supporting the Court's conclusions on the impact of segregated education (9), p. 494.

Footnote eleven immediately moved to the center stage as journalists, lawyers, and scholars debated the merits of Warren's opinion. Southern conservatives charged that the Supreme Court had departed from the law and, in effect, had amended the Constitution on the strength of certain questionable findings developed by social scientists. In Virginia, James J.

Kilpatrick, then editor of the *Richmond News Leader,* wrote a battery of editorials in 1955 which argued that the issue was not race but the Constitution, and urged his state to resist the Court's decree. Kilpatrick and others were quick to place special emphasis on the Court's inclusion of Gunnar Myrdal's *An American Dilemma* in challenging the decision. They charged that his origin and politics made him a poor judge of southern customs [Grundman (15), pp. 83–92].

The South's criticism of the use of social science evidence was not easily brushed aside by legal commentators who supported the decision. "Friendly critics" praised the result but criticized much of Warren's legal scholarship. Some wished that the Court had based its decision on neutral principles, and others regretted that it had not taken the opportunity to expose the glaring weaknesses of *Plessy v. Ferguson* and subsequent rulings on public school segregation. Many "friendly critics" agreed with Robert J. Harris's comment that *Brown* was a great decision but the opinion ". . . was not a great opinion" [Wechsler (36), p. 35; Harris (17), p. 431]. Common to all observations was the apprehension that the Court's reliance on social science evidence was a two-edged sword capable of haunting the *Brown* decision.

In 1955, Edmund Cahn (11) wrote a significant article which attempted to defuse the debate over the Court's use of social science data (pp. 150–169). In a gentle way Cahn took issue with the research and conclusions of Professor Kenneth B. Clark. During the litigation, Professor Clark, at the time an assistant professor at the City College of New York, was utilized by the NAACP as an expert witness in the Delaware, Virginia, and South Carolina cases. In South Carolina and Delaware (Virginia involved the desegregation of a high school), Professor Clark gave black children, between the ages of six and nine, a doll test which he had devised prior to the litigation. Clark showed black children brown and white dolls and asked them a variety of questions purported to demonstrate how segregation harmed the self-esteem of black children. Clark concluded that segregation had a debilitating effect on the self-concept of black children.[3] Cahn, however, pointed out that the research design of the doll test had serious flaws: the sample was small, only sixteen in South Carolina; it was impossible to determine whether shcool or other influences were responsible for the results; and Clark's research demonstrated that northern children responded the same way. At the trial level Cahn suggested that counsel for the defendants overlooked these weaknesses because they were well aware that segregation degraded blacks and, therefore, devoted their time to disparaging the geographical or ethnic background of the expert witnesses. The credibility of social scientists, he stressed, derived from the fact that their findings "happened to coincide with common knowledge." In effect, he argued that a Ph.D was not necessary to conclude that state-enforced segregation violated "universally accepted standards of right and wrong" and was "psychologically imperious and morally evil."' Cahn, therefore, disagreed with Clark and gently chided him for writing that evidence of segregation's harm "had to come from the social psychologists and other social scientists." The law professor thought it significant that the Court had not directly cited Clark's testimony and interpreted footnote eleven as merely a thoughtful gesture to some hardworking, well-intentioned scholars by a magnanimous judge [Cahn (11), pp. 159–165].

After his analysis of the social science testimony, Professor Cahn summarized briefly and prophetically the danger of coupling basic rights with social science research. The behavioral sciences, he wrote, "are so very young, imprecise, and changeful, their findings have an uncertain expectancy of life. Today's sanguine asseveration may be cancelled by tomorrow's revelations . . . or new technical fad." Legislators might wish to use social science findings for legislative experiments, but the courts should not permit "our fundamental rights to rise, fall, or change along with the latest fashion of our psychological literature." If the courts rested their decisions on social science data and social psychologists returned "to the ethnic mysticism of the past," Cahn concluded that the future of constitutional rights was dim [Cahn (11), pp. 167–168].

In addition to its changefulness, Cahn offered additional cautions to judges faced with social science evidence. He warned them that it was very difficult to use properly. Different premises and the difficulty of checking inferences empirically made it very difficult "to notice where objective science ends and advocacy begins" (11), p. 166.

Many of Cahn's comments have stood the test of time. Others not only joined Cahn in finding fault with Clark's research but extended their criticism to the work of the scholars who joined Clark in footnote eleven.[4] Some years after the decision, Chief Justice Warren confirmed Cahn's interpretation of the Court's use of social science. He observed: "We included it because I thought the point it made was the antithesis of what was said in *Plessy*. They had said there that if there was any harm intended, it was solely in the mind of the Negro. I thought these things— these cited sources—were sufficient to note as being in contradistinction to the statement in *Plessy*. It was only a note after all" [Kluger (21), p. 706]. Finally, Cahn, as this paper will show, correctly predicted that social science could cut both ways and that resourceful lawyers might use it to restrict desegregation in different circumstances. Nonetheless, Cahn's prediction that "the impact of the Brandeis brief is no longer as great as when the device was novel and judges more readily impressed by the paraphernalia of social and pseudo science" proved short of the mark [Cahn (11), p. 154]. Cahn's judgment on this issue probably was blunted by his distrust of social science and his effort to persuade courts not to take its findings too seriously.

Whatever the Supreme Court's rationale for citing social science evidence in *Brown*, the incidence of this kind of evidence in school litigation escalated rather than declined after 1954. There were several reasons for this development. First, the South was not prepared to disregard the Court's utilization of social science evidence. In addition to its usefulness as a basis for criticizing *Brown I*, the South was initially confident that it could reverse the decision by producing an alternative set of data which justified segregation. Secondly, the NAACP, for a variety of reasons, continued to stress social science evidence in litigation. Although there were limitations to Clark's research, his findings demonstrated that black children in the North suffered the same kind of damage as those in the South. Consequently liberal social scientists and lawyers were led to believe that whatever the cause of racial isolation, it was harmful. The loose language of *Brown I* also encouraged them to pursue this line of reasoning. For example, the citation from the Kansas three-judge court implied that racial separation of any kind had detrimental effects (347 U.S. 483: 49). From a practical point of view, the NAACP was attracted to this argument because it thought it would be useful in attacking segregation in the North. Originally NAACP lawyers thought that proving *de jure*-type conduct among northern school officials would be too difficult [Herbst (18), p. 47]. Although this strategy did not work, the effect was to place attention on the effects of schooling rather than the quality of the facilities or the curriculum. This increased the demand for social scientists who were trained to analyze the relationship between racial separation and achievement. This method of structuring litigation would subsequently be important in Virginia in the last years of the 1960s.

Between 1954 and 1969 social science evidence did not play a significant role in Virginia and the remainder of the South. The efforts of the social scientists on behalf of segregationists met with failure. Methodological weaknesses, racist preconceptions, and reactionary political views made it difficult for social scientists sympathetic to the South to persuade other social scientists, school boards, and courts that blacks were inherently inferior to whites [Newby (27), pp. 62–117].

Another important reason why social science played a subordinate role during this period was related to the parameters of the law. In 1955 two legal decisions were rendered which had a significant impact on school desegregation in the South. On May 31, the Supreme Court handed down its "deliberate speed" formula in the second *Brown* decision. In implementing *Brown I*, the Court delegated responsibility for desegregation to the federal district court judges who were given vague guidelines to govern their decisions (349 U.S. 294, 1955). Less than two months later, on

July 15, a three-judge federal district court, in *Briggs v. Elliott,* declared that the decision in *Brown I* did not require integration but merely forbade state-enforced discrimination by race. The combination of *Brown II* and *Briggs* meant that Virginia and the South were given the opportunity to experiment with a variety of school assignment plans aimed at limiting or preventing school desegregation. In turn, this meant that NAACP lawyers devoted all their time and energy to proving that various assignment plans either blatantly or subtly violated the *Brown* decision.

The history of Virginia's school desegregation cases serves as a demonstration of the thrust and counterthrust of law and litigation. From 1956 to 1958 Virginia's desegregation policy was guided by a collection of laws which provided for school closures whenever a black child was admitted to a white school. When state and federal courts declared these laws unconstitutional in 1959, Virginia passed another series of laws aimed at minimizing desegregation. Once again NAACP lawyers successfully challenged these laws as well as a variety of assignment plans. Between 1959 and 1964 the lawyers for the NAACP won decisions at the Fourth Circuit Court of Appeals overthrowing dual attendance zones, assignments based on academic tests limited to blacks, and minority to majority transfer plans. In every one of these cases NAACP lawyers pounded on the theme that the law required desegregation. Despite a string of legal victories, by 1964 Virginia's civil rights lawyers had succeeded in placing only 5 percent of Virginia's black children in schools with white children. There were two major barriers to desegregation at this time: the Fourth Circuit Court's acceptance of freedom-of-choice school plans and, in urban Virginia, the presence of racially segregated housing patterns. Although neutral on its face, freedom-of-choice assignment plans resulted in little desegregation. Fear, inertia, and traditional loyalties, all more pronounced in urban Virginia, meant that black students usually chose to remain in black schools.[5]

Beginning in 1968 the legal picture described above changed dramatically with the Supreme Court's decision in *Green v. New Kent County,* a rural Virginia county east of Richmond. In this case the Court held that freedom-of-choice plans were unacceptable if they did not lead to integrated schools and if other methods were available which promised to work more effectively. The Court also laid to rest the *Briggs* dictum by charging school boards with the "affirmative duty to convert to a unitary system in which racial discrimination would be eliminated root and branch" (391 U.S. 430, 1968: 437–38). The inference of *Green* was that the purpose of *Brown* was not limited to eradicating state-sanctioned school segregation but to assure that every black student could have an integrated education which was, by implication, the only test of educational equality. On the basis of this ruling and its inferences, the lawyers for the NAACP asked school boards to eliminate all black schools in the jurisdiction. They argued that a unitary school system was one in which the ratio of black to white students in each school corresponded to the racial composition of the entire school system. Where housing patterns served as obstacles to integration, civil rights lawyers considered bus transportation a legitimate tool for desegregation. If school systems were overwhelmingly black, they argued that consolidation with surrounding white systems was required by the law.

The NAACP's legal victory in *Green,* however, was accompanied by a dramatic change in the nation's mood on race relations which was unfavorable to school desegregation. The most significant developments between 1964 and 1968 were the emotional northern protests to the legal assault on racial isolation in its cities, the criticism of integration as a viable objective by a segment of black Americans, and the division among social scientists on integration as a remedy to past racial discrimination [Woodward (37), pp. 189–220].

The inference of *Brown* and *Green,* that the equality of educational opportunity and integrated schools were synonymous, was based on social science findings and depended upon them for their sustenance. After *Green,* as the NAACP proposed more controversial remedies to achieve school desegregation, it naturally utilized social science evidence. In fact, given the unpopular political climate in 1968, the NAACP may have hoped that the historic unanimity of social scientists on the desegregation issue would not only tip the scales in its favor in the courts but also at the bar of public opinion. Thus, social scientists were pushed to the center of the legal stage reminiscent of *Brown I.* The result this time, however, was legal confusion and a breakdown of unanimity among social scientists.

The new phase of the social scientists' role in the school desegregation cases actually preceded the *Green* decision by two years. In 1966, the federal government published *Equality of Educational Opportunity,* a study of the availability of equal educational opportunities in the United States which was ordered by the Office of Education and directed by James S. Coleman. The major conclusion of the *Coleman Report* was that the most significant correlates of educational achievement, in their order of importance, were the family class background of the student and the social class mix of the classroom. The report not only found that the gap in physical facilities and curricula between black and white schools was not as great as expected, but that these tangibles were overrated in determining success on achievement tests. Finally, the study did not suggest that racial integration, as an independent factor, was responsible for accelerating educational achievement [Coleman (12), pp. 298–304].

The *Coleman Report* generated a controversy among educators who debated the report's research design, conclusions, and policy inferences.

A major flaw of the study, according to one authority in educational testing, was its selection of verbal ability as the overriding criterion of academic achievement, since this skill was generally understood to be strongly influenced by the child's home. The same person thought there was absolutely no evidence in the *Report* which demonstrated that minority or lower-class children automatically benefited from classroom attendance with middle-class children [Dyer (13), pp. 38–56]. Others argued that the *Coleman Report* underrated the importance of financial resources and quality of teachers [Bowles (3), pp. 89–99].

The importance placed on a middle-class environment in public schools threatened to undermine the importance of racial integration. However, in *Racial Isolation in the Public Schools,* a study sponsored by the United States Commission on Civil Rights, a team of social scientists re-examined the Coleman data in an effort to determine its meaning for desegregation. The Commission study found that the achievement of black students improved in majority white schools. Although the survey did not offer a specific explanation for this phenomenon, it did conclude that the "combined effects of social class integration and racial desegregation are substantial" [U.S. Commission on Civil Rights, (35), pp. 90–91]. Since only one-fourth of black America was middle class, Harvard Professor Thomas Pettigrew, a co-director of *Racial Isolation,* explained later, racial integration and class integration were hardly distinguishable [Pettigrew, (30), p. 62]. In addition to achievement in school, this study also found that racial isolation penalized the black student after graduation. Negative community attitudes toward black schools, the perpetuation of racial stereotypes, and limited association with whites were considered important factors in restricting job opportunities for black public school graduates [U.S. Commission on Civil Rights, (35), p. 114]. *Racial Isolation* warned, however, that the mere mixing of black and white bodies provided no panacea to educational and social problems. Successful school desegregation needed an environment where the entire community cooperated by providing an atmosphere of positive racial acceptance (35), pp. 154–159.

Although *Racial Isolation* demonstrated that a harmony could be attained between the *Coleman Report* and racial integration, it also suffered serious shortcomings. The results of the research did not show a causal relationship between racial integration and academic achievement. Those scholars who made such a connection were engaging in an inference which required more research. In concluding that segregated schools penalized the black student after graduation by perpetuating stereotypes, the authors of *Racial Isolation* were again speculating. There was no evidence which illustrated how desegregation altered other elements of racism in society [St. John, (32), pp. 36–41, 59–60, 107–113, 119–124].

Also, in suggesting that integration required a favorable setting, the study begged the question regarding the wisdom of pursuing controversial desegregation plans in hostile settings. Finally, some scholars charged that American sociologists were, as a profession, too committed to racial assimilation. They believed that ethnicity and racial pride held out productive possibilities which were consistent with American history and democracy [Metzger (23), pp. 637–38; McCarthy and Yancey (22), pp. 647–666].

Although the *Coleman Report* offered a wealth of information on the impact of education on American children, it also demonstrated how much was yet unknown about the educational process. The findings called for more research and caution in their utilization. The politically charged atmosphere of the late 1960s, however, prevented such an approach. This atmosphere led to two important developments. One was a serious division among the social scientists, accompanied by charges and countercharges that research findings were being subordinated to personal policy preferences concerning school integration [Pettigrew *et al.*, (31), pp. 88–118]. The second development was that school boards and federal district court judges, as illustrated by two Virginia cases, were now in a position to utilize a literal and uncritical reading of social science evidence to restrict as well as to order school integration.

In 1969, black plaintiffs challenged a Norfolk, Virginia, assignment plan which left a large percentage of black children in all black schools at the elementary and junior high levels. The Norfolk school board during 1969–1970 was responsible for 56,628 students of which 24,007 were black. Its assignment plan provided that 5,918 black students would attend desegregated schools [*Beckett v. School Board of the City of Norfolk,* (2)]. The school board defended this assignment plan by arguing that it was guided by the most recent social science data, which suggested that the most important factor in determining a school's success was the socio-economic background of the school's population. From the board's perspective, the desegregation of black schools made little educational sense unless the proper social class mix was present. The school board based this argument on conclusions drawn from the *Coleman Report*. The plaintiffs charged that the law, following the *Green* case, required the elimination of all black schools and argued that the transportation of students was a legally acceptable means of achieving this goal. Lawyers for the NAACP and Civil Rights Division contended that "token desegregation of whites into black schools is better than none at all but, in general, they insist[ed] that the previously all-black schools must now constitutionally be made up of at least 25 percent whites—at all times agreeing, however, that it would be preferable to have a majority white" (2), p. 1289.

Another important element in this case was the judge, Walter E. Hoffman, who had conducted the Norfolk litigation from its inception in 1955. Because of Judge Hoffman's criticism of massive resistance and his order to integrate Norfolk's schools, he had been a favorite target of massive resisters in the late 1950s [Peltason, (29), pp. 11–12]. His refusal to bend in the face of political pressure resulted, however, from his reading of the law and not from any enthusiasm for school integration. In 1957 Hoffman wrote that he saw "no inherent right of any child to attend any particular school in which children of another race are in attendance" as long as they were not excluded for racial reasons [*Adkins v. School Board of Norfolk,* (1)]. By 1959 there was little evidence to suggest that Hoffman had departed from this position.

In *Beckett* (2), decided on December 30, 1969, Judge Hoffman accepted the school board's assignment plan and the premises upon which it was based. As far as educational achievement was concerned, he considered race "definitely a secondary factor." Courts, Hoffman continued, "are overlooking . . . the primary variable [which] is social class; not race. . . . It is the social class of the overall group *in gross* which makes desegregated schools advantageous to all." In fashioning an assignment plan for Norfolk, Hoffman observed: "We cannot believe that the Supreme Court, in requiring 'desegregation,' has merely ordered a mixing of racial bodies without consideration of the social class factor." Moreover, he feared that racial balancing would lead to the flight of the white middle class from the city. As a result, the best educational mix would be permanently unobtainable in Norfolk schools (308 F. Supp. 1274, 1969: 1284–1285, 1287–1288).

To a great extent, Hoffman's conclusions regarding social science relied on the clever use of the testimony of Professor Thomas F. Pettigrew. In establishing the credibility of Pettigrew's testimony, Hoffman commenced by describing the Harvard professor as "undoubtedly the most outstanding and knowledgeable person in the field of sociology and race relations as related to integration." To this value judgment, Hoffman added Pettigrew's personal description of himself as a "racial integrationist." With his credentials established, Hoffman quoted directly from Pettigrew's testimony which praised the Norfolk school board for attempting for the first time "to explicate principles that would guide their plans based on the best social science data we now have available" (308 F. Supp. 1274, 1969: 1286). The Norfolk judge also cited Pettigrew's approval of an assignment plan which provided for a ratio of seventy white to thirty black (with a maximum of 40 percent black) in Norfolk's schools. The Harvard professor believed that such a plan would minimize white flight, maximize black achievement, and contribute to the development of positive attitudes in all children [*Atkins v. Norfolk* (1), p. 1291].

Hoffman also devoted some attention to the argument of the NAACP and the Civil Rights Division that token desegregation of black schools was better than none at all. On this point Hoffman wrote that the *Coleman Report* concluded that the achievement of black children did not increase with the introduction of a token white enrollment. In fact, some evidence showed that the achievement of black and white children declined in these settings. Hoffman acknowledged that the poor performances of such white children might be explained by their social class background. If that were the case, however, he believed that it was another good argument for avoiding token integration. After all, he concluded, "we trust that there is just as much interest in the disadvantaged white child as with respect to the disadvantaged Negro child" (1), p. 1291.

Hoffman's use of the *Coleman Report,* other social science data, and Pettigrew's testimony was perplexing. In reading the *Coleman Report* as statement of truths, Hoffman went far beyond the findings of the *Report* and failed to appreciate their shortcomings (1), pp. 10–11. Secondly, he confused *Brown II*'s order to desegregate schools with another goal: equality of educational outcomes. His mixture of the two was understandable, given the confidence that social scientists and lawyers exhibited on behalf of school integration and its ability to produce equality of outputs. Hoffman demonstrated, however, that this latter goal could actually be used to limit rather than increase integration. Thirdly, Hoffman engaged in a selective use of social science evidence. Pettigrew disapproved of the Norfolk plans' provision for neighborhood schools for the first three grades. Hoffman preferred a neighborhood plan for all of the elementary years but compromised at the third grade because some evidence suggested that the "adverse effects" of racial isolation began at age nine [Beckett (2), p. 1302]. Yet he offered no analysis for defending the selection of the third grade over any other. A fourth characteristic of Hoffman's opinion was his enthusiastic embracement of social science evidence. He wrote: "We have no hesitancy in examining the case from the standpoint of these criteria. It was on these grounds that the Supreme Court overruled *Plessy v. Ferguson* in *Brown v. Board of Education*" (2), p. 1279. Perhaps the decision explained his enthusiasm. He had demonstrated that social science research conducted by scholars with impeccable liberal credentials could be used to limit desegregation.

Hoffman also attempted to reshape the school litigation in another significant way. In an important facet of Hoffman's opinion, he argued that the distinction between *de facto* and *de jure* had no basis in fact or history. The significance of this debate was largely related to a section of the 1964 Civil Rights Act which stated that nothing in the act "shall empower any official or court to issue any order seeking to achieve racial balance in any school requiring the transportation of pupils or students from one school to another . . . in order to achieve such racial balance . . ." (2), p. 1302. The NAACP and the Civil Rights Division argued that the above section did not apply to Norfolk since it only covered *de facto* segregation.

The Norfolk School Board, however, argued that it had exhibited "good faith" and had eliminated discriminatory school assignments. In effect, the school board held that Norfolk had eliminated *de jure* segregation and that it was not responsible for the *de facto* segregation that remained. The Civil Rights Division and the NAACP countered with the argument that discriminatory housing practices contributed to the *de jure* character of Norfolk's racial segregation. In short, pre-1954 legislation and post-1954 delays and housing practices combined to create a situation which could not be remedied, because of their cumulative effects, without racial balancing (2), p. 1303.

Hoffman rejected the NAACP's position and argued that by extending the concept of *de jure* segregation to include the discriminatory actions of all public officials and laws meant that every state was guilty of *de jure* segregation, especially if one emphasized the cumulative effects of past laws. To strengthen the argument, Hoffman added an appendix to his opinion which cited discriminatory legislation in northern states (2), Appendix C: pp. 1311–15. From this perspective, Hoffman failed to see how the South could be distinguished from the North in desegregation cases. He articulated the thoughts of many Virginians when he wrote: "We cannot believe that the Constitution may be interpreted one way for one group of states, and still another way for the remaining states" (2), p. 1305.

Hoffman's intent, however, was not to precipitate racial balancing throughout the nation. As a result of *Brown* and its progeny, Hoffman wrote that school boards had two mandates: one negative, one positive. The former prohibited a school board from excluding students from schools because of race or color *(Briggs v. Elliott);* the latter required maximum desegregation *(Green v. New Kent County),* but, according to Hoffman, "so far as it may be reasonable and feasible." This qualification was significant, since Hoffman believed that the *Green* precedent could not easily be applied to Norfolk because of the demographic differences. In distinguishing the *Green v. New Kent County* case from the Norfolk case, Hoffman saw two important differences. One was that the freedom of choice plan was defective in the *Green* case, in part, because New Kent County claimed, unlike Norfolk, that it had desegregated its schools "and not that desegregation was proceeding at an adequate pace." Secondly, Hoffman thought it regrettable that some courts had interpreted *Green's* "'desegregate now' as an indication that the mixing of bodies is of primary importance and sound educational principles must take a back seat." He interpreted the Supreme Court's opinions differently. Although the time for compliance with the negative mandate was passed, Hoffman refused to believe "that the Supreme Court had ruled out reasonable experimental plans grounded upon factors which give rise to the belief that such experimentation will lead to successful integration for the city as a whole" [*Beckett, 1969:* (2) pp. 1276–1278, 1288].[6]

The Fourth Circuit Court of Appeals held that Judge Hoffman's use of social science data was impermissible. Hoffman's effort, however, generated three opinions from the four-man court. Judge John Butzner, who wrote the court's opinion, argued that Norfolk's "rigid adherence to quotas . . . preserves traditional racial characteristics of its schools." He found that the Norfolk plan excluded many black pupils from integrated schools merely because of their race. The result was "the antithesis of a racially unitary school system." Judge Albert V. Bryan concurred with Butzner but expressed sympathy with the school board's efforts to do a good job. Despite the good intentions of the school board, Bryan thought the assignment plan incorporated racial quotas which violated *Brown* and its progeny. Judge Simon Sobeloff, with Judge Harrison Winter concurring, wrote the third opinion. Sobeloff's opinion was sparked by his displeasure with the use of social science evidence and his unwillingness to leave Bryan's praise of the school board unanswered. Sobeloff concluded that "The new, and spurious, 'principles' devised by the Board and endorsed by the Judge as justification for the failure to desegregate fly in the face of *Brown* . . . and are simply new rationalizations to perpetuating illegal segregation" [Brewer (7), pp. 408, 411, 443–444]. Unlike Hoffman, the Fourth Circuit Court of Appeals read *Brown* as simply requiring racial desegregation of the schools. Except for Sobeloff's obvious disdain for the introduction of the *Coleman Report,* this court completely avoided the issues raised by social science evidence.

The special emphasis placed on social science in the Norfolk suit was repeated in the Richmond school consolidation case. This trial had national significance, since it was one of several cases in the courts at that time which attempted to integrate schools by crossing political boundaries. The NAACP saw this remedy as the key to desegregating urban America which increasingly found majority black enrollments in city school systems.

The consolidation case was precipitated when Judge Robert R. Mehrige upheld an interim crosstown busing plan for Richmond city schools. In arriving at his decision in August 1970, Mehrige avoided all references to social science evidence. His opinion followed very closely the logic of law found in the stream of litigation from *Brown* through *Green.* Yet Mehrige's opinion evinced some theories about segregation which indicated sympathy for integration. He accepted, without qualification, Chief Justice Warren's statement in *Brown* that segregated schools were "inherently unequal." This citation acquired special significance when he coupled it with the conclusion that "the result of segregation whether *de jure* . . . or *de facto* . . . is still the same" [*Bradley* (4), pp. 555, 562, 574].

The Richmond busing decision prompted the Richmond school board and the NAACP to file a suit seeking the consolidation of the Richmond schools with the county school systems of Henrico and Chesterfield. The proposed metropolitan school system contemplated an enrollment of 105,000 students, of which 78,000 would be bused. The black enrollment was expected to reach 34 percent of the entire system (*Richmond Times-Dispatch,* August 20, 1970, p. 1).

On the surface, the Richmond school board's decision to ask the district court to join the three school districts was touched with irony. After all, the Richmond school board had invested two decades of its energy in attempting to minimize the impact of the *Brown* decision. Judge Mehrige's busing decree, however, marked the end of the success of this action. School and city officials now faced the prospect of a majority black school system for the indefinite future, and they did not like it. Underlying the school problem was a larger concern for the future stability of Richmond. The reality of rising expenditures and the specter of a shrinking tax base threatened the future of Virginia's capitol. School merger was viewed by some as a method of fostering greater regional planning, as a means of slowing white flight, and as a way of saving the Richmond schools. City and school officials were now ready to join the black plaintiffs in litigation with wide-ranging ramifications. The latter, of course, welcomed the opportunity to use Richmond as a test case for arguing that the Constitution permitted the crossing of political boundaries to integrate urban school systems [Grundman, (15), pp. 379–82].

Whereas Judge Mehrige avoided the dilemma posed by social science research in the Richmond busing case, he was inextricably entangled in the debate among educators when he ordered the consolidation of the Richmond, Chesterfield, and Henrico school systems. On January 10, 1972, in a 200-page opinion, Mehrige drew heavily on concepts developed by social science research. For example, one of the most striking parts of Mehrige's analysis was his conclusion that the "meaningful" or "effective" integration of public schools was essential to equality of education in a biracial community. In defining "meaningful integration" Mehrige rested heavily on the testimony of Thomas Pettigrew, who defined integration as "mix plus positive interaction . . . between whites and blacks." The optimum racial mix, according to Pettigrew, provided for black enrollments ranging from 20 to 40 percent. The lower percentage prevented tokenism and the ceiling discouraged white flight. The 40 percent limit on black enrollment also prevented negative racial identifiability because it eliminated majority black schools which the social scientists believed were considered inferior in the Richmond metropolitan area. Mehrige argued that "meaningful integration" would remedy the negative effects of majority black schools which, according to the experts, had negative effects not only upon "black pupils and teachers, but the entire community." Moreover, these adverse effects had a cumulative effect which was especially dramatic during the early years. Initiated at an early age, "meaningful integration" closed the educational gap because it brought about "self-perceptions and aspirations not colored by notions of artificial advantage or disadvantage related to race" [*Bradley* (5), pp. 67, 80–81, 103, 193–95].

In claiming that integration would close the educational gap between white and black students, Mehrige sidestepped the *Coleman Report*. He thought the *Coleman Report* had merit and that social class mixing would accompany racial integration "since race and class correlated to a great degree, but not completely." He stressed, however, that social class was a less important factor than integration as an educational tool, especially at the early grades. For Mehrige, the requirements of social science coincided with the requirements of the law [*Bradley,* (5), p. 196].

In addition to the educational benefits of school integration, Mehrige found that integration contributed to good race relations. The development of "realistic racial attitudes," "friendship and positive social behavior," and the "abatement of interracial hostility" were significant educational goals. In attaining them, Mehrige thought there was "no appropriate substitute." In making these judgments on the attitudinal benefits of integration, Mehrige rejected the opinion of the experts for the defendants, who testified that the consolidation plan was demeaning to black children because it implied that they could only learn in majority white classrooms. Mehrige declined to accept this argument on three grounds. First, in examining the testimony of Dr. Clifford Hooker, Dr. William McClure and Dr. James Whitlock, the leading experts for the defense, Mehrige pointed out that all of the men were experts in school administration and finance, rather than educational psychology. Secondly, cross-examination also revealed that the defense experts had previously advocated the reorganization of school districts for educational purposes, which included the advancement of such values as racial tolerance. Mehrige portrayed these men as educators who normally favored innovation, and attributed their reservations to unfamiliarity with Richmond and an undue sensitivity to area opposition to consolidation. Finally, Mehrige concluded that black opposition to consolidation was rhetoric inspired by accumulated frustrations with the failure of integration [*Bradley,* (5), pp. 194–195, 198–200, 202, 204].

Another question involving educational psychology was related to the impact of *de jure* as opposed to *de facto* segregation. The *Brown* decision found that state sanction of segregated education led to the inferiority of black education. In the Richmond case, however, the state sanction no longer existed. School children in Richmond were bused and black and white children attended the same schools in Henrico and Chesterfield counties. When Dr. Clifford Hooker of the University of Minnesota stated that "a public school is desegregated when it excludes no one because of race," he summarized the essence of the defense's case. Mehrige found two fundamental shortcomings with this argument. One was that the impact of transitional steps in the law had the same effect upon students as *de jure* segregation. Mehrige agreed with Dr. Robert Green's statement that containment strategies led black children to believe that "no matter how hard you work in life your ability to move freely is controlled by the dominant community in a very negative manner." Professor Pettigrew also testified, in Mehrige's words, that the educational harm to the black child in Richmond was "similar if not identical to the harm incurred prior to the *Brown* decision." Mehrige added that the failure to implement *Brown* "may" be an important negative variable for black children. The Richmond judge concluded that minor changes or transitional steps were not satisfactory. In effect, he argued that the negative effects of state imposed segregation were not eliminated until a state assignment program was achieved. A second reason why the mere elimination of racial assignments did not satisfy *Brown,* according to Mehrige, was that racial identifiability was the essential educational as well as legal problem. More importantly, and crucial in this case, was that racial identifiability in Richmond was a metropolitan problem and not one that was limited to the cities or the individual counties. In other words, a student compared his school assignment to others in the metropolitan area and not his school district [Bradley (5), pp. 80–81, 103, 209. 210].

In elaborating upon the Metro concept, Mehrige plunged deeply into statistical and demographic data. In order to demonstrate a community of interests, Mehrige cited statistics showing a significant level of economic interdependency and plans for regional co-operation service areas. After establishing the existence of a community of interest to his satisfaction, Mehrige cited statistics which broke down the black-white enrollment for the three school districts. In general, they indicated that by 1972 Richmond had a predominantly black school system (70 percent) and that the two counties were predominantly white (90 percent). To Mehrige, the existence of a metropolitan community of interest and disproportionate ratios of whites to blacks in the city and the counties was *prima facie* evidence of a segregated school system. He concluded by discussing evidence which tied the disproportionate racial assignment in the area to federal and local authorities who had colluded to restrict residential integration in the Richmond metropolitan area. Mehrige showed that the Federal Housing Authority and the Veterans Administration had originally pursued policies which perpetuated segregated housing. Although the federal government altered its guidelines to eliminate segregative language, Mehrige stressed that past policies had long-term effects. He bolstered this by citing a study directed by Karl E. Taeuber, a sociology professor at the University of Wisconsin, who concluded that the index of segregation in the city had increased from 79.3 percent in 1960 to 82.1 percent in 1970. Contributing to the federal government's policy were the city and county governments which opposed public housing in predominantly white areas. The long-term effects of racially restrictive covenants and the refusal of real estate agents to show blacks homes in white areas were also a part of this seamless web of racial separation in housing. Mehrige also found that state and local school authorities contributed to segregated housing through the selection of school building sites. He thought that a symbiotic relationship existed between housing segregation and school segregation. Judge Mehrige agreed that the boundary lines which separated the three political educational units were not drawn to segregate blacks. They were not, however, sufficient grounds for denying equal protection. Mehrige rested this conclusion on the voting rights and reapportionment cases. School buses, he continued, provided the means for passing over the school boundaries [*Bradley,* (5), pp. 91, 100, 178–182, 184–185, 212–227].

The pivotal question raised by this case was the procedure used by Judge Mehrige to evalute the social science data. Fortunately, his candor offered some insights into this question. At one point in his opinion he wrote: "It should be pointed out that the court in considering the testimony of the experts gives greater weight to those experts whose opinions were to the effect that equality of educational opportunity would flow from the consolidation of schools in the metropolitan areas, and that the proposed plan is both reasonable and feasible, than to the testimony of those whose opinions differ." But why did he prefer the opinions of the advocates of integration rather than those of the skeptics? Mehrige wrote: "In considering the weight to be given to the testimony of all the witnesses, the Court has considered the qualifications, experience, interest or lack of the same in the outcome of the litigation, their bias if any, as well as their actions upon the witness stand, and the weight and process of the reasoning by which they supported their respective opinions and testimony [*Bradley,* (5), p. 178].

These criteria helped to illuminate the reason why the plaintiffs' experts performed so well. First, unlike the defense experts, who were trained in administration and finance, the plaintiffs' experts were in educational psychology. Second, the star expert for the plaintiffs, Professor Pettigrew, had graduated from one of the Richmond high schools. As such, he combined educational expertise with a personal understanding of the situation. In addition, Dr. Robert Green of Michigan State had studied the Prince Edward County schools in Virginia, which had been closed for five years prior to 1963. Pettigrew and Green's firsthand knowledge of segregation in Virginia made their testimony more effective. Third, plaintiffs' experts profited from an unshaken conviction that their data demonstrated the educational and attitudinal benefits of integration. Pettigrew, in particular, was articulate, witty, and difficult to trap in cross-examination. The defense experts were less sure of themselves. Although persuaded that consolidation would fail for lack of support and, in the case of Clifford Hooker, that the requirement for majority white schools had racist implications, they avoided categorical conclusions. As a result, they were tangled up in contradictions which undermined their testimony. Finally, the experts of the plaintiffs may have profited from Judge Mehrige's view that consolidation was simply good policy. There were two statements buried in his opinion which indicated a strong sympathy for integration and for righting the wrongs of past discrimination. At one point Mehrige predicted that public resistance to consolidation would disappear if the community was made aware of the "discretionary practices to which the members of the plaintiff class and their parents and grandparents had been subjected." At another place in his opinion, Mehrige thought it unfortunate that resistance to integration had forced numerous historical expositions of the Fourteenth Amendment, when its language ;"bespeaks it all [Bradley (5), p. 178]. As history, Mehrige's interpretation of the Fourteenth Amendment was simplistic. Yet, his view of history and the struggle of blacks in America stood as evidence that Mehrige wanted to cut through the law in order to promote racial harmony.

As in the Norfolk case, Mehrige's opinion failed to reflect the differences of opinion in the debate among social scientists on the impact of racial isolation and integration. A number of his assertions were based on research findings that were hotly debated among social scientists or on inferences from these findings which needed more research. Easily his most controversial judgment was that school segregation and its cumulative effects were responsible for the condition of urban America and for black employment, income, housing, and attitudinal problems. The implication that integration offered the only solution to these problems was equally controversial. In 1976, there simply were not enough studies which demonstrated the relationship between schools and other elements of racism in society. In addition, research studies were contradictory concerning the impact of desegregation on anxiety, self-esteem, and aspirations of Negro children. Finally, Mehrige's assertion that the demands of the law and social science were identical was not persuasive. His opinion, however, suggested the opposite, i.e., that "racial identifiability" evolved into a legal concept because of the social science evidence. In other words, he used social science to find a violation of the Constitution and then retreated to the position that "racial identifiability" was "a conclusion of law ultimately." Mehrige's ultimate attempt to give primacy to the demands of the law was obviously done with an eye to the higher courts.

On June 5, 1972, the Fourth Circuit Court of Appeals reversed the Mehrige ruling with only one dissenting opinion. J. Braxton Craven, Jr., wrote the Court's opinion which concluded that the consolidation plan amounted to the adoption of a fixed racial quota. Craven concluded: "The Constitution imposes no such requirement, and imposition as a matter of substantive constitutional right of any particular degree of racial balance is beyond the power of the district court." Even if the educational experts were correct, the Appeals Court concluded that the consolidation plan was beyond the scope of the federal district court. The majority was equally emphatic in rejecting Mehrige's explanation for the predominance of blacks in the inner city. In Craven's opinion, the explanation for the housing patterns in the Richmond area was "simply not known." If the reason was known, he judged that school boards were not required to solve the housing problem [*Bradley,* (5), pp. 1058, 1064, 1066].

The lone dissenter, Harrison Winter, accepted the concept of racial identifiability in the metropolitan area. Even though the individual school systems might comply with law, in the Richmond area, because of past public and private policies, schools were identifiably black. Consolidation, he concluded, was the only remedy to past discriminatory practices (5), pp. 1076–1078.

The opinion of the Fourth Circuit Court of Appeals followed closely the Supreme Court's decision in *Swann v. Charlotte-Mecklenburg Board of Education,* delivered in April of 1971. In *Swann,* the Supreme Court unanimously held that the transportation of school children was an acceptable "tool of school desegregation." The Court accompanied this holding, however, with some guidelines which limited the scope of lower court remedies. In writing for the Court, Chief Justice Warren Burger stated that the objective of *Brown* remained to eliminate state-imposed or *de jure* discrimination. The Court, moreover, emphasized that its focus was on the discriminatory action of school and not other state authorities. Finally, Burger wrote that racial balancing was not required by the law. Under some circumstances, school systems with one-race schools were acceptable under the law [*Swann* (34), pp. 22–24, 29].

The ambiguity of the *Swann* opinion left NAACP lawyers with some hope that the consolidation case still had a chance before the Supreme Court. In 1973 the Supreme Court, however, technically affirmed the

Fourth Circuit Court's decision when it deadlocked, four to four [*School Board of City of Richmond* (33), pp. 92, 93]. In 1974 in *Milliken v. Bradley* (25), a Detroit case involving an integration plan similar to Richmond's, the Supreme Court, in a 5-4 split, reversed the district court's acceptance of interdistrict desegregation and dealt another blow to the NAACP's position. With Burger writing again, the Court stressed that the plaintiffs failed to show that the school districts outside of Detroit were responsible for segregation within the city (25), pp. 717, 744–745.

The Supreme Court's opinions in *Swann* and *Milliken,* in part, reflected the conservative mood of the country. A survey of selected Virginia cases offered another reason for the Court's caution: the ineffectiveness of social science as a desegregation tool. In general, busing and consolidation raised policy and educational questions of profoundly difficult dimensions. In comparison to *Brown I,* where the moral bankruptcy of segregation strengthened the position of social scientists, the common sense of the issue, to use Edmund Cahn's expression, was more complex in the Norfolk and Richmond cases. By 1969 it was less clear that integration at any cost was the only method of implementing *Brown I.* The *Coleman Report* and the multitude of studies which followed demonstrated that school desegregation, by itself, failed to provide the anticipated educational or attitudinal results. The mere attainment of desegregation or the mixing of black and white students, however, required remedies which often clashed with values prized by blacks and whites. Busing and consolidation plans threatened the liberty of a parent to shape a child's education and the freedom of different groups to maintain or build communities. In other words, these methods of attacking racial isolation in urban America juxtaposed equality and liberty in such a way that the "common sense" choice was less clear than in 1954. A crucial aspect of the Norfolk and Richmond cases was that, unlike *Brown I,* the use of social science evidence failed to clarify this dilemma. Considered as a whole, the opinions of Judges Hoffman and Mehrige showed that inferences from social science research could be used to limit or expand desegregation, depending upon the policy orientation of the court. As a result, the Supreme Court's refusal to take judicial notice of social science evidence in *Swann* and *Milliken* can be viewed as a response to the breakdown of the consensus among social scientists and a recognition of the difficulty of using this type of evidence properly.

FOOTNOTES

1. Studies which dispute the thesis that public schools, either today or in the past, bridged the gap between the rich and poor, black and white are Christopher Jencks, *et al., Inequality: A Reassessment of the Effect of Family and Schooling in America* (New York: Basic Books, Inc., 1972) and Colin Greer, *The Great School Legend: A Revisionist Interpretation*

of American Education (New York: Basic Books, Inc., 1972). An example of the claim by black writers that *Brown* was essentially a racist decision is found in Howard Moore, Jr., *"Brown v. Board of Education:* The Court's Relationship to Black Liberation," in *Law Against the People: Essays to Demystify Law, Order and the Courts,* ed. by Robert Lefcourt (New York: Random House, 1971), p. 58. The case for community control is made by Charles V. Hamilton in "Race and Education, A Search for Legitimacy," *Harvard Educational Review* 38 (Fall 1968), pp. 669–84. For a brief summary of the developments which have upset the civil rights consensus of 1954 see the third edition of C. Vann Woodward's *The Strange Career of Jim Crow* (New York: Oxford University Press, 1974), pp. 189–220. A useful survey of more than one hundred school desegregation studies is found in Nancy St. John, *School Desegregation Outcomes for Children* (New York: John Wiley and Sons, 1975).

2. I have selected Virginia because it was one of the companion cases before the Supreme Court in 1954 and because virtually every important legal question in the school desegregation case has been raised in this state.

3. The best discussion of the NAACP's mobilization of social scientists is Kluger's *Simple Justice.* On Professor Clark's role see in particular pp. 315–345.

4. Stephen I. Miller and Jack Kavanaugh, "Empirical Evidence," *Journal of Law and Education* 4 (January, 1975), pp. 164–165; L. Paul Metzger, "American Sociology and Black Assimilation: Conflicting Perspectives," *American Journal of Sociology* 76 (January, 1971), pp. 634–635.

5. For a general survey of the litigation see my "Public School Desegregation in Virginia." An excellent analysis of the difficulties faced by the Department of Health, Education and Welfare in Virginia between 1965 and 1968 is provided by Gary Orfield, *The Reconstruction of Southern Education* (New York: John Wiley and Sons, 1969), pp. 208–263.

6. The significance of this line of reasoning is seen in *Keyes v. School District No. 1, Denver, Colorado* where Justice William Powell, in an opinion which concurred with and dissented from the Court's holding, called for an abandonment of the *de jure–de facto* distinction and cited Hoffman's analysis with approval. See 413 U.S. 189, 219–226 (1973).

7. In 1970 the Richmond schools were 60 percent black. By 1972 the black enrollment increased to 70 percent.

8. In his opinion Mehrige and Pettigrew tried to avoid the charge that 30 to 40 percent black enrollments represented quotas. They agreed that these percentages were required by the composition of the metropolitan population.

REFERENCES

1. *Adkins v. School Board of the City of Norfolk,* 148 F. Suppl. 430 (E.D. Va. 1957).
2. *Beckett v. School Board of the City of Norfolk,* 308 F. Supp. 1274, 1307 (E.D. Va. 1969).
3. Bowles, Samuel, "Toward Equality of Educational Opportunity," *Harvard Educational Review* 38 (Winter 1968): 89–99.
4. *Bradley v. School Board of City of Richmond,* 317 F. Supp. 555 (E.D. Va. 1970).
5. ———, 338 F. Supp. 67 (E. D. Va. 1972).
6. ———, 462 F. 2d 1058 (4th Cir. 1972).
7. *Brewer v. School Board of the City of Norfolk,* 434 F. 2d 408 (4th Cir. 1970).
8. *Briggs v. Elliott,* 132 F. Supp. 77 (E.D. S.C. 1955).
9. *Brown v. Board of Education of Topeka,* 347 U.S. 483 (1954).
10. ———, 349 U.S. 294 (1955).
11. Cahn, Edmund, "Jurisprudence," *New York University Law Review* 30 (January 1955): 150–169.

12. Coleman, James S., *et al. Equality of Educational Opportunity.* Government Printing Office, Washington (1966).
13. Dyer, Henry S., "School Factors and Equal Educational Opportunity," *Harvard Educational Review* 38 (Winter 1968): 38–56.
14. Greer, Colin, *The Great School Legend: A Revisionist Interpretation of American Education,* Basic Books, Inc., New York (1972).
15. Grundman, Adolph H., "Public School Desegregation in Virginia from 1954 to the Present," unpublished Ph.D. dissertation, Wayne State University, 1972.
16. Hamilton, Charles V., "Race and Education, A Search for Legitimacy," *Harvard Educational Review* 38 (Fall 1968): 669–684.
17. Harris, Robert J., "The Constitution, Education and Segregation," *Temple Law Quarterly* 29 (Summer 1956): 409–433.
18. Herbst, Robert L., "The Legal Struggle to Integrate Schools in the North." *The Annals,* 407 (May, 1973), 43–66.
19. Jencks, Christopher, *et al., Inequality: A Reassessment of the Effect of Family and Schooling in America.* Basic Books, Inc., New York: 1972.
20. *Keyes v. School District No. 1, Denver, Colorado,* 413 U.S. 189 (1973).
21. Kluger, Richard, *Simple Justice: The History of Brown v. Board of Education and Black America's Struggle for Equality.* Alfred A. Knopf, New York: 1976.
22. McCarthy, John D., and William L. Yancey, "Uncle Tom and Mr. Charlie: Metaphysical Pathos in the Study of Racism and Personal Disorganization." *American Journal of Sociology* 76 (January 1971): 627–647.
23. Metzger, L. Paul, "American Sociology and Black Assimilation: Conflicting Perspectives." *American Journal of Sociology* 76 (January 1971): 627–647.
24. Miller, Stephen I. and Jack Kavanaugh, "Empirical Evidence," *Journal of Law and Education* 4 (January, 1975), 159–171.
25. *Milliken, Governor of Michigan v. Bradley,* 418 U.S. 717 (1973).
26. Moore, Howard Jr. "Brown v. Board of Education: The Court's Relationship to Black Liberation," *Law Against the People: Essays to Demystify Law, Order and the Courts* (edited by Robert Lefcourt), Random House, New York (1971).
27. Newby, I. A., *Challenge to the Court: Social Scientists and the Defense of Segregation, 1954–1966.* Louisiana State University Press, Baton Rouge (1954–1966).
28. Orfield, Gary. *The Reconstruction of Southern Education.* John Wiley and Sons, New York 1969.
29. Peltason, J. W., *Fifty-Eight Lonely Men: Southern Federal Judges and School Desegregation,* University of Illinois Press, Urbana (1971).
30. Pettigrew, Thomas F., *Racially Separate or Together?* McGraw-Hill Book Company, New York (1971).
31. ———, David J. Armor, and James Q. Wilson, "On Busing: An Exchange," *The Public Interest* 30 (Winter 1973), 88–118.
32. St. John, Nancy. *School Desegregation Outcomes for Children,* John Wiley and Sons, New York (1975).
33. *School Board of City of Richmond v. State Board of Education of Virginia,* 412 U.S. 92 (1972).
34. *Swann v. Charlotte-Mecklenburg Board of Education,* 40 U.S. 1 (1970).
35. U.S. Commission on Civil Rights, *Racial Isolation in the Public Schools.* Washington, D.C.: U.S. Government Printing Office, 1967.
36. Wechsler, Herbert, "Toward Neutral Principles of Constitutional Law." *Harvard Law Review* 73 (November 1959), 1–35.
37. Woodward, C. Vann, *The Strange Career of Jim Crow* (3rd ed.), Oxford University Press, New York (1974).

THE USE OF A PERSONAL SERVICE ASSISTANT IN THE TREATMENT OF MENTAL HEALTH PROBLEMS: A PROPOSAL AND SOME SPECULATIONS

R. Kirk Schwitzgebel,[1] HARVARD UNIVERSITY

Mental patients, delinquents, congressmen, musical rock groups, and college professors have at least one common problem: the management of daily personal affairs. For some people, the completion of professional and domestic tasks on time may be difficult or impossible without the assistance of another person.

Many prominent persons in public life use managers, agents, assistants, consultants, or secretaries to help them meet the social demands resulting from a busy schedule and to help them maintain a positive public image. Many other people could use the services provided by agents, managers, or assistants but instead struggle through their daily obligations. Unexpected events such as family illness produce additional stress and difficulty. Although assistance may come from family members or friends, the reduction of extended family living units and the increase of geographic

Research in Law and Sociology—Vol. 1, 1978, pages 251–264.

mobility reduce the availability of family members and friends willing or able to help, even in situations of crisis.

Mental patients often have difficulty in managing their daily business or personal affairs not only because of their mental disorders but also because people in the community may be reluctant to help them. Similarly, delinquent youths may alienate family members and persons in the community who could assist them. Much that is casually called "psychotherapy" may actually involve teaching the patient how to manage daily affairs.

The following discussion will tentatively explore the feasibility of developing the role of a personal service assistant to help persons function more effectively in their natural social environments. The role is intended to be nonstigmatizing for both the employer and the employee (the assistant). The role is also intended to be flexible so that the responsibilities of the personal service assistant can be varied from occasional assistance to the long-term detailed management of daily affairs.

Although the personal service assistant may integrate his services with those of a professional therapist, the role is not conceived as a "paraprofessional" role in the sense that the assistant must always function in cooperation with, or subordinate to, a professional. Ideally, the role should permit the occupant to function autonomously and professionally with the collaboration of other service providers as might be needed.

BACKGROUND

Use of Paraprofessionals in the Treatment of Mental Problems

As the conceptualization of the etiology of mental illness has gradually shifted from a concern with intrapsychic pathology to a concern with social and environmental causes, treatment methods have also changed. The use of paraprofessionals in mental health is not new. Psychiatric aides working with patients within hospital settings are still a major part of the staff in mental health facilities. Currently, aides are being given increasing responsibility so that their work now extends considerably beyond the custodial role of an attendant. They have not only helped to solve manpower problems, but have also been found to facilitate the earlier release of patients to the community [Ellsworth (11)].

In the late 1950s and early 1960s, a new type of paraprofessional emerged who more directly assisted the professional therapist or assumed some of the functions of the professional therapist. One of the best-known efforts of this type was the pilot study conducted by Margaret Rioch, *et al.* begun in 1960 in the Adult Psychiatry Branch of the National Institute of Mental Health [Rioch, *et al.* (27)]. The trainees in this study were eight upper middle-class women with a median age of forty to forty-four. All of them were college graduates and had children. Four of them had been psychoanalyzed. Functioning as mental health counselors, they saw forty-nine "difficult or very difficult" patients for, on the average, ten weeks. A one-year follow-up study indicated that thirteen of the patients showed marked or moderate improvement.

This widely publicized study was not followed, however, by a great increase in the use of trained lay persons as mental health counselors. In light of this and other studies which indicated the potential usefulness of lay persons,[2] Rioch *et al.* (27) suggested that professionals are interested not only in doing the best they can for the patients but also in doing the best they can for themselves. Professionals may be overly concerned about competition from paraprofessionals.

The use of college students, both undergraduate and graduate, as paraprofessional aides or lay counselors has perhaps achieved broader acceptance. College students have served both as "companions" [Holzberg, *et al.* (18)] and as "group therapists" for hospitalized, chronic schizophrenics [Posner (25)]. The latter study by Ernest Posner involved eleven female undergraduates, fifteen professional therapists, and 295 male, chronic schizophrenics who served as treated subjects and un-treated controls. After participating in group therapy over a period of five months, the patients seen in therapy improved significantly more than those who had not been in therapy, as measured by psychological tests. In addition, there were significantly better post-therapy scores on three psychological tests for those patients treated by the college students as compared to the professional therapists. College students have also been used as counselors with children in elementary schools [e.g., Goodman (14)].

Perhaps the widest acceptance of mental health intervention by lay persons has occurred in the area of peer counseling. College students have served as counselors to other students [Brown (4); Brown, *et al.* (5); Edgar and Kotrick (10)], as "therapeutic peers" in crisis situations [Dana, *et al.* (8)], and as "companions" to students receiving professional counseling [Boylin (3)]. There are, of course, many hot-line information and referral services staffed by teenage and young adult volunteers. At the secondary school level, students have been trained as peer counselors to direct group discussions and to assist school personnel with other students having personal problems [Hamburg and Varenhorst (17)].[3]

Use of Paraprofessionals in the Treatment of Delinquency

Within the past ten years, there has been a rapidly increasing use of volunteers in court settings. One well-known program, Project Misde-meanant, located in Royal Oak, Michigan, has used volunteers to work with juvenile misdemeanants. Several substantial studies of the effectiveness of this program have been conducted involving over 300 experimental and comparison juveniles. In two studies, the results appeared to be positive as measured by subsequent law violations, but questionable when measured by school attendance [Morris (23), Rosenbaum et al. (28)].[4]

The Volunteer Probation Counselor Program in Lincoln, Nebraska, was selected in 1974 by the Law Enforcement Assistance Administration as one of seventeen "exemplary projects." This program matched volunteers with high-risk misdemeanant youths according to their needs. There were four general classes of need: primary counseling, friend-companion, adult model, and direct supervision. The volunteers, most of whom had some college education, ranged from eighteen to sixty-nine years of age with an average (mean) of about twenty-seven years. The "volunteer counselors" provided assistance in employment and education and helped youths through crisis situations. During their regular probationary periods, randomly assigned, high-risk probationers in the volunteer program were found to commit about 46 percent fewer offenses than comparable high-risk probationers in the regular probation program [Ku, et al. (21)].

In a program begun in 1973 at the Community Psychology Action Center at the University of Illinois [Davidson (9)], undergraduate student volunteers worked with youths who were diverted from the criminal justice system and randomly assigned to the volunteer program or a control condition. The volunteers typically met with the youths for six to eight hours per week for four and one-half months. Behaviorally specific goals were established for each youth, e.g., attend school four days per week. The students acted as contract negotiators and youth advocates. A one-year follow-up showed statistically significant differences in favor of the experimental group as measured by police contacts and the seriousness of alleged offenses.[5]

Outside of the formal probation setting, volunteers have been frequently used in community programs, e.g., Big Brother/Big Sister programs. In a carefully structured program using behavior modification procedures, Fo and O'Donnell (12) used adults indigenous to the community as behavior change agents. This program, known as the Buddy System, involved the random assignment of 442 youths to either an experimental treatment group or no-treatment control group. The youths in the experimental group were matched with adult buddies who used contingent social and material rewards to reduce behaviors such as truancy, fighting, incomplete homework assignments, and returning home late at night. Fo and O'Donnell (12) report a statistically significant reduction of official offenses for the experimental, high-risk youths during the one year they participated in the Buddy System as compared with the control youths. However, for those low-risk experimental youths with no major prior offenses, the number of offenses they later committed significantly increased even above that of the control group. The investigators speculated that this might have been caused by the unplanned informal contacts that these low-risk youths had with high-risk youths.

The overall impression is that the results of volunteer programs with delinquents have been positive with a few program models tentatively evaluated [e.g., Hunt (19), Schwitzgebel (31)]. However, a careful, integrated analysis of program effects is clearly the exception rather than the rule. A study published by the National Information Center on Volunteers in Courts suggests that the effectiveness of these programs is not yet known [Shelley (32)]. A survey of 70 studies by Peters (24) led her to conclude that methodologically adequate studies of effectiveness are for the most part lacking. The rapid growth of volunteer services in the courts has been based more upon apparent benefits to the juveniles and volunteers rather than empirical evidence of offense reduction. The continued use of volunteers regardless of empirical findings should not be surprising because, it may be remembered, probation originally began as a volunteer service.

Focus upon Indigenous Personnel

Several of the studies cited above used persons within the patients' or delinquents' own environments as paraprofessionals in the treatment process. The federal funding of research and demonstration programs gave considerable impetus to the use of indigenous personnel. In 1963, the President's Committee on Juvenile Delinquency and Youth Development funded Mobilization for Youth, located on New York City's lower East Side. This project relied heavily upon the use of indigenous persons living around the project site to assist in school and community programs. Later, more extensive funding was provided for indigenous paraprofessionals by the Economic Opportunity Act of 1964 which emphasized the "maximum feasible participation" of those to be served. It has been estimated that by the end of OEO's first fiscal year in 1965, over 25,000 paraprofessionals were employed in community action programs [Schmais (29)]. These persons were largely adults. With the Nelson-Scheuer Amendment (1966) to the Act, funds were later extended to include youths as well as adults.

In 1968, the Juvenile Delinquency Prevention and Control Act included a special provision (Sec. 201) for the training of youths and adults for "new careers" in fields related to juvenile delinquency. A noteworthy project conducted by J. Douglas Grant in the California Men's Prison used prisoners as program developers and trainers. Several of these men have subsequently played important roles in developing, directing, and evaluating human service programs. It has been suggested that even if the persons receiving help from the paraprofessional do not appreciably benefit, it is fairly likely that the paraprofessionals offering help will benefit [e.g., Riessman (26)].

In a pioneering group therapy program at the Harlem Hospital, June Christmas (7) utilized indigenous aides who came largely from the same lower socio-economic status as the patients. Weekly group therapy sessions were led by a psychiatrist with psychotic, post-hospital patients and the aides who first acted as observers and finally "cotherapists." In addition, the aides provided case service to certain patients related to problems such as securing better housing or employment. They helped patients with applications, phone calls, and contacts with other agencies. In some instances, they also conducted home interviews. Considerable emphasis was placed upon action-oriented approaches to the solution of problems and upon the use of group interaction and reinforcement for patients and aides.

The use of peers as "helpers" may occur naturally and may be a preferred mode of assistance by young adults. In one study of crisis intervention services, college sophomores were asked whom they would personally seek out for assistance [Dana, *et al.* (8)]. Their preferences, ranging from most to least preferred, were close friend, a particular person (who could become a friend), roommate, student mental health center, psychological clinic, and office of student affairs. Regardless of whether the students lived on or off campus, they preferred, and more frequently used, peer intervention as compared with university professional services.

CONTRACTUAL AGREEMENTS FOR THE DELIVERY OF PERSONAL SERVICES

The brief and incomplete discussion above of the use of paraprofessionals in the area of mental health may nevertheless indicate some of the diversity of the roles and tasks assumed by paraprofessionals. These roles have ranged from clerical assistants to "cotherapists" [Christmas (7)]. The notion that patients or clients might enter into explicit contracts with therapists has become increasingly popular within the past few years. These treatment contracts which clarify therapist and patient responsibilities might be extended to include paraprofessionals and other personal service personnel.

Some Current Concepts in Treatment Contracts

Applying Ralph Nader's consumer advocacy approach to mental health services, the Public Citizen's Health Research Group has published a booklet titled, *Through the Mental Health Maze: A Consumer's Guide to Finding a Psychotherapist, Including a Sample Consumer/Therapist Contract* [Adams and Orgel (1)]. In responses to a questionnaire prepared by this group, 64 out of 72 psychiatrists and 124 out of 166 psychologists replied that it was their policy "to make a verbal or written contract which includes what that patient can expect from you and what you can expect from them." Although these responses may be quite biased toward a consumer viewpoint, they may indicate the practical feasibility of using treatment contracts.[6] The Health Research Group suggested that the contract process make clear that therapy is a mutual effort with mutual responsibilities. Treatment goals will differ from person to person. The flexibility of a contract is one of its advantages. "The ideal contract and the ideal therapy share the idea of the 'meeting of the minds'" [Adams and Orgel (1), p. 37]. The sample treatment contract prepared by the Health Research Group includes stipulations such as the specific goals of treatment, the type and duration of treatment, its cost, and the possibility of renegotiating the contract.

This sample contract does not differ markedly in content from the contracts suggested by others (e.g., Alexander and Szasz (2); Schwitzgebel (30), Stuart (34). Stuart (34) notes that contracts which specify the goals of treatment and the procedures to be used can expose mental health services to the test of empirical review by the one person who is in the best position to render the judgment—the client. In contracts with families involving a child, Stuart suggests the explicit recognition of the possibility that the child's behavior may be a result of the parent-child interaction. Therefore, the contract might include the statement, "The objective of this service is to change the interaction between Mr. and Mrs.——and their child——in order to achieve the following objectives . . ." (p. 8).

Treatment contracts are not new. Implicit in every treatment situation is a contract which requires at minimum the performance of some service by the therapist and payment by the patient. The use of explicit contracts may greatly increase mutual understanding and expand the types of services available as long as the parties do not intend to engage in illegal behavior or behavior clearly contrary to public policy.

DEVELOPMENT OF A MODEL ROLE: THE PERSONAL SERVICE ASSISTANT

There would probably be general agreement that the use of paraprofessionals in the delivery of mental health services has been, on the whole, useful. At the least, paraprofessionals have helped to meet in an economic manner manpower requirements. Several problems remain, however, for paraprofessionals, such as job stability, role definition, and career advancement opportunities. Of particular concern here is their role definition and its relationship to planned interventions for changing human behavior. The term "paraprofessionals" implies that they are auxiliary to a professional and often secondary in importance. Those assisting professionals are also sometimes called "nonprofessionals." Although this term clearly differentiates them from professionals, it may also imply a lack of skill or importance. The professional usually provides back-up services for the paraprofessional or may directly supervise or intervene in some situations.

It would be desirable to have a role for paraprofessionals or other personal service providers which is professional in the sense that it involves special skills and responsibilities and is independent and more nearly coequal with other professional roles. A psychologist's professional role can be independent or collateral with a psychiatrist's role. A social worker and a minister have professional roles that can be independent or collateral with the roles of a psychologist or psychiatrist. The relationships among the roles are determined by institutional structure and treatment programs. As treatment conceptualizations and treatment programs change, role relationships and definitions may change.

Current treatment programs, particularly in psychology, are placing increasing emphasis upon environmental factors (contingencies) that may produce problem behaviors or maintain them. The person receiving traditional therapeutic help may also need guidance related to his employment, money management, or interpersonal relationships. In addition, he may need active intervention (instruction or negotiation) directly within his home, business, or recreational settings until he has learned the necessary skills. In discussing the mental problems of the aging person, Stone (33), p. 175, has discussed the need for protective intervention services and has briefly alluded to "surrogate services" which would provide a "new decision maker in areas where the elderly person cannot function well."

The model role tentatively suggested here is that of a personal service provider. The term "personal service" is a generic term which, though varying somewhat from state to state, generally refers to services specifically performed for a person (the employer) at his request. Personal service roles range from maid, chauffeur, bodyguard, guardian, to accountant, lawyer, and physician. Personal service roles also include counselor and therapist. The proposed role is that of a "personal service assistant." The duties of the personal service assistant could vary according to the needs of the employer and the assistant's skill. The employer could be a businessman, actor, housewife, patient, parolee, or professor. There would be much flexibility in defining the role requirements and the title for the occupant of the role.

The term "personal service assistant" is a general term that could include a variety of subroles. The following list of roles, or combinations of them, may give some indication of the range of services that could be provided: consultant, personal manager, executive agent, social secretary, companion, attaché, valet, guardian, partner, advocate, guide, attendant, and adviser. More imaginatively, there are coaches, trainers, and golf caddies.[7] Some actors hire personal agents who not only arrange bookings, but also take care of many other arrangements such as travel, meals, and press interviews. As one actor described his personal agent's job: "He helps you get your act together." In exchange, personal agents take 15 percent of the earnings. Athletes, athletic clubs, and investment clubs may have managers. Families also may have family managers or assistants.

A legal issue often raised with regard to the employment of a person providing personal service is the extent of that person's authority. If that person may enter into agreements or contracts which legally bind his employer, he is acting in the capacity of an agent. (The person does not, however, need to be called an "agent.") The person can be given limited authority such as purchasing food or necessities or more general authority such as managing a budget and control over related checking and savings accounts. The range of authority can be specified by verbal or written agreement between the personal service assistant and his employer. If the personal service assistant has no direct authority to act on behalf of his employer, he might be called a consultant. If he has extensive authority, he might be called a manager or guardian.

Generally, the employer is legally responsible for the behavior of his employee unless that person is acting independently. Thus a person is usually not responsible for the behavior of a plumber or tennis instructor whom he hires. The plumber and tennis instructor provide a service, but they do not perform their tasks with detailed directions from him. The more the person providing service acts under the specific direction of the employer, the more the employer is responsible for the actions of this employee. In many situations, the personal service assistant will be following the instructions of his employer and therefore the employer will be responsible unless the assistant is clearly acting outside of the scope of his employment, e.g., not following instructions of his employer. The range of duties and responsibilities should be clarified prior to employment.

Ideally, the personal services role should not negatively label the employer or the employee. The role does not necessarily imply a mental health disability. Personal agents, assistants, and managers are used by persons of outstanding social accomplishment. Important political candidates often use "trip men" who accompany the candidate on his trips after the general arrangements have been made by the advance men. The trip man's responsibility is to see that the trip goes smoothly, that the candidate arrives at appointments on time, and that he is suitably dressed for the occasion. The trip man also has an extra copy of the candidate's speech in his pocket.

Although there has been an extensive use of paraprofessionals in mental health programs, the employment of these persons has usually been in hospital, clinic, school, or court settings rather than in community settings and homes. Furthermore, only a few projects have explicitly encouraged and experimentally evaluated the direct service function of paraprofessionals. As previously noted, projects by Christmas (7) and Davidson (9) directly involved paraprofessionals in some management tasks. The Streetcorner Research Project [Schwitzgebel (31)] engaged delinquents in interviews and secondary activities conducted largely by undergraduate students. These secondary activities were sometimes of a recreational type and sometimes more directly related to delinquency reduction, e.g., arranging and driving a youth to a job interview. A three-year follow-up of twenty matched experimental and control subjects in the project showed a significant reduction of subsequent arrests and months of incarceration for the experimental group. No statistically significant differences were found in recidivism rates for those youths with only interviewing as compared with interviewing and secondary activities. Although the number of youths involved is small and the activities were of a varied nature, the results suggest a need for caution in assuming that management-oriented services alone can contribute significantly to delinquency reduction without careful evaluation.

One noteworthy project, finding positive results with management-oriented services, was the Expediter Project located in Tacoma, Washington. This project used nineteen indigenous paraprofessionals as "expediters." The expediters were largely housewives or women who held semiskilled jobs. The project director, H. J. Wahler, has summarized the need for active, natural-setting intervention [Wahler, et al. (35), pp. i–ii]:

It is apparent that office- or institution-bound psychotherapy, casework, counseling or supportive relationships are often not enough. When life is badly awry, people also need help with some or many aspects of their ecological milieu. In other words, they need someone to expedite—someone to provide information, to lend a hand when and where it is needed, and to intercede if need be. The office-bound professional has neither the time nor range of information to function as a situational therapist. This is true no matter how badly his client may need intercession, specific and applicable information, or a tangible helping hand. Thus, to translate the notion of "working with the total person" into functional reality, professionals with expertise in inside processes must have a teammate who is expert in working with outside processes.

The expediters did not attempt to change directly the behavior of the clients. A large portion of the expediters' time with clients was spent in giving information to clients and visiting their homes to discuss problems. Lesser amounts of time were spent in providing transportation for clients, in assisting them with errands, letter writing, and completing forms. Using matched experimental and control groups of patients released from a state mental hospital, the experimental group receiving expediter services generally showed less in-hospital time six months following release than the control group not receiving these services.

As suggested here, it would not be necessary for the personal service assistant to be employed exclusively by one person. He might be employed by several persons as are many personal agents serving actors. Several actors may employ the same agent or one professional agency may provide the services of several personal agents for a large number of actors. The effective assistant should be well paid for tasks well performed. Payment may be made contingent upon the successful completion of certain tasks. Although contracts with service providers are often verbal, a written contract would be useful in clarifying duties and responsibilities.

FOOTNOTES

1. Assistant Professor, Department of Psychology, California Lutheran College. On leave, Department of Psychiatry, Harvard Medical School, 1976–77. I appreciate the assistance of Mark Hagen.

2. See, for example, the study by Carkhuff and Truax (6) in which significant improvement was found in the ward behavior of seventy-four patients seen by trained lay hospital personnel as compared with a control group of seventy patients not treated by lay group counselors.

3. Peer group procedures have also been used with hospitalized schizophrenics who share responsibilities and therapy interviews [e.g., Ludwig and Marx (22)] and with geriatric patients [Kosbab, *et al.* (20)].

4. Morris (23), p. 117, reports a recidivism rate of 7 percent for the probationers in the volunteer program over a period of nine years from 1960 to 1969. A study by Thomas E. Koschtial, funded by the National Institute of Mental Health, compared the Royal Oak program (N=310) with a comparison probation program in another court (N=223). Over a period of four and three-quarter years, 49.8 percent of the comparison group had committed one or more offenses as compared with 14.9 percent of the Royal Oak group.

5. A general survey of the use of students as therapeutic agents can be found in Gruver (15). Guerney (16) has edited a useful and extensive collection of papers on the use of paraprofessionals, parents, and teachers in providing mental health services.

6. The sample of responses obtained by the Health Research Group might be misleading as no procedures were apparently used to control for sample bias or to test the reliability or validity of the responses. Only slightly over one percent of the psychiatrists who were sent questionnaires responded and 17.7 percent of the psychologists responded.

7. Like most golf professionals, Johnny Miller can control his stroke to a variation of only a few yards. Estimating the required distance is not, however, one of his strong abilities. His caddie, Andy Martinez, can very accurately estimate distances for him. Martinez may spend as many as fifteen hours walking off distances, and measuring greens on a new course. Last year at age twenty-six, Martinez is reported to have earned $23,000 during twenty weeks of tour.

REFERENCES

1. Adams, S., and M. Orgel, *Through the Mental Health Maze: A Consumer's Guide to Finding a Psychotherapist, Including a Sample Consumer/Therapist Contract*. Public Citizen's Health Research Group, Washington, D.C. (1975).
2. Alexander, G. J., and T. S. Szasz, "From Contract to Status via Psychiatry," *Santa Clara Lawyer* (1973), pp. 13, 537–557.
3. Boylin, E. R., "The Use of Peers in Psychotherapy," *Psychotherapy: Theory, Research and Practice* (1971): 8, 285–286.
4. Brown, W. F., "Student to Student Counseling for Academic Adjustment," *The Personnel and Guidance Journal* 53 (1965): 811–817.
5. ———; N. O. Weke; and V. G. Zunker, "Effectiveness of Student-to-Student Counseling on the Academic Adjustment of Potential College Dropouts, *Journal of Educational Psychology* 62 (1971): 285–289.
6. Carkhuff, R. R., and C. B. Truax, "Lay Mental Health Counseling: The Effects of Lay Group Counseling," *Journal of Consulting Psychology* 29 (1965): 426–431.
7. Christmas, J. J., "Group Methods in Training and Practice: Nonprofessional Mental Health Personnel in a Deprived Community," *American Journal of Orthopsychiatry* 36 (1966): 410–419.
8. Dana, R. H., F. Heynen, and R. Burdette, "Crisis Intervention by Peers," *Journal of College Student Personnel* 15 (January 1974): 58–61.
9. Davidson, W. S., Personal communciation, December 1976.
10. Edgar, K. F., and C. Kotrick, "The Development of a Peer Counseling Center," *Psychotherapy: Theory, Research and Practice* 9 (1972): 256–258.
11. Ellsworth, R. B., *Nonprofessionals in Psychiatric Rehabilitation: The Psychiatric Aide and the Schizophrenic Patient,* Appleton-Century-Crofts, New York (1968).
12. Fo, W. S. O., and C. R. O'Donnell, "The Buddy System: Relationship and Contingency Conditions in a Community Intervention Program for Youth with Nonprofessionals as Behavior Change Agents," *Journal of Consulting and Clinical Psychology* 42 (1974): 163–169.

13. Gartner, A., *Paraprofessionals and Their Performance: A Survey of Education, Health, and Social Service Programs,* Praeger, New York (1974).
14. Goodman, G., "An Experiment with Companionship Therapy: College Students and Troubled Boys—Assumptions, Selection, and Design," in Guerney, B. G. Jr. (ed.) *Psychotherapeutic Agents: New Roles for Nonprofessionals, Parents, and Teachers,* Holt, Rinehart and Winston, New York (1969), pp. 121–128.
15. Gruver, G. G., "College Students as Therapeutic Agents," *Psychological* Bulletin 76 (1971): 111–127.
16. Guerney, B. G. (ed.), *Psychotherapeutic Agents; New Roles for Nonprofessionals, Parents, and Teachers,* Holt, Rinehart and Winston, New York (1969).
17. Hamburg, B. A., and B. B. Varenhorst, "Peer Counseling in the Secondary Schools: A Community Mental Health Project for Youth," *American Journal of Orthopsychiatry* 42 (1972): 566–581.
18. Holzberg, J. D., H. S. Whiting, and D. G. Lowy, "Chronic Patients and a College Companion Program," *Mental Hospitals* 15 (1964): 152–158.
19. Hunt, J. McV., "Message, Potpourri and the Hall-Nebraska 'Model,'" *Clinical Psychologist* 22 (1969): 127–136.
20. Kosbab, F. P., M. E. Kosbab, and S. Woolley, "A Buddy System for Hospitalized Geriatric Patients," *Archives of General Psychiatry* 7 (1962): 135–139.
21. Ku, R., R. Moore, and K. Griffiths, *The Volunteer Probation Counselor Program, Lincoln, Nebraska: An Exemplary Project.* LEAA, Office of Technology Transfer, Washington, D.C. (1975).
22. Ludwig, A. J., and A. J. Marx, "The Buddy Treatment Model for Chronic Schizophrenics," *The Journal of Nervous and Mental Disease* 148 (1969): 528–546.
23. Morris, J. A., *First Offender: A Volunteer Program for Youth in Trouble with the Law,* Funk & Wagnalls, New York (1970).
24. Peters, C., "Research in the Field of Volunteers in Courts and Corrections: What Exists and What Is Needed," *Journal of Voluntary Action Research* 2 (1973): 121–134.
25. Poser, E. G., "The Effects of Therapists' Training on Group Therapeutic Outcome," *Journal of Consulting and Clinical Psychology* 30 (1966): 283–289.
26. Riessman, F., "The 'Helper' Therapy Principle," *Social Work* 10 (1965): 27–32.
27. Rioch, M. J., C. Elkes, A. A. Flint, B. S. Usdansky, R. G. Newman, and E. Silber, "NIMH Pilot Study in Training Mental Health Counselors" *American Journal of Orthopsychiatry* 33 (1963): 678–689.
28. Rosenbaum, G., Jr. Grissell, T. Kaschtial, R. Knox, and K. Z. Leenhouts, "Community Participation in Probation: A Tale of Two Cities," *Proceedings of the American Psychological Convention* 4 (1969): 863–864.
29. Schmais, A., "Implementing Nonprofessional Programs in Human Services, (New York: Graduate School of Social Work, New York University, 1967, p. 6) cited in A. Gartner, *Paraprofessionals and Their Performance: A Survey of Education, Health, and Social Service Programs,* Praeger, New York: 1971, p. 5.
30. Schwitzgebel, R. K., "A Contractual Model for the Protection of the Rights of Institutionalized Mental Patients," *American Psychologist* 30 (1975): 815–820.
31. ————, *Streetcorner Research: An Experimental Approach to the Juvenile Delinquent.* Harvard University Press, Cambridge, Mass. (1965).
32. Shelley, E. L. V., *Volunteers in the Correctional Spectrum,* National Information Center on Volunteers in Courts, Boulder, Colo. (1971).
33. Stone, A. A., *Mental Health and the Law: A System in Transition.* NIMH Monograph Series, Government Printing Office, Washington, D.C. (1975).
34. Stuart, R. B., Guide to Client-Therapist Treatment Contract, Research Press, Champaign, Ill. (1975).

35. Wahler, H. J., R. Johnson, and K. Uhrich, *The Community Mental Health Expediter Project,* Department of Social and Health Services, State of Washington, 1972.
    Walker, C. E., M. Wolpin, and L. Fellows, "The Use of High School and College Students as Therapists and Researchers in a State Mental Hospital," *Psychotherapy: Theory, Research, and Practice,* 1967, 4, 186–188.

ADOPTION FOR BLACK CHILDREN: A CASE STUDY OF EXPERT DISCRETION

Jacqueline Macaulay, UNIVERSITY OF WISCONSIN

Stewart Macaulay, UNIVERSITY OF WISCONSIN

I. INTRODUCTION

The number of black children needing homes and available for adoption has exceeded the supply of black parents applying to adopt them for a half century or more. In the 1960s a new resource was suddenly discovered for these children—white parents. This type of transracial adoption excited

*Jacqueline Macaulay, Women's Research Institute of Wisconsin, Inc. Stewart Macaulay, Professor of Law, University of Wisconsin. We wish to acknowledge our complex debts to the following people: Jean Arndt, Harry Ball, Nettie Berkowitz, Robert Hintz, Verna Lauritzen, Katherine Ostrander, Luann Patenaude, Margaret West, and many other professionals and adoptive parents who have shared their expertness and experiences with us. We thank Gordon Baldwin, Phoebe Ellsworth, Suzanne Griggins, Joel Handler, Marygold Melli and Dawn Day Wachtel, for reviewing earlier drafts of this article, and Janet Brewer, Suzanne Griggins, Jean Morse and Gary Young for excellent research assistance.

Research in Law and Sociology—Vol. 1, 1978, pages 265-318.

strong feelings among social workers who were startled that such a thing was even possible, among some white couples who viewed integrated families as perhaps more interesting than other kinds and perhaps as a step toward the creation of a better society, and among some black people who viewed transracial adoption very negatively.

Before the 1960s, transracial adoptive placements had been very rare. However, in almost all states such placements were not prohibited by the controlling statutes which did and do little more than tell all those involved in the adoption process that they should seek to promote "the best interests of the child." The formal rules didn't change in the 1960s. Yet practice—the living law—has been characterized since then by extreme and abrupt shifts that mirrored the state of black-white relations in North American society. Transracial adoption was first regarded as unthinkable; then as something truly good and moral, to be encouraged enthusiastically; then as something to be avoided because it might be an attack on the black family and black culture—or even cultural genocide; and now in the mid-1970s, perhaps as something which might be a good thing, sometimes, in some areas, and often better than other alternatives.

In large measure, the decision to make transracial placements rests in the discretion of social workers, subject to the veto of their superiors and that of lower court judges. Social workers also have the power to make decisions that will influence the likelihood that black families will adopt black children. The professionals gained this degree of control over adoption by holding themselves out as experts and, through their organizations, by seeking legislation granting them a decisive role in the adoption process. The child-care system which evolved is but one instance of a trend that goes back at least eighty years in North America as progressive and liberal reformers have turned to experts for rational solutions to society's problems [Friedman and Macaulay (72), p. 732; Hurst (101); Nonet (169)]. But there has also been a mounting disenchantment with experts. The new reformers seek to subject expert judgments to the constraints of rule making. Now the effort often is to get expert knowledge built into the decision processes at an earlier stage—as the factual base for the drafting of rules and standards [Carlin, *et al.* (26); Davis (42); Handler (92); Lowi (137)]. However, as we shall see, those experts charged with caring for homeless black children have played a role based on skills other than a mere application of neutral scientific principles.

There are black children who need homes now and there will continue to be such children in the foreseeable future. If they are not adopted by some family, something must be done for them by the state. Most of the alternatives to adoptive placement (institutional or foster care) that are presently available are regarded as very much second best by most experts and by the public. Any creation of new, more attractive alternatives would require both legislation and appropriation of substantial funds. This would be difficult to achieve in most states. Thus, adoption of black children by black families, transracial adoption, or both, continue to have instrumental importance as partial solutions to the problem.

Transracial adoption also has strong and mixed symbolic significance. On the part of white families and social workers who promote it, it is a striking rejection of traditional North American views about the separation of the races. For blacks, it may also symbolize paternalism and a denial of black values. Thus, the study of the transracial adoption movement in itself is significant. We feel that it is also an important case study of how a social institution, supposedly created and maintained by legal norms, actually fashions changing responses to shifting social norms without losing its mantle of legitimacy.

This, then, is an article about how those who had the power to make decisions in the name of the society made some judgments, changed their judgments, and failed to make other judgments, and so determined the fate of the children in their charge for better and for worse. First, we will describe and explain, as best we can, what policy has been enunciated for homeless black children and what has actually happened to them over the years. To do this we will consider why a certain group ended up with the power to decide who could adopt whom and how this group has exercised that power. Then we will turn to an examination of what can be said for and against the present system and consider some alternatives.

II. THE PRESENT SYSTEM FOR THE CARE OF HOMELESS BLACK CHILDREN: STRUCTURE AND STRATEGIES

A. The Present System for the Care of Homeless Black Children

There have long been homeless black children in the United States. Most of them have relatives or friends to take over their care and upbringing—informal adoption apparently is much more common in the black than in the white community [Hill (100); Jones (114); Ladner (132)]. But there are always those for whom substitute families are not immediately available. In such cases public or private social welfare organizations take over. Although some of these black children are taken care of by private black-run organizations, most of them go into a caretaking system run by whites [Billingsley and Giovannoni (10)]. The adoption system was created to deal with healthy, whole, white infants, and the white middle class couples thought most likely to want to adopt. It has a history of offering poor care and few adoption opportunities to black children [Anderson (3); Community Studies, Inc. (38); Getz (78); Gruber (86); Haitch (90); M. Schapiro (193, 194); Trombley (213); Wachtel (216)]. We will briefly describe the evolution of this system and some of its consequences for black children.[1]

In the early part of this century, adoption was not a common solution for childlessness. Both the willingness to adopt and the way in which it was done were strongly affected by attitudes toward what was labeled "illegitimacy." A childless couple seeking a child might find a physician who knew of an unwed mother willing to surrender her baby to those who would provide a good home, or the couple might go shopping at an orphanage. Once a child was found, the couple would seek a court order terminating the parental rights of the birth mother and another order granting a petition for adoption. Judges always could deny a petition for adoption, but the case was not an adversary proceeding and no one argued against the adoption. Judges lacked the resources to investigate the couple's potential as parents and the skill to evaluate any information that might be found. Judges were busy with other matters, and approving the adoption seemed to make everyone concerned happy. Petitions for adoption were usually granted.

As the supply of babies from unwed mothers and potential adoptive parents grew, some felt that people with more understanding of the problems involved than doctors and lawyers were needed to fill the broker's role. The earliest adoption agencies were voluntary organizations, often connected with a religious group, and staffed by women doing good works in their spare time. These volunteers saw their job as providing children for childless couples as well as helping unwed mothers place children they could not raise.

As the care of dependent children came to be seen as "social work," those engaged in social work sought professional status. Many of them thought that adoption placement called for more than untrained volunteers. The volunteers and professionals joined issue over whether the volunteers took too cavalier an attitude toward preserving the ties of kinship between illegitimate children and their biological mothers or other relatives. On one hand, the professionals talked of conserving "human values" by keeping mother and child together [Parker, (175)]. On the other hand, the volunteers, typically married and motherly, charged that the professionals were seeking to implement academic ideas and, because of their lack of experience, that they would unnecessarily burden unwed mothers with their babies and thus force them into poverty.

The professionals won, and their victory is reflected in adoption statutes. One of the social workers' important strongholds was and still is the Children's Bureau which was part of the United States Department of

Labor until the creation of the Department of Health, Education and Welfare. The Children's Bureau has long sought to influence the content of the adoption statutes passed by the states by issuing commentaries and drafts of model statutes that bear the stamp of expert approval. Generally, judges are now directed by statute to grant petitions for adoption only if it is in the best interests of the child or if the child's interests will be promoted. [See Bodenheimer (12) for proposals for reform of adoption statutes. See Weinberg (221) for a summary of all state statutes to that date.] While such a standard is not very precise, it does tell a judge that the child's interests rather than those of biological or prospective adoptive parents have priority.[2] Moreover, this standard sets the stage for deference to expert opinion. The best interests of a child do not call for application of legal reasoning but for expertise about children and parenting. [See, for example, the Governor of Connecticut's message vetoing a bill that would have given foster parents some rights at the expense of the experts, Conn. Pub. & Special Acts, 1972 Sess., Pub. Act No. 203, p. 9. Compare Mnookin (159).] And social workers stand ready to offer expertise [cf. Parker (175); Lubov (138)].

Some statutes have made one or two specific points about where the best interests of a child lie. Seven states have, or had, laws requiring that adoptive parents be of the same religious faith as the child's biological mother "whenever possible" or "where practicable." Ten more states have, or had, statutes that may make religious matching likely since they require that the religious background of child and applicants be brought to the attention of the judge. [See *New York University Law Review* (168), for a summary of legislation concerning religion in adoption.] Two states had laws calling for racial matching and, more recently, two states (Connecticut and Kentucky) have passed statutes declaring that courts shall not *disapprove* an adoption solely because of a difference in race or religion between child and prospective parents. (Conn. Pub. & Special Acts, 1973 Sess., Pub. Act No. 73-156, Sec. 12; Ky. Rev. Stat. Sec. 199.471, Suppl. 1972.)[3]

Statutes also were passed calling for the licensing of adoption agencies. When this happened most of the agencies connected with religious groups got licenses and continued their work, but their staff changed from volunteers to full time professionals. Until relatively recently, most adoption placement was carried on by such private agencies [Kadushin (119)]. They received into their care the majority of healthy white babies released for adoption, and much of their practice appears to have continued to be oriented toward finding white children for childless white couples. Also until relatively recently, these agencies seldom dealt with black children or black couples applying to become adoptive parents [Billingsley and Giovannoni (10)].

Since the turn of the century, public agencies have been responsible for the majority of dependent children other than readily adoptable white babies. Although these agencies have always made some adoptive placements, the majority of children under their guardianship have been those whose families are temporarily unable to care for them, those whose families have permanently collapsed, and those transferred from private agencies because of problems which private agencies do not have resources to deal with. [For example, see studies of foster care loads by Gruber (86) and Wisconsin Dept. of Public Welfare (225)]. Most black homeless children can be found under public agency guardianship. In the early part of the century they usually lived in institutions; today they are most likely to be placed with a foster family paid to take care of them.

The practice of independent adoption placements did not die out and its continuation has, naturally, been seen as a problem by the professionals. This has prompted more legislation influencing the structure of adoption in ways that affect homeless black children. For most of their history, both public and private adoption placement agencies have had a shortage of white infants without physical handicaps and an oversupply of applicants who wanted to adopt [Klemesrud (128); M. Schapiro (193)].[4] Since many people who want to adopt are relatively wealthy middle-and-upper class couples, a variety of unlicensed brokers—many of them lawyers—have continued to run a market to meet the demand which licensed agencies could not satisfy or refused to do so. Some couples still are served by doctors and lawyers who know of an unwed mother or pregnant woman who does not want to or cannot raise her child, some unlicensed brokers serve out of a spirit of humanitarianism, but others are in the business for profit. (For a recent report see "The Baby Selling Racket," a series that appeared in the *Chicago Sun-Times*, June 13 to 25, 1976.)

Not surprisingly, social workers do not approve of these suppliers' unschooled ways nor of any transfers not overseen by licensed professionals [Hallinan (91); Lukas (139); *New York Times*, December 4, 1959, p. 34; M. Schapiro (193); Schoenberg (195); Smith (207); *Yale Law Journal* (228)]. They stress that the ability to be a good parent is unrelated to ability to find a broker or to buy a child and, despite evidence to the contrary [Eldred, *et al.* (53); Witmer, *et al.* (226)], that placements made without the care and protection of licensed agencies are very risky.

From the 1920s to the present, professional adoption workers and their organizations have sought to limit independent placements [Chevlin (30); Getz (78); Madison (146); Parker (175); Theis (212)]. They have been fairly successful. While the number of adoptions was rising sharply between 1957 and 1970, the number of independent placements did not increase [National Center for Social Statistics (165)]. In 41 states and the

District of Columbia, before judges can pass on petitions for adoption, they must refer them to a professional adoption worker for a report. (In a few states the judges may waive this requirement in the best interests of the child.)

However, there is reason to believe that laws controlling independent placements are not always enforced [Klemesrud (128); M. Schapiro (193); *U.S. News & World Report,* July 30, 1973, p. 62]. Thus the professionals have not ceased trying to improve regulation of independent adoptions. They favor making activity in the black market for babies a criminal offense. In Oregon, for example, the legislature declared that "No private individual, including midwives, physicians, nurses, hospital officials and all officers of unauthorized institutions, shall engage in child-placing work . . ." [Ore. Rev. Stat. §418.300 (1971); see also *Chicago Sun-Times,* June 25, 1976, pp. 4, 51].

More legal changes were prompted by other suppliers of babies who operated in an unorthodox manner. These groups sought to find homes for children who were not perfect-white-infants—particularly foreign children. The evidence available indicates that the idealists' placements have also turned out as well as agency placements [DiVirgilio (45); Isaac (106); Kadushin (118); Rathbun, *et al.* (184)]. However, at the time these unorthodox placements were made they too looked very risky to professionals. They objected that not enough was known about either parents or children before placement, and they obviously feared that many were with families who would be or had been turned down by regular agencies.

The professionals won the day here. Proxy adoptions, the procedure which made international adoption relatively easy, was outlawed, forcing parents who want to adopt a foreign child either to travel to the child's native country or to go through an expensive and time-consuming screening process [Adams and Kim (1)]. The professionals were also helped here by their successful lobbying effort directed toward control of independent adoptions. The net effect of all this was to curtail the first experiments in transracial adoption in the early 1960s and to inhibit any attempts to make an end run around the formal adoption system. And social work professionals are well organized to press for even more laws if they perceive further threats to the system.

This evolution has left us with the following structure that affects homeless black children: Many children, both black and white, are under the guardianship of public and private agencies which have wide freedom to decide what becomes of them. Suppose, for example, a private agency decided that it opposed the adoption of black children by white parents. If it openly announced this as its policy, a group favoring such adoptions might be able to bring a class action to challenge it in court. However, for many reasons this is unlikely to happen. The law is not clear, and such a suit would be expensive. A group favoring transracial adoption could instead try to mobilize public opinion against agency policy and push for favorable legislation. For example, in the *Coombs* case a court refused to accept an agency judgment that foster parents could not adopt their foster child because she was too bright for them (*New York Times,* March 7, 1960, p. 21 and March 9, 1960, p. 27; *Time,* March 21, 1960, p. 43). The case received wide publicity, most of it very hostile to the agency, and that prompted a statutory change in New Jersey so that now foster parents have the right to adopt their foster children (N.J. Stat. Ann. Sec. 30: 4C-26.5 & 26.7, Supp. 1973). However, the key to the *Coombs* outcome seems to be scandal, and many agency refusals to act are not scandalous news. Other judges have tried to change social work practice and met with defeat [Isaac (107)].

Furthermore, it is not clear that winning a court case or pushing through new legislation would have any impact beyond erasing an undesirable formal standard. An adoption agency need not openly announce its policy against, say, transracial adoption, in which case a challenger who knows that informal policy or individual caseworkers are opposed to transracial adoption would have a difficult burden of proof. Individual caseworkers can carry out their own antitransracial adoption policy by just never finding any white applicants whom they deem suitable for minority children. Generally, the wide discretion granted to adoption agencies means that, as one New York legislator put it, "For all practical purposes the state has not one but 42 different sets of adoption laws . . ." [*New York Times,* December 10, 1966, p. 36; see also Fricke (69); Merrill and Merrill (155)].

Most importantly, until recently agencies have faced few structural demands to take affirmative action for children other than white infants. Private agencies could refuse to give service to unwed mothers whose children would be hard to place for whatever reason, including race [Edwards (52); Heath (97); Trombley (213)]. The custody of any children that private agencies do take and feel they cannot place can be transferred to public agencies.

Until very recently almost all public agencies were organized in such a way that any backlog of hard to place children was made to appear small. This was the result of the organizational division of adoption and foster care services. Children deemed unadoptable or hard to place were sent to institutions or foster families. Unless some placement plan had been made and was actively being pursued, foster children were the formal responsibility of only the foster-care worker. The organizational problem was compounded by the high turnover among foster care workers and large caseloads which meant that individual children were not known to anyone who might have planned for them. In this way children who had no real chance of being brought up by a birth parent became "lost in the files," drifting to adulthood in foster care which probably was not a good substitute for adoptive placement and was actually damaging to far too many children. The separation of foster care and adoption services further compounded the situation when foster caseloads came to be seen as a problem. Instead of shifting part of the burden to the adoption section of the agency, the tendency was to seek more money to expand the number of foster homes. This situation is particularly relevant in tracing the fate of black children in the system since a disproportionate number of children adrift in foster care were (and still are) black.[5]

Black children are also affected by action at another point in the adoption system. Formal review of adoption agency practices still lies in the hands of courts at the point when they are asked to approve particular petitions for adoption. One striking recent example of the use of this power involved a county judge in Pennsylvania who announced that he would no longer approve the adoption of black, Vietnamese or Korean children by white parents. He explained that "It's great when they're little pickaninnies. They're cute and everybody's a do-gooder. But what about when they're 14 or 15?" (*Milwaukee Journal,* May 6, 1976, p. 1). This kind of judicial response is most unusual, however, and the end of the story suggests that a judge's veto itself may be subject to informal control. After a great deal of publicity and public criticism, apparently in part engineered by adoption workers, this judge seems to have changed his position. Had he not done so, the scandal might have prompted an attempt to gain legislation.

In the usual case the judge does not have much information about the child, the prospective parents, or about other resources that might exist for the child [Katz (123)]. If the agency learns to write persuasive recommendations, few trial judges will have the time, skill, or inclination to look behind them. We have no actual count, but our impression is that courts usually rule in favor of the agency when a decision is challenged. (See, for example, *Ebony,* March, 1963, p. 131, and *New York Times,* November 10, 1962, p. 15.) The possibility that a judge may veto agency action may influence agency policy at times—although not necessarily to change policy as much as to stimulate efforts to get around the judge's position. (For example, if a judge is known to frown on transracial adoption the agency might transfer some applicants and children to an agency in a different jurisdiction.) By and large, then, the legal adoption proceeding is usually regarded as purely ceremonial by judge and agency alike. [See, for example, comments by Broeder and Barrett (20) on the "unreal" quality of cases and literature dealing with the *legal* relevance of religion in adoption.]

The view just presented of how the present caretaking system for home-less black children came about is not quite the same as that presented in social work texts. For example, Bishop (11) saw it this way:

> . . . the agencies are faced with a considerable antagonism on the part of the commu-nity . . . directed toward agency restrictions, which are seen as preventing eligible couples from receiving children and as denying adoption to adoptable children . . . Some of the criticism is a natural reaction to *restriction inherent in law* and in a disciplined casework process . . ." (p. 28, emphasis added).

Similarly, when professionals began to see that there were far too large caseloads of "hard-to-place" children needing homes, it seemed to some of them that the problem stemmed from society which has rejected the children and had not given the professionals the resources to solve the problem created by rejection. [For example, see the editorial in *Child Welfare,* October, 1963, p. 368; Dunne (48); Reid (186).] At the same time, the profession is not totally forgetful of its effective lobbying arm; one can also find in social work texts blunt statements such as this from Boehm (14) in 1965; "A major social work activity has been getting suitable adoption legislation passed . . ." (p. 65). [See also Fanshel (57).]

The evolution of this system and the existence of some blindness on the part of its makers as to where it was drifting is not an unusual story; rather it is more likely typical of any bureaucratic system which evolves through incremental decision making, rationally pursued to deal with or avoid immediate problems. [See, for example, Macaulay (145).] As following sections will describe, when the system was confronted with some of the gross inequities in services to different kinds of children that had evolved, some adoption workers were among the leaders of action to correct those inequities.

B. A History of Decision-Making Affecting Homeless Black Children

1. The System Fails to Offer Acceptable Services to Black Children (1920—1960)

Professional adoption workers were largely responsible for creating a system for dealing with homeless children where the best solution to their problem was adoption. However, the adoption system as it operated was shaped by ideas developed in the placement of white infants, and these ideas may have been important reasons why the system failed to serve black children. In order to understand how the discretionary power of adoption agencies has been used in ways affecting black children, we will first sketch some important features of the usual agency procedure for placing healthy white infants. It is difficult to look back now and describe precisely the actual practices of most adoption agencies from the mid-1920s to the mid-1950s. There was wide variance between agencies and within agencies over time as supply and demand varied [Kadushin (117); Merrill and Merrill (155); *New York Times,* Feb. 16, 1962, p. 12; Riday (187)]. However, we can outline a model of the most common standards that adoption agencies said they followed, based on the professional literature and, to some extent, personal accounts found in the popular press.

The most important[6] and common of these standards were as follows:

(1) The couple had to have a good income and a middle-class life style, including a well-kept home, perhaps large enough so that the child could have a room of his or her own.

(2) The wife had to be a full-time mother, and she could not desire to work outside the home, even part-time.

(3) The couple had to offer medical evidence that they were infertile; they could have no other children.

(4) The couple's health had to be excellent, including their mental health. However, since most applicants had struggled with infertility for some time, it was assumed that they had residual emotional problems. The psychiatric input into social work ideology was heavily weighted toward a diagnosis of pathology which would, if the ideology were followed in practice, lead to labeling many idiosyncrasies and nonconforming views as symptoms of mental illness. For example, couples were turned down for wanting children too badly, for not seeming to care about their biological childlessness, for holding unusual political or religious beliefs, and for bad experiences with their own parents. Women ran a risk of being rejected if they had frequent headaches, enjoyed sex too much or not at all, and so on.

Most agencies probably did hold fairly close to the announced standards in white adoptions since the supply and demand situation assured them of placing all of their healthy white infants no matter how rigid their standards for prospective parents. Whatever the actual practices, the announced standards and known personal experiences of applicants certainly prompted an image held by many that it was difficult to adopt a child. If these standards were applied to blacks who asked for children, or if blacks believed that they would be, the standards would clearly have acted as a deterrent to many black couples wanting to adopt. Even today, the proportion of blacks with middle-class incomes and housing is far lower than the proportion of whites, and the disparity was greater from the mid-1920s to the mid-1950s. Black mothers are likely to work from necessity or from a desire for better things for their families. Proof of sterility affronts black males at least as much as it does whites. Some black couples who might be willing and able to adopt already have children of their own. Moreover, the ability of a white social worker—and almost all adoption workers were white—to make judgments about the mental health of a black couple can be questioned. Even if one were to grant a worker's capability to diagnose mental health, few white applicants accept the necessity for the kind of probing social workers think necessary; there is reason to suppose that many blacks would regard such probing as outrageous or frightening when conducted by a white. Then too, adoption agency customs assumed in this early period that those applying to be parents would be interviewed several times by a professional worker in agency offices during normal working hours. Few low-income couples have the privilege of leaving work for such purposes. Finally, experience and better judgment would tell many blacks generally to stay away from situations where they would be judged by white middle-class professionals on the agency's home ground. The net effect of such practices and standards surely limited demand from black couples for children to adopt. [For a review of these problems see Madison and Schapiro (148); see also Aldridge (2); Festinger (62); Fradkin (66); Fricke (69); Wachtel (216).]

Those most likely to consider adoption during this period were married, childless couples earning enough money to feel able to support a child. We have no way of knowing how many black couples, over the years in question, fell into this class, but it seems unlikely that it would be high. Even if we assume that no members of this group were ever deterred by agency standards and procedures and that the latter would be relaxed so that every black couple applying would have been given a child, there probably would have been many black children left unadopted.

The other side of the supply and demand equation is also part of the problem. The most common source of babies available for adoption is unmarried mothers. Known unwed parenthood tends to be more common among the poor. Among other reasons, poor women tend to have little access to contraception and abortion, and blacks, of course, are overrepresented in the ranks of the poor [Madison and Schapiro (148); Sklar and Berkov (206)]. Unmarried black women may more often want to keep and raise their babies than unmarried white mothers—at least in the past—but even so the supply of adoptable black babies is greater than the supply of adoptable white babies in proportion to the population "at risk" for producing them. It is likely that there would be even more known adoptable black babies if services to unwed black mothers equaled those available to whites. Unwed black mothers are not likely to enter maternity homes during pregnancy, and they are less apt to be visited by a hospital social worker than a white unwed mother. If they are seen by a worker, they are often discouraged from giving up their babies because workers do not think that there are enough foster and adoptive homes for black children. [See Billingsley and Giovannoni (10); Boehm (13); Boothby (15); Deasy and Quinn (44); Herzog and Bernstein (98); M. Schapiro (193); Wachtel (216).] As described above, private agencies have in the past refused adoption services to minorities because they felt that they could not find homes for minority babies. The state agencies have no right to make such refusals, but it has been reported that the State of Wisconsin makes extra efforts to find black unwed fathers and to force them to support children of "low adoptability" [Ball, *et al.* (7); see also, Community Studies, Inc. (38); Costigan (40); Platts (180); Reed (185)].

Thus it may be that adoption into black families never could have entirely solved the problem of black children needing good homes in the years before 1950. The number of black children born of unwed mothers possibly would have swamped the supply of potential black adoptive parents under the best of circumstances. Nonetheless, there is impressive evidence that the rate of placement of available black children in black homes was kept low by the system's usual response to black applicants. Adoption may not have been the solution to the whole problem, but it could have solved more of it if customs developed in the placement of white infants had not stood in the way.

2. Perception of a Problem and First Responses
(the Mid-1950s to the Early 1960s)

At any time in any society there are many potential social problems, but only a few come to be recognized and labeled as such by those who might be expected to seek solutions. There are no scientific laws explaining the process of defining the issues on the social agenda. While we cannot establish beyond doubt why many people both inside and outside the professional adoption community came to regard the treatment of homeless black children as a scandal during the late 1950s and early 1960s, we can suggest some of the elements that played a part. Then we can catalog some of the initial attempts to respond by taking small steps that would disrupt existing patterns as little as possible. All of this served to set the stage for more dramatic action which we will discuss in the next section.

First, and most obviously, in the late 1950s and early 1960s, the times were right for concern about black children. Awareness that few black children were adopted in proportion to the number coming into the child-care system can be found in the professional literature as early as 1935 [Murphy (162)]. However, we found very few references to the situation in social work journals during the next seventeen years. Blacks suffered so many social disadvantages and injustices in the Depression that it is not surprising that adoption reform was not viewed as an important priority at that time. But with the decision of the Supreme Court in *Brown v. Board of Education* (the school desegregation case) in 1954, the problems of black Americans arrived at the center of the stage [Harding (22)]. Many social workers were political liberals, and it is understandable that they would become very concerned about racism found in their own house.

In the 1950's there was also widespread uneasiness about the quality of foster care generally [Boehm (13); Getz (78); Glover (79); Maas and Engler (144); M. Schapiro (193); *New York Times,* Sept. 30, 1955, p. 28]. As we have noted, far too many children, a large proportion of whom were black, were drifting to adulthood in foster care which was supposed to be temporary, but which, in practice, ended only with the end of their childhood. Of course, many foster families have provided excellent homes for their charges. Although by definition their relationship is temporary, they establish strong bonds with their children, offering much love and good care and becoming the true psychological parent described by Goldstein, Freud and Solnit (81). [For example, see cases described by Kadushin (116).] Furthermore, we should note that foster parents for black children tend to be black, relatively poor, and not well educated [Husbands (102); Madison and Schapiro (147)]. Those who criticize the foster care offered by these families may be following their white middle-class biases and overlooking the strengths of black foster parents [Hill (100); Ladner (132); Mandell (149)].

However, although the existence of many good, loving foster families must be acknowledged, the existence of seriously inadequate foster homes must also be faced because they constitute a serious social problem (see footnote 5). Some foster parents were (and still are) indifferent to the development and future of their charges, and some were actually dangerous caretakers. Furthermore, the medical, physical and emotional needs of many of the children in these foster homes were not being attended to by anyone in the agency that was in charge of them. Social workers came to term homeless black children as "socially handicapped" because it was so difficult to find adoptive homes for them [Glover (79); Streit (210)]. While black children may have been socially handicapped by racism and poverty, they were also administratively handicapped because the adoption and foster care systems offered them far less service than was routinely given to white children [cf. Polier (182) who speaks of "professional abuse" of children.]

As one might expect, when both professional and nonprofessional critics began to assert that the care of homeless black children was a scandal, the response of many child care agencies was to do nothing. All plausible solutions seemed controversial and costly, and those who ran these agencies did not see the problem as theirs. Others took only minimal steps to deal with it just as theories of incremental decision making would predict. For example, one early effort was on behalf of children with mixed racial background whose physical features were such that they might pass as white [CWLA (32); Dunne (48); Fradkin (66); Paull (176); Taft (211); H. L. Shapiro (200)]. An attempt was made to develop scientific ways of predicting the appearance of these children when they grew up [Daniels (41); Nordley and Reed (170)].[7] White parents were educated into the genetics of racial mixture [Stern (209)]—it was emphasized that apparently white children with a black forebear will not produce black babies (unless, of course, they take black lovers or spouses).

The 1950s also saw the first of many special efforts to recruit black parents for black children, efforts which, for a variety of reasons, did little to reduce the population of black children needing homes.[8] At the outset, it was assumed that blacks were not interested in adoption of strangers' children because the ratio of applicants to the number of children available was so low [Billingsley and Giovannoni (10); Deasy and Quinn (44); Hawkins (95); Manning (150); Schapiro (194); Woods and Lancaster (227)]. In fact, when one controls for socioeconomic class, the rate of agency adoptions by blacks is slightly greater than that for whites [Herzog and Bernstein (98)]. To some extent the shortage of black homes for adoptable black children reflected little more than that in our economy there are relatively fewer black than white homes that could meet agency income standards.

Some of the recruitment efforts involved using the mass media to publicize actual children needing homes. As we might expect, many social workers found aggressive publicity methods to be highly unprofessional. However, these were the most successful methods since they did often produce a flood of inquiries [Dukette (47); Fricke (67), (69); Herzog and Bernstein (98); *New York Times,* December 25, 1956, p. 31, and April 27, 1964, p. 31; Owens (174)]. But many black couples did not follow through after making the first contact in response to these appeals.

As we have said, part of the failure of these appeals may rest on the inability of the agencies to meet inquiries with what Wachtel (216) terms "sympathetic processing." Later white-controlled agencies gained a better understanding of their problems (and of their biases), but generally throughout the 1960's, all that most adoption workers knew for sure was that they were not doing very well in finding permanent homes for the black children in their care. They usually found themselves at the end of their recruitment efforts with as great a problem as when they started out [Billingsley and Giovannoni (10); Fricke (67); Herzog and Bernstein (98)]. The pool of adoptive parents consisted of the relatively sparse generation born in the depression years of the 1930s while the babies were being produced by the more abundant generation of the 1940s. Unwed motherhood rates were rising (U.S. Bureau of the Census, 1972) and foster care loads continued to increase (*Children*, January-February, 1967, p. 39).

3. White Parents Adopt Black Children (the Late 1950s to the Early 1970s)

The limited success of attempts to solve the problems of homeless black children prompted an important social experiment. If there were not enough black parents for all of the black children, why not have them adopted by the relatively plentiful white applicants? Of course, not all white applicants were willing to embark on such an adventure, but it became clear that some were. [Whites were more willing to adopt non-whites who were not black, Chambers (27)]. In part, the idea of transracial adoption came about as campaigns to sell black children to black adoptive parents splashed over and reached an unintended audience [Fricke (69); MARCH (151)]—whites who had been turned down earlier when applying to adopt or who faced a long wait for a child; whites who wanted to strike a blow against racism; whites who wanted to integrate their own families for the benefit of themselves and their children; whites who, perhaps, wanted to defy their parents, relatives and friends or to prove how liberal they were; and many whites who just loved children and were responding to children in need. [See Madison and Schapiro (148), for a review of studies of these parents. See also Grow and Shapiro (84); Kribs (130); Ladner (133); Marmor (152); Pepper (177); Shireman and Watson (203).]

Whites had asked for black children, but in the past the conventional answer of almost all adoption agencies was that transracial adoption was impossible [Dunne (48); Lukas (139); Owens (174); M. Schapiro (193); South Carolina Law Quarterly (208); Uhlenhopp (214)].[9] According to the social workers, adoption was hard enough without adding the burdens of objections from relatives, neighbors and friends. Much of their objection rested on the doctrine of matching, developed by the agencies in placing white infants and earlier thought to be very important [Brown (23); Fradkin (66); M. Schapiro (193); Taft (211)]. Blue-eyed blond parents were not to be given brown-eyed brunettes. College-educated parents were not to be given a child of parents whose offspring were thought unlikely to be college material. The idea was that parents and child could establish a better relationship if differences were minimized. The idea was plausible since there is evidence that similarity is important in selecting friends and spouses [Byrne (25)]. However, the real purpose may have been to facilitate hiding or denying the fact of adoption. For example,

[F]oster parents . . . will accept a child with greater warmth if their parents and relatives can say that the child looks so much like his adoptive dad that one doesn't know that he isn't really an own child! [Letter from Iowa State Dept. of Social Welfare, October 29, 1954, quoted in Uhlenhopp (214).]

Perhaps more importantly, an applicant who was not interested in matching ran a risk of being suspected of being neurotically unrealistic [Ball, *et al.* (7); Doss (46); Fradkin (66); Fricke (68)].

Obviously, few friends or relatives of a white parent were likely to say that a black child "looks so much like his adoptive dad that one doesn't know that he isn't really an own child!" And if an applicant who was not interested in matching hair and eye color might be suspected of being neurotically unrealistic, think of the reaction to an applicant who was not interested in matching race.

The position taken by the most professional adoption agencies was reflected in the 1958 edition of the *Standards for Adoption Service* of the Child Welfare League of America. The CWLA Standards are not law nor a restatement of what is typical, but, rather, they are a statement of what the most prestigious organization in the field of adoption sees as the better view. The 1958 *Standards* found transracial adoption very questionable:

4.6 Race
Racial background in itself should not determine the selection of the home for a child.
 It should not be assumed that difficulties will necessarily arise if adoptive parents and children are of different racial origin. At the present time, however, children placed in adoptive families with similar racial characteristics, such as color, can become more easily integrated into the average family group and community.
4.7 Interracial background
Children of interracial background should be placed where they are likely to adjust best. A child who appears to be predominantly white will ordinarily adjust best in a white family, and should therefore be placed with a family that can accept him, knowing his background.
 In such situations it is desirable to have the participation of the appropriate consultants, including a geneticist or anthropologist, in arriving at a decision on how the child should be placed. . . . In selecting a family it is necessary to consider not only the attitude of the adoptive parents, but also that of the larger community within which the child will be living. If a suitable placement is not possible within a given community, the child should be placed elsewhere. . . .
4.11 Physical and personality characteristics
Physical resemblances should not be a determining factor in the selection of a home, with the possible exception of such racial characteristics as color.

Orthodoxy notwithstanding, some social workers and some prospective parents had begun in the late 1950s to think that nationality and strict physical (not including racial) matching were not important for everyone

[Boehm (14); DiVirgilio (45); Fradkin (66); Jenkins (110); Maas (142); *New York Times,* January 28, 1955, p. 13; M. Schapiro (193)].[10] This may have paved the way for serious consideration of transracial adoption.[11] A few cautious experiments began in the very late 1950s and early 1960s. One of these was the Indian Adoption Project, announced in 1960. [See Davis (43); Lyslo (140, 141); *New York Times,* October 31, 1960, p. 34.] Individual agencies began placing some black children with white couples in the early 1960s. [See Fricke (70); MARCH (151); Open Door Society (171); Sandusky, *et al.* (192)].

Many early placements were with white couples who had their own biological children. It was thought that these couples would not need a perfect white infant, as infertile couples might. A few childless couples who were thought to have more strengths than other couples received black children as well.

The early selection of parents to participate in transracial adoption was also affected by a common but unlabeled bureaucratic tradition that arose in placing white infants. We will call this C-matching. Some parents were just barely acceptable to the agency; if graded on an A to F scale, they would receive a C. The agency also had children who just barely passed whatever express or tacit standard it applied to decide which infants were adoptable. They may have had some minor physical defect or their parents may have had a poor social or medical history. Assuming that agency standards were relevant to predicting good parenting, children with special needs should have gone to the A parents while C parents ought to have had less trouble raising A children. However, in the process of matching parents with children, workers tended to match perfect parents with perfect children: A parents got A children and B parents got B children. This left C parents and C children represented by two piles of leftover file folders. It was then natural to match the almost unplaceable child with a couple who had to settle for second best or get nothing at all [Bradley (18); Edwards (52); Fradkin (66); Jenkins (110); Kadushin (117); Schapiro (194)].

Some black children, then, in these new transracial adoption experiments, were placed with couples who were, at best, only marginally eligible for perfect white infants. Thus the C-matching tradition was enlarged to include transracial adoption [Branham (19); Herzog, *et al.* (99)].

The C-matching tradition could cut another way. Many white couples who applied to adopt black children were college graduates. The agencies were reluctant to give these applicants children whose backgrounds were not predictive of intellectual success. Social workers were probably aware that the background of the black children in their charge was shaped more by racism than by intellectual potential, but this awareness didn't help them in matching parents with children.

Many transracial adoptive applicants were likely to explain at least part of their motivation in terms of integrationist values. (See references given at the beginning of this section.) This fit into the spirit of the early 1960s; so did organization and action to promote racial integration. Many parents organized into groups dedicated to promoting transracial adoption and, as they began to see greater problems, to expanding adoption opportunities for all parentless children.[12] Some of these groups—for example, the Open Door Society, which began in Montreal—were used as recruitment, public relations and publicity auxiliaries by agencies and workers eager to expand the movement. Members of these groups reinforced each other's decisions to adopt transracially and encouraged others to do it. Some groups functioned to give social workers much needed reinforcement for unorthodox placements, while others felt they had to push skeptical agencies into the transracial adoptive business and some lobbied for supportive legislation. (Many of the groups put out newsletters, and many have put us on their newsletter list. It is from these newsletters that our evidence for transracial adoptive parent attitudes and activities comes.)

In print the adoption professionals' enthusiasm for transracial adoption lagged behind transracial adoptive practitioners and their customers. What was happening outside the journals was publicized only informally through the colleague system of dittoed and mimeographed reports and word-of-mouth. Some suggestion of the amount of activity unreported in the literature can be found in 1965 in three letters to the editor protesting an article on the paucity of black adoptive homes that did not mention the possibility of transracial adoption (*Children*, May-June 1965, p. 128).

Transracial adoption came of age in the professional literature with the appearance of Fricke's 1965 article.[13] By the mid to late 1960s many of the experiments had become major thriving programs. This was true, for example, in Chicago, Los Angeles, Minneapolis, St. Paul, Montreal, Portland (Oregon), and Toronto. For a time transracial adoption seemed to be the "in" thing for progressive agencies [Sandusky, *et al.* (192); Seidl (197); *Wall Street Journal*, January 9, 1970, p. 1]. Social workers and right-thinking parents could do something about a social problem by making one of the most important commitments people can make. This change in professional opinion and public views was symbolized by the revision of the CWLA *Standards for Adoption Service* in 1968. Ten years made a big difference:

4.5 Race
Racial background in itself should not determine the selection of the home for a child. . . .
   It should not be assumed by the agency or staff members that difficulties will necessarily arise if adoptive parents and children are of different racial origin. The agency

should be ready to help families who wish to adopt children of another race to be prepared for, and meet, such difficulties as may occur. . . . In most communities there are families who have the capacity to adopt a child whose racial background is different from their own. Such couples should be encouraged to consider such a child. . . .

As in any adoption plan, the best interests of the child should be paramount.

4.9 Physical and personality characteristics

Physical resemblances of the adoptive parents, the child or his natural parents, should not be a determining factor in the selection of a home. . . .

One cannot prove that these standards had a significant impact on practice, but, at the least, we assume that some workers could have justified their transracial placements by quoting them to a supervisor or a board which questioned what was being done. And sometimes it took but one worker to start making such placements in an agency.

The popular press found transracial adoption very newsworthy—we found twenty-six separate articles and books considering it in the 1960s. Some of the earliest families were given very positive publicity by such publications as the *New York Times Magazine, Look, Parents Magazine,* and *Ebony*. These were, almost without exception, heart-warming stories with the message that the problems one might expect just did not occur. Many of the authors strongly advocated transracial adoption and attacked social workers for timidity and irresponsibility in tackling the problems of homeless black children.

As a result of this movement and publicity, the number of transracial adoptions increased tremendously. But it barely made a dent in the problem. In 1971, for example, there were an estimated 40,000 to 80,000 adoptable black children under agency guardianship in this country. As Table 1 shows, in that year, only 7,420 black children were placed in adoptive homes, and only 2,574 adoptions were transracial.

It seems fairly clear that adoption workers did not feel free to justify transracial adoption in the professional literature in terms of promoting integration. We found only one sentence in the professional journals in the 1960s suggesting that transracial adoption served the positive value of integration [Fellner (61)]. At the time, this view had an eloquent spokesperson, Clayton Hagen, an adoption social worker. None of his speeches or papers [see, for example, Hagen (88)] was reported in the professional journals until 1972 when one was quoted at length in a review of another's book [Seely and Seely (196)]. Instead, transracial adoption had to be justified as being in the best interest of the black child—not the white family or society in general. As long as the choice was between a white home and what was viewed as bad foster care, one could talk about transracial adoption as being in the best interests of the black child, par-

Table I

	1968	1969	1970	1971	1972	1973	1974	1975
Total black children placed	3,122	4,336	6,474	7,420	6,065	4,655	3,813	4,172
Placements in black families	2,389	2,889	4,190	4,846	4,496	3,574	3,066	3,341
Placements in white families	733	1,447	2,284	2,574	1,569	1,091	747	831
Proportion of black children placed in white families	23%	33%	35%	35%	26%	23%	20%	20%
Number of agencies responding	194	342	427	468	461	434	458	565

Source: Opportunity, A Division of The Boys and Girls Aid Society of Oregon. *1976 Opportunity Report,* January, 1977. For a discussion of problems with these data see Madison and Schapiro (148).

ticularly in the early 1960s. Later this argument would become more difficult to make in the face of black objections.

Even as the transracial adoption wave crested, the skeptics within the adoption community were never completely silent. They continued to warn that transracial adoption was risky and called for the utmost caution, [Fly (64); Grow and Shapiro (84); Herzog *et al.* (99); Sandusky *et al.* (192)]. Many workers were still not convinced that there was evidence that matching parents and child was not important.[14] It had, of course, never been demonstrated that matching *was* important, but the idea was, until the 1960s, widely accepted in the profession and well-buttressed with psychiatric opinion. Some conceded that parents could take a lot more differences between themselves and their children than social workers had thought, but they wondered if racial differences might not be too much for many.

Also, it was never established whether motivation with moral political overtones, such as that found in the case of some transracial adoption applicants, was not neurotic and likely to lead to disastrous outcomes for the child [Chestang (29); Herzog, *et al.* (99); Jenkins (110)]. Moreover, at the time the transracial adoption movement began, and for almost fifteen years thereafter, there were no studies of the impact of transracial adoption upon which to base decisions.

However, early reports of the experiences of the few transracial families were encouraging to the movement. The dire predictions of shattering rejection of transracial families by both the black and white communities were not born out in the early experiences. In fact, two of the most common problems transracial parents reported were the discomfort of facing attributions of sainthood and moral superiority and the child-raising problem of gushing relatives and neighbors [Fricke (68)]. However, the Cassandras said that the transracial families had just been lucky. The real problem would come when the children entered school, or in adolescence when the children faced problems of dating and finding mates, or problems of finding their identity in the white communities in which they were growing up. Whether or not there will be in fact serious problems for most of the adolescent black children of transracial families is still unknown. Early returns both suggest serious problems for only a few and possibly extraordinary strengths among others [Edgar (50, 51); Falk (55); Fanshel (59); Grow and Shapiro (184, 185a); Hutson (103); Isaac (106); Ladner (133); Los Angeles County (136); *Over the Doorstep*, MARCH (151) 1971 Supplement; Simon and Altstein (205); *Time*, August 16, 1971, p. 42; Whelan (222); Zastrow (232)].

4. A Time of Conflict (the Late 1960s to the Present)

a. Opposition to Transracial Adoption

In the late 1960s, blacks were beginning to fight for power in many institutions in American society, and their claims of right were being heard far more than at any time in the past. Integration no longer was an unquestioned goal, and blacks were not eager to thank whites for favors. Some transracial parents were unpleasantly surprised to meet blacks who objected to their integrated families. Some black voices began to be raised in the professional literature, mainly questioning articles supporting transracial adoption. At first, the main criticism was that it primarily benefited white families and only served to divert attention from the needs of the larger number of black children who would not be adopted by whites in any event [Billingsley and Giovannoni (9, 10); King (125)]. Later it was argued that transracial adoption could be positively harmful to black children [Chestang (29); Chimezie (36, 36a); Herzog *et al.* (99); Jones (113); Katz (122); Ladner (133)].

The counterrevolution was sparked by the National Association of Black Social Workers (NABSW). They stated their views at their national convention in 1972, and then restated them a short time later at the Third North American Conference on Adoptable Children, for the benefit of the professionals and parents most involved in the transracial adoptive movement [NABSW (164); *New York Times*, April 9, 1972, p. 27, April 12, 1972, p. 38; and April 23, 1972, p. 111]. The opponents of transracial adoption stated that no matter where black children grow up, white society will treat them as blacks if they have any black ancestry. The critics of transracial adoption did not believe that white parents could teach their black children to deal with this. Moreover, black children in white homes were being deprived of their inheritance of black culture. The opponents feared that the motive behind transracial adoption was cultural genocide, that it was a movement to force integration which would swamp black culture and destroy it, that it was an attack on the black family, and that it was but one more example of white paternalism. [See Chunn (37); Ladner (133); Nettingham (167); Williams (223); see also Fanshel (59), for a description of similar fears among Native Americans in reaction to the Indian Adoption Project.]

Not all black professionals or blacks in general bought the NABSW position. Some disagreed but quietly [*Ebony*, March 1972, p. 145 and September, 1973, p. 32; *New York Times*, April 12, 1972, p. 38, April 23, 1972, p. 111, March 16, 1975, p. 44; Rustin (191); Williams (224); see also Herzog, *et al.* (99); Young (231)]. Some accepted much of what the opponents had to say but concluded that white homes would be better than the realistically immediate alternatives [*Children Today*, January-February, 1972, p. 35; *New York Times*, April 12, 1972, p. 38; see also Howard, Royse, and Skerl (100a).]

As might be expected, many parents of interracial families were angered. [See, for example, Johnson (111); *National Adoptalk*, May-June, 1972, p. 1; *Over The Doorstep*, October 1973, p. 12; Vieni (215).] They had committed too much to accept the view that they were harming their adopted children. It was true that in the past they had paid little attention to giving their children knowledge of the black culture [*Over The Doorstep*, Fall, 1970, p. 3; Simon (204)], but this could be remedied. The Open Door Society of Montreal, for example, helped organize black history and black culture courses given by blacks for integrated families.

These parents also countered the anti-transracial adoptive arguments with the charge that they represented black racism. Those whose children were of mixed racial parentage pointed out that their children were not only half black but also half white and said it was racist to deny their white heritage. [For example, see *Over The Doorstep*, 1973, p. 12.] NABSW responded:

Those born of Black-white alliances are no longer Black as decreed by immutable law and social customs for centuries. They are now Black-white, interracial, bi-racial, emphasizing the whiteness as the adoptable quality; a further subtle, but vicious design to further diminish Black and accentuate white. We resent this high-handed arrogance and are insulted by this further assignment of chattel status to Black people. [NABSW (164), p. 9].

Whatever the merits of transracial adoption or the case against it, it seems clear that those who ran most adoption agencies listened and shuddered, possibly in fear of black power and possibly for fear that their position on transracial adoption had not been morally right. Each article in the literature that attacked transracial adoption was followed by critical letters defending it. But once again the CWLA symbolized the shift in professional views by amending its *Standards for Adoption Service*. In 1968, section 4.5 said that "racial background in itself should not determine the selection of the home for a child . . ." In 1972 the section was amended to read that "It is preferable to place children in families of their own racial background," but then went on to state that "Children should not have adoption denied or significantly delayed when adoptive parents of other races are available [CWLA (34)]."

This counterrevolution cut transracial adoption by 39% in a single year, just when the movement seemed to be growing rapidly (Table 1). Black-white transracial adoptions had jumped from 733 in 1968 to 2,574 in 1971, according to the best count available, but in 1972 dropped to 1,569. In 1974, the rate and number of transracial adoptions were close to the 1968 levels. The number increased in 1975, but not even to 1969 levels.[15]

b. New Alternative Solutions

As the criticism of transracial adoptions grew, many offered alternative solutions to the problem of finding good homes for the many black children who needed them. Blacks had, themselves, led or staffed the most successful actions to correct the neglect of homeless black children in state guardianship [Billingsley and Giovanonni (10); Michaela (156); *National Adoptalk*, May-June 1971, p. 1; Sandusky *et al.* (192)]. Thus black professionals were in a position to offer promising solutions. White workers had not paid much attention to their black colleagues' successes (or failures), but if they had read their journals they might have been aware of the probable causes of the previous failures of white-run efforts. Furthermore, these were times when social workers were hearing a great deal about institutional racism, white middle-class bias in the welfare system, and the value of community control. Viewed in the context of adoption work, these ideas led to the development of a number of innovative proprosals. The attacks on transracial adoption in 1972 served to create pressure for implementation of some of these proposals as a way of challenging the argument that transracial adoption was the only or even an acceptable solution to the problems of homeless black children. (Interestingly, the newsletters from the various adoptive parent organizations suggest that much of the lobbying effort came from organizations originally formed to promote transracial adoption.) We will catalogue these alternatives, briefly describe what has happened, and then will turn to the question of the impact of various programs on homeless black children.

Black Professionals and the Adoption of Blacks by Blacks. White workers came to understand that they were more likely to be seen as adversaries than helpers by many in the black community. If potential adoptive parents were repelled by white workers in offices in white areas, then agencies should appoint black workers to staff and run offices in black neighborhoods. At the very least, black workers should be recruited to handle black applicants. These ideas took hold in many agencies, which then changed their organization or staffing patterns drastically [King (125); Kreech (129); Lawder, *et al.* (135); Sandusky, *et al.* (192)].

For one example of many efforts, the San Diego County Department of Public Welfare established Tayari in 1971 when it decided that transracial adoption was not appropriate for children of two black parents. The Tayari office is in the black community, staffed by blacks and effectively controlled by blacks. At the outset the staff interviewed black couples who had made inquiries about adoption but then had dropped out of the regular agency program. Results from this survey led to easing access to the agency through such things as meeting prospective parents in their homes after working hours and redesigning forms and bureaucratic procedures to make them less of a deterrent to black couples. Great efforts have been made to gain the confidence of the black community and to deal with relevant problems not previously handled by the regular agency. For example, Tayari has helped grandparents through the procedure of officially adopting grandchildren left in their care so that government benefits might be obtained [Neilson (166)].

Tayari's staff feel very strongly that the black community should be making decisions regarding black children. The concept is not a new one; Catholic and Lutheran agencies have always been allowed by the child welfare system to maintain a proprietary interest in "their own" children. Ball, *et al.* (7) suggested that one advantage of this system was to minimize religious conflict. [Compare the concern of Jewish leaders about the placing of Jewish dependent children in gentile institutions in the early 1900s as reported by Romanofsky (190).] If blacks had control over black children, it might similarly help reduce racial conflict.

Whatever the rationale for black control, the Tayari type of system seems likely to produce better results than the old routines. Wachtel (216) reported that the number of black children placed for adoption rose as the proportion of blacks in an agency rose. Regardless of the racial composition of the area served, the source of agency funding, and the size of the agency, the greater the white control, the fewer the black placements. Interestingly, Wachtel also found, still controlling for the racial composition of the area served, that the more evidence of professional involvement (meetings attended, journals read, etc.), the fewer the black placements reported. Apparently, there is something about orientation toward presumably white-dominated professional concerns that mitigates against helping black children find homes.

Wachtel's correlations cannot explain the reasons for the relatively great success of black-dominated agencies. On the basis of the literature on successful programs (cited above) we can speculate that black, community-oriented workers are more sensitive than others to barriers to agency access, have more intuitive understanding of a black applicant's chances of making a good parent, and can make more precise judgments of the risks involved in any situation, thus allowing them to take more chances.

Subsidized and Quasi-Adoption and Permanent Foster Care.   If blacks don't adopt because of financial problems, the agencies could pay them a subsidy to adopt. One can argue for adequate state appropriations to fund such a program on the ground that in the long-run this will save money. [See the review by Madison and Schapiro (148).] This idea is not a new one; mention of it can be found in the CWLA Adoption Standards of 1958. A related idea is permanent foster care or quasi-adoption. If the risk of having a child removed discourages foster parents from becoming attached to the child (and this is what a child needs), or if good foster parents want to keep their ward permanently but fear they don't have enough income to do what they want to do for their child, then the agency should make a contract for permanent support or a commitment to respect the permanence of foster parent-child bonds. This too might save money in the long run.

Many states have passed statutes authorizing subsidized adoption for low income parents or programs to give continued support to existing foster families that want to make their arrangements permanent. However, legislatures have not been generous in appropriating money to support these programs and statutory schemes are often structured to limit what the state must pay out. In our interviews with agency and state personnel we learned that few agencies have pushed usage of subsidized adoption or permanent foster care arrangements; many families who might very much want to make use of these programs do not know about them [Illinois Dept. of Children and Family Services (105); Katz (124)].

One source of the difficulty may be conventional social work theory which holds that all foster placements are temporary by definition and, further, that foster parents should be discouraged from becoming too attached to their wards since this makes removal to better permanent homes difficult. [See, for example, Weaver (220).] Some professionals view giving foster parents rights to adopt or to keep their long-term wards as erosion of the agency's power to do what is best for each child [Katz (123); *Chicago-Kent Law Review* (31)].

These views, however, often do not seem to fit reality. Many children are in foster care arrangements that have been permanent in all but name. Furthermore, it would seem to be a contradiction in goals to expect good parenting from people forbidden to love their wards. Goldstein, *et al.* (81) have written an impassioned plea that such nonsense be cut out of child welfare policy. The "real" parents, they say, are the psychological parents—the loving caretakers—and having a committed constant parent is the sine qua non of good child rearing. Also, it seems unlikely that many agencies would really have plans to move foster children who have been in a home for a long time, particularly if they are black, since it is difficult to find adoptive parents for older black children.

Another source of the reluctance to pursue subsidized adoption and permanent foster care solutions may lie with the foster parents. Foster families exercising their rights under some of these statutes would lose money. Fees for foster care won't make anyone rich, but they may be critical income for a family that is poor and particularly for families of foster children with disabilities—the "hard to place" children that are often found in foster care. The expenses covered by foster care payments sometimes are more than welfare would cover for one's biological or adopted children. Furthermore, although the popular press reports many cases of foster parents who have very strong desires to claim their foster children as their own, it is not clear what proportion of foster families they represent. All in all, it is difficult to predict how great the usage of these statutes giving foster and adoptive parents new rights and permanent support would become if the states did provide sufficient funds.

Technology to Make the System Work for All Children. If the system tends to lose track of children in foster care and to neglect finding permanent homes for all children who need them, then one remedy is to establish a monitoring system backed by computer "tracking" [Fellner (61); Gallagher (75)]. Tracking systems are being devised in several states, either as a result of critical self-analysis by agencies or as a result of publicity which brought legislative attention to the problem. Such systems require minimally that someone take note of where each child is and that plans for the child's future be made, reviewed, and updated at specified intervals after case opening. Computer-programmed data retrieval systems mean that all concerned are repeatedly confronted with a record on each child's situation that must be justified. Michigan's experience suggests that even without sanctions for failing to plan for a child, the hoped-for improvement in planning can be achieved (interview with Michigan officials [Sherman, *et al.*, (201)].

The model tracking system means that not only does someone become aware of the child periodically (which happened only with very troublesome children in the past), but that periodic review is not perfunctory. In Illinois, for example, if a child is in a temporary situation for eighteen months the responsible agency receives a warning that they have only six months left to do something because temporary placements are not allowed to go beyond two years. Previously workers with large caseloads usually had time only to tend to the future of children in collapsing foster situations; now they must attend to the future of all children spending more than a year and a half in temporary care. If this makes too much work for the caseworker, the existence of mandatory action provides a hefty weapon for the agency to use when demanding funds for more staff.

These systems have not been in use long enough or in enough states to allow us to gauge their impact [Sherman, *et al*. (201)]. However, states other than Michigan and Illinois have reported great delays in getting their systems running smoothly [Festinger (63); Young (230)].

c. Transracial Adoption in the 1970s.

Despite the criticism and opposition of many black professionals, transracial adoption still takes place. One placement worker in Florida told us that she places the child of two black parents in a black home, but she looks for a white home for the child of a black and a white. Often she has to send such children to northern states. She finds that black families tend not to want "biracial" children who look too white. We have no way of knowing whether her perceptions are totally accurate or typical, but we were told much the same thing by members of parent groups organized to foster transracial adoptions in two other states (see footnote 15).

Many other agencies apparently will not make transracial adoption placements. A black adoption supervisor in Texas stated, "You don't integrate a community with a child." A northern California organization of parents who had adopted transracially reported that agencies in its area abandoned placing so-called biracial children in white families because of the strong objections of an organization of black adoptive parents. Other agencies will make transracial placements if the applicants request them and are seen as qualified but these agencies do nothing to promote such adoptions.

d. Where Do We Stand Now?

Thus, we have arrived at a system where transracial adoption rests within the discretion of adoption agencies, importantly influenced by the attitudes of blacks. It no longer can be seen as a major tool for dealing with homeless black children, but it may be the solution for any particular black child. It is probably still more likely to be used if one of the child's parents or grandparents is white than where all are black.

Representatives of some adoption agencies have declared that the problem is solved, that most black and mixed race children coming into their system are placed immediately [Katz (122)]. Those children who remain in the system are, they claim, older or have physical or mental handicaps and, as before, are still hard to place. Certainly, methods of contraception are better and more widely available than in the earlier days of our story, as is abortion. In most parts of the United States it is now easier for unwed parents to raise their children without being ostracized by the community, and this probably encourages more black as well as white unwed mothers to keep their children rather than giving them up for adoption.

Not everyone is convinced that this describes the whole situation, however [see Haring (94)]. Several representatives of transracial adoptive parent organizations have voiced their suspicion that there is a cover-up by adoption professionals who are unwilling to face criticism from blacks, to acknowledge the existence of children in foster care who need adoptive placement, or even to admit that the difficulty in placing the "hard to place" child still lies more with system rather than in lack of potential parents. Effective tracking systems exist in only a very few states; one critic of the agencies wondered how they could say there were no children when they had no way of knowing. The critics find it difficult to believe that suddenly, without tracking systems, all children previously lost in the files have been found and given permanent homes and that children are not still being inadvertently set adrift in foster care when there is no evidence that foster care loads have greatly decreased or that agency staff and funding have greatly increased.

Without subpoena power and great resources it would be difficult to do the research necessary to resolve this argument. We would have to search a national sample of agencies' records, discover the proportion of foster children who would never return to a biological parent, determine that parental rights could be terminated, and then see if there were families for all the children we came up with. There are some studies which give us a clue as to what we might find. As late as March of 1973, for example, some 200 children, mostly black, were found to be "uncovered" (drifting in foster care) in a single district office in Chicago [Illinois Dept. of Children and Family Services (105)]. Similarly, Gruber (86) judged that about two thirds of the children in foster care in 1971 in Massachusetts were adoptable. Mott (161) estimated that there were 300,000 children in foster care in the nation. Other figures have ranged above 400,000 [4th North American Conference on Adoptable Children (65)]. Mott (161) estimated that 100,000 of these children in foster care needed permanent homes. Gallagher put the figure at 120,000 (*Milwaukee Journal,* April 8, 1975, p. 2). If we take Gruber's finding that two thirds of the children in foster care are adoptable, the national total may be over 200,000. Most estimates find that from one-third to one-half of the adoptable children in foster care are black.

Furthermore, there may be many black children who, if they were white, would come into the childcare system and be brought up in adoptive families. We do not know how many more black unwed mothers would elect to give up their babies for adoption if they were given a real option of placing their children in good homes. Perhaps it is best that this is not done [Mandell (149)]. We do know that often the family of a black unwed mother rallies around and the child is raised with love in the homes of grandparents or other relatives or even friends. Nonetheless, this option is not available to all black women and neither do they as yet have the options white women have.

C. An Explanation for Professional Responses to Transracial Adoption.

In writing a descriptive history of the problems of homeless black children, it was necessary to offer explanations for much of what we reported since explanation is part of description. For example, we considered the application of the white middle-class model of an adoption agency to poorer blacks when we reported changes that were made as agencies tried to attract black applicants. Yet there is an important matter left unexplained: How could professionals, whose control over the adoption process rests on their standing as experts, swing so widely in their judgments about transracial adoption in the short space of twenty years? In 1957, it was almost unthinkable to allow whites to adopt blacks; in 1968, transracial adoption was the progressive policy enshrined in the Child Welfare League of America's Standards; in 1972, transracial adoption was cultural genocide; and, in 1977, while transracial adoption is generally disapproved by the professionals, it all depends on where you are and whom you ask.

It is not easy to defend grants of discretion to experts in a democratic society. Normative decisions are supposed to be made by the elected representatives of the people subject to constitutional limitations. Experts are not elected, and, as a practical matter, they are seldom subject to the rule of law or even review by those who are affected by their choices. Questions are given to experts where political solutions are thought inappropriate. We can distinguish three models of expert decision making, although one tends to blur into the other: The process of granting discretion to experts often is legitimated by the assumption that experts merely apply the findings of science and technology to achieve goals that have been set by statute or are generally accepted. A more relaxed view sees experts as using what science and technology may be available but learning primarily by trial and error as they repeatedly deal with problems. The third model is very different. Here the expert is one who can find solutions to problems that are acceptable to those who might object and cause trouble. In this view, science and technology are but rhetorical tools serving to legitimate prudent decisions [Friedman and Macaulay (72), pp. 732–737].

As we have seen, no legislature considered the matter and then granted discretion to the adoption professionals to decide whether there should be transracial adoption. The power to make such decisions was just part of a general charge to seek the best interests of children. Normative decisions were always inherent in the charge, but it is not clear whether those who passed the statutes recognized the extent to which this is true.

It is hard to view an adoption professional contemplating transracial adoption as an example of the first model—an expert making judgments based on knowledge gained by testing hypotheses using standard research techniques. As Billingsley and Giovannoni (1969) pointed out, "There really is little systematic knowledge concerning ordinary adoption, even of Caucasian-Caucasian placements, to use as a yardstick for purposes of comparison in evaluating the outcome of interracial adoption. [See to the same effect, Jaffee (108); Eldred, *et al.* (53); Gruber (86); Isaac (106); Wald (218).] There still are no studies that would tell us enough about the outcomes of existing transracial adoptions to make decisions easy.

The lack of studies is understandable. People do not devote energy to research until they are aware of a problem, and few, if any, researchers recognized the possibility of transracial adoption before the decisions were made about whether it should be tried. And could the decisions about trying transracial adoption have waited until scientific findings were available? Indeed, could scientific evidence have ever resolved what, in essence, seems to have been a normative dispute?

Research that would resolve the debate about transracial adoption would not be easy to design and carry out so that it would be useful to adoption professionals. The very concept of a "successful" transracial adoption is heavily value-laden. A researcher would have to transform normative concepts into objective indicators for which tests could be made. This step alone is likely to lead to great dispute. For example, in order to determine success, would it be enough to compare children who were transracially adopted with children adopted in racially matched families in terms of how many of each group are seen in psychiatric clinics? Or would we not have to examine the mental health of each child individually—and what tests of mental health could we use that would be acceptable to all concerned? [Compare the well-taken criticisms of findings that more adopted than biological children have emotional problems by Kadushin (118).] Suppose we try to determine whether black children in white homes have lost their cultural identity? This would require us to define the concept "cultural identity" and then to devise indicators of its presence or absence—another task bound to provoke controversy. And, furthermore, we would have to wait until 1980 or later to do any research that could claim to be more than suggestive, because until then there won't be enough adult or older teenage children to study. (The number of children adopted transracially was not substantial before the mid 1960s.)

Finally, the actual question faced by adoption professionals was a comparative one which made matters even more difficult: It was not whether transracial adoption was the best solution conceivable but whether it was the best of the practical alternatives—even framing the question this way might offend some, which only reinforces our point. Research cannot resolve a problem of determining what is *best* unless all the normative judgments have been made and accepted. This is certainly not true of transracial adoption. For example, is it *better* for a black child to suffer the social problems an integrated family must inevitably face and lose some cultural identity as a black, or is it *better* for that child to grow up not really belonging to any family? The transracial adoption question may, thus, differ importantly from those areas of child welfare where many enthusiastically seek aid from social science [Ellsworth and Levy (54); Wald (217, 218, 219)]. On the other hand, the aspects of child welfare investigated by these authors also may have important normative conflicts lurking beneath the surface.

Actually, few experts would claim to be merely social engineers applying reliable, neutral, scientific principles. Most experts use whatever knowledge is available, the bulk of which is usually gained through trial and error. The idea that the practice of medicine is as much an art as a science captures this point. However, even this relaxed second model of expert status does not describe very well those who have been making decisions about transracial adoption. [See Brown and Brieland (21).] When the first transracial adoptions were made, in the late 1950s and early 1960s, there was no feedback available, of course. The first programs were called experiments. Actually, they were not true experiments at all, and the only feedback available for a long time was sparse, unsystematic, and largely unanalyzed. Most agencies, as is their usual custom, make placements, do follow-up visits for six months to a year, recommend adoption and send a representative to the court when it is made permanent, and then lose track of parents and child. The success of a transracial placement in the first year obviously does not predict success in the supposedly problematic teenage years nor in adulthood.

What adoption workers do have are a few inadequate studies about what leads to successful adoption quite apart from racial factors—and these studies don't even support the traditional basis of their decision-making very well [cf. Witmer, *et al*. (226); Eldred, *et al*. (53); Di Virgilio (45); Kadushin (118)]. They also have a body of ideas originally drawn from the clinical experiences of psychologists and psychiatrists about parents and children plus the theories and data offered by psychologists interested in child development. One can draw analogies from this material for adoption practice, but only analogies [cf. Mech (154)]. We found only one study that even concerned biological children of mixed marriages or unions—a study which suggests that such children have better than average psychological health [Chang (28)]. One could apply psychologists' and psychiatrists' ideas on the assumption that other things were equal—but they probably are not. Transracial adoptive families are very distinct from the average family in many important ways. As we have mentioned earlier, they started out distinct and obviously have out-of-the-ordinary family histories once they are formed. We found that we could generate from these psychological ideas plausible hypotheses that transracial adoption is very risky and also that there is no reason to fear trying it.

If the scientist in a research facility and the doctor in her office are not appropriate models of transracial adoptive decision-making, how was it done? Adoption professionals are formally responsible to legislatures, boards, vocal members of the public, their fellow professionals and themselves for producing acceptable problem solutions. If no one complains, they have in a sense, successfully carried out the mission given them. Many transracial adoptive parents did complain (cf. newsletters from adoptive parent groups from the early 1960s on), but these are apparently only one source of legitimate complaints in a professional's eyes. Of equal and more importance is the reward and punishment structure of the agency involved, a structure which seems to be well attuned to professional politics and ideology. The agency is influenced by its board of directors and the legislature, and by what "society" as represented by the press says about its actions. Agency heads, in turn, exercise some degree of control over adoption workers—and over who is hired in the first place. Supervisors reward workers who do well (by the supervisors' standards) and criticize those who do not. Finally, group meetings are held in most agencies to discuss particular cases and one must be prepared to justify one's action before fellow professionals or lose one's job or good reputation. Perhaps the most important influence over decision making is exercised in these meetings and in the political activity preparatory to meetings.

In the past adoption workers were rewarded for placing white infants with good white parents, and this was a full-time job. It would not have been clear, had anyone thought about it, what the rewards for trying to deal with black children might be while the risks of punishment were perfectly clear [cf. Fricke (68); *New York Times,* April 27, 1964, p. 31; Wachtel (216)]. It was hard for white workers to find black couples acceptable by usual standards, and it was hard to be sure of one's judgments about black clients of very different backgrounds. Moreover, the known risk of placing a black child with white parents would have been obvious had the possibility even been considered. A judge might refuse to approve it. Publicity might make it hard for the agency to get funding. The white parents might not be able to withstand the pressure of relatives or neighbors and might return the child, thereby harming both the child and the agency's reputation. [We found stories of only two such cases, both early; see *Newsweek,* April 5, 1966, p. 30, and Owens (174). But the literature had clear warnings of the dangers of transracial adoption.] And later on, there was a real risk of bringing black wrath down on the agency.

Most adoption workers in this period (but not all) had no incentive to run any risks. As described above, few of them were aware that there might be many adoptable children not in their files of active cases. Then when their perceptions changed, the risks really had changed. In the mid-1960s to the early 1970s, making transracial adoptive placements was likely only to generate heartwarming newspaper stories praising the agency, and there was the possibility that adoptive parent groups or fellow professionals would come down on them if they did not make transracial adoptive placements. They cannot be faulted for not foreseeing that the "We shall overcome" era would give way to a time of black pride. When the black social work community turned professional attitudes around, it seemed prudent to do such things as to turn responsibility for all black children over to black social workers and agencies. The transracial adoptive parent organizations might be unhappy, but they were less of a threat than black power exercised directly or through the workers' professional peers.

In addition to public opinion and the structural imperatives of the existing system, decisions about adoption are influenced by the not totally consistent theories, scientific findings, norms and biases that constitute professional ideology about good practice. It is manifested in such things as the CWLA *Standards for Adoption Service,* articles in professional journals, conversations with colleagues, and courses in schools of social work. Not every worker is exposed to all of this, and professionals do not agree with all that appears in print or with each other. However, the literature does reflect views that are widely repeated and that come to be regarded by many as common knowledge or just common sense. It serves to put some problems on the agendas of most workers and to keep others from view. Professional ideology also serves to provide blueprints for how to do a job, particularly when one is new at a task, such as transracial adoption. And once a decision is taken, professional ideology has use as backup authority if the decision needs defending. This is not to say that the ideology is consistent and unified. Actually, its usefulness includes its flexibility since one can usually find good support for more than one side of an argument in the social work literature. We cannot assess the total influence of professional ideology on transracial adoption, but we can point out that the CWLA Standards and the preponderance of articles in the professional journals neatly reflect the twists and turns of what actually happened.

Finally, adoption workers bring their own characteristics, values, and biases to the interpretation of the professional role. Adoption agencies have been criticized for running largely on white middle-class assumptions. But these are built into the white middle-class people who go into social work and end up staffing and running the agencies. People who go into social work are probably more concerned with helping others than the rest of the white middle class. When American middle-class society rediscovered racial discrimination, not surprisingly the social work profession was very receptive to calls to do something in their professional capacity. When the white middle-class members of civil rights groups learned that many blacks viewed their efforts as unwanted paternalism, white middle-class social workers quickly saw that the charge could be leveled at transracial adoption.

There have been social workers all along, of course, who did not fit the model presented above. Some have been very innovative, recognizing the problem of homeless black children early and working out trial solutions. The loose system we described allows for individual innovation, at least within certain limits.[16] There was a set legitimate vocabulary for innovations: One could not work directly for racial integration but one could seek the best interests of the child in new ways. A working definition of the best interests of a child had been learned on the job, and innovations cast in terms of that definition were often acceptable in an agency.

The power of individual workers to innovate depends on what resources are needed. Some might have foreseen the need for black workers in black-run agencies in the 1950s, but at that time there did not appear to be resources available to develop the necessary staff. Instead, most innovations were and are piecework incremental steps. A worker could recommend one transracial adoption and see if her supervisor and then the judge approved. No resources are needed for such "experiments." But then such efforts don't bring about permanent changes in agency policy and practice very often. The turnover of workers is so great that the only thing sure to endure in many agencies is the standard reporting form. Innovators come and go and their programs come and go with them. This has been the story of a number of workers and programs in individual agencies which we observed or which were described to us in interviews.

III. A SUMMARY EVALUATION

We have shown a gap between the formal normative model of how the child-care system was supposed to work, and the empirical picture of how it did work. Experts were supposed to act basing judgments on scientific knowledge and experience, but, instead, they did the best they could with what they had to accommodate a clash of norms. The existence of this gap should not be a surprise. The legal system often is forced to mediate between norms that speak of the way we would like to be and the changing social and economic reality of the way we are. We have a tradition of attempting to handle such contradictions by passing statutes that honor the norms while relying on the police and those cloaked with expert status to work things out some way or another in an acceptable, if not normatively correct, fashion. Yet there are costs in promising more than can be delivered, and short run accommodations may be bought at the price of undercutting the value of the promises made by the legal system.

In this section, we will look at the functions that were served by delegating so many of the decisions about homeless black children and transracial adoption to adoption professionals. Then we will look at the costs of carrying out these functions. Finally, we will consider the difficulties of doing anything else in a nation where, for a long time, racism has been as American as apple pie.

A. FUNCTIONS OF NORMATIVE DECISION-MAKING BY THOSE LABELED AS EXPERTS

In about twenty years, we have moved from a time when few recognized that the response of the child-care system in the United States to homeless black children was a scandal, to a period of experiments with transracial adoption, to a time of normative clash over integration and black identity, to our present position. One defending the child-care system could argue that we now have a number of new programs which eventually may solve much of the problem. Certainly some homeless children have been helped by the programs now in existence. And all of this has been done in a climate of intense conflicts about values and without the help of solid scientific data for predicting the consequences of possible courses of action.

But we could also still view the child-care system as lagging far behind our vision of what should have been done. Perhaps, as Friedman and Ladinsky (71) said in another context:

> What appears to some as an era of "lag" was actually a period in which issues were collectively defined and alternative solutions posed, and during which interest groups bargained for favorable formulations of law. It was a period of "false starts"—unstable compromise formulations by decision makers armed with few facts, lacking organizational machinery, and facing great, often contradictory demands from many publics. There was no easy and suitable solution, in the light of the problem and the alignment of powers. . . . If there was "lag" in the process, it consisted of acquiescence in presently acceptable solutions which turned out not to be adequate or stable in the long run (pp. 76–7).

By their nature, conflicts of value are hard to resolve in a way that is totally satisfactory: If one is right, the other is wrong. Losers in normative battles tend to be bitter. Compromises to avoid total victories or defeats are difficult to arrange because they smell of sell-out. Transracial adoption involved at least two important value conflicts. At first, if a white family living in a white neighborhood adopted a black child, this would challenge views about segregation of the races held by white neighbors and symbolize a commitment to integration of the races. In the late 1960s, however, the same adoption symbolized to some blacks that making blacks acceptable to whites on the whites' terms was an appropriate goal and that blacks were unable even to raise their own children—views they rejected strongly. At the time feelings were most intense, it would have been difficult to have made an authoritative final decision that would have resolved the matter so that the losing side would have accepted it.

One way that decision by expert helped resolve these value conflicts was by avoiding firm and final decisions whereby one side won a victory while the other clearly suffered a real defeat. Transracial adoption was always an experimental program pushed by some adoption agencies and not others rather than a formal public determination that integration of the races was now the social goal. The National Association of Black Social Workers was able to reverse the party line in adoption workers' ideology about transracial adoption, and this had great impact on practice. Yet reversal of the official ideology did not totally reverse practice. Some transracial adoptions are still being made, and the proponents see that they have lost a battle but not necessarily the war.

The imprecise "best interests of the child" standard may have helped avoid symbolic victories and losses with resulting bitterness. By its nature, it allowed adoption agencies to have a general policy with exceptions to fit particular cases. Black social workers could be placated by a general declaration against transracial adoption, but some agencies could still place, for example, at least mixed race children in a white home in communit es where neither black nor white views were felt to be intensely opposed. Moreover, to some degree, the best interests standard helped deflect debate from themes of segregation, integration and black separation into what the best interests of particular children might be. People were not forced to take principled ideological stands. Since there were no hard data and definitive experiences, all that was needed was a plausible argument. Hard data might have narrowed debate, forced normative choice, and thus engaged the profession in a very tough battle that it would prefer to avoid.

Thus, the decision-making process was insulated from those who insisted on hard normative victories. Those who criticized professional practices but who lacked recognized credentials found it difficult to get experts to listen, let alone respond or change. They also found it hard to get courts or legislatures to listen and to substitute their judgment for that of the experts. As Edelman (49) has pointed out,

> The ability to get the public to perceive the exercise of authority and the allocation of values as a 'professional' rather than a political issue is one of the most common and one of the most effective political techniques in contemporary society for it discourages and weakens political criticism [pp. 8–9].

The adoption system that had evolved was equipped with just this protection against pressure to make hard normative choices that might have been premature and certainly very disrupting. Instead we saw accommodations that delayed final decisions until some of the fire behind intensely held feelings burned lower.

At the same time, a few crusading adoption workers, together with various organizations of transracial adoptive parents were able to spread the transracial adoption movement to many parts of the country in a relatively short time and at a relatively low cost. These few groups and individuals had enough access to decision-making power to begin some experiments—no revolution, just experiments. The looseness of the system made this possible. If one agency balked at trying some of these experiments, there were others serving the same area (Catholic or Lutheran instead of the state agency, for example) that might be willing to host an innovative program.

Even these crusaders had some checks on their freedom. They were not totally insulated from effective criticism; most adults consider themselves knowledgeable about what the best interests of a child are. This, plus some natural sympathy for children, added up to a threat of scandal if the innovators went too far in affronting common sense. Transracial adoption was never used, for example, as a tool to integrate white neighborhoods in the South. There were more transracial adoptions in states with low black populations than those with large black populations [Opportunity, Inc. (172)].

Another characteristic of the existing adoption system was that it was able to react very quickly to the attacks of the National Association of Black Social Workers. The NABSW had a professional forum, its protests were heard and heeded by some. The opponents of transracial adoption had a great advantage since decision-making power had been so completely delegated to the professionals who were listening to them. If the NABSW had had to seek to get legislation passed, its members might have found it difficult to get even the attention of many legislators. More importantly to this organization, any statute that banned the adoption of black children by white parents probably would be an unconstitutional denial of equal protection of the law.[17]

A constitutional challenge by pro-transracial adoption forces might have been possible all along. One with standing to sue could have tried to prove that adoption agencies had a policy against transracial placements that was unconstitutional. Practically, however, the agencies did not have to worry a great deal about such a suit being brought or about losing it. One such suit ended in a settlement that did change agency practices, but it took place in the early period when the transracial adoption movement was beginning and served to push a particular agency to join in what was then a growing trend. (For an interesting legal ethics issue raised by this case because plaintiffs were recruited by advertisements in newspapers, see Jarmel (109), pp. 2–18 to 2–21.) There was a similar settlement in Ohio in 1973. [See *Chartoff v. Montgomery Co. Children Services Board* (S.D. Ohio, 1973), reported in 4th North American Conference on Adoptable Children (65).] In still another case, adoption agencies in New York City were sued by the New York Civil Liberties Union. It was alleged that the seven children representing a class were outrageously neglected and subjected to institutional warehousing as a result of racial and religious discrimination. Adoption professionals initially were very concerned about the possible impact of the case. However, a three-judge federal court decided that the New York statutes concerning religious matching in adoption were not unconstitutional on their face [*Wilder v. Sugerman*, 385 F. Supp. 1013 (S.D.N.Y. 1974)]. The United States District Judge then decided that children did not represent a class but could sue on their own behalf and finally decided, after trial, that the attorneys for the black children who had not been adopted could not prove that adoptive parents could have been found for them. The suit was dismissed (*New York Times,* January 21, 1977, p. B12). One can wonder how far the judge was influenced by a concern for the difficulties of intervening in an area of normative conflict where there seem to be so few easy solutions. Undoubtedly, he was hesitant to try to run the adoption system for black children in New York City. Of course, other suits could be brought other places. Nonetheless, the results to date are likely to discourage attempts to solve the problems of homeless black children by litigation.

B. The Costs of the Expert Façade: Has the Problem Been Solved or Only Hidden?

It is not clear that the problems of homeless black children have been solved very well. The measures taken could have been very effective, but no one really knows. Tracking systems may eventually assure individual planning for each child, but what comes out of a tracking system's computer will be no better than what goes in. Tracking systems will not affect the discretionary nature of decisions as to whether a particular child is labeled "unadoptable" or whether a child is likely to be returnable to a biological parent. There is no way of knowing how many black infants will continue to be excluded from the child-care system because unwed mothers think adoption of black infants is impossible. The alternative is the perpetuation in society of a fair-sized group of not only unwed but unwilling mothers.

It may be that in order to accommodate conflicting values, the actual impact of programs which send black children to black adoption workers or into subsidized adoption programs will be hidden. Or we may see the creation of tokens—a few black adoption agencies to serve in cities with a large black population—in the place of large scale programs, or the passage of legislation without appropriations to make them meaningful. But who will know? The price of some accommodations is a lack of accountability.

Another price is that paid by the children. It is clear that a substantial number of children have spent time in bad foster homes because of the way the system worked. The original refusal to consider transracial adoption, rationalized on the basis of the necessity of matching parents and children, certainly kept some black children from going into white homes. One cannot prove that the long-run damage to these children from inadequate foster care was greater than that which the black opponents of transracial adoption assert would have been inflicted had the children gone into white homes, but the best current evidence suggests that the damage actually inflicted was not inconsequential (see Footnote 5). Some of the steps to improve the system could have been taken much sooner and cut down this damage, if not eliminated it. It is easy, of course, to shoot at fifteen-to-twenty year old mistakes in the light of present knowledge. But it is worth doing if only as a reminder that we've let things slide in the past and those who paid the price—the children—are not those we like to see pay.

The opponents of transracial adoption did not win a total victory but they probably came out better than the pro-transracial adoptive forces. The statistics in Table 1 do not suggest that transracial adoption is a major activity, given the number of black children who are without permanent homes. One of the reasons for the apparent success of NABSW in the cutback of adoptions of black children by white parents may be that NABSW's members are social workers who could operate inside the system, as fellow professionals whose views were salient to those workers contemplating transracial placements. The parent groups, on the other hand, were outsiders who lacked legitimate qualifications so that their views could be dismissed.

We do not know to what extent NABSW spoke for most blacks, but some recent evidence suggests that they did not [Howard, *et al.* (100a)]. We do not know either whether the social workers who advocated transracial adoption represented the views of even the majority of white liberals, let alone all whites. So we can't say what greater social forces are represented on the winning or losing sides. ·

The end result, the tolerance of transracial adoption only in pockets of the country where neither blacks nor whites will strongly object, is probably unconstitutional insofar as this pattern is systematically supported by professionals and enforced by subtle sanctions. Advocates of transracial adoption probably had the constitution on their side and still lost. Would they be impressed by arguments about the value of keeping the peace and accommodating conflicting values? Probably not. They, as well as the opponents of transracial adoption, have expressed as their major concern the fear that the children are but pawns in this ideological game. Perhaps it would have been better to leave the whole matter to experts after all—muddling through sometimes has an advantage over head-on reform attempts that lead to unintended consequences. On one hand, faith in rational planning and problem solving may be the most utopian position of all. On the other hand, there is the possibility that the necessary research could be done and that the system could start operating as it was originally envisioned in the social work literature. Perhaps legislation or administrative rules could be drafted to limit or guide discretion. Just as war is too important to leave to the generals, this area seems too important to leave to the adoption professionals. But the area is a mine field of normative choices. None of the principal players in the system (legislators, judges, workers) would seem to have any reason to invest resources to find answers that might set off some of those normative bombshells. It is often safe to look the other way. Kenneth Boulding (16) tells us that:

> The legal and political subculture is not the result of pure chicanery and foolishness. It has evolved over many generations for some very good reasons. The main reason is that where decisions . . . make some people better off and some people worse off, problem-solving in the scientific sense would not come up with any answers. Legal and political procedures, such as trials and elections, are essentially social rituals designed to minimize the costs of conflict. The price of cheap conflict, however, may be bad problem-solving in terms of the actual consequences of decisions. So far, the social invention that will resolve this dilemma does not yet seem to have been made.

Our story indicates that we can add decisions by experts using the words of science to Boulding's list of legal and political procedures that are essentially social rituals designed to minimize the costs of conflict. Yet as he warns, the price of cheap conflict may indeed be bad problem-solving in terms of the actual consequences of decisions.

FOOTNOTES

1. Many of our data on the history of adoption policy are in the material that appears in the list of references—that is, we take the social work literature itself as representing the views of professional leaders and scholars about what policy is or should be. Of course, this literature reflects only imperfectly what went on in individual adoption agencies and what happened in specific cases, and we know that there is much variability between agencies. However, there is no reason to think that the literature does not reflect typical agencies and cases as well as the standards that most agencies intended to meet.

We, of course, also reviewed the legislation and cases, and we interviewed some who have reason to know what went on in the past. In addition, we have relied on historical accounts by Bishop (11); Jones (112); Parker (175) and Romanofsky (189). For views less critical of adoption agency practices and which, at some points, disagree with what we report here, see Dunne (48); Kadushin (120); Madison and Schapiro (148); M. Schapiro (193); and Reid (186a). Here, as so often is the case when one is dealing with real problems involving normative conflict, the data are less clear cut than one would like and there is room for differing interpretations.

2. In the mid 1970s, forty-one states and the District of Columbia used the best interests of the child standard or some variant such as "the child's interests will be promoted." Eight states used standards that referred to the prospective parents' ability to properly rear and educate the child. Two states had no express standard. We have no reason to believe that the differences in standards affect practices among the states.

3. The Texas and Louisiana statutes that required adoptive parents and children to be of the same race were declared unconstitutional. See *Compos v. McKeithen,* 341 F.Supp. 264 (E.D.La. 1972); *In re Gomez,* 424 S.W.2d 656 (Tex. Civ. App. 1967). Section 10-2585 of the 1962 South Carolina Code provided that no one could adopt the child of one white and one black parent, but this provision was not included in a 1964 revision of the laws relating to adoption. See South Carolina Code §§ 10-2587.9 et seq. (Supp. 1971). Another provision of

the 1962 South Carolina Code, dating from 1910, would bar black parents from adopting a white child. South Carolina Code § 16-553 (1962).

During the 1960s and 1970s, statutes in another fifteen states and in the District of Columbia call or called for a statement of the racial background of both child and applicants to appear in the documents before the court when a petition for adoption was considered, and six of these specified or specify that racial factors be taken into account.

Four other states barred adoption where the parents and the child were of races that were prohibited from marrying. Presumably these statutes also fell when prohibitions on racial intermarriage were declared unconstitutional in *Loving v. Virginia*, 338 U.S. 1 (1967).

In 1972, at the high point of the transracial adoption movement, substantial numbers of transracial placements were reported in all jurisdictions outside of the South. This suggests that this statutory language did not preclude transracial adoption; indeed, it seems likely that it had little deterrent effect at all [Opportunity, Inc. (172)].

4. It was reported that there was an oversupply of white babies during the 1960s [see, *e.g.*, Trombley, (213)]. However, this was not true; the ratio had just shrunk somewhat [Brown, *et al.* (24); Hylton (104)].

It is also important to recognize that the definition of adoptability has changed over the years and that this has affected the official estimates of the supply of parentless children. At first, adoptability meant near physical perfection, background characteristics (such as school achievement of mother and occupational status of her father) which were thought to predict success in life, and infant or toddler status. Professionals believed, apparently without justification, that applicants wanted only perfect, young children that matched them physically. This led to the definition of children with physical defects, problematic backgrounds (mental illness or retardation in the family, known hereditary problems, etc.) or mixed racial background as "unadoptable." In the 1950s the definition of adoptability began to change, and this group was redefined as "hard to place." By about 1958 all parentless children were officially considered adoptable and most (but not all) professionals decided that many applicants were willing and capable of adopting the "hard-to-place." The history of these definitions (and variations in professional opinion to this date) can be traced through the following: Beavan (8); Bishop (11); Chambers (27); Chevlin (30); Cook (39); Fanshel (59); Gallagher (73); Getz (78); Haber and Haber (87); Hagen (89); Hylton (104); Lahe (134); Maas (142); *New York Times* (January 27, 1955, p. 18, and December 6, 1958, p. 24); M. Schapiro (193), and Young (229).

5. A full description of the foster care system is beyond the scope of this article. A view of the enormity of the problem—and of its elements of scandal—can be found in the following sources: Billingsley and Giovannoni (10); Fanshel and Shinn (60); Festinger (63); Geiser (76); Maas (143); Mnookin (158); Mott (161); Murphy (163); Sherman, *et al.* (201); Wachtel (216); Weaver (220); Young (230). Studies of individual states' caseloads can be found in Gruber (86), Illinois Dept. of Children and Family Services (105), and Wisconsin Dept. of Public Welfare (225).

6. We did not find any studies of rejection rates which would indicate the relative importance of various standards, but various semi-official discussions suggest that those listed in the text were quite important. [For descriptions of various standards, see Anderson (4); Andrews (5); Aronson (6); Ball, *et al.* (7); Braden (17); Brown (22); Child Welfare League of America (32); Edwards (52); Kadushin (120); Kuhlman and Robinson (131); *New York Times*, January 28, 1955, p. 13; M. Schapiro (193).]

7. Two states (Kentucky and Missouri) had statutes allowing adoptive parents of one race to annul the adoption and return the child if, within five years, the child "reveals definite traits of ethnological ancestry different from those of the adoptive parents" [Ky. Rev. Stat. Sec. 199.540(1) (1971); Mo. Stat. Ann. Sec. 543.130 (1952)]. A right to annul for any reason is not given in most states; the only other states with such a right (Alabama, Arkansas, Iowa and Minnesota) base it on physical illness or defects.

8. Such campaigns were described in sixteen separate articles in the social work publications from 1948 to 1960. Most of these are mentioned by Madison and Schapiro (148). Presumably other efforts were taking place in this decade or earlier but were not written up for professional publication. Curiously, we found only one mention [Fradkin (66)] and no extensive descriptions of several major programs in the 1950s such as Adopt-A-Child in New York City, the nationwide Urban League effort, and an innovative public agency program in Los Angeles County. Also, transracial adoption had been common in Alaska, Hawaii, Puerto Rico and the Virgin Islands all along. For a description of activities not reported in the journals, see Billingsley and Giovannoni (10).

9. Explicit statements opposing transracial adoption and reports that agencies discouraged applicants who requested a child of a race other than their own were found in the social work literature up to 1964. In addition there were less explicit reports of discouragement. For example, in the "Mid-Point Report" of Adopt-A-Child (January 1955 to June 1956), we found the statement, "A number of white families, *after discussion with the agencies,* decided they were not interested in adopting children of interracial background" (p. 7, emphasis added). Similarly, in 1964 the Louise Wise agency decided to try transracial placements but found no acceptable applicants in the six months following the "flurry" of inquiries prompted by their publicity (*New York Times,* April 27, 1964, p. 31). [See also Durkette (47); MARCH (151).] For suggestions that social worker attitudes were more of a barrier to transracial adoptions than applicant attitudes, see Billingsley and Giovannoni (9); Braden (17); Fricke (70); Isaac (107); Kahn (121); and McCrea (153).

10. A follow-up study by Ripple (188) of children adopted between 1955 and 1958 indicated that, if anything, matching was related to poor emotional adjustment in later childhood. See also Chang (28).

11. The earliest approving mentions of transracial adoption which we found in the social work literature concerned placement of foreign children, mostly oriental, in caucasian homes [DiVirgilio (45); Pettis (178)]. These studies indicated that transracial adoptions might turn out, but the authors were not enthusiastic partisans of them. Before 1960, the only strong support of transracial adoption that we found was by a German who felt that, on both moral and pragmatic grounds, Germans should take responsibility for mixed race offspring of American servicemen [Pfaffenberger (179)].

12. The Adoption Resource Exchange of North American listed 148 organizations in thirty-four states and the District of Columbia as of 1973. Sixty-six of these were clearly focused on transracial adoption or the situation of homeless black children or both, and other organizations on the list may have the same interests. Some of these organizations were promoted by adoption workers but others have been independent of or antagonistic to the agencies [Children's Service Center (35); Griffin and Arffa (82); Open Door Society (171); McCrea (153); Mitchell (157); Sandusky, *et al.* (192); Selden and Gumbiner (198)]. Newsletters from these organizations over the years document these activities and orientations and show that they have continued to be active in the late 1970s.

13. The following articles in professional journals published between 1964 and 1971 mention transracial adoption: Chevlin (30); *Children,* Jan.–Feb., 1971, p. 35; Falk (55); Fellner (61); Fricke (70); Gallagher (73), (74); Griffin and Arffa (82); Hawkins (96); Jordan and Little (155); Kahn (121); Madison (146); Mitchell (157); Polier (181); Priddy and Kirgan (183); Sellers (199); Shireman (202). Most of these articles only treat transracial adoption in passing. See also Marmor (152) for an approving report in a professional text.

14. A rather convincing argument has been made by Kirk in *Shared Fate* (126) that acknowledgement of differences is, in fact, conducive to psychological health in adoptive families. For an exchange of views on this matter see Fanshel (57, 58) and Kirk (127). See also footnote 10.

15. One factor in the decline of transracial adoptions may have been the increasing availability of abortion to white women, including white women pregnant with children of black fathers which would decrease the supply of mixed race progeny. Most transracial adoptions have been of mixed race children with white families [Billingsley and Giovannoni (9); Grow and Shapiro (84); Priddy and Kirgan (183)]. Kahn (121, p. 160) has criticized workers placing light complexioned black children with white families as "implicitly sanctioning the elimination of that which is black in the child." We were told of one famous adoption agency which refused to make mixed race placements before the child was a year old since it wanted to be sure how dark the child would be, and children considered too dark would not be placed with white parents (interview with adoption agency official, 1974).

16. The sex and social status of adoption workers is relevant here. The great majority of adoption work is carried on by women. Our observation of several programs indicates that women who become adoption workers tend to have relatively high socioeconomic status to start with because they often are married to men with good jobs. This gives them the confidence and status insurance that they need in order to try innovations that could backfire and cost them their job. Also many did not plan on a lifetime career with a particular agency and were, thus, somewhat freer of organizational sanctions. [See Mandell (149), for an analysis of the relation of the status of women in our society to our system of caring for unwed mothers and their children.]

17. See *Compos v. McKeithen,* 341 F.Supp. 264 (E.D.La. 1972); *In re Gomez,* 424 S.W.2d 656 (Tex. Civ. App. 1967). Compare *Loving v. Virginia,* 388 U.S. 1 (1967). But see *Commonwealth ex rel. Lucas v. Kreischer,* 221 Pa. Super. 196, 289 A.2d 202 (1972). For a discussion of the constitutionality of racial classifications in the adoption area, see Grossman (83).

REFERENCES

1. Adams, J. E., and Hyung Bok Kim, "A Fresh Look at Intercounty Adoptions," *Children* 18, no. 6 (1971): 214–221.
2. Aldridge, Delores P., "Problems and Approaches to Black Adoptions," *Family Coordinator* 23, no. 4 (1974): 407–410.
3. Anderson, J. W., "A Special Hell for Children in Washington," *Harpers* (November 1965): 51–56.
4. ———, *Children of Special Value: Interracial Adoption in America,* St. Martin's Press, New York (1971).
5. Andrews, Robert G., "Casework Methodology with Adoptive Applicant Couples," *Child Welfare* 42 (1963): 488–92.
6. Aronson, Howard G., "Evaluating Adoptive Applicants," *Child Welfare* 34 (1955): 1–6.
7. Ball, Harry V., Richard G. Bauman, and Jeffrey E. Mandell, "A Working Paper on the Legal Process of Adoption in Wisconsin," unpublished paper, University of Wisconsin-Madison (1963).
8. Beavan, P. W., "The Adoption of Retarded Children," *Child Welfare* 35 (1956): 20–22.
9. Billingsley, Andrew, and Jeanne Giovannoni, "Research Perspectives on Interracial Adoption," pp. 57–77 in R. R. Miller (ed.), *Race, Research and Reason: Social Work Perspectives.* National Association of Social Workers, New York (1969).
10. ———, *Children of the Storm: Black Children and American Child Welfare,* Harcourt Brace Jovanovich New York (1972).

11. Bishop, Julie Ann, "Adoption," pp. 26–9 in M. B. Hodges (ed.), *Social Work Yearbook,* Russell Sage Foundation, New York (1951).
12. Bodenheimer, Bridgette M., "New Trends and Requirements in Adoption Law and Proposals for Legislative Change, Southern California Law Review 49 (1975): 10–109.
13. Boehm, Bernice, "Deterrents to the Adoption of Children in Foster Care," *Child Welfare* 37 (1958): 20–26.
14. ———, "Adoption," pp. 63–8 in H. L. Lurie (ed.), *Encyclopaedia of Social Work,* National Association of Social Workers, New York (1965).
15. Boothby, Margaret, Child Welfare Services for Black Children, *Child Welfare* 48 (1969): 170.
16. Boulding, Kenneth E., "Truth or Power," *Science* 190 (1975): 423.
17. Braden, Josephine A., "Adoption in a Changing World," *Social Casework* 51 (1970): 486–490.
18. Bradley, Trudy, "An Exploration of Caseworkers' Perceptions of Adoptive Applicants," *Child Welfare* 45 (1966): 433–443.
19. Branham, Ethel, "One Parent Adoptions," *Children* 17, no. 3 (1970): 103–107.
20. Broeder, Dale W. and Frank J. Barrett, "Impact of Religious Factors in Nebraska Adoptions," *Nebraska Law Review* 38 (1959): 641–691.
21. Brown, Edwin G., and Donald Brieland, "Adoptive Screening: New Data, New Dilemmas," *Social Work* 20 (1975): 291–295.
22. Brown, Florence G., "What Do We Seek in Adoptive Parents?" *Social Casework* 32 (1951): 155.
23. ———, "Adoption," pp. 85–89, in R. H. Kurtz (ed.), *Social Work Yearbook,* 1960, National Association of Social Workers, New York.
24. ———, Ann M. Jamieson, and Rita Dukette, "Reduction in Adoptive Applicants: Implications for Agencies—A Symposium," *Child Welfare* 43 (1964): 292–303.
25. Byrne, Donald, *The Attraction Paradigm,* Academic Press, New York (1971).
26. Carlin, Jerome, Jan Howard, and Sheldon Messinger, "Civil Justice and the Poor: Issues for Sociological Research," *Law and Society Review* 1 (1966): 66–67.
27. Chambers, Donald E., "Willingness to Adopt Atypical Children," *Child Welfare* 49 (1970): 275–279.
28. Chang, Theresa S., "The Self-Concept of Children of Ethnically Different Marriages," *California Journal of Educational Research* 25, no. 5 (1974): 245–252.
29. Chestang, Leon, "The Dilemma of Biracial Adoption," *Social Work* 17, no. 3 (1972): 100–105.
30. Chevlin, Myron R., "Adoption Outlook," *Child Welfare* 46, no. 1 (1967): 75–82.
31. *Chicago-Kent Law Review* 50 (1973): 86–102.
32. Child Welfare League of America. *Standards for Adoption Service* CWLA, New York (1958).
33. ———, Standards for Adoption Service, CWLA, New York (1968).
34. ———, Statement on Revisions of CWLA Standards on Transracial Adoption. CWLA. New York (1973).
35. Children's Service Centre, Historical Sketch of Interracial Placement Programme of Children's Service Centre, Montreal, and Formation of the Open Door Society, Montreal (1965).
36. Chimezie, Amuzie, "Transracial Adoption of Black Children," *Social Work* 20, no. 4 (1975): 296–301.
36a. ———, "Bold but Irrelevant: Grow and Shapiro on Transracial Adoption." *Child Welfare* 56 (1977): 75–.
37. Chunn, Jay, "Black Children and Public Policy: Realities and Organizational Strategies," *NABSW Journal* 5, no. 3 (1973): 15–19.

38. Community Studies, Inc., Hard-to-Place Children, Part 2: Illegitimate Negro Children," Publication No. 99, Community Studies, Inc., Kansas City (1956).
39. Cook, Annabelle, "Myths and Realities of Matching," in *Proceedings*. 4th Annual North American Conference on Adoptable Children. Metropolitan Washington Council on Adoptable Children, Washington, D.C. (1974).
40. Costigan, Barbaratt, "The Unmarried Mother: Her Decision Regarding Adoption," *Social Service Review* 39 (1965): 347.
41. Daniels, Bernice J., "Significant Considerations in Placing Negro Infants for Adoption," *Child Welfare* 29, no. 1 (1950): 8–9, 11.
42. Davis, Kenneth C., *Discretionary Justice*. University of Illinois Press, Urbana, (1969).
43. Davis, Mary J., Adoptive Placement of American Indian Children With Non-Indian Families—Part II," *Child Welfare* 40 (1961): 12–15.
44. Deasy, Leila C., and Olive W. Quinn, "The Urban Negro and Adoption of Children," *Child Welfare* 41 (1962): 400–407.
45. DiVirgilio, Letitia, "Adjustment of Foreign Children in Their Adoptive Homes," *Child Welfare* 35 (1956): 15–21.
46. Doss, Helen, *The Family Nobody Wanted*, Little, Brown, Boston (1954).
47. Dukette, Rita, "Improving Agency Services for Full Utilization," *Child Welfare* 31 (1964): 299–302.
48. Dunne, Phyllis, "Placing Children of Minority Groups for Adoption," *Children* 5, no. 2 (1958): 43–48.
49. Edelman, Murray, "The State as a Provider of Symbolic Outputs," Discussion Paper 164–73, Institute for Research on Poverty, University of Wisconsin-Madison (1973).
50. Edgar, Margaret, "Some Experiences in Inter-Racial Adoptions. Open Door Society, Inc., Montreal (1966).
51. ———, "Black Children-White Parents: A Problem of Identity," Open Door Society, Inc., Montreal (1973).
52. Edwards, Jane, "The Hard-to-Place Child," *Child Welfare* 40, no. 4 (1961): 24–28.
53. Eldred, Carolyn A., David Rosenthal, Paul H. Wender, Seymour S. Kety, Fini Schulsinger, Joseph Weiner and Birgit Jacobson, "Some Aspects of Adoption in Selected Samples of Adult Adoptees," *American Journal of Orthopsychiatry* 46 (1976): 279–290.
54. Ellsworth, Phoebe, and Robert J. Levy, "Legislative Reform of Child Custody Adjudication: An Effort to Rely on Social Science Data in Formulating Legal Policies," *Law and Society Review* 4 (1969): 167–233.
55. Falk, Laurence A., "A Comparative Study of Transracial and In-Racial Adoptions," *Child Welfare* 49, no. 2 (1970): 82–8.
56. Fanshel, David, "Indian Adoption Research Project," *Child Welfare* 43 (1964): 486–8.
57. ———, "An Upsurge of Interest in Adoption," *Children* 2, no. 5 (1964): 193–196.
58. ———, "Fanshel: More on *Shared Fate*," *Children* 12 (1965): 87–88.
59. ———, *Far from the Reservation: The Transracial Adoption of American Indian Children*, Scarecrow Press, Metuchen, N.J. (1972).
60. ———, and Eugene Shinn, *Dollars and Sense in the Foster Care of Children—A Look at Cost Factors*. Child Welfare League of America, New York (1972).
61. Fellner, I. W., "Recruiting Adoptive Applicants," *Social Work* 47 (January 1968): 92–100.
62. Festinger, Trudy, *Why Some Choose Not to Adopt Through Agencies*. Metropolitan Applied Research Center, New York (1972).
63. ———, "The New York Court Review of Children in Foster Care," *Child Welfare* 54 (1975): 211–245.

64. Fly, Selby, "Our Commitment: Adoption for Every Child Who Needs Parents," pp. 68–73, in *The New Face of Social Work,* Spence-Chapin Adoption Service, New York (1968).

65. Fourth North American Conference on Adoptable Children, *Proceedings,* (March 1974), Metropolitan Washington Council on Adoptable Children, Washington, D.C.

66. Fradkin, Helen, "Adoptive Parents for Children with Special Needs," *Child Welfare* 37 (January 1958): 1–8.

67. Fricke, Harriet, "TV or Not TV—Minnesota Settles the Question," *Child Welfare* 35, no. 9 (1956): 1–7.

68. ———, "White Adoptive Applicants and Non-White Children," unpublished paper (1962).

69. ———, "PAMY's Progress," Parents to Adopt Minority Youngsters, Minneapolis (1963).

70. ———, "Interracial Adoption: The Little Revolution," *Social Work* 10, no. 3 (1965): 92–97.

71. Friedman, Lawrence M., and Jack Ladinsky, "Social Change and the Law of Industrial Accidents," *Columbia Law Review* 67 (1967): 50–82.

72. ———, and Stewart Macaulay, *Law and the Behavioral Sciences,* 2d edition. Bobbs-Merrill, Indianapolis (1977).

73. Gallagher, Ursula M., "Adoption: Current Trends," *Welfare in Review* 4, no. 2 (1967): 12–20.

74. ———, "Adoption Resources for Black Children," *Children* 18, no. 2 (1971): 49–53.

75. ———, "Adoption in a Changing Society," *Children Today* 1, no. 1 (1972): 2–6.

76. Geiser, Robert L., *The Illusion of Caring: Children in Foster Care.* Beacon Press, Boston (1973).

77. ———, "The Shuffled Child and Foster Care," *Trial* 10, no. 3 (1974): 26–29, 35.

78. Getz, Clyde, "Adoption," pp. 26–30, in R. Kurtz (ed.), *Social Work Yearbook, 1954,* Russell Sage Foundation, New York.

79. Glover, E. Elizabeth, "Discussion," *Child Welfare* 36, no. 19 (1957): 12–14.

80. ———, "The Agency's Responsibility to Meet Children's Specific Needs," *Child Welfare* 37 (1958): 25.

81. Goldstein, Joseph, Anna Freud, and Alfred J. Solnit, *Beyond The Best Interests of The Child.* Free Press, New York (1973).

82. Griffin, Barbara P., and Marvin S. Arffa, "Recruiting Adoptive Homes for Minority Children—One Approach," *Child Welfare* 49, no. 2 (1970): 105–107.

83. Grossman, Susan J., "A Child of a Different Color: Race as a Factor in Adoption and Custody Proceedings. *Buffalo Law Review* 17 (1967): 303–347.

84. Grow, Lucille J., and Deborah Shapiro, *Black Children—White Parents: A Study of Transracial Adoption.* Child Welfare League of America, New York (1974).

85. ———, *Transracial Adoption Today: Views of Adoptive Parents and Social Workers,* Child Welfare League of America, New York (1975).

85a. ———, "Not So Bold and Not So Irrelevant: A Reply to Chimezie." *Child Welfare* 56 (1977): 86–91.

86. Gruber, Alan R., "Foster Home Care in Massachusetts: A Study of Foster Children—Their Biological and Foster Parents," Governor's Commission on Adoption and Foster Care, Boston (1973).

87. Haber, Barbara, and Lawrence Haber, "Identifying All the Children Who Need Permanent Homes," Background Paper, *Proceedings,* North American Conference on Adoptable Children. Metropolitan Washington Council on Adoptable Children, Washington, D.C. (March 1974).

88. Hagen, Clayton H., "Matching Values: Matching the Value of a Child with Parent's Values," pp. 19–35 in *Mixed Race Adoption*. Open Door Society, Inc., Montreal (1970).

89. ———, "Myths and Realities of Matching," in *Proceedings,* Fourth North American Conference on Adoptable Children, Metropolitan Washington Council on Adoptable Children, Washington, D.C. (March 1974).

90. Haitch, Richard, "Children in Limbo," *The Nation,* April 6, 1963, p. 279–281, and April 13, 1963, p. 306–309.

91. Hallinan, Helen W., "Who Are the Children Available for Adoption? Combatting the Black Market," *Social Casework* 32 (1951): 161–167.

92. Handler, Joel, *Reforming The Poor: Welfare Policy, Federalism, and Morality*. Basic Books, New York (1972).

93. Harding, Vincent, "The Black Wedge in America: Struggle, Crisis and Hope," *Black Scholar* 7 (1975): 28+46.

94. Haring, Barbara, "Adoption Trends," *Child Welfare* 54 (1975): 524–525.

95. Hawkins, Mildred, "Negro Adoptions—Challenge Accepted," *Child Welfare* 39 (1960): 20–27.

96. ———, "The New Look in Adoptions," *Catholic Charities Review,* (December 1969): 4–9.

97. Heath, W. A., "Mass Communication Methods in Recruiting Minority Group Adoptive Homes," *Public Welfare* 13 (1955): 110–114, 134.

98. Herzog, Elizabeth, and Rose Bernstein, "Why So Few Negro Adoptions?" *Children* 12 (Jan-Feb 1965): 14–18.

99. ———, Cecelia E. Sudia, and Jane Harwood, "Some Opinions on Finding Families for Black Children," *Children* 18, no. 4 (1971): 143–148.

100. Hill, Robert, *The Strengths of Black Families,* Emerson Hall, New York (1971).

100a. Howard, Alicia, David D. Royse, and John A. Skerl. "Transracial Adoption: The Black Community Perspective." *Social Work* 22 (May 1977): 184–189.

101. Hurst, Willard, *The Growth of American Law: The Law Makers*. Little-Brown, Boston (1950).

102. Husbands, Ann, "The Developmental Task of the Black Foster Child," *Social Casework* 51 (1970): 406–9.

103. Hutson, Leighton, "A Question of Identity," pp. 61–63 in *Mixed Race Adoptions,* Open Door Society, Inc., Montreal (1970).

104. Hylton, Lydia F., "Trends in Adoption, 1958–1962," *Child Welfare* 44 (1965): 377–386.

105. Illinois Department of Children and Family Services, "Utilization of Subsidies to Increase Black Adoptions," Report to the Office of Child Development, Children's Bureau, U.S. Department of Health, Education and Welfare (1973).

106. Isaac, Rael Jean, "Children Who Need Adoption: A Radical View," *Atlantic,* Nov. (1963): 45–50.

107. ———, *Adopting a Child Today,* Harper & Row, New York (1965).

108. Jaffee, Benson, "Adoption Outcome: A Two-Generation View," *Child Welfare* 53 (1974): 211.

109. Jarmel, Eli, *Problems in the Legal Representation of The Poor: Cases and Materials,* Matthew Bender, New York (1972).

110. Jenkins, Alma, "Some Evaluative Factors in the Selection of Adoptive Homes for Indian Children," *Child Welfare* 40 (1961): 16–18.

111. Johnson, C. Lincoln, "Transracial Adoption: Victim of Ideology," *Social Work* 21 (1976): 241–2.

112. Jones, C. C., "Child Welfare," pp. 98–114 in R. Kurtz (ed.), *Social Work Yearbook, 1941,* Russell Sage Foundation, New York (1941).
113. Jones, E. D., "On Transracial Adoption of Black Children," *Child Welfare* 51, no. 3 (1972): 156–164.
114. Jones, Lewis W., "Informal Adoption in Black Families in Lowndes and Wilcox Counties, Alabama," Tuskegee Institute, Tuskegee, Ala. (1975).
115. Jordon, Velma L., and William F. Little, "Early Comments on Single—Parent Adoptive Homes," *Child Welfare* 45 (1966): 536–538.
116. Kadushin, Alfred, "The Legally Adoptable, Unadopted Child. *Child Welfare* 37 (1958): 19–27.
117. ———, A Study of Adoptive Parents of Hard-to-Place Children. *Social Casework* 43 (1962): 227–233.
118. ———, "Adoptive Parenthood: A Hazardous Adventure?" *Social Work* 11 (July 1966): 30–39.
119. ———, "Adoption and Foster Care," pp. 103–111 in Robert Morris (ed.), *Encyclopaedia of Social Work. Vol. 1. Child Welfare,* National Association of Social Workers, New York (1971).
120. ———, *Child Welfare Services,* Macmillan, New York (1974).
121. Kahn, Roger, "Black and White," *Children* 18, no. 4 (1971): 160.
122. Katz, Linda, "Transracial Adoption: Some Guidelines," *Child Welfare* 53, no. 3 (1974): 180–188.
123. Katz, Sanford, "Foster Parents Versus Agencies: A Case Study in the Judicial Application of "the Best Interests of the Child Doctrine." *Michigan Law Review* 65 (1966): 145–170.
124. ———, "Subsidized Adoption in America," *Family Law Quarterly* 10, no. 1 (1976): 3–54.
125. King, Helen N., "It's Easier to Adopt Today," *Ebony* (December, 1970): 120.
126. Kirk, H. David, *Shared Fate: A Theory of Adoption and Mental Health,* Free Press of Glencoe, New York (1964).
127. ———, "Fanshel: Author Defends Data," *Children* 11 (1964): 244.
128. Klemesrud, Judy, "Adoption Costs Soar as Births Decline," *New York Times,* Feb. 20, 1973, pp. 1, 40.
129. Kreech, Florence, "Adoption Outreach," *Child Welfare* 52, no. 10 (1973): 669–675.
130. Kribs, Nancy E., "A Comparison of Characteristics of Women Who Have Adopted a Black Child and Women Who State an Unwillingness to Adopt a Black Child," *Dissertation Abstracts International* 33, no. 1-A (1972): 192.
131. Kuhlman, Frieda M., and Helen P. Robinson," Rorschach Tests as a Diagnostic Tool in Adoption Studies," *Social Casework* 32 (1951): 15–22.
132. Ladner, Joyce, *Tomorrow's Tomorrow.* Doubleday-Anchor, Garden City, N.Y. (1972).
133. ———, *Mixed Families: Adopting Across Racial Boundaries,* Anchor Press/Doubleday, Garden City, N.Y. (1977).
134. Lahe, Alice, "Babies for the Brave," *Saturday Evening Post,* (July 31, 1954): 27.
135. Lawder, Elizabeth A., Janet L. Hoopes, Robert G. Andrews, Katherine D. Lower, and Susan Y. Perry, *A Study of Black Adoptive Adoptive Families: a Comparison of a Traditional and a Quasi-Adoption Program.* Child Welfare League of America, New York (1971).
136. Los Angeles County Department of Adoptions, *Report* (1968).
137. Lowi, Theodore, *The End of Liberalism.* Norton, New York (1969).
138. Lubov, R., *The Professional Altruist: The Emergence of Social Work As a Career: 1880–1930.* Harvard University Press, Cambridge (1965).

139. Lukas, Edwin J., "Babies are neither vendible nor expendable," *Record of The New York City Bar Association* 5: 88–109.

140. Lyslo, Arnold, "Adoption for American Indian Children," *Child Welfare* 39 (1960): 32–33.

141. ———, "Adoptive Placement of American Indian Children with non-Indian Families—Part 1," *Child Welfare* 40, no. 5 (1961): 4–6.

142. Maas, Henry S., "The Successful Adoptive Parent Applicant," *Social Work* 5, no. 1 (1960): 14–20.

143. ———, "Children in Long-Term Foster Care," *Child Welfare* 48, no. 6 (1969): 321–333.

144. ———, and Richard Engler, *Children In Need of Parents,* Child Welfare League of America, New York (1959).

145. Macaulay, Stewart, "Law Schools and the World Outside Their Doors: Notes on the Margins of 'Professional Training in the Public Interest.' " *Virginia Law Review* 54 (1968): 617–636.

146. Madison, Bernice Q., "Adoption: Yesterday, Today, and Tomorrow—Part 2," *Child Welfare* 45, no. 6 (1966): 341–348.

147. ———, and Michael Schapiro, "Long-Term Foster Family Care: What is its Potential for Minority-Group Children? *Public Welfare* 27 (April 1969): 167–194.

148. ———, "Black Adoption—Issues and Policies: Review of the Literature," *Social Service Review* 47, no. 3 (1973): 531–561.

149. Mandell, Betty Reid, *Where Are The Children?* Heath, Lexington, Mass. (1973).

150. Manning, Seaton W., "The Changing Negro Family: Implications for the Adoption of Children," *Child Welfare* 43 (1964): 480–85.

151. MARCH, "Adoptive Placement of Minority Group Children In The San Francisco Bay Area: A Study of MARCH," Minority Adoption Recruitment of Children's Homes, San Francisco (1959).

152. Marmor, Judd, "Psychodynamic Aspects of Transracial Adoptions," pp. 200–209 in *Social Work Practice*. Columbia University Press, New York (1964).

153. McCrea, Muriel B., "Agency Co-Operation with Adoptive Parents," pp. 53–56, in *Mixed Race Adoptions*. Open Door Society, Inc., Montreal (1970).

154. Mech, Edmund V., "Adoption: A Policy Perspective, pp. 467–508, in B. M. Caldwell and H. N. Ricciuti (eds.), *Review of Child Development Research, Vol. 3, Child Development and Social Policy,* University of Chicago Press, Chicago (1974).

155. Merrill, Maurice H. and Orpha A. Merrill, "Toward Uniformity in Adoption Law," *Iowa Law Review* 40 (1955): 299–328.

156. Michaela, Mother Ann, "Community Centered Foster Family Care," *Children* 13, no. 1 (1966): 8–9.

157. Mitchell, Marion M., "Transracial Adoptions: Philosophy and Practice," *Child Welfare* 48 (1969): 613–619.

158. Mnookin, Robert H., "Foster Care: In Whose Best Interest?" *Harvard Educational Review* 43 (1973): 599–639.

159. ———, "Child Custody by Adjudication: Judicial Functions in the Face of Indeterminacy," *Law and Contemporary Problems* (1975): 226–293.

160. Morris, Steven, "The Fight for Black Babies: Social Try to Stem the Rising Tide of Interracial Adoptions, *Ebony* (September 1973): 32–42.

161. Mott, Paul E., *Foster Care and Adoptions: Some Key Policy Issues,* Subcommittee on Children and Youth, U.S. Senate Committee on Labor and Public Welfare, Washington, D.C. (1975).

162. Murphy, J. P., pp. 164, in F. S. Hall (ed.), *Social Work Yearbook, 1935*, Russell Sage Foundation, New York.
163. Murphy, Henry B. M., "Long-Term Foster Care and Its Influence on Adjustment to Adult Life," pp. 425–446, in E. James Anthony and C. Koupernic (eds.), *The Child in His Family, Vol. 3. Children At Psychiatric Risk*, Wiley Interscience, New York (1974).
164. National Association of Black Social Workers, "NABSW's Position on Trans-Racial Adoption," *NABSW Journal* 5, no. 3 (1973): 9–12.
165. National Center for Social Statistics, *Adoptions in 1972*, NCSS Report E-10 (1972). U.S. Department of Health, Education, and Welfare, Washington, D.C.
166. Neilson, Jacqueline, "Tayari: Black Homes for Black Children," *Child Welfare* 55, no. 1 (1976): 41–50.
167. Nettingham, Gracie B., "My Experience with Trans-Racial Adoption," *NABSW Journal* 5, no. 3 (1973): 13–14.
168. New York University Law Review, 51 (1976): "Religious Matching Statutes and Adoption," 262–284.
169. Nonet, Philippe, *Administrative Justice: Advocacy and Change in Government Agencies*, Russell Sage Foundation, New York (1969).
170. Nordlie, Esther B., and Sheldon C. Reed, "Follow-Up of Adoption Counseling for Children of Possible Racial Admixture," *Child Welfare* 41, no. 7 (1962): 297–304.
171. Open Door Society, *Mixed Racial Adoption: A Community Project*. Open Door Society, Inc., Montreal (1967).
172. Opportunity, Inc., *National Survey of Black Children Adopted in 1972*, Boys and Girls Aid Society, Portland, Oregon.
173. ——, *National Survey of Black Children Adopted in 1975*, Boys and Girls Aid Society, Portland, Oregon.
174. Owens, Joseph A., "Adopting Negro Children," *America* 97 (1957): 622–624.
175. Parker, Ida R., "Adoption," pp. 23–25 in F. S. Hall (ed.), *Social Work Yearbook, 193M* Russell Sage Foundation, New York.
176. Paull, Joseph E., "An Agency Cleans House," *Child Welfare* 39 (1960): 19–21.
177. Pepper, Gerald W., "Interracial Adoptions: Family Profile, Motivation and Coping Methods," *Dissertation Abstracts* 27, no. 8-A (1966): 2621.
178. Pettis, Susan T., "Effect of Adoption of Foreign Children on U.S. Adoption Standards and Practices," *Child Welfare* 37 (1958): 27.
179. Pfaffenberg, Hans, "Planning for German Children of Mixed Racial Background," *Social Service Review* 30 (1956): 33–37.
180. Platts, Hal K., "Mothers Seeking to Relinquish Baby for Adoption," *Children* 17 (1970): 27–30.
181. Polier, Justine Wise, "The Invisible Legal Rights of the Poor," *Children* 12 (1965): 217.
182. ——, "Professional Abuse of Children: Responsibility for the Delivery of Services," *American Journal of Orthopsychiatry* 45, no. 3 (1975): 357–362.
183. Priddy, Drew, and Kirgan, Doris, "Characteristics of White Couples Who Adopt Black/White Children. *Social Work* 16, no. 3 (1971): 105–107.
184. Rathbun, Constance, Helen McLaughlin, Chester Bennett, and James A. Garland, "Later Adjustment of Children Following Radical Separation from Family and Culture," *American Journal of Orthopsychiatry* 35 (April 1965): 604–609.
185. Reed, Ellery F., "Unmarried Mothers Who Kept Their Babies," *Children* 12 (1965): 118–119.
186. Reid, Joseph H., "Ensuring Adoption for Hard to Place Children," *Child Welfare* 35 (March 1956): 4–8.
186a. ——, "Principles, Values and Assumptions Underlying Adoption Practice," *Social Work* 2 (January 1957): 22–29.

187. Riday, Edwin, "Supply and Demand in Adoption," *Child Welfare* 48, no. 8 (1969): 489–491.
188. Ripple, Lillian, "A Follow-Up Study of Adopted Children," *Social Service Review* 42 (1968): 479–499.
189. Romanofsky, Peter, "Professionals vs. Volunteers: A Case Study of Adoption Workers in the 1920's," *Journal of Voluntary Action Research* 2, no. 2 (1973): 95–101.
190. ———, " 'To Save . . . Their Souls' ": The Care of Dependent Jewish Children in New York City, 1900–1905," *Jewish Social Studies* 36 (1974): 253–261.
191. Rustin, Bayard, "Open Door Society Newsletter," October (1973) 5–7.
192. Sandusky, Annie Lee, Jane Harwood Rea, Ursula Gallagher and Elizabeth Herzog, *Families for Black Children: The Search For Adoptive Parents. II. Programs and Projects.* Children's Bureau, Department of Health, Education, and Welfare, Washington, D.C. (1972).
193. Schapiro, Michael, *A Study of Adoption Practice. Vol. 1. Adoption Agencies and the Children They Serve.* Child Welfare League of America, New York (1956).
194. ———, *A Study of Adoption Practice, Vol. 3. Adoption of Children With Special Needs.* Child Welfare League of America, New York (1957).
195. Schoenberg, Carl, "Adoption: The Created Family," *Annals of The American Academy of Pediatrics* 355 (1964): 69.
196. Seely, Jo Ann and James Seely, "Book Review," *Children Today,* 1 (May-June 1972): 33–34.
197. Seidl, Frederick W., "Transracial Adoption: Agency Response to Applicant Calls," *Social Work* 17, no. 3 (1972): 119–120.
198. Selden, Jean, and Josephine S. Gumbiner, "A Parent's Adoption League," *Child Welfare* 48 (1969): 165, 171.
199. Sellers, Martha G., "Transracial Adoption," *Child Welfare* 48, no. 6 (1969): 355–356.
200. Shapiro, H. L., "Anthropology and Adoption Practice," pp. 34–38 in M. Schapiro (ed.), *A Study of Adoption Practice. Vol. 2. Selected Scientific Papers Presented at the National Conference On Adoption, January 1955,* Child Welfare League of America, New York (1956).
201. Sherman, E. A., R. Neuman, and A. Shyne, *Children Adrift In Foster Care: A Study of Alternative Approaches.* Child Welfare League of America, New York (1973).
202. Shireman, Joan F., "Adoptive Applicants Who Withdrew," *Social Service Review* 44, no. 3 (1970): 285–292.
203. ———, and Kenneth W. Watson, "Adoption of Real Children," *Social Work* 17, no. 4 (1972): 29–38.
204. Simon, Rita James, "An Assessment of Racial Awareness, Preference and Self Identity Among White and Adopted Non-White Children," *Social Problems* 22 (1974): 43–57, 23 (1974): 109–110.
205. ———, and Howard Altstein, *Transracial Adoption,* John Wiley & Sons, Inc., New York (1977).
206. Sklar, June, and Beth Berkov, "Teenage Family Formation in Postwar America," *Family Planning Perspectives* 6, no. 2 (1974): 80–90.
207. Smith, I. E., "Adoption," pp. 20–27, in M. B. Hodges (ed.). *Social Work Yearbook, 1949,* Russell Sage Foundation, New York.
208. South Carolina Law Quarterly, "Recent Cases: Interracial Adoption." *South Carolina Law Quarterly* 9 (1957): 630–632.
209. Stern, Curt, "Hereditary Factors Affecting Adoption," pp. 47–58, in M. Schapiro (ed.), *A Study of Adoption Practice. Vol. 2. Selected Scientific Papers Presented at the National Conference On Adoption, January, 1955,* Child Welfare League of America, New York (1956).

210. Streit, Peggy, "Time of Adoption," *New York Times,* August 23, 1964: 48.
211. Taft, Ruth, "Adoptive Families for "Unadoptable" Children," *Child Welfare* 32 (1953): 5–9.
212. Theis, Sophie Van S., "Wisconsin Substantially Decreases Independent Adoptions," *Child Welfare* 33 (1954): 133.
213. Trombley, William, "Babies Without Homes," *Saturday Evening Post,* Feb. 16, 1963: 15–20.
214. Uhlenhopp, Harvey, "Adoption in Iowa," *Iowa Law Review* 40 (1955): 228–298.
215. Vieni, Miriam, "Transracial Adoption Is a Solution Now," Social Work 20 (1975): 419–421.
216. Wachtel, Dawn Day, "Adoption Agencies and the Adoption of Black Children," unpublished doctoral dissertation, University of Michigan (1972).
217. Wald, Michael S., "State Intervention on Behalf of Neglected Children: A Search for Realistic Standards," *Stanford Law Review* 27 (1975): 985–1040.
218. ——, "Legal Policies Affecting Children: A Request for Aid," *Child Development* 47, no. 1 (1976): 1–5.
219. ——, "State Intervention on Behalf of Neglected Children: Standards for Removal of Children from Their Home, Monitoring the Status of Children in Foster Care, and Termination of Parental Rights," *Stanford Law Review* 28 (1976): 623–706.
220. Weaver, Edward, "Long-Term Foster Care: Default or Design? The Public Agency Responsibility," *Child Welfare* 67 (1968): 339–45.
221. Weinberg, R., *Law of Adoption, Third Revised Edition.* Oceana, Dobbs Ferry, N.Y. (1968).
222. Whalen, G., "Adoption and Racial Differences: Experiences of the School Age Child," pp. 65–66, in Open Door Society, *Conference Proceedings,* Montreal (1970).
223. Williams, Cenie J., Jr., "The Black Child," *NABSW Journal* 5, no. 3 (1973): 5–8.
224. Williams, Helen, "The Black Social Workers' Dilemma," in *The Black Woman,* pp. 170–179, Signet Books, New York (Toni Cade, ed., 1970).
225. Wisconsin Department of Public Welfare, *Foster Family Care: A Program in Transition.* Division of Children and Youth, Department of Public Welfare, Madison (1965).
226. Witmer, Helen, Elizabeth Herzog, E. Weinstein, and M. Sullivan, *Independent Adoptions—A Follow-Up Study.* Child Welfare League of America, New York (1963).
227. Woods, Sister Frances Jerome, and Alice C. Lancaster, "Cultural Factors in Negro Adoptive Parenthood," *Social Work* 7: 14–21.
228. Yale Law Journal, "Moppets on the Market: The Problem of Unregulated Adoptions." *Yale Law Journal* 59 (1950): 715.
229. Young, R. E., "From Matching to Making in Adoption: The Interest of Adoptive Applicants in the 'Hard to Place' Child," unpublished Ph.D. dissertation, University of Pennsylvania (1971).
230. Young, D. W., "Referral and Placement in Child Care: The New York City Purchase-of-Service System" *Public Policy* 22 (Summer 1974): 293–327.
231. Young, Whitney M., Jr., "Social Welfare in a Crisis of Conscience," pp. 92–96 in *The New Face of Social Work,* Spence-Chapin Adoptive Service, New York (1969).
232. Zastrow, Charles H., "Outcome of Negro Children–Caucasian Parents of Transracial Adoptions," unpublished doctoral dissertation, University of Wisconsin-Madison, (1971).

RESEARCH IN LAW AND SOCIOLOGY
An Annual Compilation of Research

Guest Editor: Steven Spitzer, Department of Sociology, University of Northern Iowa, Cedar Falls

Volume 2   May 1979   Cloth   Approx. 365 pages
ISBN NUMBER: 0-89232-111-3

TENTATIVE CONTENTS:

A 10 percent discount will be granted on all institutional standing orders placed directly with the publisher. Standing orders will be filled automatically upon publication and will continue until cancelled. Please indicate which volume Standing Order is to begin.

JAI PRESS INC.

P.O. Box 1285
321 Greenwich Avenue
Greenwich, Connecticut 06830

(203) 661-7602   Cable Address: JAIPUBL.

OTHER SERIES OF INTEREST FROM JAI PRESS INC.

Consulting Editor for Sociology: Rita J. Simon, Director, Program in Law and Society, University of Illinois

ADVANCES IN LAW AND PSYCHOLOGY
Series Editor: Robert L. Sprague, Director, Institute for Child Behavior and Development, University of Illinois

COMPARATIVE STUDIES IN SOCIOLOGY
Series Editor: Richard F. Tomasson, University of New Mexico

POLITICAL POWER AND SOCIAL THEORY
Series Editor: Maurice Zeitlin, University of California—Los Angeles

RESEARCH IN COMMUNITY AND MENTAL HEALTH
Series Editor: Roberta G. Simmons, University of Minnesota

RESEARCH IN ECONOMIC ANTHROPOLOGY
Series Editor: George Dalton, Northwestern University

RESEARCH IN LAW AND ECONOMICS
Series Editor: Richard O. Zerbe, Jr., SMT Program, University of Washington

RESEARCH IN ORGANIZATIONAL BEHAVIOR
Series Editors: Barry M. Staw, Graduate School of Management, Northwestern University and Larry L. Cummings, Graduate School of Business, University of Wisconsin

RESEARCH IN RACE AND ETHNIC RELATIONS
Series Editors: Cora B. Marrett, University of Wisconsin, and Cheryl Leggon, University of Illinois, Chicago Circle

RESEARCH IN SOCIAL MOVEMENTS, CONFLICTS AND CHANGE
Series Editor: Louis Kriesberg, Syracuse University

RESEARCH IN SOCIAL PROBLEMS AND PUBLIC POLICY
Series Editor: Michael Lewis, University of Massachusetts

RESEARCH IN SOCIAL STRATIFICATION AND MOBILITY
Series Editor: Donald J. Treiman, University of California—Los Angeles

RESEARCH IN SOCIOLOGY OF EDUCATION AND SOCIALIZATION
Series Editor: Alan C. Kerckhoff, Duke University

RESEARCH IN SOCIOLOGY OF KNOWLEDGE, SCIENCES AND ART
Series Editor: Robert Alun Jones, University of Illinois

RESEARCH IN THE INTERWEAVE OF SOCIAL ROLES: Women and Men
Series Editor: Helena Z. Lopata, Center for the Comparative Study of
  Social Roles, Loyola University of Chicago

RESEARCH IN THE SOCIOLOGY OF HEALTH CARE
Series Editor: Julius A. Roth, University of California—Davis

STUDIES IN SYMBOLIC INTERACTION
Series Editor: Norman K. Denzin, University of Illinois

**ALL VOLUMES IN THESE ANNUAL SERIES ARE AVAILABLE AT INSTITU-
TIONAL AND INDIVIDUAL SUBSCRIPTION RATES.**

PLEASE WRITE FOR DETAILED BROCHURES ON EACH SERIES

A 10 percent discount will be granted on all institutional standing orders
placed directly with the publisher. Standing orders will be filled automatically upon publication and will continue until cancelled. Please indicate
with which volume standing order is to begin.

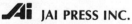 **JAI PRESS INC.**
P.O. Box 1285
321 Greenwich Avenue
Greenwich, Connecticut 06830
(203) 661–7602   Cable Address: JAIPUBL.

ANNUAL SERIES

RESEARCH IN LAW AND ECONOMICS
An Annual Compilation of Research
Series Editor: Richard O. Zerbe, SMT Program, University of Washington.

The contributions to be included in this series represent original research by scholars internationally known in their fields. A few articles generally based on outstanding dissertations by younger scholars will also be included. The contributions will include theoretical, empirical and legal studies considered to belong to the law-economics genre.

Volume 1.   Sept. 1978   Cloth   350 pages (Tent.)   Institutions: $25.00
ISBN NUMBER 0-89232-028-1   Individuals: $12.50

CONTENTS: Towards a Theory of Government Advertising, Kenneth W. Clarkson, University of Miami, and Robert D. Tollison, Virginia Polytechnic Institute. **Protecting the Right to Be Served by Public Utilities,** Victor P. Goldberg, University of California, Davis. **Comparison of American and Canadian Airline Regulation,** William Jordon, York University. **The Dynamics of Traditional Rate Regulation,** Patrick Mann, University of West Virginia. **Price Discrimination and Peak Load Pricing Subject to Rate of Return Constraint,** David L. McNicol, University of Pennsylvania. **Airline Market Shares vs. Capacity Shares and the Possibility of Short-Run Loss Equilibrium,** James Miller, III, American Enterprise Institute. **The Role of the Compensation Principle in Society,** Warren J. Samuels, Michigan State University. **Dynamic Elements in Regulation: The Case of Occupational Licensure,** William D. White, University of Illinois, Chicago Campus. **The Public Interest Theory of Regulation,** Richard O. Zerbe, Jr. and Nicole Urban, University of Washington. **Third Degree Price Discrimination in the Municipal Electric Industry,** Daniel R. Hollas, University of Mississippi, and Thomas S. Friedland, University of Illinois. **The Political Rationality of Federal Transportation Policy,** Ann F. Friedlander and Richard deNeufville, MIT. **The Incentive Effects of Medical Malpractice Claims,** Douglas Conrad, University of Chicago. **Market Equilibrium and the Informative Value of Advertising,** Thore Johnson, Columbia University.

A 10 percent discount will be granted on all institutional standing orders placed directly with the publisher. Standing orders will be filled automatically upon publication and will continue until cancelled. Please indicate with which volume standing order is to begin.

 JAI PRESS INC.
P.O. Box 1285
321 Greenwich Avenue
Greenwich, Connecticut 06830

(203) 661-7602   Cable Address: JAIPUBL.